THE BIG BOOK
OF DATES

THE BIG BOOK
OF DATES

LAURIE ROZAKIS, Ph.D.

McGraw-Hill

New York   San Francisco   Washington, D.C.   Auckland   Bogotá   Caracas
Lisbon   London   Madrid   Mexico City   Milan   Montreal   New Delhi
San Juan   Singapore   Sydney   Tokyo   Toronto

Library of Congress Cataloging-in-Publication Data

Rozakis, Laurie.
    The Big Book of Dates / Laurie Rozakis.
            p.   cm.
        ISBN 0-07-136102-2
            1. Chronology, Historical.   2. History—Miscellanea.   I. Title.
    D11 R69 2001
    902'.02—dc21   00-048184

McGraw-Hill

A Division of The McGraw·Hill Companies

1 2 3 4 5 6 7 8 9 0   DOC/DOC   0 9 8 7 6 5 4 3 2 1 0

ISBN 0-07-136102-2

This book was designed by Robert Freese and set in Baskerville by North Market Street Graphics.

Printed and bound by R. R. Donnelley & Sons.

To J.R., a cherished friend, confidant, and beauty consultant who enriches my life in more ways than I can name, even in a book this size. I am truly blessed to have you in my life. (And there's no way I can fit in the names of all the other people who feel the same way about you!)

Contents

Acknowledgments

So many people helped me work on this monumental project. Among my angels:

- My thanks to Nancy Mikhail for conceiving this book and working with me to develop the idea.
- My deep gratitude to Mary Glenn, Janice Race, Charles Annis, and the staff of McGraw-Hill for their commitment to this project.
- Copyeditors Richard H. Adin and Carolyn H. Edlund worked long and hard on this complex book, and I very much appreciate their work.
- My thanks also to the marvelous employees of the Farmingdale Public Library. Not only do you always find the material I need, but you are all a really nice group of people. (And I promise to return those overdue books!)

To all these dedicated professionals: I an indebted to your wisdom, expertise, and devotion. You make me look really good!

PART 1

FINE ARTS

Part 1 Fine Arts

	Art and Architecture	Music	Literature	Popular Culture
−2,400,000	Africa: Oldest stone tools found			
−45,000	Neanderthal carvings on mammoth tooth, discovered near Tata, Hungary; earliest cave artwork	Africa: Oldest known musical instruments		
−38,000	Africa: First composite tools			
−30,000	Germany: Ivory horse, oldest known animal carving			
−25,000				Poland: First boomerang; 13,000 years before first Australian boomerang
c. −10,000	France: Antler baton engraved with seal and salmon figures			
	Japan: First pottery; first boats			

Did You Know?

Beer here? Before −6000, the Sumerians made beer from malted barley. Clay tables found in Babylonia record ancient drinking songs and suggest that the Mesopotamians liked variety: nineteen different beers are listed.

	Art and Architecture	Music	Literature	Popular Culture
−5000	Colonization of Caribbean islands			
−4000 to −3501	Egypt and Europe: Painted pottery	Egypt: Harps and flutes	Sumer: Pictographs on clay tablets	Egypt/Mesopotamia: Women use henna

3

	Art and Architecture	Music	Literature	Popular Culture
	Australia: First Aboriginal paintings Russia: Ceramic ware			dyes to color their hands and feet. Eye shadow called *kohl* (lead ore, antimony, malachite) believed to repel danger
−3500 to 3001	Sumerian temple of Janna China: Potter's wheel	Egypt: Lyres and double clarinets	Sumer: Earliest writing Sumerian cuneiforms Egyptian hieroglyphs	
−3000 to −2501	Egypt: Cheops Pyramid at Giza Great Sphinx at Giza c. −2750 Stonehenge built in England	China: Bamboo pipe	*Epic of Gilgamesh* (−2500 to −1500) Egypt: Scribes used	Wrestling begins Egypt: Dogs tamed; mirrors used
−2500 to −2001	China: Painted pottery, black pottery	China: Five-tone musical scale	Egypt: First libraries; writing changes from horizontal/left to right to vertical/right to left	

KEY DOCUMENT

The Epic of Gilgamesh is a long narrative poem about a Sumerian king named Gilgamesh who lived between −2700 and −2500. Although the poem is ancient, its concerns are timeless: how to become famous and respected; how to cope with the loss of a close friend; how to accept one's own inevitable decline and death. Here is an excerpt:

> *Hear me, great ones of Uruk,*
> *I weep for Enkidu, my friend,*
> *Bitterly moaning like a woman mourning*
> *I weep for my brother,*
> *O Enkidu, my brother,*
> *You were the ax at my side,*
> *My hand's strength, the sword in my belt,*
> *The shield before me,*
> *A glorious robe, my fairest ornament;*
> *An evil Fate has robbed me.*

	Art and Architecture	Music	Literature	Popular Culture
–2000 to –1500	c. –2000 First palaces built in Crete	Denmark: Trumpets	–1500 Phoenician alphabet Egypt: Alphabet of twenty-four signs; Earliest "novel" China: First literature	

Did You Know?

The Great Pyramid at Giza, the largest pyramid in Egypt, is 450 feet high, consists of 2.3 million stones, and weighs more than 6 million tons. Thousands of Egyptian laborers spent 23 years building the tomb for the pharaoh Khufu; many workers died in the construction, crushed to death by the heavy stones.

	Art and Architecture	Music	Literature	Popular Culture
–1500 to –1001	Foundation of Corinth	Egypt: Harp music	India: Upanishad hymns China: First dictionary	–1370 Queen Nefertiti of Egypt paints her nails red, a color reserved for royalty
–1000 to –901	China: Brush and ink painting Europe: Gold jewelry North America: Pinto Indian huts built in California		China: Writing developed Hebrew alphabet developed Hebrew *Song of Songs*	Egypt: Wigs used Israel: Caftans worn

Did You Know?

All alphabets used today can be traced to a north Semitic alphabet that emerged around 1700 BCE at the eastern end of the Mediterranean. From this came the Hebrew, Arabic, and Phoenician alphabets. The Greeks adapted the Phoenician alphabet and introduced it into Europe around 1000 BCE. The Greeks standardized the lines to read from left to right and added some symbols for vowels. The Greek alphabet gave rise to the Roman alphabet and the Cyrillic alphabet. The word alphabet comes from the first two Greek letters: alpha and beta.

	Art and Architecture	Music	Literature	Popular Culture
−900 to −801	Ishtar Temple rebuilt at Nineveh		Greece: *Odyssey* and *Iliad*	−750 Women dye their hair black, whiten skin with lead powder
−800 to −701	Asia Minor: Arts and crafts flourish	Earliest recorded hymn Greece: music key part of daily life	Greece: Phonetic alphabet written left to right China: Poems Greece: Hesiod's "Theogony"	
−700 to −601	Babylon rebuilt Peloponnesus: First Doric columns Samos: First Ionic columns Greece: Acropolis built Babylon: Tower of Babel begun		Kallinos, Greek poet Archilochus, Greek writer of poems and fables Stesichorus of Sicily creates heroic ballad Sappho of Lesbos, Greek poet Indian Vedas, religious and educational tracts	

Did You Know?

Along with the Temple of Artemis at Ephesus, the Seven Wonders of the Ancient World are the Egyptian pyramids (the only Wonder still standing); the Colossus of Rhodes; the Hanging Gardens of Babylon; the Mausoleum at Halicarnassus; the lighthouse at Alexandria (world's first lighthouse); and the statue of Zeus at Olympia.

	Art and Architecture	Music	Literature	Popular Culture
−600 to −501	Hanging Gardens at Babylon Burma: Shwe Dragon Pagoda Turkey: Temple of Artemis at Ephesus		Aesop's Fables −525 to −456 Aeschylus, Greek dramatist	Delphi theatre built

	Art and Architecture	Music	Literature	Popular Culture
–500 to –451			–500 "Ramayan," Hindu poem	
			–500 Pindar's *Odes*	
	c. –498 Rome: Temple of Saturn			
	Egypt: Amun temple			
			–496 to –406 Sophocles, Greek dramatist	
	–484 Rome: Temple of Castor and Pollux		–484 to –406 Euripides, Greek dramatist	
			–458 Aeschylus' "Oresteia"	
–450 to –410	–440 "Elgin marbles" from the Parthenon			
			–423 Aristophanes' *The Clouds*	Greece: Carrier pigeons used
			–415 Euripides' *The Trojan Women*	
			–414 Aristophanes' *The Birds*	
	–407 Erechtheum completed on the Acropolis at Athens			
–400 to –351			Pentateuch finalized	
			–396 Plato's *Apologia*	
			Chinese write on silk, wood, bamboo	

Did You Know?

Two of our modern wedding traditions date from the ancient Romans. First, a bride was carried over the threshold of her new home to avoid the risk that she might stumble or enter with her left foot, both thought to bring bad luck. Second, brides wore wedding rings on the third finger of their left hand because the Romans believed that the nerve in that place led directly to the heart.

	Art and Architecture	Music	Literature	Popular Culture
−350 to −301	Greek theater of Epidaurus		India: Heroic epic *Mahabharata*	
	c. −350 Greek Corinthian columns		−342 to −290 Meander, Greek comedic writer	
		−340 Aristotle begins music theory		
−300 to −251			−293 to −215 Greek poet Apollonius of Rhodes	
	−275 Colossus of Rhodes completed (destroyed −224)			
	−275 Lighthouse at Alexandria completed			
−250 to −201			−239 to −170 "Father of Latin literature" Ennius	
	−230 Egypt: Temple to the sun god Horus			
			−205 Plautus' *Miles gloriosus* comedy	
−200 to −151			Books written on parchment, vellum	

KEY DOCUMENT

A major Roman historian and tutor to the future emperor Claudius, Livy recorded the history of Rome—all 142 papyrus books.

He wrote: "I invite the reader's attention to the much more serious consideration of the kind of lives our ancestors lived, of who were the men and what the means, both in politics and war, by which Rome's power was first acquired and subsequently expanded. I would then have him trace the process of our moral decline, to watch first the sinking of the foundations of morality as the old teaching was allowed to lapse, then the final collapse of the whole edifice, and the dark dawning of our modern day when we can neither endure our vices nor face the remedies needed to cure them."

Art and Architecture	Music	Literature	Popular Culture
		–195 to –159 Terence, Roman dramatist	
c. –170 Pons Aemilius, first stone bridge in Rome			
c. –170 first paved streets in Rome			
–150 to –101			–150 Romans apply gold saffron around eyes; blacken lids with wood ash

Did You Know?

Can't tell the Roman gods from the Greeks? Here's your scorecard for the most common gods and goddesses:

Roman name	Greek name
Bacchus	Dionysus
Ceres	Demeter
Cupid	Eros
Diana	Artemis
Faunus	Pan
Furies	Erinyes
Hercules	Heracles
Juno	Hera
Jupiter	Zeus
Lucifer	Phosporus
Mars	Ares
Mercury	Hermes
Minerva	Athena
Neptune	Poseidon
Proserpina	Persephone
Saturn	Cronus
Sol	Helios
Ulysses	Odysseus
Venus	Aphrodite
Victoria	Nike
Vulcan	Hephaestus

	Art and Architecture	Music	Literature	Popular Culture
	c. −130 to −120 Venus de Milo sculpture			
	China: Dictionary of 10,000 characters			
−100 to −51	c. −105 First college of Technology, at Alexandria		−70 to −19 Roman poet Virgil	
			c. −59 to 17 Titus Livius (Livy)	
			−65 to −8 Roman poet Horace	
			India: *The Bhagavad-Gita*	
−50 to −1		−50 Earliest oboe	Library of Ptolemy I of Alexandria destroyed in fire	−50 Cleopatra rouges her cheeks with red ocher and paints her upper eyelids blue-black and her lower eyelids green
			−43 to 18 Roman poet Ovid	
	−38 "Laocoon" marble sculpture			
	−30 Rome: Pantheon begun			

Part 1 Fine Arts
1 TO 500

	Art and Architecture	Music	Literature	Popular Culture
1 to 50			5 Ovid's *Metamorphoses*	
			43 to 120 Roman poet Martial	
			47 to 120 Greek historian Plutarch	
				50 Gauls use soap

Did You Know?

Publius Ovidius Naso (Ovid) was the most brilliant poet of his generation. The fifteen books of his masterpiece, the Metamorphoses, record the history of the world from chaos to the apotheosis of Julius Caesar and the reign of Augustus. During his life, Ovid enjoyed great literary success, and later poets imitate him often—from Dante to Ezra Pound. For example, his tale of Pyramus and Thisbe (Metamorphoses, book 4)—two star-crossed youths whose parents forbid their relationship—is the source of Shakespeare's Romeo and Juliet.

	Art and Architecture	Music	Literature	Popular Culture
51 to 100			58 to 138 Roman poet Juvenal	
				64 Great Fire of Rome
	79 Vesuvius erupts, burying town of Pompeii			Pompeii graffiti includes this inscription: "What use to have a Venus, if she is made from marble?"
	c. 80 Rome: Coliseum amphitheater			
	81 Rome: Arch of Titus			
	100 Africa: Meroe (capital of Kush) is well-known iron-making center		c. 100 to 250 The *Tamil* anthologies	

	Art and Architecture	Music	Literature	Popular Culture
101 to 150	122 to 138 Hadrian's Wall built to defend Britain			
	140 Roman theatre built			

KEY DOCUMENT

The poems of the *Eight Anthologies* and the *Ten Songs* are the earliest literary works in classical Tamil. Of the nearly 2,500 poems, most are signed. Here is a typical poem:

What She Said

Bless you, my heart.
The shell bangles slip
from my wasting hands.
My eyes, sleepless for days,
are muddied.
             Get up, let's get out
             of this loneliness here.

	Art and Architecture	Music	Literature	Popular Culture
151 to 200	c. 164 Oldest Mayan monuments		Chinese literature flourishes	
	c. 200 India: Carvings on Amaravati stupa			

Did You Know?

The 220 sacred wooden buildings erected at Japan's Shinto shrine at Ise have been pulled down and replaced by identical buildings every 20 years since they were first built in the fifth century. Only unpainted cypress wood is used, which is held together with dowels and joints rather than nails.

	Art and Architecture	Music	Literature	Popular Culture
201 to 250	212 to 217 Rome: Baths of Caracalla			
			220 Sanskrit drama	

	Art and Architecture	Music	Literature	Popular Culture
251 to 300	271 to 276 Aurelian walls around Rome			
	290 Amphitheater of Verona			
	300 Russia: Palace of Diocletian			
301 to 350				
351 to 400	360 China: Caves of a Thousand Buddhas		c. 360 Books replace scrolls	
		390 First "Hallelujah" hymns		
401 to 450	432 Basilica of S. Maria Maggiore			

KEY DOCUMENT

The Justinians had many laws. Here's the law for prostitution: "We absolutely forbid any women to be led by artifice, fraud, or compulsion to such debauchery; it is permitted to no one to support a prostitute or to prostitute them publicly, and to use the profits for any other business; we forbid them to undertake agreements for this and to require sureties and to do any such thing which compel the wretched women unwillingly to destroy their chastity." (529)

	Art and Architecture	Music	Literature	Popular Culture
451 to 500	446 Galla Placidia's Mausoleum at Ravenna	Peru: Flutes, horns, tubas, and drums	First anthology of Greek literature	Anglo-Saxons wear coats, shirts, and tunics
	476 China: Figures of Buddha in temples			Tea comes to China from India

Part 1 Fine Arts

501 TO 1000

	Art and Architecture	Music	Literature	Popular Culture
501 to 550		521 Greek musical notation enters West		
	522 Oldest known pagoda from the Sung Yuen temple of Honan, China			
	525 Buddhist caves with stone carvings			
	526 Tomb of Theodoric, Ravenna			
	527 Church of the Nativity, Bethlehem, rebuilt			
	532 St. Sophia Basilica, Constantinople			
			540 First Welsh poets	Pointed shoes are popular
				549 Sassania Empire: Music, dancing, hunting, chess flourish
			550 Encyclopedia of Greek writers	
			Epic Greek poem "Hero and Leander"	

Did You Know?

The Horyuji Temple in Japan is the oldest surviving wooden building in the world.

	Art and Architecture	Music	Literature	Popular Culture
551 to 560				
561 to 570				
571 to 580				
581 to 590	585 Japan: Horyuji temple (finished 607)			
	589 Great Wall of China rebuilt			589 First reference to toilet paper
591 to 600	600 Arles Cathedral		600 China: Books printed	Canterbury: First English school

KEY DOCUMENT

The *Koran*'s revelations were received by Mohammad, known to Muslims as the Prophet of God, during the last two decades of his life, from roughly 610, when the angel Gabriel first appeared to him, to his death in 632. During Mohammad's lifetime, these revelations were recorded by his followers, and gathered together in one volume after his death. The volume is called the *Koran* (al-qur'an), or *The Recitation*. Here is an excerpt from 4. Women:

Men, have fear of your Lord, who created you from a single soul. From that soul He created its mate, and through them He bestrewed the earth with countless men and women.

Fear God, in whose name you plead with one another, and honor the mothers who bore you. God is ever watching over you.

Give orphans [girls] their property which belongs to them. Do not exchange their valuables for worthless things or cheat them of their possessions; for this would surely be a great sin. If you fear that you cannot treat orphans with fairness, then you may marry other women who seem good to you: two, three, or four of them. But if you fear that you cannot maintain equality among them, marry only one or any slavegirls you wish. This will make it easier for you to avoid injustice.

	Art and Architecture	Music	Literature	Popular Culture
601 to 650	607 Buddha in yoga position			
			610 to 632 The *Koran*	
	625 Japan: First Ise shrine			
	646 Nara period of Japanese art			

Art and Architecture	Music	Literature	Popular Culture
650 China: Wood block prints			650 Caliphs introduce first news service

651 to 700

Art and Architecture	Music	Literature	Popular Culture
		671 Caedmon, earliest English poet	
			695 Arab coinage
			700 Peru: Tapestry weaving

KEY DOCUMENT

Li Po, born in western China without family connections or money, brilliantly reinvented himself as a cross between a court poet and a jester. Here is one of his poems:

Dialogue in the Mountains

You ask me why I lodge in these emerald hills;
I laugh, don't answer—my heart is at peace.
Peach blossoms and flowing waters
go off to a mysterious dark,
And there is another world,
not of mortal men.

701 to 750 701 to 762 Li Po

Art and Architecture	Music	Literature	Popular Culture
			710 Egypt: Sugar planted
715 Islam: Earliest paintings		Beijing: First printed newspaper	
749 China: "The Neighing Stallion" famous sculpture			
750 Indian Shore Temple	Gregorian church music in Germany, France, and England	750 Tamil language	750 Beds become popular in France and Germany
750 Pueblo period in southwest US			

	Art and Architecture	Music	Literature	Popular Culture
751 to 800		Church music schools at Paris, Cologne, and Metz	Li Po, Chinese poet Cynewulf, Anglo-Saxon poet	793 Kyoto, Japan established
801 to 850	Palatine Chapel at Aix-la-Chapelle		Korea: Flowering of culture	Charlemagne outlaws prostitution
			Separation of French and Latin	802 Rose bushes planted in Europe
	Acropolis of Zimbabwe		Norway: Bragi, poet	850 Earliest use of gunpowder
			Louis the Pious destroys German epics collected by his father Charlemagne	
851 to 900	Danes sack Canterbury Cathedral	Earliest polyphonic music	Salerno University established	851 Crossbow used in France

KEY DOCUMENT

Shah-nama or *Book of Kings,* the national epic of the Persian people, was penned by Abu'l-Qasim Firdawsi from several different versions of the mythic story already in circulation. The *Shan-nama,* comprised of more than 60,000 couplets, is presented as a history of Persia from the beginning of the world until the Arab conquest of Iran. Here is a sample from the portion called *Rustam and Suhrab,* considered by many readers and critics to be among the most tragic works ever written:

> *The Rustam choked, and his heart was full of fire,*
> *His eyes of tears. He mounted quick as dust*
> *And came with lamentation to the host*
> *In grievous consternation at his deed.*
> *The Iranians catching sight of him fell prostrate*
> *And gave God praise that Rustam had returned;*
> *But when they saw the dust upon his head,*
> *His clothes and bosom rent, they questioned him:*
> *"What meaneth this? For whom art thou thus troubled?"*
> *He told the fearful deed, and all began*
> *To mourn aloud with him. His anguish grew.*
> *He told the nobles: "I have lost today*
> *All strength and courage. Fight not with Turan [the Turkmans]:*
> *I have done enough harm."*

Did You Know?

Beowulf, the oldest European epic, is an uneasy blend of pagan morality and Christian ethics. Filled with blood and guts, the 3,128-line poem nonetheless embodies the highest ideals of its time and place: loyalty, courage, selflessness, and fairness. The hero Beowulf, a Geat from the region that is today Sweden, sails from his homeland to try to free Danish King Hrothgar's great banquet Hall, Herot, from the monster Grendel, who has been ravaging it for 12 years. The action takes place in sixth-century Scandinavia, and was recited by minstrels called "scops" for 300 years before it was written down. Here is an excerpt:

> *So Grendel ruled, fought with the righteous,*
> *One against many, and won; so Herot*
> *Stood empty, and stayed deserted for years,*
> *Twelve winters of grief for Hrothgar, king*
> *Of the Danes, sorrow heaped at his door*
> *By bell-forged hands. His misery leaped*
> *The seas, was told and sung in all*
> *Men's ears: how Grendel's hatred began.*
> *How the monster relished his savage war*
> *Of the Danes, keeping the bloody feud*
> *Alive, seeking no peace . . .*

First important
Japanese painter,
Kudara Kuwanari

Second Pueblo
period in US

863 Cyrillic alphabet
created

881 First German
ballad

Arabia: Coffee
discovered

KEY DOCUMENT

When Angles and Saxons came hither from the east,
Sought Britain over the broad-spreading sea,
Haughty war-smiths overcame the Britons,
Valiant earls got for themselves a home.
　　—*from* The Anglo-Saxon Chronicle

890 Earliest French
poem

	Art and Architecture	Music	Literature	Popular Culture
				900 Paper manufactured in Cairo
901 to 950			Farces appear on the stage	
	913 Warwick Castle		Arabian tales *A Thousand and One Nights* begins	
	936 Ottonian period in architecture		*Kokinshu*, official imperial anthology of Japanese poetry	
			940 to 1020 Firdawsi, Persian poet	
		942 Arabs bring		

Did You Know?

The earliest known cultivated species of coffee is Coffea arabica, *the coffee shrub of Arabia; it is now cultivated mostly in Latin America. Coffee may derive its name from the Arabic* qahwah, *but some scholars connect it with the name Kaffa, a province in southwest Ethiopia, reputedly its birthplace.*

	Art and Architecture	Music	Literature	Popular Culture
		trumpets to Europe		
951 to 1000			960 First Chinese plays with music	
	961 St. Paul's Cathedral rebuilt after fire			
	963 First record of London Bridge			
	970 Cairo: El-Ahzar Mosque		970 *Exeter Book*, English poetry	
				972 Cairo University established
		990 Musical notation	978 to c. 1031 Japanese court lady Murasaki Shikibu's novel *Tale of Genji*	

Art and Architecture	Music	Literature	Popular Culture
		998 to 1061 Sung Chi, Chinese poet	
1000 Italy: Artistic revival		1000 *Beowulf,* Old English heroic epic	1000 Millennium madness; fears of end of world
		1000 *The Pillow Book,* Japanese diary of imperial court	

Part 1 Fine Arts

1001 TO 1500

	Art and Architecture	Music	Literature	Popular Culture
1001 to 1050	c. 1001 Africa: Benin people use lost-wax method to cast realistic brass heads	*Plainsong* or church chants dominate music	1007 to 1072 Chinese poet Ou Yang Hsiu	
	1012 Cairo: Hakin Mosque			
	1012 Bamberg: Heinrich Cathedral			
	1018 India: Brihadisv Rasvamin Temple			
				1021 St. Vitus' Dance epidemic in Europe
	1025 Japan: Tosa school of painting			
		1026 Guido d'Arezzo do, re, mi, fa, sol, la		
		1050 Musical notes get time value	1050? to 1132? Omar Kayyam, Persian poet	
		1050 Polyphonic singing replaces Gregorian chant		
1051 to 1100	1052 England: Westminster Abbey			
	1053 Japan: Byodo Temple			

Did You Know?

The lost-wax method of sculpting is West Africa's oldest art. First, the head was sculpted in wax and covered in clay. Next, the clay mold was baked in a kiln, where the wax melted and was "lost." Molten brass was then poured into the clay mold. When the mold cooled, it was broken, leaving the sculpture intact.

Art and Architecture	Music	Literature	Popular Culture

Did You Know?

The Bayeux Tapestry: The Norman cavalry charge at the shieldwall at the Battle of Hastings *illustrates the story of the Norman Conquest of England. The tapestry is embroidered wool on linen, 20 inches high and 230 feet long, and now hangs in the town hall at Bayeux, France. The tapestry is one of the best surviving examples of Middle Ages art.*

Art and Architecture	Music	Literature	Popular Culture
1066 Norman (Romanesque) architecture			1066 First appearance of Halley's Comet
1068 England: Warwick Castle			
		1070 to 1142 Abelard, poet and theologian	
1074 England: Tower of London begun		Monks produce *illuminated* (illustrated) manuscripts	
1077 England: St. Albans Cathedral			
1080 England: Bayeux Tapestry			
1084 England: Worcester Cathedral			
1087 London: St. Paul's burns down and is rebuilt		India: Allegorical plays	1087 *Domesday Book* (tax matters)
1092 England: Tewkesbury Abbey			
1094 Venice: St. Mark, Cathedral	Beginning of secular music		1094 Venice: First gondolas
1100 Gothic architecture		1100 "Gitagovinda," Indian love poem	Middle English supersedes Old English
1100s First statues erected in Easter Island		"Chanson de Roland," heroic French poem	

	Art and Architecture	Music	Literature	Popular Culture
1101 to 1150	1101 to 1125 Under Hui Tsung, Chinese landscape painting reaches its zenith			
			1110 England: First miracle plays	
	1113 Russia: St. Nicholas, one of first onion-domed churches			
	1113 Cambodia: Temple of Angkor Wat begun			

KEY DOCUMENT

The Persian poet, scientist, and mathematician Omar Kayyam is probably the best known Islamic poet in the West, where his Rubaiyat have been read for centuries. The poems, written in a literary form called the *rubia*, address religious and philosophical issues. Here are several lines from Edward FitzGerald's classic 1859 translation:

The Worldly Hope me set their Hearts upon
Turns Ashes—or it prospers; and anon,
Like Snow upon the Desert'd dusty Face,
Lighting a little hour or two—is gone.

	Art and Architecture	Music	Literature	Popular Culture
				1120 China: Playing cards likely invented
		1127 First troubadours		
	1134 France: Chartres Cathedral begun			
			1135? to 1190? Chretien de Troyes, author of Arthurian romances	
	1137 Germany: Mainz Cathedral completed			

Art and Architecture	Music	Literature	Popular Culture

Did You Know?

Romanesque *architecture is* characterized by rounded arches and sturdy pillars. Gothic *architecture, which* developed around the 1100s, had pointed arches and slender pillars.

1151 to 1200

Cambodia: Khmer Empire reaches peak of wealth and power; ruler Suryavarman II (1113 to 1150) directs crowning glory: Temple-tomb of Angkor Wat

c. 1155 to 1190 Marie de France, storyteller

1151 First fire and plague insurance

England: Chess game arrives

Engagement rings become fashionable

1158 England: Oxford Cathedral

1161 Chinese use explosives

Did You Know?

The miracle plays *described the* lives of the saints.

1166 Egypt: Cairo citadel

1170 de Troyes, "Lancelot" ballad of courtly love

1174 Italy: "Leaning   Cymbals introduced
Tower" of Pisa

c. 1175 *Mystère d'Adam,* French vernacular rather than Latin

1176 First version of *Reynard the Fox* fable

	Art and Architecture	Music	Literature	Popular Culture
	c. 1190 US: Flat-topped mounds used as temple bases in Mississippi river area			
			c. 1191 The *Nibelungenlied*	
	c. 1200 to 1230 Africa: King Lalibela of Ethiopia has churches cut from rock	Ireland: Professional bards India: Sitar played Southern India: Vina	c. 1200 *El cantar de mio Cid* (*The Song of the Cid*) Spanish epic	
	c. 1200 to 1250 US: Apartments and round kivas built in Colorado			
1201 to 1250	1201 France: Façade of Notre Dame cathedral			

Did You Know?

The ballad, a *folk song that tells a story*, was a popular poetic form of the day. One surviving series of ballads concerns Robin Hood, a legendary hero who may have existed around the turn of the thirteenth century. Robin, an outlaw, lived in the woods with his band of "merrye" men, robbing from the rich and helping the poor.

	Art and Architecture	Music	Literature	Popular Culture
			1207 to 1273 Rumi, Persian poet	
			Italy: Sonnet form develops	1209 England: Cambridge University founded
			Germany: Drama develops	First court jesters
			Goose quills used for writing	London: Newgate Prison
				Europe: Giraffes shown
		1226 "Laudi" (praise to God) religious songs		England: Coal mined in Newcastle

Art and Architecture	Music	Literature	Popular Culture
	c. 1230 to 1306 Jacapone da Todi, Franciscan friar, melds mystical love of God with awareness of secular world		Hats become fashionable
	1232 to 1315 Raymond Lully, poet and mystic		
	c. 1240 "Sumer is icumen in," first recorded canon; four-part round over two-part repeated pattern	India: First bardic period; epic *Prithvi Rah Raso*	
1248 Spain: Work starts on Alhambra, Granada			
	c. 1250 to 1318 Heinrich von Meissen, poet of theology, philosophy		

KEY DOCUMENT

Some historians believe that the ballad "Sir Patrick Spence" is based on a real event. In 1281, Margaret, daughter of Alexander III of Scotland, traveled by ship to Norway to marry Eric, King of Norway. On the way back to Scotland, the ship vanished in the rough seas. Here is an excerpt from the ballad:

The king has written a broad letter,
And signed it with his hand,
And sent it to Sir Patrick Spence
Was walking on the sand.

The first line that Sir Patrick read,
A loud laugh launched he,
The next line that Sir Patrick read,
A tear blinded his eye.

"O, who has done this deed,
This ill deed done to me,
To send me out this time of the year,
To sail upon the sea!"

	Art and Architecture	Music	Literature	Popular Culture
1251 to 1300	Africa: Ife create beautiful brass work	*Motet,* polyphonic form with different words sung in each part		
			c. 1260 to 1300 Italy: Cavalcanti, love poetry	
			1265 to 1321 Italy: Dante Alighieri, *Divine Comedy*	1278 Mirror invented
			The Travels of Marco Polo, the most famous and important travel book ever written	c. 1290 Italy: Eyeglasses invented
				Italy: Gold currency first used

KEY DOCUMENT

The Divine Comedy, the greatest poem of the Middle Ages, has three main divisions: Hell (Inferno), Purgatory (Purgatorio), and Paradise (Paridiso). Written in Italian, the poem describes Dante's descent through the concentric circles of hell, from the least to the greatest kind of evil. For example, first comes ante-Hell, the home of those who refuse to choose between right and wrong. This is followed by a series of circles occupied by those guilty of sins of self-indulgence of all kinds: illicit lovers, gluttony, hoarding, and violence. At the very bottom is the fallen angel, Satan or Lucifer. Here is an excerpt:

> *Midway in our life's journey, I went astray*
> *from the straight road and woke to find myself*
> *alone in a dark wood. How shall I say*
> *what wood it was! I never saw so drear,*
> *so rank, so arduous a wilderness!*
> *Its very memory gives shape to fear.*

1301 to 1350		c. 1301 to 1377 Guillame de Machaut, *ars nova*		
		Italy: Madrigal form develops	1304 to 1347 Petrarch, greatest Italian poet of fourteenth century.	

Art and Architecture	Music	Literature	Popular Culture
1305 Italy: Giotto paints first realistic frescoes			
		1313 to 1375 Boccaccio, the *Decameron,* Italian novella	

Did You Know?

The Decameron *(1353) is an enormously influential collection of 100 witty and bawdy tales set in the time of plague.*

		1320 to 1388 Persia: Hafiz, mystic poet	
			1328 274,000 people in Paris
		c. 1332 England: Christian allegorical poem "Piers Plowman"	
		1333 to 1384 Japan: Kanami Motokiyo, No plays	
		1341 Rome: Petrarch made Poet Laureate	

Did You Know?

Between the twelfth and the fourteenth centuries, many beautiful cathedrals were built in France, including Lyon, Notre Dame, Bourges, Rheims, Amiens, Le Mans, and Chartres. These Gothic cathedrals have tall, pointed arches and beautiful stained glass windows.

| | | 1343? to 1440 England: Geoffrey Chaucer, writer | |

	Art and Architecture	Music	Literature	Popular Culture
1351 to 1400		*Dissonance*	1352 *Arab Chronicles:* Ibn Battuta on ancient Mali	Open sewers run down city streets
			1363? to 1443 Japan: Zeami, No playwright	

KEY DOCUMENT

In his own lifetime, Geoffrey Chaucer was considered the greatest English poet, and time has not tarnished his reputation. His unfinished masterpiece, *The Canterbury Tales*, ranks as one of the world's finest achievements. It also provides our best contemporary re-creation of fourteenth-century England.

The work includes twenty-four stories of pilgrims who made the journey to the sacred shrine of Canterbury, where the archbishop Thomas à Becket had been murdered in 1170. Readers first meet the pilgrims at the Tabard Inn in Southwark, near London, and follow their trip to Canterbury. By using the concept of the pilgrimage, Chaucer is able to bring together people from the three main strata of medieval society: the church, the court, and the common people. Here is an excerpt in the original middle English:

> *A Knyght ther was, and that a worthy man*
> *That fro the tyme that he first bigan*
> *To riden out, he chivalrie,*
> *Trouthe and honour, fredom and curteisie*

1367 to 1368 Russia: First stone fortifi-cations on Kremlin

c. 1370 England: *Sir Gawain and the Green Knight,* medieval romance

India: Paper comes to India from Persia

Did You Know?

The No Theatre is a traditional Japanese dramatic form with a firm set of rules. The plays involve lyrical language, music, masks, elaborate costumes, and dance. Men play all the parts. The plays are firmly grounded in the Shinto and Buddhist religions and also reflect the Japanese folk belief that Japan's mountains and rivers are inhabited by demons and ghosts. The plays, which are almost always tragic, often focus on a deceased character who has been wronged and is seeking delivery from tortures.

	Art and Architecture	Music	Literature	Popular Culture
			c. 1370 to c. 1460 Spain: Perez de Guzman, historian and poet	
			c. 1375 to 1425 Celtic tales: *Red Book of Hergest*	
				c. 1400 Africa: Great Zimbabwe thrives on gold trade
1401 to 1450	c. 1401 to 1428, Masaccio, first great *quattrocento* painter			
	1403 Ghiberti sculpts figure realistically, heralding the Renaissance		c. 1403 to 1409 China: *Yongle dadian,* encyclopedia	
				1407 Italy: Casa di San Giorgio, one of first public banks, founded in Genoa
				1407 London: Bethlehem Hospital (Bedlam), becomes institution for the insane

KEY DOCUMENT

Sir Gawain and the Green Knight has been called the best English example of the medieval romance. It is admired for its descriptive language, vivid descriptions, skillful organization, penetrating characterizations, and re-creation of the pageantry of medieval life. Sir Gawain was one of King Arthur's knights; the Green Knight is commonly interpreted as a vegetation myth. Here is an excerpt:

> *There were stares on all sides as the stranger spoke,*
> *For much did they marvel what it might mean*
> *That a horseman and a horse should have such a hue,*
> *Grow green as the grass, and greener, it seemed,*
> *That green fused on gold more glorious by far.*

Art and Architecture	Music	Literature	Popular Culture
1419 Italy: Brunelleschi's Foundling Hospital in Florence begins Renaissance architecture			
1420 Italy: Brunelleschi designs dome of Florence Cathedral			
1423 Italy: de Fabriano: *Adoration of the Magi*			
		1424 Chartier's "La Belle Dame Sans Merci," attack on courtly love	
		1431 to c. 1463 Francois Villon, father of modern French poetry	
1432 Flemish painter Jan van Eyck: *Adoration of the Lamb*			
		1434 Italy: Alberti's *Della Farmiglia*	
1435 Donatello: *David*			
1438 to 1445 Fra Angelico paints San Marco Monastery, Florence			
		c. 1440 India: Kirttivasa's *Ramayana,* Bengali literature	
1450 Under the Medicis, Florence becomes center of Renaissance arts and learning			c. 1450 Korea: King Sejong introduces official Korean script

	Art and Architecture	Music	Literature	Popular Culture
1451 to 1500	1452 to 1519 Italy: Leonardo da Vinci	Religious mass becomes more varied		
	1454 to 1457 Uccello's *Battles* show perspective and an eerie mood			
	1455 Mexico: Huge temple to Aztec war god Huitzilopochtli built in Tenochtitlan		1455: Gutenberg prints first Bible	
	c. 1460 China: Imperial Ming porcelain exported			
			1469 to 1527 Italy: Niccolò Machiavelli	
			1469 to 1470 England: Malory's *Morte D'Arthur*, epic prose romance of Arthurian legend	
	1475 to 1564 Michelangelo			
	1478 Italy: Botticelli: *Primavera*			
				1480 da Vinci invents the parachute
	1482 First great Renaissance villa built for Pope Leo X by Sangallo			
	1483 Japan: Ashikaga Yoshimasa completes Silver Pavilion Temple, or Ginkakuji, at Kyoto			
	1485 Botticelli: *The Birth of Venus*			

Art and Architecture	Music	Literature	Popular Culture
1488 Great Wall of China rebuilt to ward off invaders			
1488 Bellini: *Madonna and Saints*			
			1490 Italy, Holland: First orphanages
			1492 Profession of book publishing starts
		1494 Germany: Brant's *Ship of Fools*, satire	
1495 to 1497 da Vinci: *The Last Supper*			
1497 Michelangelo: *Bacchus* sculpture			
	1498 Ottaviano dei Petrucci patents process of music printing		1498 First pawnshops
1499 Michelangelo: *Pieta* statue			
1500 First faience and majolica (types of pottery)			1500 England: Lead pencils used

Part 1 Fine Arts

1501 TO 1800

	Art and Architecture	Music	Literature	Popular Culture
1501 to 1510	c. 1500 Oval stone houses built on Easter Island			Handkerchiefs first used
	1501 Durer: *Life of the Virgin*			
	1501 Lippi: *St. Catherine*			
		1502 Ottaviano de Petrucci: *First Book of Masses*		
	c. 1503 da Vinci: *Mona Lisa*		1503 to 1542 Thomas Wyatt, English poet	
	1503 to 1519 Gothic art: Henry VII's Westminster Chapel			
	1504 Michelangelo: *David* sculpture	1504 to 1571 Francesco di Bernardo Corteccia, Italian composer		
	1504 Durer: *Nativity*			
	1504 Michelangelo: *The Holy Family* sculpture			
	1504 Raphael: *Marriage of the Virgin*			
		1505 to 1585 Thomas Tallis, English composer		1505 Africa: Factories built by Portuguese
	1506 to 1612 Rome: Construction of St. Peter's Basilica		c. 1506 to 1581 Wu Ch'eng-en: *Journey to the West* or *Monkey* (pub. 1592)	
	1507 Durer: *Adam and Eve*			

Art and Architecture	Music	Literature	Popular Culture
		1508 Rodriguez de Montalvo, *Amadis of Gaul,* chivalric romance that inspired conquistadors	
			1509 First attempt to license doctors
			1509 Constantinople: rocked by earthquake
1508 to 1512 Michelangelo paints Sistine Chapel ceiling			
1510 Titian: *The Gypsy Madonna*	1510 to 1561 French musician Louis Bourgeois *La Mandragola*		

1511 to 1520

Art and Architecture	Music	Literature	Popular Culture
1511 Durer: *Adoration of the Trinity*		1511 Erasmus: *In Praise of Folly*	
1512 Raphael: *Julius II*		1512 "Masque" first used to describe poetic drama	
c. 1512 to 1516 Grunewald: Isenheim altarpiece			
		c. 1513 Leo Africanus: *History and Description of Africa*	Corn imported to Spain from the West Indies
1514 Bosch: *The Garden of Worldly Delights*			1514 Europe: Pineapples first sold
1514 Titian: *The Tribute Money*			
1515 to 1530 London: Hampton Court Palace		1515 England: John Skelton's morality play	1515 Switzerland: In 3 months, more than 500 "witches" burnt
1515 Titian: *Flora*			
1516 Raphael: *The Sistine Madonna*	1516 to 1565 Composer Cyprien de Rore *Magnificence*	1516 Sir Thomas More's *Utopia*	1516 Europe: Indigo dye used
1516 Titian: *The Assumption*			

Art and Architecture	Music	Literature	Popular Culture
1517 Raphael: *The Transfiguration*		1517 to 1547 English poet Henry Howard, Earl of Surrey, the first to use blank verse	1517 Europe: Coffee becomes popular
			1518 Europe: Asian porcelain sold
			Europe: Eyeglasses used
c. 1520 to c. 1550 China: Wu school of painting	1520 to 1591 Composer and musician Vincenzo Galilei, Galileo's father		1520 Chocolate brought to Spain from Mexico
	1520s German hymns and chorales, four to five parts		

1521 to 1530

			1521 France: Silk first made
		1522 China: *Romance of Three Kingdoms*	

Did You Know?

According to an ancient tale, Quetzalcoatl stole the cocoa tree from his brother and sister gods and gave it to the Toltecs, an Aztec people, and taught them to make chocolate. Wherever it came from, chocolate was prized by the Aztec Indians of Mexico. They demanded it from other tribes as a tribute—during Montezuma's reign, nearly 50,000 pounds of cocoa beans were brought to Tenochtitlan every year. Some of the beans were used for money, others were offered to the gods, and the rest were ground into a frothy drink for the wealthy.

1523 Titian: *Bacchus and Ariadne*	1523 First manual for lute players		
			1524 Europe: Turkeys first eaten
c. 1525 to 1569 Peter Brugel the Elder, landscapes		1525 to 1585 French poet Pierre de Ronsard established Alexandrine meter of twelve-syllable line	

Art and Architecture	Music	Literature	Popular Culture
1526 Durer: *The Four Apostles*			
		1527 Castiglione: *The Courtier*	
	Fantasia, toccata, and ricercar are new instrumental forms	1528 *Annals of Tlatelolco*, earliest Latin script chronicle in the Aztec language	
			1529 Italy: Women allowed on the stage for the first time
		1530 to 1566 English writer Sir Thomas Hoby	Europe: Matches being used, almost 1,000 years after their invention in China
		1530 England: Morality play *Everyman* first printed	
1531 to 1540		1532 France: Rabelais' *Gargantua*	

Did You Know?

Michelangelo (1475 to 1564), a sculptor, architect, painter, and poet, exerted a tremendous influence on his contemporaries and Western art in general. The great Renaissance poet Ludovico Ariosto described the famous artist this way: "[He] is more than mortal, divine angel." His achievement changed the course of Western art and architecture. For example, his dome for St. Peter's became the model for domes all over the Western world, including most of the state capitol buildings in America.

Art and Architecture	Music	Literature	Popular Culture
		1532 Machiavelli: *The Prince*	
		1532 Italian poet and satirist Ludovico Ariosto's *Orlando Furioso*, epic of romantic chivalry	

Art and Architecture	Music	Literature	Popular Culture

KEY DOCUMENT

From Castiglione's *The Courtier, Book 1:*
Perhaps I am able to tell you what a perfect Courtier ought to be, but not to teach you how ye should do to be one. Notwithstanding, to fulfill your request in what I am able, although it be (in manner) in a proverb that *Grace is not to be learned,* I say unto you, whoso mindeth to be gracious or to have a good grace in the exercises of the body (presupposing first that he be not of nature unapt) ought to begin betimes [early], and to learn his principles of cunning men.

1533 Holbein: *The Ambassadors*

1533 First madrigals printed in Rome

1533 First asylums for mentally ill

1533 to 1592 French essayist Montaigne

1535 Holbein: *King Henry VIII*

1536 Michelangelo: *Last Judgment* on wall in Sistine Chapel

1536 Spain: First song book with lute accompaniment

1537 Italy: First conservatories of music established

1538 Titian: *Venus of Urbino*

Did You Know?

Indian Moghul art of this era assimilated the Persian tradition of miniature painting, which stressed elaborate decoration and vivid colors.

1539 Holbein: *Anne of Cleves*

1539 to 1578 George Gascoigne, English poet

1539 France: First Christmas tree, at Strasbourg Cathedral; Public lottery held

1540 Titian: *A Young Englishman*

	Art and Architecture	Music	Literature	Popular Culture
1541 to 1550	1541 to 1614 El Greco	The lute becomes a popular instrument		
				1542 King Charles I rules that Indians could not be made slaves
	1543 Titian: *Ecce Homo*			
	1546 Titian: *Pietro Aretino*			Rich Elizabethans shunned vegetables; only the poor ate produce (which they grew)
	1546 to 1611 Spranger			
			1547 to 1616 Miguel de Cervantes	
			1547 to 1579 *Florentine Codex* collection of Aztec lore and literature	
	1548 to 1556 Michelangelo: *Pieta* sculpture			1548 France: First roofed theatre
	1548 Titian: *Charles V on Horseback*			
	1548 Tintoretto: *St. Mark Rescuing a Slave*			
			1549 Joachim du Bellay, manifesto of French poets *Défense et illustration de la langue française*	1549 Europe: Dwarfs and other handicapped people used as jesters
	c. 1550 Palladio, Villa Rotunda, Vicenza		1550 to 1581 *Cantares Mexicanos* main source of Aztec poetry	1550 Sweden: First stage play
	c. 1550 Japanese "Ukiyoe" painting		1550 to 1617 Chinese dramatist T'ang Hsien-tsu	1550 Italy: Billiards played for first time

Art and Architecture	Music	Literature	Popular Culture
		1550 *The Booke of Common Praier noted,* first English prayer set to music	
		1550 to 1607 William Bradford: *Of Plymouth Plantation*	
South Pacific: Maoris build fortified enclosures			Tobacco grown in Spain
			About 7 million Indians in South America; by 1600, will decline to 1 million due to European diseases.
1551 to 1560 Renaissance reaches height in England			1551 England: Licenses first given to alehouses and taverns
		1552 to 1599 Edmund Spencer, English poet	Europe: Most people had teeth blackened by decay. Experts advised brushing teeth with sugar to reduce and remove decay!
		1552 Rabelais, bawdy and satiric *Gargantua* and *Pantagruel*	
		1552 to 1618 Sir Walter Raleigh	

Did You Know?

Sir Walter Raleigh was a true Renaissance man: soldier, philosopher, courtier, explorer, colonist, historian, scientist, poet. He fought in Ireland and Cadiz, directed the colonization of Virginia, and introduced the potato to Ireland and tobacco to Europe.

	1553 Modern violin develops		

Art and Architecture	Music	Literature	Popular Culture
1554 Titian: *Venus and Adonis*		1554 to 1586 Sir Philip Sidney, English poet	Most people still eating with their fingers and perhaps a knife
		1554 to 1606 English poet John Lyly	
		1554 to 1558 *Popul Vox,* sacred books of Quiche Mayan	
1555 Michelangelo: *Pieta* sculpture		1555 Aztec dictionary	1555 Tobacco brought from America to Spain
1555 Tintoretto: *St. George and the Dragon*			
1555 to 1636 China: Tung Ch'i-ch'ang shows spiritual message in landscapes			
1555 Bruegel: *The Fall of Icarus*			
1556 Suleiman's Mosque in Constantinople completed		1556 *Book of Chilam Balam,* Maya lore	1556 Earthquake kills over 800,000 people; worst earthquake in history
		1557 *Tottel's Miscellany,* has poems by Wyatt, Howard, etc.	1557 First play censored in England
			1557 Influenza epidemic devastates Europe
	Japan: Bamboo pipes, three-stringed guitars, zithers popular	1558 *Legend of the Sun,* Aztec view of the world	
1559 to 1584 Madrid: Escorial palace			
		1560 Hsu Wei *Ching P'Ing Mei,* first classical Chinese novel	

	Art and Architecture	Music	Literature	Popular Culture
1561 to 1570	High point of Dutch Renaissance: painters Rubens, Van Dyck, Hals, Rembrandt	1561 to 1663 Italian composer Jacopo Peri	1561 to 1626 Francis Bacon	
	1562 Brueghel: *Two Chained Monkeys*	1562 Gasparo da Salo, first great Italian violin maker		1562 England: Witchcraft made a capital offense
	1562 Tintoretto: *Christ at the Sea of Galilee*			
				1563 93,000 people living in London
	1564 Brueghel: *Christ Carrying the Cross*		1564 to 1616 William Shakespeare	1564 England: Horse-drawn coach introduced
			1564 Vasari *Lives*	
			1564 to 1593 Christopher Marlowe	

Did You Know?

Along with Francisco de Goya and Diego Velazquez, El Greco is considered a master of Spanish art. Born Domenikos Theotokopoulos in 1541 in Crete, he traveled to Venice in 1570 and worked in Titian's studio. In 1577, he arrived in Toledo, Spain, where he settled and received his nickname—El Greco ("the Greek"). His 1586 masterpiece, Burial of Count Orgaz, manifests El Greco's typical elongated figures, horror vacuii (dread of unfilled spaces), and mystical atmosphere.

	Art and Architecture	Music	Literature	Popular Culture
	1565 Tintoretto: *Flight into Egypt*			1565 Spain: Potatoes arrive from America
	1565 Brueghel: *A Country Wedding*			1565 England: Pencils manufactured
				1565 US: St. Augustine FL, established
	1567 Brueghel: *Adoration of the Magi*		1567 to 1601 Thomas Nash	
			1567 to 1643 Venetian composer Claudio Monteverdi	

Art and Architecture	Music	Literature	Popular Culture
			1568 England: Beer first bottled
			1569 Spain: Sunflowers arrive from America
1570 Tintoretto: *Moses Striking the Rock*			
1571 to 1580		1572 to 1631 John Donne, English metaphysical poet	
		1572 to 1637 Ben Jonson	
		1572 de Ronsard: Epic poem on French kings	
		1572 Luis Camoes, *The Lusiads,* epic Portuguese poems	
1573 to 1652 English architect Inigo Jones	Germany: *Meistersang,* poetic songs based on minstrels	1573 Gascoigne poems	
1573 to 1615 Japan: Monoyama period, castle at Azuchi			
1573 Mexico City Cathedral started (completed 1813)			
		c. 1575 China: Realistic, erotic novel *The Golden Lotus*	
		1575 Torquato Tasso: *Jerusalem Liberated*	
			1576 The Theatre, first permanent theatre in England
1577 to 1660 Peter Paul Rubens, Dutch baroque painter		1577 Holinshed's *Chronicles*	

Art and Architecture	Music	Literature	Popular Culture
		1578 to 1580 John Lyly: *Euphues*	
1579 da Bologna: *The Rape of the Sabines* sculpture		1579 Spencer: *The Shepheaders Calendar*	1579 First glass eyes
	1580 English folk tune "Greensleeves"	1580 Montaigne: *Essays*	
1581 to 1590	c. 1581 France: Ballet danced in court		
			1582 Pope Gregory institutes Gregorian calendar

Did You Know?

Oratorio *is a form of opera with sacred themes and no acting or scenery.*

			1583 England: First life insurance
	1584 Chu Tsai-Yu invents equal temperament in music		
1586 El Greco: *Burial of Count Orgaz*		1586 Japan: Kabuki theater starts	1586 England: Smoking imported from Virginia

Did You Know?

Expeditions headed by Sir Walter Raleigh tried twice (1585, 1587) to establish colonies on Roanoke Island. Virginia Dare's grandfather, mapmaker John White, one of the colony's leaders, found it deserted when he returned with supplies in 1590 or 1591. The letters "C R O" were carved on a tree. Croatan was the name of a nearby island and an Indian tribe; had the colonists gone to the island? Had the Indians attacked? The fate of the colonists has never been established. You can see the excavated remains of the colonists' fort at the Fort Raleigh National Historic Site.

Art and Architecture	Music	Literature	Popular Culture
			1586 327-ton Egyptian obelisk raised to vertical position
1587 Japan: Osaka Castle completed	1587 Monteverdi *First Book of Madrigals*	1587 Marlowe: *Tamburlaine*	1587 US: Virginia Dare, first British child born in America, on Roanoke Island
	1587 Collection of Jewish songs	1587 to 1679 Joost van den Vondel, Dutch poet	
		c. 1588 Marlowe: *Dr. Faustus*	c. 1588 to 1592 Shakespeare in London as actor and playwright
			1588 Vatican library opens
1589 Caravaggio: *Bacchus*		1589 Puttenham: *The Arte of English Poesie*	1589 France: Forks first used in court
1590 Rome: Dome of St. Peters completed		1590 Spenser: *The Faerie Queene*	
1590 El Greco: *St. Jerome*		1590? Aesop's *Fables* translated into Aztec	
		1590 Sidney: *Arcadia*	
		1590 Marlowe: *The Jew of Malta*	
		1590 Italy: Commedia dell'arte company	
		1590 Spenser: *The Faerie Queene*, Books 1 to 3	
1591 to 1600		1591 Sidney: "Astrophil and Stella"	1591 Ireland: Trinity College founded
		1591 to 1674 Robert Herrick, English poet	
1592 Tintoretto: *The Last Supper*		1592 China: *Monkey*	

Art and Architecture	Music	Literature	Popular Culture
		1592 to 1598 Shakespeare: histories, comedies	
		1592 Marlowe: *Hero and Leander*	
		1592 Kyd: *The Spanish Tragedy*	
1593 El Greco: *The Crucifixion, The Resurrection*		1593 to 1633 George Herbert, English metaphysical poet	1593 England: London theatres closed due to plague
	1594 First opera: Peri's *Dafne*		1594 England: Theatres reopen
			1595 Heels first used on shoes
1596 Caravaggio: *Basket of Fruit*		1596 Spenser: *The Faerie Queene,* Books 4 to 6	1596 England: Tomatoes introduced
			1596 England: Toilets installed in Queen's palace
1597 El Greco: *St. Martin and the Beggar*	1597 Gabrieli: *Sonata, Pian'e Forte,* first ensemble piece that specified instruments		
1598 to 1680 Giovanni Lorenzo Bernini, architect		1598 Shakespeare: *Henry IV*	
1598 to 1666 Francois Mansart, Classical French architect		1598 Ben Jonson: *Every Man in His Humor*	
1599 to 1641 Anthony Van Dyke, Dutch baroque painter		1599 Sidney's essay "In Defence of Poesy"	1599 Original Globe Playhouse built
1599 to 1660 Diego Velázquez, Spanish baroque painter			

Art and Architecture	Music	Literature	Popular Culture
1599 to 1667 Francesco Borromini, Italian architect			
c. 1600 Caravaggio: *Doubting Thomas* shows vivid realism and simplicity		1600 Thomas Nash poems	1600 Wigs become the fashion rage
		c. 1600 Raleigh: "The Nymph's Reply to the Shepherd"	

Did You Know?

Opera, a drama in which all or part of the dialogue is sung, contains instrumental overtures, interludes, and accompaniments. Developed in Italy in the late sixteenth and early seventeenth centuries by a group of musicians and scholars who called themselves the Camerata (salon). Claudio Monteverdi, the first great composer to turn his attention to opera, sparked its development throughout Italy.

1601 to 1610	Dances for lutes, leading to musical forms: *pavane, galliard, allemande, gavotte*	1601 to 1609 Shakespeare's tragedies and romantic comedies	1601 England: Poor Law makes the parishes take care of the needy
			1602 England: Bodleian Library
		1603 Shakespeare: *Hamlet*	
		1604 to 1605 Shakespeare: *King Lear*	
		1604 Lope de Vega: *Comedias* (25 vol.)	
		1605 Cervantes: *Don Quixote de la Mancha,* first modern novel	1605 225,000 people in London
1606 to 1669: Rembrandt van Rijn	1606 Italy: Open-air opera	1606 to 1616 Beaumont and Fletcher, English dramatists	

Art and Architecture	Music	Literature	Popular Culture
		1606 to 1684 Pierre Corneille, French writer	
		1606 Ben Jonson: *Volpone*	
Baroque period in art; spectacular effects and realism	1607 Claude Monteverdi: *Orfeo,* early European opera	1607 Marston: *What You Will*	Tea introduced to Europe
1608 El Greco: *Golgatha, Cardinal Taverna*	1608 Monteverdi: *Lamento d'Arianna*	1608 to 1674 John Milton, Puritan poet	
1609 Constantinople: Blue Mosque built		1609 to 1617 Garcilas de la Vega: El Inca, *Royal Commentaries of the Incas*	1609 Holland: Delft: Tin-enameled ware made
		1609 to 1642 John Suckling, English poet	1609 Japan: Commercial publishing begins
1610 El Greco: *The Opening of the Fifth Seal*	c. 1610 Violin appears in an orchestra	1610 Ben Jonson: *The Alchemist*	
Easter Island: Stone towers with inner chambers			

Did You Know?

Cervantes took part in the Battle of Lepanto and was enslaved by the Turks for 5 years.

1611 to 1620	1611 Rubens: *Descent from the Cross*		1611 King James version of the Bible	
	1613 Reni: *Aurora*	1613 Cerone: Musical history and theory	1613 de Vega: *Fuenteovejuna*	1613 Globe Theatre burns down when spark from stage cannon sets fire to thatch roof; Globe rebuilt on original foundation

Art and Architecture	Music	Literature	Popular Culture

Did You Know?

Between 1526 and 1870, nearly 10 million slaves were shipped to Europe (175,000), Spanish America (1,552,000), Brazil (3,647,000), British Caribbean (1,665,000), British North America and the United States (399,000), French America (1,600,000), Dutch America (500,000), and the Danish West Indies (28,000).

Art and Architecture	Music	Literature	Popular Culture
		1614 Webster: *The Duchess of Malfi*	
1615 Rubens: *The Battle of the Amazons*			
1616 Inigo Jones' Queen's House, classical Palladian-style line develops		1616 to 1664 Andreas Gryphius, German writer	1616 Shakespeare dies
		1616 England: Ben Jonson appointed Poet Laureate	
1617 to 1682 Spain: Bartolome Esteban Murillo, painter who established Seville Academy		1617 Lyly: *Euphues, the Anatomy of Wit*	1617 Stuart collars become the fashion rage

Did You Know?

Shakespeare's The Tempest *(1611) was inspired in part by Silvester Jourdain's* A Discovery of the Bermudas.

Art and Architecture	Music	Literature	Popular Culture
	1618 Bass in Italian lute songs		
1619 Velázquez: *Adoration of the Kings*	1619 Shutz: *Psalms*		1619 US: First black slaves arrive in Virginia
	1620 Praetorius: *Syntagma musicum,* musical encyclopedia	1620 Bacon: English philosopher, *Novum Organum*	

	Art and Architecture	Music	Literature	Popular Culture
	c. 1620 to 1689 China: Kung Hsien, vast landscapes including *A Thousand Peaks and Myriad Rivers*			
1621 to 1630	1621 Van Dyck: *Rest on the Flight Into Egypt*	c. 1621 to 1676 Grimmelshausen: *Simplicissimus,* start of the German novel	1621 to 1678 Andrew Marvell	
	1622 Rubens: *The Medici Cycle*		1622 to 1673 Jean Baptiste Poquelin Moliere, French actor and dramatist	
	1622 to 1625 Bernini: *Apollo and Daphne* sculpture			
	1623 Inigo Jones: Queen's Chapel, Westminster			
	1624 Poussin: *The Rape of the Sabine Women*	1624 Fugue develops in Germany as contrapuntal treatment of main theme	1624 Japan: First theatre opened 1624 England: Middleton's *A Game of Chess* played nine times to become first "long run"	
	1625 Inigo Jones: Covent Garden Church	1625 Moscow: Bells installed in the Gates of Salvation		1625 England: Hackney coaches used in London
	1626 Poussin: *Triumph of David*			1626 US: Deal between Peter Minuit and Native American chiefs for purchase of Manhattan
	1627 Rembrandt: *The Money-Changer*			1627 France: Registered mail first used
	1628 Velázquez: *Christ on the Cross*		1628 Juan Ruiz de Alarcon, Spanish comedies	

Art and Architecture	Music	Literature	Popular Culture
1629 Van Dyke: *Rinaldo and Armida*			
1629 Shah Jahan has Peacock Throne built			
1630 Rubens: *Blessings of Peace*	c. 1630 Italy: Bel canto, lyrical style of singing, develops		
1630 Italy: Beginning of high baroque period			

Did You Know?

According to legend, Peter Minuit, the director general of the Dutch colony of New Amsterdam, purchased Manhattan island from the Canarsee Indians with trinkets and cloth valued at 60 guilders, then about $24. Historians have disputed the amount of money that Minuit paid.

1631 to 1640

Art and Architecture	Music	Literature	Popular Culture
		1631 to 1700 John Dryden	
1632 to 1723 Christopher Wren, architect of St. Paul's Cathedral dome	*Castrati* singers reach greatest prominence in seventeenth- and eighteenth-century opera	1632 Bernal Diaz del Castillo, *True History of the Conquest of New Spain*	
1632 to 1643 India: Taj Mahal			
1633 to 1639 de Cortona: Ceiling of the Grand Salone, Palazzo Barberini		1633 Donne: *Poems*	1633 Adam Roelantse establishes first school in colonies
		1633 to 1703 Samuel Pepys	
1633 Van Dyke: *Charles I*		1633 John Ford: *'Tis a Pity She's a Whore*	
1633 Van Dyke: *Equestrian Portrait of Charles I*			
		1634 Milton: *Comus*	

Art and Architecture	Music	Literature	Popular Culture
		1634 *Passion Play* at Oberammergau	
		1634 to 1693 Madame de Lafayett: *La Princess de Cleves,* French court romance	

Did You Know?

The castrato are male singers castrated before puberty. The practice of castration, illegal, and often done without the child's consent, produced an adult voice of great power and sweetness. By the eighteenth century, the majority of male opera singers were castrati. The most famous of the castrati was Carlo Broschi, known as Farinelli.

Art and Architecture	Music	Literature	Popular Culture
1635 Velázquez: *Surrender of Breda*		1635 Calderón de la Barca: *La Vida es sueno*	1635: England: Speed limit on hackney coaches, 3 mph
1635 Poussin: *Kingdom of Flora*		1635 Corneille: *Medee*	
1636 Van Dyke: *Charles I on Horseback*		1636 Corneille: *El Cid,* beginning of modern French drama	1636 Harvard College founded
	1637 Italy: First public opera house opens in Venice	1637 Milton: *Lycidas*	1637 Holland: Tulip trade collapses
1638 Rubens: *The Three Graces*	1638 Monteverdi: *Madrigals* (book 8)		1638 England: Torture abolished
	1638 Dynamic markings (p for *piano* and f for *forte*) used for first time by Domenico Mazzochi		
1639 Rubens: *Judgment of Paris*			1639 US: First printing press
1640 Rembrandt: *Self-Portrait*			

	Art and Architecture	Music	Literature	Popular Culture
			1640 Plays of de la Barca and Lope de Vega translated into Aztec	
			1640 Brome: *The Antipodes*	
1641 to 1650		1641 Barnard: *First Booke of Selected Church Musick*	1641 England: Evelyn's *Diary*	
	1642 Rembrandt: *Night Watch*			1642 England: Puritans close theatres
				1642 England: Property and income tax made law
	1643 Velázquez: *Venus and Cupid*	1643 Cavalli: *Egisto* (opera)		1643 France: Moliere establishes *Comedie Francaise*
	1643 Taj Mahal completed	c. 1643 France: Ballet develops in court		1643 France: Coffee becomes popular

---

KEY DOCUMENT

Matsuo Bashō (1644 to 1694), generally regarded as the greatest Japanese haiku poet, lived a simple life as a Zen Buddhist. The haiku, which consists of three lines of five, seven, and five syllables, evolved from a form of collaborative poetry called *renga*. Here are two of Bashō's characteristic haiku:

The sun's way:	*Summer grasses*
Hollyhocks turn toward it	*All that remains*
Through all the rain of May.	*Of soldier's visions.*

	Art and Architecture	Music	Literature	Popular Culture
	1644 Ribera: *St. Paul the Hermit*		1644 to 1694 Bashō Matsuo: Haiku reaches its peak	1644 England: Globe Theatre pulled down
	1645 Rembrandt: *The Rabbi*		1645 Kornaros: *Rotokritos*, Greek epic poem	

Art and Architecture	Music	Literature	Popular Culture
1645 Velázquez: *King Philip IV on a Boar Hunt*		1645 Milton: *L'Allegro, Il Penseroso*	
1646 Rembrandt: *Adoration of the Shepherds*			
1646 Lorrain: *Hagar and the Angel*			
			1647 England: First newspaper ad
1648 Rembrandt: *The Pilgrims at Emmaus*	c. 1648 Japan: Koto becomes national instrument; strings produce five-toned scale	1648 Herrick: *Hesperides*	1648 Italy: Mirrors, chandeliers made
1648 Ribera: *The Holy Family with St. Catherine*	1648 Aria and recitative become two clear-cut parts of opera	1648 to 1718 China K'ung Shang-jen: *Peach Blossom Fan*	
		1649 Luis Lasso de la Vega: *Huei Tlamahuicoltica,* one legend of Virgin of Guadeloupe	
		1649 Lovelace: *Lucasta*	
1650 Murillo: *The Holy Family with the Little Bird*	1650 Overture emerges as musical form	1650 US: Anne Bradstreet, poetry	

Did You Know?

The Great Fire of London destroyed most of the city, including 13,000 houses, St. Paul's Cathedral, and 84 churches, the Guildhall, markets, wharves, and even shipping on the river Thames.

		1650s Marvell's poetry	

	Art and Architecture	Music	Literature	Popular Culture
	c. 1650 de la Tour: *St. Sebastian*	1650 Modern harmony starts; modulation develops	1650 Japan: Modern No drama starts	
			1650 Corneille: *Andromede*	
		c. 1650 to 1740 Italy: Stradivari family perfects the violin		
1651 to 1660	France replaces Italy as the center of the arts in Europe		1651 Hobbs: *Leviathan*	
	1651 Rembrandt: *Girl with a Broom*			

Did You Know?

Alice Clawson, who lived on Virginia's eastern shore in the mid-1600s, didn't take any nonsense from anyone. When her husband came home from a stay with Nanticoke Indians with an Indian woman, Alice hauled her two-timing husband off to the local court. They agreed with her outrage, and Alice became the first Virginia woman to obtain a divorce.

	Art and Architecture	Music	Literature	Popular Culture
		1652 Hilton: Collection of rounds and canons	1652 to 1725 Chikamatsu Monzaemon, Japanese dramatist, wrote Kabuki and jojuri (puppet) plays	1652 France: Minuet becomes fashionable
		1653 to 1713 Arcangelo Corelli: Will develop concerto		1653 France: First mail boxes (Paris)
	1654 Rembrandt: *Portrait of Jan Six*		1654 Joost van den Vondel: religious drama, *Lucifer*	1654 Germany: First picture book for children
	1655 Rembrandt: *Woman Bathing in a Stream*			
	1656 Vermeer: *The Procuress*	1656 England: First opera house opens in London		

Art and Architecture	Music	Literature	Popular Culture
1656 Velázquez: *Las Meninas,* realism			
1657 Vermeer: *The Spinners*			
1659 Vermeer: *Young Girl With Flute*			
1660 Vermeer: *The Cook*	First public concerts in modern sense	1660 to 1669 Pepys: *Diary*	1660 Germany, England: Women allowed to act on stage
		c. 1660 to 1731 Daniel Defoe	1660 England: Toilets imported from France

Did You Know?

Louis XIV's palace of Versailles took 47 years to complete and cost millions of dollars. The facade measures 1,361 feet and is surrounded by sumptuous gardens. During Louis' life, 5,000 courtiers lived in the palace and another 5,000 servants lived close by.

Art and Architecture	Music	Literature	Popular Culture
1661 to 1670 France: Louis XIV starts building Versailles			
1661 to 1674 Murillo: Paintings for almshouse of St. Jorge			
1662 Andre Le Notre: Designs park and gardens at Versailles		1662 Butler: *Hudibras*	
		1662 Wigglesworth: *The Day of Doom*	
1663 France: Charles Le Brun, director of French Academy, responsible for Salons de la Guerre and de la Paix	1663 England: First collection of anthems	1663 Davenant: *The Siege of Rhodes*	1633 England: Turnpike toll introduced

Art and Architecture	Music	Literature	Popular Culture
1663 Poussin: *The Four Seasons*			
1664 Vermeer: *The Lacemaker*	1664 French horn becomes part of orchestra	1664 Moliere: *Tartuffe*	1664 Wigs get bigger
1665 Gian Lorenzo Bernini, baroque master, attempts to redesign Louvre, but plans rejected		1665 de La Rochefoucauld: *Reflections*	1665 Canada: First modern census
1665 Murillo: *Rest on the Flight into Egypt*		1665 Moliere: *Don Juan*	
1665 Rembrandt: *The Jewish Bride*			
	c. 1666 Germany, Italy: Trio sonata develops	1666 Dryden: *Annus Mirabilis*	1666 Great Fire of London
	1666 Stradivari labels his violins for first time	1666 Moliere: *Misanthrope*	1666 Cheddar cheese first made

Did You Know?

A popular form of entertainment in Burma is the pwe, *a type of folk opera that combines story with music and dance.*

		1667 Milton: *Paradise Lost* begun	
		1667 Racine: *Andromaque*	
		1667 to 1745 Jonathan Swift	
1668 Rembrandt: *Return of the Prodigal Son*		1668 de la Fontaine: *Fables*	
		1668 Aphra Behn: *Oroonoko*	

Art and Architecture	Music	Literature	Popular Culture
		1688 Etherege: *She Wou'd If She Cou'd*	
1669 Hobbema: *The Avenue of Middleharnis,* Dutch landscapes			
1669 France: Louis Le Vau: leading baroque architect, remodels Versailles			
1669 Vermeer: *Girl at the Spinet*			
c. 1670 van Ruisdael: *Windmill at Wijk*		1670 to 1727 William Congreve, English dramatist	
1671 to 1680 1672 France: Lorrain's *Evening* shows classical landscape tradition			
1672 China: Kao-ts'en: *Autumn Landscape*			
		1674 Milton: *Paradise Lost,* greatest epic poem in English	Clocks equipped with minute hands
		c. 1674 to 1675 US: Edward Taylor, metaphysical poems	
		c. 1674 Wycherley: *The Country Wife,* a bawdy play	
1675 England: Christopher Wren, greatest English architect, begins work on St. Paul's Cathedral			1675 Paris becomes center of European culture
		1676 Etherege: *A Mode of Mode*	

Art and Architecture	Music	Literature	Popular Culture
		1677 Racine: *Phedre*	1677 France: Ice cream becomes popular in Paris
		1677 Wycherley: *The Plain Dealer*	
	c. 1678 Chorale prelude for organ develops	1678 Bunyan: *Pilgrim's Progress*	
		c. 1678 Mexico: Spanish nun Juana Inez de la Cruz: *A Nosegay of Poetic Flowers*	
		1678 Dryden: *All for Love*	
		1679 P'u-Sungling: *Liao Chai*	Dodo bird extinct
	c. 1680 Continuo played on keyboard instrument (often, harpsichord) in Scarlatti's cantatas		
	1680 Stradivari makes first known cello		
1681 to 1690		1681 Marvell: *Poems*	
		1681 Dryden: *Absalom and Achitophel*	
		1682 Ihara Saikaku: *Life of a Sensuous Man* (Japanese comic realism)	1682 France: Royal family moves into Versailles
	1685 to 1750 Johann Sebastian Bach		
		1686 Japan: *Shusse Kagekiyo,* puppet play	
1688 to 1745 Lukas von Hildebrandt: will bring "Austrian Baroque" style to its peak		1688 to 1744 Alexander Pope, English poet and critic	

Art and Architecture	Music	Literature	Popular Culture

Art and Architecture	Music	Literature	Popular Culture
	1689 Purcell: *Dido and Aeneas* (opera)		
	c. 1690 Modulation makes music more harmonic	1690 Locke: *Essay Concerning Human Understanding*	
	c. 1690 Corelli: Develops concerto, including soloist and orchestra	1690 to 1644 Bashō: Japan's foremost haiku poet, *The Narrow Road of the Interior*	
1691 to 1700 1691 to 1694 Italy: Andrea dal Pozzo, leader of baroque style of illusionist decoration		1691 Sor Juana Ines de la Cruz: *Reply to Sor Filotea de la Cruz*	1691 France: First directory of addresses
		1692 Purcell: *The Fairy Queen*	1692 US: Salem witchcraft trials
			1692 Manual of language for deaf-mutes
1693 Spain: Churri-guera's *St. Salamanca* shows rich style called *Churriguesque*	1693 Scarlatti: *Teodora* (opera)		
		1694 Congreve: *The Double Dealer*	
		1694 to 1778 Voltaire: dramatist, wit, novelist	

Did You Know?

Voltaire was the pen name of Francois Marie Arouet, one of France's greatest satirical writers.

Art and Architecture	Music	Literature	Popular Culture
		1695 Congreve: *Love for Love*	
1696 England: John Vanbrugh and Nicolas Hawksmoor use baroque architecture on Castle Howard	c. 1696 Organ music fugues develop; shown in music of Bach and Buxtehude	1696 Cibber: *Love's Last Shift* 1696 Regnard: *Schelmuffsky,* German adventure novel	
1697 Yucatan: Spanish destroy last parts of Maya civilization		1697 Perrault: fairy tales	1697 Sedan chair becomes popular means of transportation
1698 France: Place Vendome, Paris			
	1699 Manual on dance notation	1699 Dryden: *Fables Ancient and Modern*	1699 Russia: Tax on beards
		1700 Congreve: *The Way of the World*	1700 Germany: Unmarried women taxed in Berlin
		1700 Japan: Kabuki theatre flourishes	1700 Toilet becomes popular piece of furniture

---

KEY DOCUMENT

In his best-selling *Poor Richard's Almanack,* Benjamin Franklin said: "Early to bed, and early to rise, makes a man healthy, wealthy, and wise;" "He that lives on hope will die fasting;" "Love your neighbor: yet don't pull down your hedge;" "Three may keep a secret if two of them are dead."

Art and Architecture	Music	Literature	Popular Culture
			1700 New York: Reading room established that becomes New York Library Society in 1754
1701 to 1710	1701 Joseph Sauveur uses "acoustics" in relation to tone		1701 Yale College founded
			1701 University of Venice founded

Art and Architecture	Music	Literature	Popular Culture
			1701 Captain Kidd hanged for piracy
1702 Japan: Kano and Yamato types of painting combined			1702 England's first daily newspaper, the *Daily Courant*

Did You Know?

William Kidd (c. 1645 to 1701) went to sea when he was still a teenager and early showed a keen aptitude for piracy. In 1697 and 1698, he seized several ships off the coast of Africa, including the loaded Quedagh Merchant. When he heard a warrant had been issued for his arrest, Kidd headed from the West Indies to Oyster Bay, Long Island, and then to Boston. Kidd tried to talk his way out of the predicament, but he was convicted of piracy and hanged. Some of his treasure was later found on Gardiners Island, off the east coast of Long Island, and the belief has long persisted that a great deal more booty is hidden in the region.

Art and Architecture	Music	Literature	Popular Culture
1703 Russia: St. Petersburg shows influence of Versailles			
1703 England: Work started on Buckingham Palace			
	1704 George Frideric Handel: *St. John Passion*	1704 Swift: *Tale of a Tub*	1704 *Boston News Letter,* first newspaper in US
	1704 J. S. Bach: First cantata		
1705 England: Blenheim Palace shows influence of Versailles			
		1706 to 1790 Benjamin Franklin: Statesman, writer, scientist, printer	
		1706 Defoe: *The Apparition of One Mrs. Veal*	

Art and Architecture	Music	Literature	Popular Culture
			1707 Eau-de cologne made in Cologne
1708 France: Coypel uses Roman baroque style in Versailles' ceiling			
	1709 "For He's a Jolly Good Fellow" becomes well-known song	1709 Pope: *Pastorals*	1709 US: New York City: Slave market set up on the corner of Wall and Water Streets; men, women, and children were bought and sold there
		1709 to 1784 Samuel Johnson	
	1709 Cristofori invents pianoforte	1709 Steele's journal: *Tatler*	
	1710 Handel becomes Kapellmeister to George of Hanover		1710 England: First copyright law
	1711 Clarinet first used in an orchestra	1711 Pope: *Essay on Criticism*	1710 Three-color printing invented
	1711 Handel: *Rinaldo*	1711 Addison's journal: *Spectator*	
	1711 Tuning fork invented		
	1712 Handel: *Il Pastor fido* (opera)		1712 England: Last witch executed
	1713 Handel: *Utrecht Te Deum*		
	1713 France: School of dance established at Paris opera		
			1714 Prussia: Witch trials abolished
1715 France: Rococo style exemplified in Giles Marie Oppenordt's fountains, complete with shells, swirls, and scrolls	c. 1715 Europe: Italian becomes language of opera	1715 to 1735 Le Sage: *Gil Blas,* picaresque novel	1715 France: Vaudeville

(row label, left margin) 1711 to 1720

Art and Architecture	Music	Literature	Popular Culture
		1716 Japan: Hakuseki *Ori-Taku-Shiba*	
		1716 US: First English actors perform	
1717 Watteau: *Departure for the Island of Cythera*		1717 Pope: *The Rape of the Lock*	1717 Prussia: School attendance mandatory
1718 Watteau: *Parc Fete*			1718 US: Blackbeard blockades North Carolina; the Governor of Virginia offers a bounty for the pirate's head; after a fierce battle, Blackbeard's head is impaled on the victor's mast

Did You Know?

Robinson Crusoe *is often called the first true novel in English.*

Art and Architecture	Music	Literature	Popular Culture
	1719 Handel composes Italian-language operas	1719 Defoe: *Robinson Crusoe*	
	1719 First book on Turkish music		
	1720 Handel: *Harpsichord Suite No. 5*		1720 Novels first serialized in newspapers
			1720 England: Wallpaper becomes popular
1721 to 1730	1721 J. S. Bach: *The Brandenburg Concertos*	1721 Monzaemon: *The Love Suicides* at Anijima (written for puppet theatre)	

Art and Architecture	Music	Literature	Popular Culture
		1722 Defoe: *Moll Flanders,* realistic novel	

Did You Know?

Although a severe childhood illness stunted his growth (he grew to a mere four feet six inches) and left him crippled and tubercular, Alexander Pope was the literary dictator of his age in English letters. Poet, critic, philosopher, he was often on the attack, which earned him the nickname "Wicked Wasp of Twickenham," from the village where he lived.

Art and Architecture	Music	Literature	Popular Culture
	1723 J. S. Bach: *St. John Passion*		
	1723 Handel: *Ottone* (opera)		
	1724 Handel: *Giulio Cesare* (opera)		1724 England: Gin becomes a fashionable drink
	1726 Reinhard Keiser comic opera uses spoken dialogue rather than recitative, marking emergence of light opera	1726 Swift: *Gulliver's Travels*	1726 Scotland: First circulating library
			1727 Brazil: Coffee first planted
			1727 England: First marriage ad in a newspaper
			1727 Quakers demand slavery be abolished
	1728 John Gay: *The Beggar's Opera* first performed; new style of political satire	1728 Pope: *The Dunciad*	
	1729 J. S. Bach: *St. Matthew Passion*	1729 Swift: "A Modest Proposal"	1729 China: Opium smoking prohibited

Art and Architecture	Music	Literature	Popular Culture

KEY DOCUMENT

Here's an excerpt from Swift's "A Modest Proposal for Preventing the Children of Poor People in Ireland from Being a Burden to their Parents or Country, and for Making them Beneficial to the Public":

"I shall now therefore humbly propose my own thoughts, which I hope will not be liable to the least objection.

"I have been assured by a very knowing American of my acquaintance, in London, that a young healthy child well nursed is at a year a most delicious, nourishing, and wholesome food, whether stewed, roasted, baked, or boiled; and I have no doubt that it will equally serve in a fricassee or a ragout.

"I do humbly offer it to public consideration that of the hundred and twenty thousand children, already computed, twenty thousand may be reserved for breed, whereof only one fourth part to be males, which is more than we allow to sheep, black cattle, or swine . . . that the remaining hundred thousand may, at a year, be offered for sale to the persons of quality and fortune through the kingdom, always advising the mother to let them suck plentifully in the last month, so as to render them plump and fat for a good table. A child will make two dishes at an entertainment for friends; and when the family dines alone, the fore or hind quarters will make a reasonable dish, and seasoned with a little pepper or salt will be very good boiled on the fourth day, especially in winter."

	Art and Architecture	Music	Literature	Popular Culture
	1730 Hogarth: *Before and After*		1730 Gottsched: *Critische Dichtkunst,* German Enlightenment	
1731 to 1740	1731 Hogarth: *The Harlot's Progress*	1731 Guistini: *Sonate da Cimbalo di piano e forte,* likely first modern piano work	1731 Abbe Prevost: *Manon Lescaut,* foreshadows Romanticism	
	1732 Paris: Facade of Ste. Sulpice shows reaction against rococo	1732 England: Covent Garden opera house opens	1732 Franklin: *Poor Richard's Almanack*	
		1733 J. S. Bach *Mass in B Minor* (short version)		
			1734 Montesquieu: *Considerations of the Causes of the Grandeur of the Romans and their Decadence,* sociopolitical analysis	1734 Mme. de Lambert recommends women get college education

Art and Architecture	Music	Literature	Popular Culture
1735 Hogarth: *The Rake's Progress*			1735 John Peter Zenger, New York City editor, acquitted of libel, establishing freedom of press

---

> ## KEY DOCUMENT
>
> If you would not be forgotten,
> As soon as you are dead and rotten,
> Either write things worth reading,
> Or do things worth the writing.
> —Benjamin Franklin

Art and Architecture	Music	Literature	Popular Culture
			1735 US: First musical theatre in America, at Charleston, SC
1736 Hogarth: *The Good Samaritan*		1736 Voltaire: *Le Mondain*	
	1737 Rameau: *Castor et Pollux*		
1738 Chardin: *La Gouvernante*	1738 J. S. Bach: *Kyrie* in *Mass in B Minor* shows mastery of contrapuntal writing	1738 Voltaire: *Discours sur l'Homme*	1738 Herculaneum excavated
1740 Hogarth: *Captain Coram*		1740 to 1795 James Boswell	1740s US: Population of 13 colonies is 1.5 million, including 250,000 slaves; Boston and Philadelphia largest cities
		1740 Richardson: *Pamela*	
			1740 Russia: Freedom of the press
1741 to 1750	1741 Gluck: *Artaserse* (opera)		1741 England: David Garrick's stage debut
	1741 Handel: *The Messiah*		

Art and Architecture	Music	Literature	Popular Culture
1742 Boucher: *Bath of Diana*		1742 Fielding: *Joseph Andrews*	c. 1742 Japan: Color printing developed
1742 Hogarth: *The Graham Children*			
1743 Hogarth: *Marriage a la Mode*	1743 Handel: *Samson*	1743 Pope: *The Dunciad*, mock heroic attack on betrayal of literature by hack writers	
1743 to 1772 Church at Vierzehnheiligen, richly painted in gold, pink, and white, shows Italian baroque skill of Balthasar Neumann			

Did You Know?

Handel composed The Messiah *in eighteen days.*

Art and Architecture	Music	Literature	Popular Culture
1745 Hogarth: *Self-Portrait*		1745 Goldoni: *The Servant of Two Masters*, comic play	
1746 Boucher: *The Milliners*			1746 France: Quadrille becomes popular dance
1746 Reynolds: *The Eliot Family*			1746 Princeton University founded
			1746 England: People forbidden to wear tartans

Did You Know?

Johnson's Dictionary *was immense: Writing in 80 large notebooks, Johnson defined more than 40,000 words, illustrating many of their meanings with more than 100,000 quotations drawn from English writing on every subject. Unlike his predecessors, Johnson treated English as a living language and acknowledged shades of meaning. His Dictionary did not have a rival for more than a century.*

	Art and Architecture	Music	Literature	Popular Culture
		1747 Handel: *Judas Maccabaeus*	1747 to 1755 Johnson's *Dictionary*	
		1748 American barn dances add new type of music	1748 Izumo II: *The Treasury of Loyal Retainers* (Japanese play about samurai)	1748 Pompeii discovered
			1748 Richardson: *Clarissa*	
	1749 Gainsborough: *Mr. and Mrs. Robert Andrews*	1749 Handel: *Music for the Royal Fireworks*	1749 Fielding: *Tom Jones*	1749 Portugal: Sign language invented
	1749 Horace Walpole's Strawberry Hill House made Gothic rococo fashionable			
	Neoclassicism spreads across Europe		1750 Gray: "Elegy Written in a Country Church Yard"	1750 US: First theatre opens
	Chinoiserie, a taste for Chinese art and design, becomes popular in Europe			
1751 to 1760		1751 Handel: *Jephta*	1751 *Encyclopédie* "bible" of the Enlightenment	1751 Minuet becomes popular dance
			1752 Fielding: *Amelia*	Chippendale makes his furniture
	1753 to 1806 Japan's Kitagawa Utamaro, one of the greatest exponents of the ukiyoke school of painting			
	1754 Boucher: *Judgment of Paris* series			1754 Germany: University of Halle graduates first female medical doctor
	1754 Allan Ramsay: *Dialogue on Taste* sparks an interest in antiquity			1754 Scotland: St. Andrews Golf Club founded

Art and Architecture	Music	Literature	Popular Culture
1754 to 1762 St. Petersburg Winter Palace melds rococo forms with baroque			
1755 Gainsborough: *Milkmaid and Woodcutter*		1755 Samuel Johnson: *Dictionary of the English Language*	1755 US: Postal service established
		1755 Mikhail Lomonosov: Father of modern Russian literature, *Grammar*	1755 Great Lisbon earthquake; thousands killed
			1755 University of Moscow founded
1756 Reynolds: *Admiral Holbourne and His Son*	1756 to 1791 Wolfgang Amadeus Mozart: Austrian composer		
1757 Gainsborough: *The Artist's Daughter with a Cat*			
	1758 First book on how to play the guitar		1758 Halley's comet

Did You Know?

Rousseau was a pioneer in the Romantic movement in which writers, artists, and musicians stressed emotion over reason. His writing influenced William Wordsworth, William Blake, and Johann von Goethe.

Art and Architecture	Music	Literature	Popular Culture
	1759 Haydn: *Symphony No. 1 in D Major*	1759 Voltaire: *Candide*	1759 England: British Museum opens
		1760 Sterne: *Tristram Shandy*	
1761 to 1770 1761 Boucher: *Girl and Birdcatcher*		1761 Rousseau: *La Nouvelle Heloise*, advances idea of "noble savage"	1761 France: First veterinary school
	1762 Mozart tours Europe, 6 years old	1762 Rousseau: *Social Contract*	1762 Paris: Sorbonne Library opens

Art and Architecture	Music	Literature	Popular Culture
1762 Syon House mixes English Palladian with Roman architecture and Renaissance palaces	1762 Benjamin Franklin turns the harmonica into a practical instrument		
			1763 England: Boswell first meets Johnson
	1764 Haydn: *Symphony No. 22 in E-flat*		1764 London houses first numbered
			1764 US: Brown University established
		1765 Walpole: *The Castle of Otranto,* gothic novel	1765 US: First medical school at College of Pennsylvania
	1766 Haydn: *Great Mass in E-flat*	1766 Goldsmith: *The Vicar of Wakefield*	1766 London: First paved sidewalk
			1766 England: Theatre Royal in Bristol
			1766 India: Famine in Bengal
	1767 Gluck: *Alceste* String quartets become popular	1767 US: Godfrey: *The Price of Parthia,* first American play 1767 Sterne completes *Tristram Shandy*	
	1768 Mozart's first produced opera Mozart is one of the first great composers who tries to live independently without a patron, but he dies a pauper		1768 England: Royal Academy of Art founded
1769 Fragonard: *The Study*			

Art and Architecture	Music	Literature	Popular Culture
1769 Falconet: Statue of Peter the Great shows Russian classicism in hands of foreign artists			
1770 Gainsborough: *The Blue Boy*	1770 to 1827 Ludwig van Beethoven		1770 France: First public restaurant
1771 to 1780 1771 West: *The Death of Wolfe*		1771 *Encyclopedia Britannica*	
	1772 First barrel organ	1772 Lessing: *Emilia Galotti*	A dollar is nicknamed "buck" because in the mid-1700s, a buckskin is worth about a dollar
1773 Reynolds: *The Graces Decorating Hymen*		c. 1773 US: Phillis Wheatley: poems	1773 Germany: Waltz becomes chic dance
		1773 Goldsmith: *She Stoops to Conquer,* comedy of manners	
		1774 Goethe: *Sorrows of Young Werther* began a cult of hero ruled by heart rather than head	
1775 Gainsborough's *William Henry, Duke of Gloucester,* glamorous and richly colored, challenges Reynold's supremacy in English portrait painting		1775 Beaumarchais: *The Barber of Seville*	1775 Franz Mesmer suggests that "animal magnetism" causes attraction between certain people
		1775 Sheridan: *The Rivals*	
		c. 1775 Akinari: *Tales of Moonlight and Rain* (Japanese supernatural stories)	1775 US: Patrick Henry's "liberty or death" speech
1776 Fragonard: *The Washerwoman*	1776 Mozart: *Haffner Serenade*	1776 Gibbon: *Decline and Fall of the Roman Empire*	
	1776 Mozart: *Serenade in D Major*	1776 Paine's *Common Sense*	
		1776 *Sturm und Drang* movement named	

Art and Architecture	Music	Literature	Popular Culture

> ### KEY DOCUMENT
>
> Thomas Paine was an obscure corset-maker when he rocketed to fame as a fiery proponent of separation from Britain. His first pamphlet, *Common Sense,* appeared in 1776, a time when most colonists still hoped the quarrel with England could be settled amicably. Paine pointed out the advantage, necessity, and obligation of a break with England and urged "an open and determined DECLARATION OF INDEPENDENCE." The pamphlet's opening has become famous: "These are the times that try men's souls: The summer soldier and sunshine patriot will, in this crisis, shrink from the service of his country; but he that stands it NOW, deserves the love and thanks of man and woman. Tyranny, like hell, is not easily conquered; yet we have this consolation with us, that the harder the conflict, the more glorious the triumph."

Art and Architecture	Music	Literature	Popular Culture
		1776 to 1787 Gibbon *Decline and Fall of the Roman Empire*	
1777 Gainsborough: *The Watering Place*	1777 Haydn: *Symphony No. 63 in C Major*	1777 Sheridan: *The School for Scandal*	1777 US: Stars and Stripes becomes flag of Continental Congress
			1778 England: Bramah builds a better toilet
1780 Copley: *Death of Chatham*	1780 Spain: "Bolero" dance created		1780 England: About 70,000 Catholics
	1780 Haydn: "Toy" Symphony		1780 Circular saw invented
			1780 First fountain pen
1781 to 1790	1781 Haydn: "Russian" string quartets		
	1782 Mozart: *The Abduction from Seraglio* (opera)	1782 to 1788 Rousseau: *Confessions*	
		1782 Crèvecoeur: *Letters from an American Farmer*	

Art and Architecture	Music	Literature	Popular Culture

KEY DOCUMENT

In one of his *Letters,* Hector St. John de Crèvecoeur attempted to define an "American": "What, then, is this American, this new man? He is neither an European nor the descendant of an European; hence that strange mixture of blood, which you will find in no other country. I could point out to you a family whose grandfather was an Englishman, whose wife was Dutch, whose son married a French woman, and whose present four sons have now wives of different nations. He is an American, who, leaving behind him all his ancient prejudices and manners, receives new ones from the new mode of life he has embraced, the new government he obeys, and the new rank he holds. He becomes an American by being received in the broad lap of our great Alma Mater. Here individuals of all nations are melted into a new race of men, whose labors and posterity will one day cause great changes in the world. . . . The American ought therefore to love this country much better than that wherein he or his forefathers were born."

		1782 de Lacios: *Liasons Dangereuses*	
	1783 Mozart: *Mass in C Minor*	1783 William Blake: poems	
		1783 Noah Webster: *Spelling Book;* 60 million copies will be sold	
1784 Goya: *Don Manuel de Zungia*	1784 Salieri: *Les Danaides*	1784 Beaumarchais: *The Marriage of Figaro*	1784 US: *Pennsylvania Packet and General Advertiser* is first long-term daily paper

KEY DOCUMENT

Here are the opening stanzas to William Blake's *The Tyger:*

*Tyger! Tyger! burning bright
In the forests of the night,
What immortal hand or eye
Could frame thy fearful symmetry?*

*In what distant deeps or skies
Burnt the fire of thine eyes?
On what wings dare he aspire?
What the hand dare seize the fire?*

Art and Architecture	Music	Literature	Popular Culture
1784 David: *Oath of the Horatii* establishes Neoclassical painting in France			1784 France: First school for the blind
1785 Thailand: Emerald Buddha Chapel 1785 Richmond, VA: Capitol brings Neoclassic architecture to US		1785 Cowper: poet; "The Task," shows deep love of nature and prefigures Romantics	1785 Mexico: Academy of Fine Arts established; brings Neoclassicism to Mexico
1786 Reynolds: *The Duchess of Devonshire* 1786 Gilray: "A New Way to the National Debt" develops art of caricature	1786 Mozart: *The Marriage of Figaro*	1786 Scotland: Robert Burns: first book of poems, *Kilmarnock Edition,* widely acclaimed 1786 Bourgoyne: *The Heiress*	
1787 David: *Death of Socrates* 1787 Reynolds: *Lady Heathfield*	1787 Mozart: *Don Giovanni*	1787 US: Tyler: *The Contrast,* satiric comic play 1787 Schiller: *Don Carlos*	1787 US: Dollar bill first used as currency
1788 David: *Love of Paris and Helena*	1788 Mozart: Symphonies in E-flat, G Minor, and "Jupiter" (considered greatest symphonies)	1788 Goethe: *Egmont*	1788 France: Bread riots
1789 Gerard: *Joseph and His Brothers*	1789 Ernst Chladni: Invents *euphonium,* musical instrument in tuba family	1789 US: William Hill Brown: *The Power of Sympathy,* first American novel, published anonymously 1789 Blake: "Songs of Innocence"	
	1790 Mozart: *Cosi fan tutte*	1790 Burns: "Tam O'Shanter"	1790 US: First session of Supreme Court
1791 to 1800	1791 Haydn: *Surprise Symphony*	1791 Boswell: *Life of Johnson*	

Art and Architecture	Music	Literature	Popular Culture
	1791 Mozart: *The Magic Flute*		
1792 Soane: Bank of England Stock Office design shows height of classicism	1792 Claude-Joseph Rouget de Lisle: *La Marseilles*	1792 Mary Wollstonecraft: *Vindication of the Rights of Women*	1792 England: Gas lights first used
	1792 Cimarosa: *Il Matrimonio Segreto* (opera); called "Italian Mozart"		
1793 David: The *Murder of Marat* shows political element in some French art	1793 Paganini, master violinist, makes his debut	1793 Marquis de Sade: *La philosophie dans le boudoir*	1793 US: Yellow fever epidemic in Philadelphia
			1793 US: Capitol built in Washington, DC
			1793 France: Education compulsory
1794 Goya: *Procession of the Flagellants*	1794 Burns: Scottish poet, *Auld Lang Syne*	1794 Blake: *Songs of Innocence and Experience*	1794 France: First Technical college
1794 Trumbull signs *The Declaration of Independence*			
1795 Carstens: *Night and Her Children*	1795 Haydn: Twelve London symphonies	1795 Goethe: *Wilhelm Meisters Lehrjahre*	1795 France adopts metric system
1795 Goya: *The Duchess of Alba*	1795 Beethoven: Three piano trios		1795 England: First horse-drawn railroad
1796 Goya: *Los Caprichos*		1796 Fanny Burney: British writer, *Camilla*	1796 British rulers take violin to India, where it is used in their music
1797 Turner: *Millbank, Moon Light*	1797 Haydn: *Emperor Quartet*	1797 Coleridge: "Kubla Khan," first edition	
		1798 Wordsworth and Coleridge: *Lyrical Ballads*	

Art and Architecture	Music	Literature	Popular Culture
		1798 Coleridge: *The Rime of the Ancient Mariner*	
		1798 Brown: *Wieland, or The Transformation*	
1799 Goya: *Capichos* etching	1799 to 1800 Beethoven: First symphony		1799 Egypt: Rosetta Stone discovered
1799 David: *Rape of the Sabine Women*	1799 Haydn: *The Creation*		
1800 Goya: *Portrait of a Woman*		1800 Edgeworth: *Castle Rackrent*	1800 US: Library of Congress established in Washington, DC with a $5,000 stipend
		1800 Morton: *Speed the Plough*	

Part 1 Fine Arts
1801 TO 2000

	Art and Architecture	Music	Literature	Popular Culture
1801 to 1810		1802 Beethoven: *Symphony No. 2 in D Major, Op. 36*	1802 Coleridge: *Dejection: an Ode*	1802 Babylonian cuneiforms deciphered
			1802 de Chateaubriand: *Le Genie de Christianisme* will greatly influence French Romantic writers	
	1803 West: *Christ Healing the Sick*	1803 Beethoven: *Sonata for violin and piano, Op. 47*		
		1804 Beethoven: *Symphony No. 3 in E-flat, Op. 55* ("Eroica")	1804 Schiller: *Wilhelm Tell* describes the need for political freedom	
	1805 Turner: *Shipwreck*	1805 Beethoven: *Fidelio* (opera)	1805 Bretano and von Arnim: *Des Knaben Wunderhorn,* collected folk poems	
	1806 Ingres: *Napoleon I on the Imperial Throne*	1806 Beethoven: *Symphony No. 4 in B-flat, Op. 60*		
	1807 David: *Coronation of Napoleon* 1807 Turner: *Sun Rising in a Mist*	1807 Beethoven: *Leonora Overture No. 3* 1807 Beethoven: *Coriolanus Overture*	1807 Wordsworth: *Ode on Intimations of Immortality*	1807 London streets lit by gas lights
	1808 Goya: *Execution of the Citizens of Madrid* 1808 Girodet: *Entombment of Atala*	1808 Beethoven: *Fifth and Sixth Symphonies* ("Pastoral") Orchestral concerts become popular in London, Paris, and Vienna as the middle class begins to support music	1808 Goethe: *Faust* Part I 1808 Kleist: *Penthesilea*	1808 Source of Ganges River discovered

Art and Architecture	Music	Literature	Popular Culture
1809 Constable: *Malvern Hill*		1809 to 1849 Edgar Allan Poe	1809 Men's pigtails pass from fashion
1809 Ingres: *Charles-Francois Mallet*		1809 Washington Irving: *Rip Van Winkle*	
1809 to 1810 Friedrich: *Abbey Under Oak Trees*			
		1810 Scott: "Lady of the Lake"	
		1810 Madame de Stael: *De L'Allemagne*	

KEY DOCUMENT

Jane Austen's *Pride and Prejudice* begins this way:
    "It is a truth universally acknowledged, that a single man in possession of a good fortune, must be in want of a wife.
    "However little known the feelings or views of such a man may be on his first entering a neighborhood, this truth is so well fixed in the minds of the surrounding families, that he is considered as the rightful property of some one or other of their daughters."

	Art and Architecture	Music	Literature	Popular Culture
1811 to 1820	1811 Ingres: *Jupiter and Thetis*		1811 to 1896 Harriet Beecher Stowe	1811 England: Luddites (persons opposed to technological advances) destroy machines
			1811 Jane Austen: *Sense and Sensibility*	
	1812 Elgin Marbles brought from Egypt to England	1812 Beethoven: *Symphonies No. 7 (Op. 92) and No. 8 (Op. 93)*	1812 Germany: Brothers Grimm fairy tales	1812 England: First tin cans for preserving food
	1812 Goya: *Portrait of the Duke of Wellington*		1812 to 1870 Charles Dickens	1812 Egypt: Great Temple of Abu Simbel discovered
	1813 Turner: *Frosty Morning*	1813 to 1883 Richard Wagner: German composer	1813 Austen: *Pride and Prejudice*	1813 Waltz becomes the "in" dance
		1813 to 1901 Guiseppe Verdi: Italian composer	1813 Mary Shelley: "Queen Mab"	

Art and Architecture	Music	Literature	Popular Culture
		1813 Hoffmann: *The Devil's Elixir*	
1814 Goya: *The Second of May, 1808*		1814 Austen: *Mansfield Park*	
1814 Goya: *The Third of May, 1808*		1814 Scott: *Waverley*, first historical novel	
1814 Ingres: *L'Odalisque*			

Did You Know?

In 1814, when Ferdinand VII returned to the Spanish throne, y Lucientes Goya painted two pictures to commemorate Spanish resistance to French occupation. The first, entitled The Second of May, 1808, portrays the Spanish uprising against Napoleon's cavalry; the second and more famous, The Third of May 1808, depicts the French reprisals.

Art and Architecture	Music	Literature	Popular Culture
			1815 Miner's safety hat invented
1816 von Klenze: Palais Leuchtenberg, Munich, shows Neo-Renaissance architecture	1816 Rossini: *The Barber of Seville*	1816 Austen: *Emma*	
		1816 Coleridge: "Kubla Khan," second edition	
		1816 Keats: "On First Looking Into Chapman's Homer"	
1817 Géricault: *The Raft of the Medusa*			
1818 Spain: Prado Museum established	1818 Huber and Mohr's "Silent Night" Christmas carol	1818 Mary Shelley: *Frankenstein*	
1818 Géricault: *Decapitated Heads*		1818 Austen: *Northanger Abbey*	
1819 Turner: *Childe Harold's Pilgrimage*	1819 Ludwig von Beethoven goes deaf	1819 to 1820 Mary Shelley and John Keats write poems	1819 Egypt gives Cleopatra's Needle to England
1819 Géricault: *The Raft of the Medusa*	Franz Schubert popularizes the *lieder,* a German lyric song		

	Art and Architecture	Music	Literature	Popular Culture
			1819 to 1892 Walt Whitman: American poet	
			1819 Byron: *Don Juan* (first two cantos)	
	1820 Biedermeier style becomes fashionable		1820 Washington Irving: *The Sketch Book of Geoffrey Crayon, Gent*	1820 Venus de Milo discovered
	1820 Constable: *The Hay Wain*		1820 Keats: "Ode to a Nightingale"	1820 Conductor's baton introduced
	1820 Constable: *Dedham Lock and Mill*		1820 Scott: *Ivanhoe*	
			1820 to 1865 Mirza Asadulla Khan Ghalib, top Urdu poet, writes *ghazal* lyric poems on Islamic culture	
1821 to 1830	1821 Constable: *Study of Clouds at Hampstead*	Field composes short pieces for the piano	1821 Cooper: *The Spy*	1821 Champollion: deciphers Egyptian hieroglyphics using Rosetta Stone
		1821 von Weber: *Der Freischutz*		

Did You Know?

The Rosetta Stone turned out to be the key to unlocking the mystery of Egyptian hieroglyphics.

	Art and Architecture	Music	Literature	Popular Culture
	1822 Delacroix: *Dante and Virgil Crossing the Styx*	1822 Schubert: *Eighth Symphony* ("The Unfinished")	1822 Pushkin: *Eugene Onegin*	
	1822 to 1823 Géricault: *Portrait of a Child Murderer*		1822 De Quincey: *Confessions of an Opium Eater*	
		1823 "Home Sweet Home" song	1823 Cooper: *The Pioneers*, first "Leatherstocking" tale	
		1823 Beethoven: *Ninth Symphony*		

Art and Architecture	Music	Literature	Popular Culture
c. 1824 Friedrich: *Man and Woman Gazing at the Moon*			
1825 Constable: *Leaping Horse*	1825 Pushkin: *Boris Godunov* 1825 Musical Fund Society founds first important musical school in Philadelphia	1825 Manzoni: *I Promessi Sposi*	1825 France: Sacrilege becomes capital offense 1825 England: Tea roses introduced
	1826 Mendelssohn: Overture to *A Midsummer Night's Dream*	1826 Cooper: *The Last of the Mohicans* 1826 Hugo: *Odes et Ballades*	
1827 Constable: *The Cornfield* 1827 Delacroix: *Death of Sardanapalus* 1827 to 1838 Audubon: *Birds of America*		1827 Russia: Pushkin, foremost Russian writer, dies in duel 1827 Heine: *Book of Songs* 1827 Cenacle poets (Victor Hugo, Sainte-Beuve, etc.) 1828 Noah Webster: *The American Dictionary of the English Language* 1828 Hugo: *Odes Odes*	1827 Baedeker publishes travel guides Oil paints first sold in tubes, which made painting outdoors much easier
1829 to 1896 Sir John Everett Millais: English painter 1829 Constable: *Hadleigh Castle*	1829 Chopin: debut 1829 Chinese *sheng*, the mouth organ, brought to Vienna	1829 Irving: *The Conquest of Granada* 1829 to 1843 Balzac writes over ninety stories and novels	1829 US: First cooperative stores
1830 Structural ironwork used on buildings	1830 Berlioz: *Symphonie Fantastique*	1830 Stendhal: *The Red and The Black*	1830 Women's hemlines rise; sleeves and hats become huge; men's shirts have stiff collars

	Art and Architecture	Music	Literature	Popular Culture
1831 to 1840	Greek revival in European architecture at its height	Chopin writes piano nocturnes, mazurkas, and polonaises 1831 "My Country, 'Tis of Thee"; until 1931, one of US national anthems	1831 Hugo: *Notre Dame of Paris* 1831 Poe: *Poems*	1831 Charles Darwin sails on HMS *Beagle* to South America, New Zealand, and Australia 1831 Cholera pandemic 1831 New York: First horse-drawn buses
	1832 Constable: *Waterloo Bridge from Whitehall Stairs* 1832 Hiroshige: *Fifty-three Stages of the Tokaido* (color prints)		1832 Bulwer-Lytton: *Eugene Aram* 1832 Tennyson: *Lady of Shallot*	
		1833 Chopin: *Twelve Etudes, Op. 10* 1833 Mendelssohn: *Italian Symphony, Op. 90*	1833 Dickens: *Sketches by Boz*	1833 England: Charity bazaars catch on 1833 *New York Sun*, first successful penny daily newspaper 1833 US: Patent granted for first soda fountain
	1834 Delacroix: *Women of Algiers* 1834 Mulready: *Giving A Bite* 1834 to 1835 Hokusai: *The Thirty-Six Views of Mt. Fuji*	1834 Glinka: *A Life for the Tsar*	1834 Hugo: *The Hunchback of Notre Dame* 1834 Bulwer-Lytton: *The Last Days of Pompeii* 1834 Pushkin: *The Queen of Spades* 1834 Pushkin: *The Dead Princess*	1834 France: Fann Elssler ballet debut 1834 Shorthand method invented
	1835 Constable: *The Valley Farm* 1835 Phrase "Art for Art's Sake" coined	1835 Donizetti: *Lucia di Lammermoor*	1835 Hans Christian Anderson: Fairy tales 1835 to 1910 Samuel Clemens (Mark Twain)	1835 Halley's Comet reappears 1835 P. T. Barnum begins his career

Art and Architecture	Music	Literature	Popular Culture
			1835 Burglar-proof safe patents
1836 to 1868 Houses of Parliament show Gothic revival		1836 Dickens: *Pickwick Papers*	1836 "The Lancers" becomes fashionable dance
		1836 Carlyle: *Sartor Resartus*	
		1836 Leopardi: *La Ginestra*	
		1836 Gogol: *The Government Inspector*	
		1837 Hawthorne: *Twice-Told Tales*	1837 England starts registering births
		1837 Leopardi: *The Broom*	1837 US: Widespread financial panic
1838 Thorvaldsen: *Christ and the Twelve Apostles*	1838 Berlioz: *Benvenuto Cellini* (opera)	1838 Elizabeth Barrett Browning: *The Seraphim and Other Poems*	1838 Frédéric Chopin and George Sand have a torrid affair that rivets public attention
1839 Spitzweg: *The Poor Poet*		1839 Poe: "The Fall of the House of Usher," short story	1839 Maya culture rediscovered
1839 Turner: *The Fighting Temeraire*			1839 Cunard shipping line begun

Did You Know?

Popular from the day it was first exhibited, Turner's The Fighting Temeraire *satisfied the public's taste for emotion and drama. The* Temeraire *was famous for having avenged the death of Admiral Nelson in the Battle of Trafalgar, 1805. The* Temeraire *retaliated by blowing up the French ship; winning the Battle of Trafalgar, saving England from Napoleon's invasion.*

Art and Architecture	Music	Literature	Popular Culture
1840 Delacroix: *Entry of the Crusaders into Constantinople*	1840 France: First harmonium	1840 Cooper: *The Pathfinder*	1840 England: First postage stamps sold
		1840 Lermontov: *A Hero for Our Times*	

Art and Architecture	Music	Literature	Popular Culture
1840 England: Nelson's Column erected in Trafalgar Square			Greater range of oil colors available, including violets, bright greens, intense yellows
1840 to 1860 Barry and Pugin design the Houses of Parliament, London			

1841 to 1850

	Music	Literature	Popular Culture
	1841 Saxophone patented	1841 Elizabeth Barret Browning: *Pippa Passes*	1841 London: *Punch* humor magazine debuts
	1841 Schumann: *Symphony No. 1 B-flat Major, Op. 38* ("The Spring")	1841 Cooper: *The Deerslayer*	1841 Hypnosis discovered
		1841 Dickens: *The Old Curiosity Shop*	1841 P. T. Barnum opens "American Exhibition," museum of freaks
		1841 Poe: "Murders in the Rue Morgue," first detective story	1841 US: First university degrees granted to women

KEY DOCUMENT

Elizabeth Barrett Browning's *Sonnets from the Portuguese* contains the famous "Sonnet 43":

How do I love thee? Let me count the ways.
I love thee to the depth and breadth and height
My soul can reach, when feeling out of sight
For the ends of Being and ideal Grace.
I love thee to the level of everyday's
Most quiet need, by sun and candlelight.
I love thee freely, as men strive for Right;
I love thee purely, as they turn from Praise.
I love thee with the passion put to use
In my old griefs, and with my childhood's faith.
I love thee with a love I seemed to lose
With my lost saints—I love thee with the breath,
Smiles, tears, of all my life!—and, if God choose,
I shall but love thee better after death.

Art and Architecture	Music	Literature	Popular Culture
1842 Rousseau: *Under the Birches*		1842 Tennyson: *Ulysses*	1842 Polka becomes popular dance
		1842 Gogol: *Dead Souls*	Brass bands become popular
	1843 Wagner: *The Flying Dutchman*	1843 Dickens: *A Christmas Carol*	1843 US: Social reformer Dorothy Dix reveals shocking conditions in prisons and mental asylums
		1843 Tennyson: "Morte d'Arthur"	
			1843 France: First nightclub opens in Paris
			1843 Conjoined twins Chang and Eng Bunker marry the Yates sisters
1844 to 1856 Ingres: *Madame Moitessier*	1844 to 1908 Nikolai Rimsky-Korsakov, Russian composer	1844 Dumas père: *The Count of Monte Cristo*	1844 England: YMCA founded
1844 Turner: *Rain, Steam and Speed—The Great Western Railway*	1844 Verdi: *Ernani*	1844 Thackery: *Barry Lyndon*	
1845 Ingres: *La Comtesse d'Haussonville*	1845 Wagner: *Tannhauser*	1845 Poe: "The Raven" poem	1845 US Naval Academy opens
		1845 Douglass: *Narrative of the Life of Frederick Douglass, An American Slave*	
1846 Millais: *Pizarro Seizing the Inca of Peru*			1846 Elias Howe patents sewing machine
			1846 First painted Christmas cards sold
			1846 US: Smithsonian Institution opens in Washington, DC
	1847 Verdi: *Macbeth*	1847 Charlotte Bronte: *Jane Eyre*	1847 Evaporated milk invented

Art and Architecture	Music	Literature	Popular Culture
		1847 Emily Bronte: *Wuthering Heights*	
		1847 Thackery: *Vanity Fair*	
1848 Millet: *The Winnower*		1848 Karl Marx: *The Communist Manifesto*	1848 US: Spiritualism becomes popular
1848 Holman Hunt, Millais, D. G. Rossetti: found Pre-Raphaelite Brotherhood		1848 Dickens: *David Copperfield*	1848 First appendectomy
1848 Courbet: *After Dinner at Ornans*			
1849 Millet: *Stonebreakers*			1849 California gold rush
1849 Millais: *Christ in the House of His Parents*			1849 US: Amelia Bloomer agitates for reform in women's clothing

Did You Know?

In Sower and Stonebreakers, Jean-François Millet was turning away from the myths and allegories favored by the Academy and exploring the social realities of the time.

	Art and Architecture	Music	Literature	Popular Culture
	1850 Courbet: *The Stone Breakers*	1850 Jenny Lind, "The Swedish Nightingale," tours America	1850 Hawthorne: *The Scarlet Letter*	1850 Levi Strauss: Invents jeans
	1850 Millet: *Sower*		1850 E. B. Browning: *Sonnets from the Portuguese*	
	1850 Crystal Palace, London	1850 Wagner: *Lohengrin*	1850 Tennyson: *In Memoriam, A.H.H.*	
1851 to 1860	1851 to 1891 Baron Haussmann introduces squares, parks, and boulevards to Paris	1851 Verdi: *Rigoletto*	1851 Melville: *Moby Dick*	1851 England: Great Exhibition
			1851 Hawthorne: *The House of the Seven Gables*	1851 I. M. Singer improves the sewing machine

Art and Architecture	Music	Literature	Popular Culture

Did You Know?

In 1850, 21-year-old Levi Strauss went to San Francisco to peddle notions such as thread and pots and larger items such as canvas to the gold miners. The small items sold well, but Strauss found himself stuck with the rolls of canvas. While talking to one of the miners, Strauss learned that sturdy pants that would stand up to the rigors of digging were almost impossible to find. On the spot, Strauss measured the man with a piece of string. For six dollars in gold dust, Strauss had a piece of the left-over canvas made into a pair of stiff but rugged pants. The miner was delighted with the results, and word got around about "those pants of Levi's." Business was so good that Levi Strauss was soon out of canvas. He wrote to his two brothers in New York to send more. He received instead a tough brown cotton cloth made in Nimes, France, called serge de Nimes. Almost at once, the foreign term was shortened to denim. Strauss had the cloth dyed a rich blue called "indigo," which became a company trademark.

			1851 England: First double-decker bus
1852 to 1857 The rebuilt Louvre shows the influence of Neo-Renaissance and Neo-Baroque architecture		1852 Hawthorne: *Twice-Told Tales*	1852 US: Suspension bridge over Niagara Falls
1852 Hunt: *The Light of the World*		1852 Harriet Beecher Stowe: *Uncle Tom's Cabin*	
1852 Millais: *Ophelia*		1852 Hawthorne: *The Blithedale Romance*	
1852 Hunt: *Awakening Consciousness*		1852 Dickens: *Bleak House*	
		1852 Turgenev: *A Sportsman's Sketches*	
	1853 Steinway and Sons begin piano firm		1853 England: Queen Victoria uses chloroform during birth of seventh child, making anesthesia popular
	1853 Verdi: *La Traviata*		
1854 Millais: *The Reaper*		1854 Dickens: *Hard Times*	

Art and Architecture	Music	Literature	Popular Culture
		1854 Thoreau: *Walden*	
		1854 de Nerval: *Les Chimeres*	
		1854 Tennyson: "The Charge of the Light Brigade"	

Did You Know?

Tennyson's "The Charge of the Light Brigade" celebrates the Battle of Balakava.

Art and Architecture	Music	Literature	Popular Culture
1855 Daumier: *La Ronde*	1855 Berlioz: *Te Deum*	1855 Whitman: *Leaves of Grass*	1855 Florence Nightingale: Brings cleanliness to nursing
1855 to 1860 Corot: *The Valley*		1855 Longfellow: *The Song of Hiawatha*	
			1856 England: "Big Ben," 13.5 ton bell created
1857 Millais: *The Gleaners*		1857 Flaubert: *Madame Bovary*	1857 England: Victoria and Albert Museum
		1857 Baudelaire: *Flowers of Evil*	1857 US: *Atlantic Monthly* magazine
	1859 Gounod: *Faust*	1859 Darwin: *Origins of Species*	1859 Charles Blondin: crosses Niagara Falls on a tightrope
		1859 John Stuart Mill: *On Liberty*	
		1859 Fitzgerald: Translation of *The Rubaiyat of Omar Khayyam*	1859 Port Said, Egypt, founded
		1859 Dickens: *A Tale of Two Cities*	

	Art and Architecture	Music	Literature	Popular Culture
			1859 Goncharov: *Oblomov*	
	1860 to 1961 painter "Grandma Moses," Anna Mary Robertson	1860 to 1911 composer Gustave Mahler	1860 Hawthorne: *The Marble Faun*	
			1860 Eliot: *The Mill on the Floss*	
	1860 Manet: *Spanish Guitar Player*			
1861 to 1870	1861 Dore: *Inferno*	First American musical: *The Black Crook*	1861 Dickens: *Great Expectations*	1861 US: Passports first used
		US: Black spirituals flourish in South	1861 Dostoevsky: *The House of the Dead*	1861 England: First daily weather forecasts
			1861 Eliot: *Silas Marner*	
			1861 Datta: *Meghanadvadh*	
			1862 Turgenev: *Fathers and Sons*	

KEY DOCUMENT

Here is an excerpt from *The Battle Hymn of the Republic* by Julia Ward Howe.

Mine eyes have seen the glory of the coming of the Lord
He is trampling out the vintage where the grapes of wrath are stored,
He has loosed the fateful lightening of His terrible swift sword
His truth is marching on

Glory! Glory! Hallelujah!
Glory! Glory! Hallelujah!
Glory! Glory! Hallelujah!
His truth is marching on.

I have seen Him in the watch-fires of a hundred circling camps
They have builded Him an altar in the evening dews and damps
I can read His righteous sentence by the dim and flaring lamps
His day is marching on.

Glory! Glory! Hallelujah!
Glory! Glory! Hallelujah!
Glory! Glory! Hallelujah!
His truth is marching on.

Art and Architecture	Music	Literature	Popular Culture
		1862 Hugo: *Les Miserables*	
1863 Manet: *Dejeuner sur l'herbe*		1863 to 1933 Constantine Cavafy: Egyptian-born Greek poet	1863 US: Roller-skating debuts
1863 France: Salon des Refuses, Impressionist painters			
1863 Manet: *Olympia*		1863 Hale: *Man Without a Country*	
1863 Cabanel: *Birth of Venus*			
		1864 Dostoevsky: *Notes from Underground*	1864 US: "In God We Trust" first appears on US coins
			1864 US: While attacking Confederate forces in Alabama, Admiral Farragut says, "Damn the torpedoes! Full speed ahead!"
1865 Homer: *Prisoners from the Front*	1865 Wagner: *Tristan and Isolde*	1865 Lewis Carroll: *Alice's Adventures in Wonderland*	1865 US: Ku Klux Klan founded
1865 Saint Pancras Station, London, is one of the largest buildings in Europe: 698 feet long, 100 feet high, roof span 243 feet.			1865 US: First carpet sweeper; housewives rejoice
			1865 US: *The Nation* magazine
			1865 US: First Pullman RR cars (sleepers)
			1865 US: First train robbery
1866 Degas: begins painting his ballet scenes	1866 Thomas: *Mignon* (opera)	1866 Dostoevsky: *Crime and Punishment*	1866 Coca-Cola invented
1866 Monet: *Camille*		"Naturalism" in literature begins; belief that human fate is determined by environment and heredity in a cold, indifferent universe	

Art and Architecture	Music	Literature	Popular Culture
1867 Cézanne: *Rape*	1867 Strauss: *Blue Danube*	1867 Ibsen: *Peer Gynt*	
1867 World's Fair introduces Japanese art to West	1867 Gounod: *Romeo and Juliet*		
	1867 Strauss: *The Blue Danube*		
	1867 Verdi: *Don Carlos*		

Did You Know?

The Meghanadvadh *is a Bengali version of the Ramayana epic in blank verse.*

1868 Degas: *The Orchestra*	1868 Tchaikovsky: *Symphony No. 1*	1868 Louisa May Alcott: *Little Women*	1868 Badminton created
1868 France: Development of Impressionism		1868 Collins: *The Moonstone*	1868 Croquet craze
1868 Renoir: *The Skaters*		1868 Dostoevsky: *The Idiot*	

Did You Know?

The "Impressionists"—Paul Cézanne, Edgar Degas, Claude Monet, and Pierre Renoir being the most famous—held an independent exhibition after their work had been rejected by the official French Salon. A derisive journalist coined the name "Impressionists" for them from a painting Monet had called Impression, Sunrise. The group had eight exhibitions, the last in 1886.

1869 to 1954 Henri Matisse	1869 Wagner: *Rheingold*	1869 Twain: *Innocents Abroad*	1869 Suez Canal completed
1869 Manet: *The Execution of Emperor Maximillan of Mexico*		1869 Tolstoy: *War and Peace*	

	Art and Architecture	Music	Literature	Popular Culture
			1870 Verne: *Twenty Thousand Leagues Under the Sea*	1870 Schliemann begins digs at Troy
1871 to 1880	1871 Rossetti: *The Dream of Dante*	1871 Verdi: *Aida*	1871 Carroll: *Through the Looking Glass*	1871 US: Barnum opens his circus
	1871 Ward: Albert Buildings, London		1871 Eliot: *Middlemarch*	1871 US: Chicago Great Fire
				1871 Africa: Stanley meets Livingstone

Did You Know?

The Albert Buildings, designed in the so-called Gothic arcaded model, were the most modern commercial buildings of the time. Built on cleared slums, they are an early example of urban renewal.

	Art and Architecture	Music	Literature	Popular Culture
	1872 Whistler: *The Artist's Mother*		1872 Verne: *Around the World in 80 Days*	
	1872 to 1873 Monet: *Impression: Sunrise*		1872 Turgenev: *A Month in the Country*	
	1873 Cézanne: *The Straw Hat*	1873 Bruckner: *Symphony No. 2*	1873 Tolstoy: *Anna Karenina*	1873 Germany: Adopts mark as currency
	1873 Monet: *Field of Poppies*	1873 Rimsky-Korsakov: *Ivan the Terrible* (opera)		1873 Cities of Buda and Pest are united to form Hungarian capital
		1873 Tchaikovsky: *Symphony No. 2*		
	1874 First Impressionist exhibition, Paris	1874 Brahms: *Hungarian Dances*	1874 to 1963 Robert Frost	1874 US: First zoo, Philadelphia
	1874 Renoir: *La Loge*	1874 Moussorgsky: *Boris Gudunov*	1874 Hardy: *Far from the Madding Crowd*	
	1874 Whistler: *Nocturne in Black and White: The Falling Rocket*	1874 Strauss: *Die Fledermaus*		
		1874 Verdi: *Requiem*		

Art and Architecture	Music	Literature	Popular Culture
1875 Eakins: *The Gross Clinic*	1875 to 1937 Maurice Ravel	1875 Twain: *The Adventures of Tom Sawyer*	1875 England: First roller-skating rink
	1875 Bizet: *Carmen*		
	1875 Gilbert and Sullivan: *Trial by Jury*		
	1875 Tchaikovsky: *Piano Concerto No. 1, Op. 23*		
			1876 Telephone invented
1877 Homer: *The Cotton Pickers*	1877 Tchaikovsky: *Swan Lake*	1877 James: *The American*	1877 US: First public telephones
1877 Manet: *Nana*		1877 Flaubert: *A Simple Heart*	1877 Frozen meat shipped for the first time
1877 Rodin: *The Age of Bronze*			
1877 Degas: *La Repetition*			
	1878 Gilbert and Sullivan: *HMS Pinafore*	1878 Hardy: *The Return of the Native*	1878 Milk first delivered in bottles
			1878 Salvation Army gets its current name
1879 Renoir: *Mme. Charpentier and Her Children*	1879 Tchaikovsky: *Eugen Onegin*	1879 Ibsen: *A Doll's House*	
1879 Rodin: *John the Baptist*		1879 James: *Daisy Miller*	
1879 Degas: *Scenes de Ballet*			
1880 Rodin: *The Thinker*	1880 Gilbert and Sullivan: *The Pirates of Penzance*		1880 Bingo developed
1880 Cassatt: *Woman in Black at the Opera*			1880 Canned foods first offered for sale
			1880 US: NY streets lit by electric lights
1881 to 1890 1881 to 1973 Pablo Picasso		1881 James: *Portrait of a Lady*	

Art and Architecture	Music	Literature	Popular Culture
1881 Gerome: *Pygmalion and Galatea*	1881 Brahms: *Academic Festival Overture, Op. 80*		1881 England: Flogging abolished in navy
1881 Renoir: *Luncheon of the Boating Party*			
1882 Paul Gauguin gives up his career as as a Paris stockbroker to paint	1882 Tchaikovsky: *1812 Overture*	1882 Stevenson: *Treasure Island*	1882 Japan: Bank of Japan established
1882 Manet: *Bar at the Foliese-Bergere*	1882: Chatterjee: *Ananda Math*, allegorical novel of resistance to colonial rule	1882 Ibsen: *Enemy of the People*	
1882 Cézanne: *Self-Portrait*	1882 Wagner: *Parsifal*		
	1882 Debussy: *Le Printemps*		
	1883 NY: Metropolitan Opera House opens		1883 US: First skyscraper 10 stories, Chicago
			1883 US: "Buffalo Bill" Cody's "Wild West Show"
			1883 US: Brooklyn Bridge opens
1884 Rodin: *The Burghers of Calais*	1884 Brahms: *Symphony No. 3 in F Major, Op. 90*	1884 Twain: *The Adventures of Huckleberry Finn*	1884 France: Divorce allowed
		1884 Ibsen: *The Wild Duck*	
1885 Van Gogh: *The Potato Eaters*	1885 Brahms: *Symphony No. 4 in E Minor, Op. 98*	1885 Zola: *Germinal*	1885 German Karl Benz sells first automobiles
	1885 Gilbert and Sullivan: *The Mikado*		
1886 Suerat: *Sunday Afternoon on the Grande Jatte*		1886 Stevenson: *Dr. Jekyll and Mr. Hyde*	1886 Statue of Liberty dedicated
1886 Rodin: *The Kiss*		1886 Rimbaud: *Illuminations*	

Art and Architecture	Music	Literature	Popular Culture
		1886 Tolstoy: *The Death of Ivan Illyich*	1886 Nietzsche: *Beyond Good and Evil* proclaims a "life force," a "will to power," and a "superman" who embodies these powers

Did You Know?

Given by the people of France to the people of the United States as a symbol of a shared love of freedom and everlasting friendship, the Statue of Liberty is the largest freestanding sculpture ever created. It weighs 450,000 pounds and rises 151 feet above its pedestal. More than 100 feet around, Ms. Liberty boasts eyes 2½ feet wide, a mouth 3 feet wide, and a nose 4½ feet long. Her upraised right arm extends 42 feet; her hand is nearly 17 feet long. Her fingers are close to 10 feet long. The statue has an interior framework of iron that keeps it from toppling over.

Art and Architecture	Music	Literature	Popular Culture
1887 to 1986 painter Georgia O'Keefe	1887 Verdi: *Otello*	1887 Conan Doyle: First Sherlock Holmes story "A Study in Scarlet"	1887 Esperanto invented (an artificial international language)
1887 Rodin: *Age of Bronze*		1887 Strindberg: *The Father*	1887 Eiffel Tower built for 1889 Paris World's Fair
		1887 Mallarme: *Poesies*	1887 Daimler's internal combustion engine
1888 to 1889 Van Gogh produces over 200 paintings	1888 Gilbert and Sullivan: *The Yeomen of the Guard*		1888 "Jack the Ripper" murders six women in London

KEY DOCUMENT

The poet Emma Lazarus composed the sonnet for the inscription at the base of the Statue of Liberty. It ends:

> *Your huddled masses yearning to breathe free,*
> *The wretched refuse of your teeming shore,*
> *Send these, the homeless, tempest-tost, to me,*
> *I lift my lamp beside the golden door!*

Art and Architecture	Music	Literature	Popular Culture
1888 Van Gogh: *Night Cafe*	1888 Tchaikovsky: *Symphony No. 5*		1888 First beauty contests
	1888 Rimsky-Korsakov: *Sheherazade*		
1889 Van Gogh: *Self-Portrait with Bandaged Head*	1889 Strauss: *Don Juan*		
1889 Gauguin: *The Yellow Christ*			
1890 Cézanne: *The Cardplayers*		1890 Ibsen: *Hedda Gabler*	
1890 van Gogh: *Cornfield with Crows*		1890 Wilde: *The Picture of Dorian Gray*	
1890 to 1892 Cézanne: *Woman with Coffee Pot*		1890 Dickinson: *Poems* (published posthumously)	
1890 to 1894 Cézanne: *Still Life with Basket of Apples*			
1890 to 1891 Louis Sullivan: Wainwright Building, St. Louis			

KEY DOCUMENT

"There is a minute of life passing," Cézanne said. "Paint it in its reality and forget everything to do that!"

1891 to 1900	Matisse leads Fauvist movement in painting	1891 Mahler: *Symphony No. 1*	1891 Hardy: *Tess of the D'Urbervilles*	1891 Russia: Famine
				1891 Japan: Severe earthquake
	1892 Toulouse-Lautrec: *At the Moulin Rouge*	1892 Tchaikovsky: *The Nutcracker*	1892 to 1950 Edna St. Vincent Millay	
			1892 Shaw: *Mrs. Warren's Profession*	

Art and Architecture	Music	Literature	Popular Culture
1892 Gauguin: *Spirit of the Dead Watching*			
1893 Art Nouveau becomes fashionable	1893 to 1964 Cole Porter	1893 Tagore: *Punishment*	
1893 Munch: *The Cry*	1893 Patty Smith Hill and Mildred Hill: "Happy Birthday"		

KEY DOCUMENT

Edvard Munch, who once spent several months in a hospital being treated for depression, said: "One cannot forever paint women knitting and men reading. . . . I want to represent people who breathe, feel, love, and suffer." Munch's disturbing painting *The Cry* is probably the best known of all his works.

Art and Architecture	Music	Literature	Popular Culture
1894 Munch: *Puberty*	Scott Joplin plays ragtime	1894 Kipling: *The Jungle Book*	1894 Hershey's chocolate bar debuts
		1894 Shaw: *Arms and the Man*	1894 X-rays discovered
1895 Kollwitz: *Revolt of the Weavers*		1895 H. G. Wells: *The Time Machine*	1895 US: Gillette introduces safety razor
1895 Rodin: *Balzac*		1895 Ichiyo: *Child's Play*	1895 England: Wilde's unsuccessful libel action against the Marquis of Queensberry
	1896 Puccini: *La Boheme*	1896 Chekhov: *The Sea Gull*	1896 Nobel prizes established
	1896 Strauss: *Also Sprach Zarathustra*		1896 Canada: Klondike gold rush
	1896 Gilbert and Sullivan: *The Grand Duke*		
1897 Matisse: *Dinner Table*	1897 Sousa: *Stars and Stripes Forever*	1897 to 1962 William Faulkner	1897 India: Great famine

	Art and Architecture	Music	Literature	Popular Culture
	1897 Rodin: *Victor Hugo*		1897 Wells: *The Invisible Man*	1897 England: Queen Victoria's Diamond Jubilee
			1897 Rostand: *Cyrano de Bergerac*	1897 US: *The Katenjammer Kids,* first comic strip
			1897 Shaw: *Candida*	
		1898 Sibelius: *Symphony No. 1 in E Minor*	1898 Twain: *A Connecticut Yankee in King Arthur's Court*	1898 Marie and Pierre Curie discover radium
			1898 James: *The Turn of the Screw*	
			1898 Wells: *The War of the Worlds*	
			1898 Wilde: The *Ballad of Reading Gaol*	
	1899 to 1904 Sullivan: Carson Pirie Scott and Company Store		1899 Wilde: *The Importance of Being Earnest*	
	1900 Picasso: *La Moulin de la Galette*	1900 Puccini: *Tosca*	1900 Conrad: *Lord Jim*	1900 Boys wear sailor suits
	1900 Cézanne: *Still Life with Onions*		1900 Dreiser: *Sister Carrie*	1900 Otis installs first modern escalator (Gimbles, Philadelphia)
	1900 Renoir: *Nude in the Sun*		1900 Chekhov: *Uncle Vanya*	
	1900 Sargent: *The Sitwell Family*			1900 Paper clip invented
				1900 US: One person in every hundred owns a telephone
				1900 US: Fourteen percent of homes have a bathtub
1901 to 1910	1901 to 1966 Swiss sculptor Alberto Giacometti	1901 Enrico Caruso's first gramophone recording	1901 Mann: *Buddenbrooks*	Women wear big upswept hairstyles and big showy hats, often with feathers and stuffed birds
			1901 Norris: *The Octopus*	

Art and Architecture	Music	Literature	Popular Culture
1901 Gauguin: *The Gold in their Bodies*	1901 "Tell Me, Pretty Maiden" by Harry McDonough and Grace Spences is #1 song	Beginning of Celtic literary Renaissance: Yeats, Synge, O'Casey	1901 General Electric sells the first Christmas lights
1901 Munch: *Girls on the Bridge*			1901 Ping-pong craze sweeps US
1901 to 1905 Picasso's "Blue period"	1901 Strauss: *Feuersnot*		1901 US Steel organized
1901 Klimt: *Judith*	1901 Dvorak: *Rusalka*		
Beginning of Cubist movement, including Gris, Picasso, Leger, Braque	1901 Rachmaninoff: *Piano Concerto No. 2*		
	1901 US: Ragtime develops		
1902 Gauguin: *Riders by the Sea*	1902 Sibelius: *Symphony No. 2*	1902 Du Bois: *The Souls of Black Folk*	1902 Egypt: Aswan Dam completed
1902 Monet: *Waterloo Bridge*		1902 Doyle: *The Hound of the Baskervilles*	
1902 Rodin: *Romeo and Juliet*		1902 Chekhov: *Three Sisters*	
		1902 Potter: *Peter Rabbit*	
		1902 Conrad: *Heart of Darkness*	
1903 Picasso: *Celestine*	1903 NY: Manhattan Opera house	1903 James: *The Ambassadors*	1903 *Great Train Robbery,* first narrative film. It's eight minutes long
1903 Convalescent Home in Vienna shows reaction to Art Nouveau	1903 First recording of an opera (Verdi's *Ernani*)	1903 Shaw: *Man and Superman*	1903 England: Women's Social and Political Union formed (suffrage)
		1903 London: *The Call of the Wild*	1903 Wright brothers invent the powered airplane
1904 Picasso: *Two Sisters*	1904 Puccini: *Madame Butterfly*	1904 Hudson: *Green Mansions*	1904 Woman arrested in NY for smoking in public
1904 Rousseau: *The Wedding*		1904 Barrie: *Peter Pan*	

Art and Architecture	Music	Literature	Popular Culture
1904 Wright: Larkin Company Administration Building, Buffalo, NY		1904 Chekhov: *The Cherry Orchard*	1904 NY city subway opens
			1904 St. Louis World's Fair
1904 to 1983 George Balanchine, American dance choreographer			1904 Ireland: Abbey Theater founded
			1904 Helen Keller, deaf and blind, graduates from Radcliffe
1905 Cézanne: *Les Grandes Baigneuses*	1905 Lehar: *Merry Widow*	1905 Wharton: The *House of Mirth*	1905 Teddy bears first sold
1905 "Les Fauves" style of art	1905 Debussy: *La Mer*	1905 Orczy: *The Scarlet Pimpernel*	1905 Milton Hershey opens world's largest chocolate factory
1905 Rousseau: *Jungle with a Lion*	Blues become popular in US		1905 US: First regular movie theater (Pittsburgh, PA)
1905 Matisse: *Portrait with Green Stripe*			
1905 Derain: *Effects Sunlight on Water*			1905 First neon lights
Beginning of Fauvist period: flat patterns and unnatural colors			1905 Rotary Club founded
	1906 Voice and music first broadcast by radio	1906 O. Henry "The Four Million"	1906 Finnish women get the vote
		1906 Sinclair: *The Jungle*	1906 Ruth St. Denis introduces modern dance
		Shaw's plays open in NY; promptly censored	1906 US: Pure Food and Drug act passed as a result of Sinclair's *The Jungle*
			President Theodore Roosevelt advocates the "Big Stick" policy: "Speak softly and carry a big stick"

Art and Architecture	Music	Literature	Popular Culture
			1906 Stanford White, America's foremost architect, killed by Evelyn Nesbit's husband, after he discovered White's affair with Evelyn

Did You Know?

Picasso's Les Demoiselles d'Avignon, one of the most influential paintings of the twentieth century, has been called the first Cubist painting.

Art and Architecture	Music	Literature	Popular Culture
1907 Picasso: *Les Demoiselles d'Avignon*	1907 Mahler: *Symphony No. 8 in E-flat Major (The Symphony of a Thousand)*	1907 Kipling wins Nobel Prize for Literature	1907 Boy Scouts started
1907 Picasso: *Self-Portrait*		1907 Strindberg: *The Ghost Sonata*	1907 Mother's Day established
1907 France: First Cubism show (Paris)	New Orleans becomes the cradle of jazz	1907 Ivanov: *Kormichiye*, leading work of the Russian symbolist movement	1907 US: First Ziegfeld Follies, NY
1907 Rousseau: *The Snake Charmer*			1907 First daily comic strip, *Mutt and Jeff*
1907 Bellows: *Stag at Sharkey's*		1907 George: *The Seventh Ring*	

KEY DOCUMENT

Matisse's *Red Room* fulfills his stated ambition: "What I want is an art of equilibrium, of purity and tranquillity, free from unsettling or disturbing subjects, so that all who work with their brains, and this includes businessmen as well as artists and writers, will look on it as something soothing, a kind of cerebral sedative as relaxing in its way as a comfortable armchair."

Art and Architecture	Music	Literature	Popular Culture
1908 Matisse: *Red Room*	1908 Mahler: *Song of the Earth* (symphony)	1908 Grahame: *The Wind in the Willows*	1908 Henry Ford produces first Model T car
	1908 Elgar: *Symphony No. 1, Op. 55*	1908 Montgomery: *Anne of Green Gables*	

Art and Architecture	Music	Literature	Popular Culture
	1908 Strauss: *The Chocolate Soldier*	1908 Stein: *Three Lives*	1908 England: First old age pensions
			1908 Isadora Duncan leading modern dancer
1909 Matisse: *The Dance* 1909 Frank Lloyd Wright designs Robie House 1909 Kandinsky's abstract canvases	1909 Strauss: *Elektra* (opera) 1909 Mahler: *Symphony No. 9* 1909 Ballet Russe	1909 Toson, Agai: *Vita Sexualis*, start of modern Japanese fiction	1909 London hairdressers introduce first permanent wave 1909 Mary Pickford is first movie star

Did You Know?

"It will be the greatest disappointment of my life if I don't go out with Halley's Comet," Mark Twain wrote in 1910. *"The Almighty has said, no doubt, 'Now here are two unaccountable freaks; they came in together and they must go out together."* Twain did indeed die in 1910.

Art and Architecture	Music	Literature	Popular Culture
1910 Modigliani: *The Cellist* 1910 Frank Lloyd Wright becomes famous 1910 Post-Impressionist Exhibition in London 1910 Schiele: *Standing Female Nude with Crossed Arms* 1910 Picasso: *Girl with Mandolin*	1910 Stravinsky: *The Firebird* 1910 Herbert: *Naughty Marietta* (operetta) Charles Ives: *Concorde Sonata*	1910 Forster: *Howard's End*	1910 V-neck sweaters called unhealthy and immoral 1910 Father's Day first celebrated in US 1910 US: Tango catches on 1910 US: The "weekend" becomes popular
1911 Braque: *Man with a Guitar* Matisse: *The Red Studio*	Stravinsky: *Petrouchka* Strauss: *Der Rosenkavalier*	Cavafy: "Ithaca" Wharton: *Ethan Frome*	Arabian look popularized by ballets such as *Scheherazade*

Art and Architecture	Music	Literature	Popular Culture

Did You Know?

The Red Studio was a lightning bolt on the art scene. Matisse's biographer Hilary Spurling noted that the painting "discards perspective, abolishes shadows, repudiates the academic distinction between line and color." This made Matisse's work a "threat to undermine civilization as they knew it."

Art and Architecture	Music	Literature	Popular Culture
Klee: *Self-Portrait*	Berlin: *Alexander's Ragtime Band*		Sarah Bernhardt is popular actress
Picasso: *Still-Life with Chair Caning and Guitar*	Elgar: *Symphony No. 2 in E-flat, Op. 63*		Russia: *War and Peace* (movie)
Nolde: *Masks*			
1911 to 1914 Gropius: Fagus Factory, Alfeld-au-der-Leine, Germany			

1912	Picasso: *The Violin*	Ravel: *Daphnis and Chloe*	Synge: *Playboy of The Western World*	Girl Scouts established
	Chagall: The *Cattle Dealer*	Handy: "Memphis Blues"	Tagore: *Gitanjali* (poems)	First airmail
	Balla: *Dog on a Leash*			*Titanic* sinks on maiden voyage
	Duchamp: *Nude Descending a Staircase* shocks public			Movie: *Quo Vadis* (Italian)
				First successful parachute jump

Did You Know?

Juliette Gordon Low started the Girl Scouts of America in 1912. When she died in 1927, there were 168,000 Girl Scouts in the US. Today, more than 200,000 girls are involved in Scouting.

1913	"Armory Show" introduces Postimpressionism and Cubism to NY	Stravinsky: *The Rite of Spring*	Cather: *O Pioneers!*	US: Sixteenth Amendment allows income tax
			Gorki: *My Childhood*	

Art and Architecture	Music	Literature	Popular Culture

Did You Know?

The "muckrakers" attacked corruption in business and politics. Key books include Upton Sinclair's The Jungle, Frank Norris' The Octopus and The Pit, and John Spargo's The Bitter Cry of the Children.

Art and Architecture	Music	Literature	Popular Culture
Boccioni: *Unique Forms of Continuity in Space* Sargent: *Portrait of Henry James* Kirchner: *Berlin Street Scene* Kandinsky: *Composition VII (No. 2)* Mondrian: *Composition VII* Tatlin: *Constructions* made of wood, metal, glass	Weatherly: "Danny Boy" Scriabin: *Prometheus* Elgar: *Falstaff*	Mann: *Death in Venice* Nobel Prize: Indian poet Rabindranath Tagore Proust: *Swann's Way*, first volume of *Remembrance of Things Past* (1913 to 1927) Lawrence: *Sons and Lovers*	First Charlie Chaplin movies US: Grand Central Terminal opens in NY The foxtrot becomes a popular dance Albert Schweitzer opens his hospital in French Congo

Did You Know?

With its violent syncopations, sudden changes of meter, and "barbaric" repetitions, Stravinsky's ballet The Rite of Spring sparked a riot at its debut. Not incidentally, it ushered in the beginning of atonal music.

	Art and Architecture	Music	Literature	Popular Culture
1914	Braque: *Music* de Chirico: *Melancholy and Mystery of a Street* Gris: *Bottle of Anis del Mono* shows Synthetic Cubism movement	Irving Berlin's songs are hits Williams: *A London Symphony* Stravinsky: *Le Rossignol*	Joyce: *Dubliners* Burroughs: *Tarzan of the Apes*	"Kool-Aid" drink mix invented US: First ski tow, Woodstock, VT *Perils of Pauline* movie serial Panama Canal opens

	Art and Architecture	Music	Literature	Popular Culture
				1914 to 1918 World War I
1915	Chagall: *The Birthday* Duchamp: Dada style paintings	New Orleans jazz flourishes	1915 to . . . Arthur Miller, American dramatist Maugham: *Of Human Bondage* Masters: *Spoon River Anthology* Frost: *A Boy's Will, North of Boston*	Margaret Sanger, author of first book on birth control, jailed *The Birth of a Nation,* first American epic film "Raggedy Ann" doll first sold Cadillac Series 51 US Coast Guard established Albert Einstein's Theory of Relativity Americans average forty phone calls a year

Did You Know?

The twentieth century liberated many people, especially women, from the grind of everyday chores. From the first electric washing machine (1911) to frozen food (1924) to dishwashers (1932) to microwave ovens (1955) to disposable diapers (1961)—consumer convenience wins the day.

	Art and Architecture	Music	Literature	Popular Culture
1916	Matisse: *The Three Sisters* Monet: *Water Lilies*	Jazz sweeps US	Ibanez: *The Four Horsemen of the Apocalypse* Joyce: *Portrait of the Artist as a Young Man* Dreiser: *The Genius* Sandburg: *Chicago Poems* Kafka: *The Metamorphosis*	US: Jeannette Rankin first woman elected to Congress England: Daily Savings Time introduced US: National Park Service established

Art and Architecture	Music	Literature	Popular Culture

Did You Know?

During the 1890s, Monet's garden at Giverny became his main subject. Although he had planted water lilies for pleasure, they became his only theme for the last two decades of his life.

1917	Modigliani: *Crouching Female Nude* Sargent: *Portrait of John D. Rockefeller* Grosz: *Dedication to Oskar Panizza* Duchamp: *Fountain,* the urinal that became one of the most celebrated works of the Dada movement	Prokofiev: *Classical Symphony, Op. 25* Busoni: *Turandot* Cohan: "Over There," WW I war song First jazz records	Eliot: *Prufrock and Other Observations* Garland: *Son of the Middle Border*	Women wear close-cropped ("bobbed") hair, often under hats or turbans Russian Revolution

KEY DOCUMENT

"The cinema is little more than a fad. What audiences really want to see is flesh and blood on the stage." Charlie Chaplin (actor, producer, director, studio founder), 1916.

1918	Gris: Cubic painter Klee: *Gartenplan* Kokoschka: *Friends* (Expressionist paintings) Legere: *Engine Rooms* (glorifies modern machines) Munch: *Bathing Man* Matisse: *Odalisques*	Bartok: *Bluebeard's Castle* Creamer and Layton: "After You've Gone" Kern: "Rock-a-Bye Baby" Stravinksy: *The Soldier's Story*	John Reed's *Ten Days That Shook the World,* his firsthand account of the Russian Revolution Cather: *My Antonia* Dada movement starts in Germany Strachey: *Eminent Victorians* Tarkington: *The Magnificent Ambersons*	US: Compulsory education Women's skirts become narrower; hemlines above the ankle US: Daylight Savings Time introduced Worldwide influenza epidemic

Art and Architecture	Music	Literature	Popular Culture
Miro: First works		Adams: *The Education of Henry Adams* Lu Xun: *Diary of a Madman*	Women over 30 years old given the vote in England

Did You Know?

In dedicating his work to Panizza, Grosz said: "I am unshaken in my view that this epoch is sailing down its destruction."

	Art and Architecture	Music	Literature	Popular Culture
1919	Bauhaus School of design revolutionizes painting, sculpture, architecture Kandinsky: *Dreamy Improvisation* Klee: *Dream Birds* Leger: *Follow the Arrow* Munch: *The Murder* Picasso: Theater sets Schwitters: *Picture with Light Center* Tatlin: *Model for the Monument to the Third International* Legere: *Mechanical Elements* Wright: Imperial Hotel, Tokyo	Elgar: *Concerto in E Minor for Cello* Jazz arrives in Europe Julliard School of Music starts George Gershwin's first hit, "Swanee"	Anderson: *Winesburg, Ohio* Lofting: First of Dr. Doolittle stories Maugham: *The Moon and Sixpence* Mencken: *The American Language* Tagore: *The Home and the World* Sandburg: *Corn Huskers*	First trans-Atlantic nonstop flight First practical zipper RCA founded
1920	Gris: Spanish Cubism Mies van der Rohe: *Glass Skyscraper Project*	Enrico Caruso's last performance at New York's Metropolitan Opera Kern: "Sally"	Agatha Christie: *The Mysterious Affair of Style*	German expressionist film *The Cabinet of Dr. Caligari*

Art and Architecture	Music	Literature	Popular Culture

Did You Know?

Lu Xun's Diary of a Madman *is the first story written in the Chinese vernacular.*

Paul Whiteman and orchestra release "Whispering," the first record to sell a million copies.

Maurice Ravel: *La Valse*

Hadley: *Cleopatra's Night*

Fitzgerald's *This Side of Paradise* sells 3,000 copies in 3 days.

O'Neill: *The Emperor Jones, Beyond the Horizon*

Pound: "Hugh Selwyn Mauberley"

US: Post Office rules children may not be sent by parcel post

Trojan condoms debut

American Civil Liberties Union founded

Did You Know?

Long-time Boston residents might recall the molasses flood that engulfed the city's North end on January 15, 1919. Many people were sitting near the Purity Distilling Corporation's fifty-foot high molasses tank enjoying the unseasonably warm day. The tank was filled with over 2 million gallons of molasses—and it was about to burst apart. First, molasses oozed through the tank's rivets. The metal bolts popped out, the seams burst, and tons of molasses burst out in a surge of deadly goo. The first wave, over twenty-five feet high, smashed buildings, trees, people, and animals like toys. Residents were carried into the Charles River, which was soon a gooey brown sludge. Sharp pieces of the tank sliced through the air, injuring scores of people. After the initial destruction, molasses continued to clog the streets for days. The disaster left more than twenty people dead and more than fifty hurt.

Wharton: *The Age of Innocence;* wins 1921 Pulitzer Prize

Lewis: *Main Street*

Kafka: *A Country Doctor*

Nobel Prize: Knut Hamsun

US: Dept. of Justice "red hunt" nets; aliens deported

US: Eighteenth Amendment— Prohibition

Art and Architecture	Music	Literature	Popular Culture

Did You Know?

Pirandello's Six Characters in Search of an Author *challenges the conventional distinction between illusion and reality, as well as authorial omniscience. This sets the stage for postmodernism and the notion that the reader, not the writer, is the final arbiter of a work's meaning.*

	Art and Architecture	Music	Literature	Popular Culture
1921	The Metropolitan Museum of Art features Matisse Manet, Degas, and Millet	Prokofiev: *The Love for Three Oranges* (opera)	Lawrence: *Women in Love*	*Four Horsemen of the Apocalypse* helps make Rudolph Valentino a star
	Picasso: *Three Musicians*	W. C. Handy sets up his own record label, Black Swan; scores a hit with Ethel Water's version of "St. Louis Blues"	Sabatini: *Scaramouche*	First Miss America Pageant; Atlantic City
	Braque: *Still Life with Guitar*		Nobel Prize: Anatole France	US: One hundred percent divorce rate increase since 1896
	Ernst: *The Elephant Celebes*		Dos Passos: *Three Soldiers*	
	Klee: *The Fish*		O'Neill: *Anna Christie*	France: Chanel introduces Chanel No. 5 perfume
	Leger: *Three Women*		Shaw: *Heartbreak House*	
	Man Ray: "Rayographs"		Pirandello: *Six Characters in Search of an Author*	US: Rebecca Latimer Felton first woman senator
	Munch: *The Kiss*			US: Ku Klux Klan on a rampage
	Picasso: *Three Women at the Spring*			1921 to 1929 NY: Harlem Renaissance, black artistic and literary movement
1922	Beerbohm drawings	Fats Waller's first record: "Muscle Shoals Blues"	Joyce: *Ulysses*	King Tut's tomb opened
	Klee: *The Twittering Machine*		Eliot: *The Waste Land*	Germany: *Nosferatu*, first vampire film
	Miro: *The Farm*	Louis Armstrong becomes famous	Claude McKay's *Harlem Shadows* sparks Harlem Renaissance	
	El Lissitzky: *Proun Composition*	Bax: *Symphony No. 1*		Lincoln Memorial dedicated in Washington, DC
	Hood and Howells: Tribune Tower, Chicago	Berlin: "April Showers"	Galsworthy: *The Forsyte Saga*	First documentary: *Nanook of the North*
			Lewis: *Babbit*	

Art and Architecture	Music	Literature	Popular Culture

Did You Know?

Joyce's Ulysses *and Eliot's* The Waste Land *are both portraits of hellish urban landscapes. In addition, both works consciously parade their learning to undermine what they see as the outmoded heritage of the past.*

Art and Architecture	Music	Literature	Popular Culture
	Bliss: *A Color Symphony*	Cather: *One of Ours* (Pulitzer)	US: First portable radio and first car radio
		Fitzgerald: *The Beautiful and the Damned*	US: *Abie's Irish Rose* a Broadway hit
		Hesse: *Siddhartha*	American cocktails fashionable in Europe
		O'Neill: *The Hairy Ape*	
		E. A. Robinson: *Collected Poems* (Pulitzer)	US: Emily Post's books of etiquette become popular
		Tarkington: *Alice Adams* (Pulitzer)	US: *Reader's Digest* founded
		Rilke: *Sonnets to Orpheus*	Turkey becomes a republic
		Knud Rasmussen documents Inuit culture and collects Inuit songs.	

KEY DOCUMENT

James Joyce's novel *Ulysses* is finally an affirmation: "I put my arms around him yes I drew him down to me so he could feel my breasts all perfume yes and his heart was going like mad and yes I said yes I will yes."

| 1923 | Beckmann: *The Trapeze* | Morton: "Yes, We Have No Bananas" | William Butler Yeats wins the Nobel Prize in Literature | US: First old-age pensions |
| | Chagall: *Love Idyll* | George Gershwin: *Rhapsody in Blue* | | Neon advertising signs invented |

	Art and Architecture	Music	Literature	Popular Culture
	Dada movement over	Bessie Smith, "Empress of the Blues," makes first record	Millay: *The Ballad of the Harp Weaver* (Pulitzer)	US: First legal birth control clinic, NYC
	Kandinsky: *Circles in the Circle*			Patent for first electric razor granted to Jacob Schick
	Nash: *The Coast*	Schoenberg: *Piano*	Salten: *Bambi*	
	Picasso: *Lady with The Blue Veil*	Bartok: *Dance Suite*	Wodehouse: *The Inimitable Jeeves*	Dance marathons craze
	Picasso experiments with Neoclassicism, Expressionism, Surrealism	Sibelius: *Symphony No. 6 in D Minor*	Cummings: *The Enormous Room*	Rin Tin Tin's film debut
		Songs from *No! No! Nanette* hits	Kapek: *R.U.R.*	First issue of *Time* magazine
	Utrillo: *Ivry Town Hall*		Rilke: *Duino Elegies*	US: Popsicles invented
				Japanese director Kenji Mizoguchi: *Yoru* (The Night)
				Douglas Fairbanks, Harold Lloyd, Charlie Chaplin, Mary Pickford big movie stars
1924	Picasso: *Still Life with Biscuits and Green Table Cloth*	Wendell Hall: "It Ain't Gonna Rain No Mo' " is #1 song	Forster: *A Passage to India*	Mah-Jongg craze
	Surrealism movement	Berg: *Chamber Concerto*	Anderson/Stallings: *What Price Glory?*	Kleenex invented
	Braque: *Sugar Bowl*	Gershwin: "Lady Be Good"	Mann: *The Magic Mountain*	Spiral-bound notebooks
	Chagall: *Daughter Ida at the Window*	Romberg: *The Student Prince*	O'Neill: *Desire Under the Elms*	*NY Times'* first crossword puzzle
			Shaw: *St. Joan*	Clarence Birdseye invents process for quick frozen food

Did You Know?

African "Highlife" pop music fuses traditional music with sea shanties, regimental brass bands, hymns, and other Western influences. Guitars, accordions, and harmonicas were added to the sound of African drums. Osibisa, formed in London in 1969, bought Highlife to a Western audience.

	Art and Architecture	Music	Literature	Popular Culture
	Michelucci and others: Stazione Centrale, Santa Maria Novella, Florence	Sibelius: *Symphony No. 7 in C Major* Swing bandleader Paul Whiteman performs George Gershwin's symphonic work *Rhapsody in Blue* Paul Whiteman's "An Experiment in Modern Music" sparks swing music	Robert Frost wins first of four Pulitzers O'Casey: *Juno and the Paycock* Wodehouse: *Jeeves* Melville: *Billy Budd* published; written 1891 Breton: *First Surrealist Manifesto* Premachand: *The Road to Salvation*	*Little Orphan Annie* comic strip debut Leopold and Loeb convicted in "thrill killing" of Bobby Franks; defended by Clarence Darrow; first successful insanity defense Wheaties introduced Steinway grand piano costs $1,425 US: Entertainer Will Rogers at the height of his career
1925	Paris: Art Deco George Balanchine becomes famous for his ballet choreography Chagall: *The Drinking Green Pig* Picasso: *Three Dancers* Miro: *The Birth of the World* Gropius: *Bauhaus*	Berg: *Wozzeck* (opera) Louis Armstrong becomes famous for his jazz trumpet Bax: *Symphony No. 2* Copeland: *Symphony for Organ and Orchestra* Friml: *The Vagabond King* Shostakovich: *Symphony No. 1* Fats Waller's first song, "Squeeze" "Highlife" pop music develops in Ghana and Sierra Leone	Fitzgerald: *The Great Gatsby* Nobel Prize: George Bernard Shaw First issue of *The New Yorker* Dreiser: *An American Tragedy* Woolf: *Mrs. Dalloway* Kafka: *Trial* (published posthumously) Dickinson: *Complete Poems* (published posthumously) Dos Passos: *Manhattan Transfer* Ferber: *So Big* (Pulitzer) Lewis: *Arrowsmith* (Pulitzer)	Baggy pants become college fashion fad Chaplin's *The Gold Rush* Josephine Baker takes Paris by storm World's first motel, CA US: Al Capone rises in power US: Flagpole sitting, dance marathons, and trenchcoats become fads US: Team of sled dogs race 650 miles with medicine; saves diphtheria-ravaged citizens of snowed-in Nome, Alaska US: Charleston and cloche (hat) are fads US: Madison Square Garden opens (NY)

Art and Architecture	Music	Literature	Popular Culture
		Robinson: *The Man Who Died Twice* (Pulitzer)	US: Ten and one half percent of all homes wired for electricity
		Uo: *Geriguigatugo*	
		Sholokhov: *Tales from the Don*	
1926 O'Keeffe: *Black Iris*	Clarinetist Benny Goodman makes first records	Hemingway: *The Sun Also Rises*	US: Route 66 gets official numerical designation
Paris: Surrealist gallery opens	Duke Ellington's first recordings	Gide: *Les Faux Monnayeurs*	NY: Home telephones $4 per month
Chagall: *Lover's Bouquet*	D'Albert: *The Golem*	Pound: Poems	
Moore: *Draped Reclining Figure*	Bartok: *The Miraculous Mandarin*	Milne: *Winnie the Pooh*	The Book of the Month Club debuts
Munch: *The Red House*	Berg: *Lyric Suite*	Lawrence: *The Seven Pillars of Wisdom*	Rin Tin Tin is biggest box office star
John: *Lady Morrell*	Hindemith: *Cardillac*	O'Casey: *The Plough and the Stars*	Will Rogers travels to Europe as goodwill ambassador; 40 million people read the daily reports he sends home
	Weill: *The Protagonist*	O'Neill: *The Great God Brown*	
	Gershwins: *Oh Kay!*, including the hit song, "Someone to Watch Over Me"	Kafka: *The Castle* (published posthumously)	
	Glenn Miller joins Ben Pollack's dance band, and his career as big band leader begins		

Did You Know?

Glenn Miller's hit songs include "Moonlight Serenade," "Little Brown Jug," "Pennsylvania 6-5000," "Tuxedo Junction," "When You Wish Upon a Star," and "Blueberry Hill."

Art and Architecture	Music	Literature	Popular Culture
1927 Braque: *Glass and Fruit*	First country music records	Nobel Prize: Henri Bergson	Academy of Motion Picture Arts and Sciences established
Burra: *Terrace*			

	Art and Architecture	Music	Literature	Popular Culture
	Demuth: *Egyptian Impression*	Alfano: *Madonna Imperia*	Cather: *Death Comes for the Archbishop*	Mae West guilty of obscenity NYC; ten days in jail
	Epstein: *Madonna and Child*	Gershwins: *Funny Face*	Hesse: *Steppenwolf*	Laurel and Hardy gain popularity
	Hopper: *Manhattan Bridge*	Kern/Hammerstein: *Show Boat*	E. A. Robinson: *Tristram* (Pulitzer)	It takes thirty-two hours to fly from NY to SF
	Le Courbusier, landmark architecture	Rogers and Hart: *A Connecticut Yankee*	Lewis: *Elmer Gantry*	Al Jolson: *The Jazz Singer,* first talking
			Proust: *Remembrances of Things Past*	full-length film
	Matisse: *Figures with Ornamental Background*	Shostakovich: *Symphony No. 2*	Traven: *The Treasure of Sierra Madre*	*Napoleon,* first widescreen film
		Stravinksy: *Oedipus Rex*	Wilder: *The Bridge of San Luis Rey*	Lang: *Metropolis,* vision of technology gone awry
		Electronic musical instrument invented	Woolf: *To the Lighthouse*	
		"Old Man River" hit song		Buster Keaton: comedy classic, *The General*
		"Let a Smile Be Your Umbrella" hit song	Bloomsbury group in England: Woolf, Forster, etc.	
			"Lost Generation" of American writers: Fitzgerald, Hemingway, Stein, Miller	US: Ruth Snyder and Judd Gray convicted of murdering Albert Snyder; they were executed at Sing Sing, 1928
				B & B Baked Beans introduced
				Dancer Isadora Duncan killed when her scarf tangled in car's wheels
				Slow fox trot is popular dance
				Model T Ford costs $550
1928	O'Keeffe: *Nightwave*	Louis Armstrong: "West End Blues"	O'Neill: *Strange Interlude*	Walt Disney's first talking cartoon, *Steamboat Willie*
	Braque: *Still Life with Jug*			

Art and Architecture	Music	Literature	Popular Culture
Chagall: *Wedding*	Weill and Brecht: *Threepenny Opera*	Huxley: *Point Counterpoint*	Mickey Mouse debut: *Plane Crazy*
	Gershwin: *An American in Paris*	Waugh: *Decline and Fall*	TV sets sold in US
		Oxford English Dictionary published after 44 years of research	Radclyffe Hall's *The Well of Loneliness* banned in Britain for lesbian content
		Benet: *John Brown's Body* (Pulitzer)	US: First Academy Award to *Wings*
		Lawrence: *Lady Chatterley's Lover*	US: 26 million cars on the road
		Nobel Prize: Sigrid Undset Woolf: *Orlando*	US: Betty Boop debuts as a cartoon short
		Yeats: *The Tower*	Amelia Earhart: First woman to fly across Atlantic
			Penicillin discovered

Did You Know?

In a contemporary review of Meis van der Rohe's Seagram Building, Time maga-zine noted that "By day [the building] is a soaring column the color of an old cannon; by night it is a giant, glowing shaft punctuating . . . the skyline. It is the definitive statement of what a skyscraper can be by the architect whom most purists hail as the master of glass-and-steel design."

	Art and Architecture	Music	Literature	Popular Culture
1929	NY: Museum of Modern Art opens	Count Basie: *Blue Devil Blues*	Hemingway: *Farewell to Arms*	US: First airport hotel (CA)
	"International Style" of modern architecture (flat, functional, streamlined)	*Showboat*, breakthrough play	Wolfe: *Look Homeward, Angel* Remarque: *All Quiet on the Western Front*	US: *Amos and Andy* on the radio (to 1960) Hitchcock's *Blackmail*
	Mies van der Rohe designs landmark buildings		Faulkner: *The Sound and the Fury*	Gerber Co. invents canned, strained baby food

	Art and Architecture	Music	Literature	Popular Culture
	Dali turns to Surrealism, as in *Illuminated Pleasures*		Woolf: *A Room of One's Own*	US: St. Valentine's Day gangland massacre, Chicago
	Brancusi: *Bird in Space*		Nobel Prize: Thomas Mann	"Talkies" destroy silent films
	Le Corbusier: Villa Savoye, Poissy, Seine-et-Oise			Stock market crash; Great Depression begins
	Chagall: *Love Idyll*			*Singin' in the Rain*
				Scotch Tape invented
1930	Gross: *Offspring*	Bartok: *Cantata Profana*	Auden: Poems	A&P, first grocery store chain
	Grosz: *Cold Buffet*	Stravinsky: *Symphony of Psalms*	Noel Coward: *Private Lives*	Ellen Church, first flight attendant
	Wadsworth: *Composition*	Hoagy Carmichael: "Georgia On My Mind"	Hart Crane: "The Bridge"	Movie: *All Quiet on the Western Front*
	Wood: *American Gothic*	Gershwin: "I Got Rhythm"	Eliot: "Ash Wednesday"	Contract bridge becomes a popular card game
	Hopper: *Early Sunday Morning*	Green: "Body and Soul"	Faulkner: *As I Lay Dying*	Passenger airlines begin regular service
		Louis Armstrong performs Fats Waller's "Ain't Misbehaving"	Hammett: *The Maltese Falcon*	*Blondie* comic strip debuts
		Bing Crosby almost single-handedly invents modern pop singing	Nobel Prize: Sinclair Lewis	
			Maugham: *Cake and Ale*	
		Gershwins: "Embraceable You"	Ferber: *Cimarron*	
1931	Beckmann: *Still Life with Studio Window*	"Star Spangled Banner," made official US national anthem	Buck: *The Good Earth*	Gangster Al Capone jailed for income tax evasion
	Bonnard: *The Breakfast Room*	Elgar: *Nursery Suite*	Faulkner: *Sanctuary*	Movie: *City Lights* (Chaplin)
	Chagall: *The Trick-Rider*		Frost: *Collected Poems* (Pulitzer)	Movie: *The Front Page*

	Art and Architecture	Music	Literature	Popular Culture
	Dali: *Persistence of Memory*	Gershwin: *Of Thee I Sing*	O'Neill: *Mourning Becomes Electra*	
	Klee: *The Ghost Vanishes*	Still: *Afro-American Symphony*		
	NY: Rockefeller Center building starts	Calloway: "Minnie the Moocher"		
		Johnson and Woods: "When the Moon Comes Over the Mountain"		
1932	Burra: *The Cafe*	Barber: *Overture to School for Scandal*	Caldwell: *Tobacco Road*	US: 25% of country on public assistance
	Calder's "stabiles" (mobiles) exhibited	Bax: *Symphony No. 5 in C-sharp Minor*	Dos Passos: *1919*	Canada: Dionne quintuplets born
	Wood: *Daughters of the American Revolution*	Grofe: *The Grand Canyon Suite*	Faulkner: *Light in August*	US: Jack Benny radio debut
	Picasso: *Head of a Woman*	Porter: *The Gay Divorcee*	Nobel Prize: John Galsworthy	Fritos corn chips introduced
	Sheeler: *River Rouge Plant*	Prokofiev: *Piano Concerto No. 5 in G Major*	Hammett: *The Thin Man*	US: Amelia Earhart first woman to fly Atlantic solo
		Ravel: *Piano Concerto in G Major*	Hemingway: *Death in the Afternoon*	
			Huxley: *Brave New World*	Movie: *A Farewell to Arms*
		Fats Waller's career flourishes	Bunzel: *Zuni Ritual Poetry*	Johnny Weissmuller debuts in Tarzan movies
				Shirley Temple's film debut

Did You Know?

In a contemporary review of Pablo Picasso, Time magazine noted that "He was the artist with whom virtually every other artist had to reckon, and there was scarcely a 20th century movement that he didn't inspire, contribute to . . . or beget."

| **1933** | Giacometti: *The Palace at Four a.m.* | School of American Ballet opens | Joyce's *Ulysses* allowed into US | US: *King Kong* |

	Art and Architecture	Music	Literature	Popular Culture
	Matisse: *The Dance*	Copeland: *The Short Symphony* Harris: *Symphony No. 1*	Nobel Prize: Ivan Bunin Caldwell: *God's Little Acre*	Germany: Books by non-Nazi and Jewish authors burned
		Strauss: *Arabella*	Lorca: *Blood Wedding*	Mass immigration of German artists (actors, musicians, etc.)
		Koehler and Arlen: "Stormy Weather"	Hamsun: *The Road Leads On*	Movie: *Little Women* (Katherine Hepburn)
		Berlin: "Easter Parade"	O'Neill: *Ah, Wilderness*	Movie: *She Done Him Wrong* (Mae West)
			Stein: *The Autobiography of Alice B. Toklas*	Nazis built first concentration camps
				Sophie Tucker, Fred Allen, Al Jolson, Ed Wynn, Eddie Cantor, and Fanny Brice are popular entertainers
				Spam invented, beginning a new era of processed foods
				Paul Getty earned $1,000 in his first year in the oil business
				Movie: *Calvacade* wins Academy Award

Did You Know?

The 1933 movie, King Kong, starring Fay Wray and Bruce Cabot, is the classic version of the beauty-and-the-beast theme. Willis O'Brien's special effects and animated monsters are still unsurpassed; the final sequence atop the Empire State Building is cinema legend.

1934	Dali: *William Tell*	Porter: *Anything Goes* Britten: *Fantasy Quartet*	Hilton: *Lost Horizons* and *Good-bye, Mr. Chips* Christie: *Murder in Three Acts*	England institutes driving tests First coin laundromat

	Art and Architecture	Music	Literature	Popular Culture
		Rachmanioff: *Rhapsody on a Theme of Paganini*	Fitzgerald: *Tender is the Night*	Movie: *It Happened One Night*
			Graves: *I, Claudius*	Movie: *Of Human Bondage*
		Brown and Freed: "All I Do Is Dream of You"	O'Hara: *Appointment in Samarra*	Movie: *The Thin Man*
			Nobel Prize: Luigi Pirandello	Flash Gordon, Buck Rogers, and the Lone Ranger rule the airwaves, as far as kids are concerned
1935	Dali: *Giraffe on Fire*	Gershwin: *Porgy and Bess*	Laura Ingalls Wilder: *Little House on the Prairie*	US: Monopoly invented
		"Swing" becomes popular	Akins: *The Old Maid* (Pulitzer)	US: Roller-skating fad
		Gershwin: "I Got Plenty O' Nothing"	Eliot: *Murder in the Cathedral*	US: Saddle shoes with ankle socks and pillbox hats are fads; jitterbug, platform shoes, and sunglasses reign
		Brown and Freed: "Alone"	Odets: *Waiting for Lefty*	
		Porter: "Just One of Those Things"	Steinbeck: *Tortilla Flat*	Movie: *David Copperfield*
		Electric organs become popular	1935 to 1947 Yasunari: *Snow Country*	Movie: *Mutiny on the Bounty*
				Movie: *The 39 Steps* (Hitchcock)
				Rumba becomes the fashionable dance
				Alcoholics Anonymous organized
				The eagle graces the back of the dollar bill

Did You Know?

Frank Lloyd Wright's concept of the hearth as the center of the home is clear in Falling Waters, as the fireplace is formed by the rocky ledge.

	Art and Architecture	Music	Literature	Popular Culture
1936	Mondriaan: *Composition in Red and Blue*	Woodie Guthrie becomes the voice of the Depression with his folk songs, such as "I Ain't Got No Home," and "John Henry"	Anderson: *High Tor*	First issue of *Life* magazine
	Wright: Falling Waters, Bear Run, PA		Fitzgerald: *The Crack-Up*	Dale Carnegie: *How to Win Friends and Influence People*
	Dorothea Lange: *Migrant Mother, California* (photograph)	Gospel becomes the dominant church music among Blacks	Huxley: *Eyeless in Gaza*	Movie: *Modern Times* (Chaplin)
			Sherwood: *Idiot's Delight*	
		US: Tanglewood music festival begins	Kaufman/Hart: *You Can't Take It With You*	Movie: *Mr. Deeds Goes to Town*
		Porter: "Easy to Love"	Nobel Prize: Eugene O'Neill	Movie: *The Great Ziegfeld*
			Frost: *A Further Range* (Pulitzer)	Bruno Hauptman convicted of killing Lindbergh baby
			Premchand: *The Cow*	
			Frobenius: *History of African Civilizations*	

Did You Know?

In 1937, to draw attention to the dire plight of the American farmer, the Farm Security Administration began documenting the shattering effects of the Depression on American farms. Under the direction of Roy Stryker, a group of talented photographers, including Dorothea Lange, Ben Shawn, Gordon Parks, and Arthur Rothstein (in addition to Stryker), provided a clear, harrowing record of one of the bleakest periods in America's countryside.

	Art and Architecture	Music	Literature	Popular Culture
1937	Picasso: *Guernica*	Shostakovich: *Symphony No. 5*	Dos Passos: *U.S.A.*	US: First feature-length cartoon, *Snow White*
	Klee: *Revolution of the Viaducts*	Rogers and Hart: *I'd Rather Be Right*	Marquand: *The Late George Apley* (Pulitzer)	US: Golden Gate bridge opens in San Francisco
	Miro: *Still Life with Old Shoe*	Rogers and Hart: *Babes in Arms*	Odets: *Golden Boy*	
	Braque: *Woman with a Mandolin*	Rome: *Pins and Needles*	Steinbeck: *Of Mice and Men*	England: Duke of Windsor marries Wallis Simpson
			Roberts: *Northwest Passage*	US: Amelia Earhart lost on Pacific flight

Art and Architecture	Music	Literature	Popular Culture
	Rogers and Hart: "The Lady Is a Tramp"	Stevens: *The Man with the Blue Guitar*	Hindenberg disaster
	Chaplin and Cahn: "Bei Mir Bist du Schoen"		
	Bessie Smith, "Empress of the Blues," dies in a car crash		

Did You Know?

A strong supporter of the Spanish Civil War, Picasso painted Guernica *for the Spanish government building at the Paris World's Fair of 1937. The painting was a protest against the actions of General Franco and his Fascist allies. The painting has since become a universal symbol of the destruction and horror of war.*

	Art and Architecture	Music	Literature	Popular Culture
1938	Wright builds Taliesin West, AZ

The Cloisters, medieval museum, built in NYC | Bartok: *Violin Concerto*

Benny Goodman's band ushers in a new style of jazz

Strauss: *Daphne*

Egk: *Peer Gynt*

Weill: *Knickbocker Holiday*

Fitzgerald and Alexander: "A Tisket, a Tasket"

Warren and Mercer: "Jeepers, Creepers" | Wilder: *Our Town* (Pulitzer)

du Maurier: *Rebecca*

Faulkner: *The Unvanquished*

Isherwood: *Goodbye to Berlin*

Rawlings: *The Yearling* (Pulitzer)

Nobel Prize: Pearl S. Buck | US introduces forty-hour work week

Douglas "Wrong-Way" Corrigan flies from NY to Dublin

Orson Welles's radio broadcast *War of the Worlds*

Movie: *You Can't Take It With You*

Lambeth Walk becomes "in" dance

Porsche designs Volkswagen "Beetle" to meet Hitler's requirements |
| 1939 | Picasso: *Night Fishing at Antibes* | DAR refuses to allow Marian Anderson to sing because she is Black | Katherine Anne Porter: *Pale Horse, Pale Rider* | Nylon stockings first sold

Movie: *Gone With the Wind* |

Art and Architecture	Music	Literature	Popular Culture
"Grandma Moses" (Anna M. Robertson) becomes famous	Rogers and Hart: *The Boys from Syracuse*	Crouse and Lindsay: *Life with Father*	NY World's Fair opens
Kandinsky: *Neighborhood*	Copeland: *Billy the Kid*	Joyce: *Finnegan's Wake*	Movie: *The Wizard of Oz*
Moore: *Reclining Figure*	Novello: *The Dancing Years*	Steinbeck: *The Grapes of Wrath* (Pulitzer)	US: Average wage 62¢ per hour
		Saroyan: *The Time of Your Life* (Pulitzer)	US: *The Shadow* and *Captain Midnight* radio shows (to 1949)
		Kaufman and Hart: *The Man Who Came to Dinner*	US: First transatlantic airmail service
		Cesaire: *Notebook of a Return to the Native Land*	US: First televised baseball game

Did You Know?

On September 12, 1940, four teenage boys set out to explore a cave in central France. To their astonishment, the boys discovered cave paintings later estimated to be about 15,000 years old. The ancient renderings included astonishing ten-foot high red bulls, magnificent horses, and other amazing creatures, perhaps painted as ritual magic to aid the hunters who sought them. In 1994, explorers discovered a second trove of Cro-Magnon cave paintings in southern France. These were more than twice as old as the Lascaux gallery. Some experts believe these ancient artists blew the pigment from their mouths.

	Art and Architecture	Music	Literature	Popular Culture
1940	France: Caves of Lascaux discovered Kandinsky: *Blue Sky*	Stravinksy: *Symphony in C*	Greene: *The Power and the Glory*	US: Pasadena Freeway, first freeway in US
	Matisse: *The Rumanian Blouse*	Rogers and Hart: *Pal Joey*	Hemingway: *For Whom the Bell Tolls*	US: Selective Service Act
		Duke Ellington becomes famous	O'Neill: *Long Day's Journey Into Night*	US: NBC first official network television broadcast
		Leadbelly (Huddie William Ledbetter) elevates the public perception of blues and folk songs	Wright: *Native Son* Hellman: *Watch on the Rhine*	Movie: *The Grapes of Wrath*
			Koestler: *Darkness at Noon*	Movie: *Rebecca* Movie: *Fantasia*

	Art and Architecture	Music	Literature	Popular Culture
			Williams: *The Corn is Green*	
			Wolfe: *You Can't Go Home Again*	
1941	Hopper: *Nighthawks*	Harris: *Folk Song Symphony*	Fitzgerald: *The Last Tycoon*	Movie: *Citizen Kane*
	Leger: *Divers Against Yellow Background*	Britten: *Violin Concerto*	Coward: *Blithe Spirit*	US: Toy balloons and toy boats catch on
		Rogers and Hart: "Bewitched, Bothered, and Bewildered"	Wilder: *The Skin of Our Teeth*	Movie: *The Big Store* (Marx Brothers)
			Brecht: *Mother Courage and Her Children*	Movie: *How Green Was My Valley*
		Rausch: "Deep in the Heart of Texas"		
		Miller: "Chattanooga Choo-Choo"		
1942	Sutherland: *Red Landscape*	Copland: *Rodeo*	Benet: *The Dust Which Is God* (Pulitzer)	Movie: *Mrs. Minniver*
	Braque: *Patience*	Menotti: *The Island God*	Glasgow: *This is Our Life* (Pulitzer)	Movie: *Bambi*
	Calder: *Red Petals*	Strauss: *Capriccio*		Movie: *Holiday Inn*
		Frank Sinatra electrifies fans	Camus: *The Stranger*	Movie: *Tortilla Flat* (Spencer Tracy)
		"White Christmas" by Bing Crosby is year's #1 song	Faulkner: *Go Down, Moses*	Americans face wartime shortages; coffee, sugar, and gasoline rationed
			Wilder: *The Skin of Our Teeth*	
		Carmen Miranda, "Brazilian Bombshell," typifies Hollywood version of Latin American music	Douglas: *The Robe*	Lloyd's of London insures Betty Grable's legs for $1 million
			Musil: *The Man Without Qualities*	Film star Carole Lombard dies in plane crash
1943	Mondriaan: *Broadway Boogie-Woogie*	*Oklahoma!*, first of five hit musicals by Rodgers and Hammerstein	E. B. White: *Stuart Little*	US: Income tax withholding begun
	Moore: *Madonna and Child*		Smith: *A Tree Grows in Brooklyn*	Martha Graham interprets modern dance

Art and Architecture	Music	Literature	Popular Culture

Did You Know?

Calder's sculptures often have a whimsical, charming quality. This quality is enhanced by their seemingly random movements.

Art and Architecture	Music	Literature	Popular Culture
Kokoschka: *Portrait of Ivan Maisky* Chagall: *The Juggler* Mies van der Rohe: Illinois Institute of Technology Campus, Chicago Soutine: *Page Boy at Maxim's*	Dinah Washington starts working with Lionel Hampton, singing "Baby Get Lost," "Trouble in Mind," "Cold, Cold Heart," and more	Sinclair: *Dragon's Teeth* (Pulitzer) Saroyan: *The Human Comedy* Eliot: *Four Quartets*	Movie: *Jane Eyre* Movie: *Casablanca* US: Polio epidemic US: Shoes, sugar, meat, fat, gas still rationed US: "Zoot suits" are the "in" clothing for "hepcats" US: Jitterbug becomes popular dance

Did You Know?

Oklahoma! marked a radical breakthrough in the stage musical, with a dynamic integration of book, song, and dance on a scale never before seen. As with many shows that followed in its model, this narrative strength enabled Oklahoma! to transfer to the movie screen virtually unchanged.

	Art and Architecture	Music	Literature	Popular Culture
1944	Matisse: *The White Dress* Picasso: *The Tomato Plant* Braque: *The Slice of Pumpkin* Rivera: *The Rug Weaver* Dove: *That Red One*	Bartok: *Violin Concerto* Copland: *Appalachian Spring* Shostakovich: *Symphony No. 8* Bernstein: *On the Town* Prokofiev: *War and Peace*	Myrdal: *An American Dilemma* Benet: *Western Star* (Pulitzer) Eliot: *Four Quartets* Maugham: *The Razor's Edge* Sartre: *No Exit*	US: GI Bill helps educate millions Movie: *Henry V* Movie: *Going My Way* England: "Blackout" conditions eased

Art and Architecture	Music	Literature	Popular Culture
	Burke and Van Heusen: "Swinging on a Star"	Druten: *I Remember Mama*	
		Winsor: *Forever Amber*	
	Mercer: "Accentuate the Positive"	Williams: *The Glass Menagerie*	
	Martin and Blanc: "Have Yourself a Merry Little Christmas"	Borges: *The Garden of Forking Paths*	
		Ellison: *King of the Bingo Game*	

Did You Know?

After World War II, Ezra Pound was imprisoned in an open cage in Italy, punishment for his treasonous radio broadcasts during the war. Found "insane and mentally unfit for trial," Pound was incarcerated in St. Elizabeth's Hospital for the insane rather than being tried for treason.

Art and Architecture	Music	Literature	Popular Culture
1945 Moore: *Family Group*	Strauss: *Metamorphosen*	US: Ezra Pound found insane	Eisenhower jackets, bubblegum, crewcuts, pageboy hairstyles catch on
Epstein: *Lucifer*	Britten: *Peter Grimes*	Chase: *Harvey* (Pulitzer)	
Wright: Design for Guggenheim Museum	Prokofiev: *Cinderella*	Orwell: *Animal Farm*	Movie: *The Lost Weekend*
	Rogers and Hammerstein: *Carousel*	Waugh: *Brideshead Revisited*	Movie: *Brief Encounter*
	"Anchors Away" helps spark Frank Sinatra's career	Thurber: *The Thurber Carnival*	Dior's "New Look": Full, calf-length skirts, tight waist
	Behop emerges as as reaction to jazz	Nobel Prize: Gabriel Mistral	"Black market" develops for hard-to-find goods

KEY DOCUMENT

"Television won't be able to hold on to any market it captures after the first six months. People will soon get tired of staring at a plywood box every night."
—Darryl Zanuck, 20th Century Fox studio executive, 1946.

	Art and Architecture	Music	Literature	Popular Culture
			Senghor: *Chants d'ombre*	World War II ends with dropping of atomic bombs on Hiroshima and Nagasaki
1946	Leger: *Composition with a Branch*	Britten: *The Tape of Lucretia*	Dead Sea Scrolls discovered	Bugsy Siegel opens the Flamingo Hotel, Las Vegas' first resort casino
	Chagall: *Cow with Umbrella*	Menotti: *The Medium*	Warren: *All The King's Men* (Pulitzer)	
	Buckminster Fuller designs structures	Ashton: *Symphonic Variations*	Miller: *All My Sons*	Levittown, NY: First suburb
		Balanchine: *Nightshadow*	O'Neill: *The Iceman Cometh*	Dr. Benjamin Spock's *Baby and Child Care*
		Berlin: *Annie Get Your Gun*	Nobel Prize: Hermann Hesse	Movie: *The Best Years of Our Lives*
		Berlin: "Anything You Can Do"	Hersey: *Hiroshima*	Movie: *Notorious*
1947	de Vlaminck: *A Bunch of Flowers*	Lerner and Loewe: *Brigadoon*	Anne Frank: *The Diary of a Young Girl*	NBC's *Meet the Press* launched
	Moore: *Three Standing Figures*	Wrubel and Gilbert: "Zip-a-dee-doo-dah"	Camus: *The Plague*	US: CIA formed
	Giacometti: *The Pointing Man*	Arlen and Mercer: "Come Rain or Come Shine"	Williams: *A Streetcar Named Desire*	Marionette Howdy Doody thrills kids from 1947 to 1960
			Lowell: *Lord Weary's Castle* (Pulitzer)	Movie: *Gentleman's Agreement*
	Matisse: *Young English Girl*		Mann: *Doctor Faustus*	US: Invasion from space scare
			Diop: *Tales of Amadou Koumba*	
1948	Leger: *Homage to David*	Hanson: *Piano Concerto No. 1*	Williams: *A Streetcar Named Desire* (Pulitzer)	12″, 33-rpm vinyl record
	Shahn: *Miners' Wives*	Berlin: "Better Luck Next Time"	Auden: *Age of Anxiety* (Pulitzer)	Alfred Kinsey: *Sexual Behavior in the American Male*
	Pollock: *Composition No. 1*	Britten: *Beggar's Opera* (new version)	Mailer: *The Naked and the Dead*	Academy Award: *Hamlet* starring Laurence Olivier
	Moore: *Family Group*	Gardner: "All I Want for Christmas is My Two Front Teeth"	Nobel Prize: T. S. Eliot	Nestle's Quick introduced

Art and Architecture	Music	Literature	Popular Culture
	Miles Davis plays brilliant jazz	Paton: *Cry, the Beloved Country*	Movie: *The Red Shoes*
			Movie: *Oliver Twist*
		Williams: *Summer and Smoke*	Movie: *Macbeth*
		Pound: *Pisan Cantos*	British National Health Service founded

Did You Know?

Assessing Miles Davis, Time *magazine noted that: "Back in 1948, when everybody was trying to blow like Diz, Miles Davis' nine-man pickup band was trimming Gillespie's blast-furnace sound to a clean, low Bunsen flame."*

Art and Architecture	Music	Literature	Popular Culture
1949 Clark: *Landscape Into Art*	Porter: *Kiss Me Kate*	Miller: *Death of a Salesman*	7", 45-rpm vinyl record
Epstein: *Lazarus*	Bliss: *The Olympians*	Algren: *The Man with the Golden Arm*	The samba becomes popular
Chagall: *Red Sun*	Britten: *Let's Make an Opera*		
	Weill: *Lost in the Stars*	Cozzens: *Guard of Honor* (Pulitzer)	Movie: *All the King's Men*
	Rodgers and Hammerstein: *South Pacific*	Orwell: *Nineteen Eighty-Four*	Movie: *The Third Man*
	Bernstein: *The Age of Anxiety*	Miller: *Death of a Salesman* (Pulitzer)	Milton Berle hosts the first telethon
	Antheil: *Symphony No. 6*	Nobel Prize: William Faulkner	
	Bartok: *Viola Concerto*	McCullers: *The Member of the Wedding*	
	Styne: "Diamonds are a Girl's Best Friend"		

Did You Know?

"Crooners," including Dean Martin, Dick Haymes, Eddie Fisher, and Tony Bennett, sent pulses soaring.

	Art and Architecture	Music	Literature	Popular Culture
		Marks: "Rudolph the Red-Nosed Reindeer"		
		Hank Miller has a run of hits, including "Lovesick Blues," "Long Gone Lonesome Blues," and "Hey Good Lookin' "		
1950	DeKooning's series *Women*	Menotti: *The Consul*	Bradbury: *The Martian Chronicles*	1.5 million TV sets in US
	Chagall: *King David*	"Cool jazz" develops	Hemingway: *Across the River and Into the Trees*	Diners Club Card: First nationwide credit card
	Giacometti: *Seven Figures and a Head*	Loesser and Burrows: *Guys and Dolls*		
	Pani and del Moral design Mexico City	Loesser and Burrows: "A Bushel and a Peck"	Heyerdahl: *Kon-Tiki*	Movie: *Rashomon*
	Pollock: *Lavender Mist*		Nobel Prize: Bertrand Russell	Brink's robbery in Boston; almost $3 million stolen
	Le Corbusier designs Chandigarh, the new capital of the Punjab	*On the Town*, starring Frank Sinatra, is a Broadway hit	Brooks: *Annie Allen* (Pulitzer)	Mr. Potato Head toy debuts
	De Kooning: *Woman I*			Movie: *Sunset Boulevard*
				Movie: *All About Eve*

Did You Know?

Cole Porter's hit songs include "Night and Day," "What Is This Thing Called Love," and "I've Got You Under My Skin."

	Art and Architecture	Music	Literature	Popular Culture
1951	Dali: *Christ of St. John on the Cross*	Britten: *Billy Budd*	Salinger: *Catcher in the Rye*	US: 15 million TV sets
	Sutherland: *Lord Beaverbrook*	Stravinsky: *Rake's Progress*	Jack Kerouac writes *On the Road* in three weeks	US: First color TV set
	Matisse completes Venice Chapel	Williams: *The Pilgrim's Progress*	Sandburg: *Complete Poems* (Pulitzer)	US: *I Love Lucy* debuts

Art and Architecture	Music	Literature	Popular Culture
Picasso: *Massacre in Korea*	Rogers and Hammerstein: *The King and I*	Wouk: *The Caine Mutiny* (Pulitzer)	US: Computers sold commercially
Dix: *Peasant Girl with Child*	Rogers and Hammerstein: "Hello, Young Lovers"	Greene: *The End of the Affair*	US: 7-Up debuts
Mies van der Rohe designs Lake Shore Drive apartment building	Seeger: "Kisses Sweeter than Wine"	Jones: *From Here to Eternity*	Movie: *The African Queen*
		Williams: *The Rose Tattoo*	US: *Roy Rogers Show* premieres on NBC
Wright designs Friedman House		Styron: *Lie Down in Darkness*	Movie: *An American in Paris*
		Carson: *The Sea Around Us*	Movie: *A Streetcar Named Desire*

Did You Know?

Akira Kurosawa's Rashomon *tells the tale of a brutal murder from four points of view, posing paradoxical questions about the nature of truth. Kurosawa's elegant meditations on violence spawned imitators:* The Seven Samurai *was remade as* The Magnificent Seven; Yojimbo *was reborn as* A Fistful of Dollars.

	Art and Architecture	Music	Literature	Popular Culture
1952	Buckminster Fuller's Geodesic dome	Henze: *Boulevard*	Ellison: *Invisible Man*	US: First bank credit card
	Chagall: *The Green Night*	Liebermann: *Lenore 40/45*	E. B. White: *Charlotte's Web*	NBC: *The Today Show*
	Dufy: *The Pink Violin*	Connor: "I Saw Mommy Kissing Santa Claus"	Hemingway: *The Old Man and the Sea* (Pulitzer)	Movie: *High Noon*
	Pollock: *Number 12*	Kubik: *Symphony Concertante* (Pulitzer)	Kramm: *The Shrike* (Pulitzer)	Movie: *The Greatest Show on Earth*
	Epstein: *Madonna and Child*	Creston: *Symphony No. 4*	Moore: *Collected Poems* (Pulitzer)	Agatha Christie's *The Mousetrap* debuts
		Haieff: *Piano Concerto*	Thomas: *Collected Poems*	Argentina: Eva Peron dies
		Harris: *Symphony No. 7*	Nobel Prize: Francois Mauriac	Christian Dior becomes well-known fashion designer
		Read: *The Temptation of St. Anthony*	Beckett: *Waiting for Godot*	

Art and Architecture	Music	Literature	Popular Culture
	Bernstein: *Trouble in Tahiti* (opera)	Steinbeck: *East of Eden*	
	Kreutz: *Acres of Sky*		
	Tcherepnin: *The Farmer and the Fairy*		

Did You Know?

In a contemporary review of Ellison's Invisible Man, Time *magazine noted that "This is no simple catalogue of hard-luck adventures in a world where might is white. Before it's over, [the novelist's] hero can face up to one of life's bitterest questions, 'How does it feel to be free of illusion?,' and give an honest answer: 'Painful and empty.' "*

	Art and Architecture	Music	Literature	Popular Culture
1953	Bazin: *Chicago*	*Kismet* Broadway show	Miller: *The Crucible*	*From Here to Eternity* wins Academy Award
	Braque: *Apples*	Britten: *Gloriana*	Fleming: *Casino Royale*	Bikinis, petticoats, head scarves, jeans become fads
	Chagall: *Eiffel Tower*	Williams: *Sinfonia antartica*	Nobel Prize: Winston Churchill	
	Moore: *King and Queen*	von Einem: *The Trial*	Anderson: *Tea and Sympathy*	Frisbee's pie plates used as toys in CT; later in the decade, Wham-O begins making Frisbee discs
		Bernstein: *Wonderful Town*	MacLeish: *Collected Poems* (Pulitzer)	
		Antheil: *Volpone*	Bellow: *The Adventures of Augie March*	Movie: *Roman Holiday*
		Bennett, Stanley, and Wiggs: "Stranger in Paradise"	Uris: *Battle Cry*	GM introduces the Chevrolet Corvette, first laminated fiberglass sports car, for $3,250
		Paige: "Doggie in the Window"		Films of Kurosawa and Satyajit Ray shown in US

Did You Know?

Popular doo-wop groups included The Ink Spots, The Mills Brothers, The Moonglows, The Drifters, The Five Royals, The Isley Brothers, and Little Anthony & the Imperials.

Art and Architecture	Music	Literature	Popular Culture
			First microwave oven developed
			US: A&P sells 10-pound bags of potatoes for 39¢

Did You Know?

Arthur Miller is regarded as one of the major playwrights of the twentieth century, but many people know him best as Marilyn Monroe's second husband.

Art and Architecture	Music	Literature	Popular Culture
1954 Bissiere: *Composition*	"Rock Around the Clock" a hit for Bill Haley & the Comets	Tolkien: *Lord of the Rings*	Swanson: TV dinner debuts
Campigli: *Diavolo Player*	Berkeley: *Nelson* (opera)	Nobel Prize: Ernest Hemingway	Movie: *On the Waterfront*
Chagal: *The Red Roofs*	Britten: *The Turn of the Screw* (opera)	Faulkner: *A Fable* (Pulitzer)	Howard Johnson: First hotel chain
Dubuffet: *Les Vagabonds*	Copland: *The Tender Land* (opera)	Hyman: *No Time for Sergeants*	Movie: *Rear Window*
Ernst: *Lonely*	Schoenberg: *Moses and Aaron*	Patrick: *The Teahouse of the August Moon*	NBC's *The Tonight Show* debuts
Leger: *Acrobat and Horse*	Menotti: *The Saint of Bleecker Street* (Pulitzer)	Williams: *Cat on a Hot Tin Roof*	Movie: *The Seven Samurai*
Picasso: *Sylvette*	Walton: *Troilus and Cressida*	Amis: *Lucky Jim*	
Sutherland: *Portrait of Churchill*	Adler and Ross: *The Pajama Game*	Golding: *Lord of the Flies*	
Jasper Johns: *Flag*	Porter: *Concerto for Two Pianos and Orchestra* (Pulitzer)	Sagan: *Bonjour Tristesse*	
Le Corbusier: Notre-Dame-du-Haut, France	Stravinsky: *Four Russian Peasant Songs*	Thomas: *Under Milk Wood*	
1954 to 1956 Nervi designs UNESCO Building in Paris	Diamond: *Ahavah*	Catton: *Stillness at Appomattox* (Pulitzer)	
		Lindbergh: *The Spirit of St. Louis* (Pulitzer)	

Art and Architecture	Music	Literature	Popular Culture
	Hovhaness: *Concerto No. 5*	Nobuo: *The American School*	
	First annual Newport Jazz Festival	Theater of the Absurd explored by Beckett, Ionesco, Genet	
	Adler and Ross: "Hernando's Hideaway"	Robbe-Grillet and Sarraute develop "new novel" without form or plot	
	Styne and Cahn: "Three Coins in the Fountain"		
	Sinatra's "Young at Heart" hits the top of the charts		
	Jerry Lee Lewis is wild man of 1950s rock n' roll with his pumping boogie piano and off-the-wall vocals. Hits include "Whole Lotta Shakin' " and "Great Balls of Fire"		
	Ray Charles' first hit, "It Should Have Been Me," followed by R&B hits "I Got a Woman" and "Hallelujah! I Love Her So"		

Did You Know?

McDonalds' first day revenues? $366.12!

Art and Architecture	Music	Literature	Popular Culture
1955 Buffet: *Circus*	Prokofiev: *Fiery Angel*	Christie: *Witness for the Prosecution*	*Gunsmoke* begins a 20-year TV run
Dali: *The Lord's Supper*	Tippett: *The Midsummer Marriage*	Greene: *The Quiet American*	Ann Landers begins giving advice

Art and Architecture	Music	Literature	Popular Culture
Jacobsen uses International Style as he designs Rodovre Town Hall, Copenhagen	Liebermann: *School for Wives*	Nabokov: *Lolita*	Disneyland, world's first theme park
	Adler and Ross: *Damn Yankees*	Miller: *A View from the Bridge*	Ray Kroc creates McDonald's
	Porter: *Silk Stockings*	Lawrence and Lee: *Inherit the Wind*	*Lawrence Welk Show* premieres on ABC
	Antheil: *The Wish*	Inge: *Bus Stop*	Special K introduced
	Adler and Ross: "Whatever Lola Wants"	Wilson: *Man in the Gray Flannel Suit*	US: Rosa Parks refuses to move to the back of the bus; civil rights movement intensifies
	Fain: "Love is a Many-Splendored Thing"	Wouk: *Marjorie Morningstar*	
		Robbe-Grillet: *The Voyeur*	Movie: *Marty*
		Nobel Prize: Halldor K. Lazness	Movie: *The Rose Tattoo*
			Movie: *The Seven Year Itch*

Did You Know?

Opening day at Disneyland was inauspicious: rides malfunctioned, refreshment stands ran out of food, and women's high heels sunk into Main Street's fresh asphalt on an unseasonably hot July day. Even Walt Disney called it "Black Sunday." Despite the shaky start, Disneyland became a phenomenon. By 1992, three additional Disney parks had been built in Orlando, Tokyo, and Paris.

1956	Chadwick: *Teddy Boy and Girl*	Elvis Presley's first major single: *Heartbreak Hotel* (Mae Axton, composer)	Beckett: *Waiting for Godot*	Prince Rainier of Monaco, Grace Kelly marry
	Hepworth: *Orpheus*		Ginsberg: *Howl*	Seat belt added to cars
	Rothko: *Orange and Yellow*	Duke Ellington has many hit songs	Osborne: *Look Back in Anger*	Movie: *The Man with the Golden Arm*
	Pop Art emerges in the work of Hamilton, Blake, Paolozi	Woody Guthrie: *This Land is Your Land*	Goodrich and Hackett: *The Diary of Anne Frank* (drama, Pulitzer)	Movie: *The King and I*
		Bernstein: *Candide*		

	Art and Architecture	Music	Literature	Popular Culture
		Lerner and Lowe: *My Fair Lady*	Metalious: *Peyton Place*	Movie: *The Ten Commandments*
		Perkins: "Blue Suede Shoes"	Kennedy: *Profiles in Courage* (Pulitzer)	Movie: *Lust for Life*
		Leiber and Stoller: "Hound Dog"	Dennis: *Auntie Mame*	Sabin develops oral polio vaccine
		Maria Callas makes singing debut	Jun'ichiro: *The Key*	First Congress of Black Writers meets in Paris
		Buddy Holly cuts first record; hits will include "That'll Be the Day," "Maybe Baby," and "It Doesn't Matter Anymore"	1956 to 1957: Mahfouz: *The Cairo Trilogy* Nobel Prize: Juan Jimenez	
		Day: "Que Sera, Sera"		
		Matson and Darby: "Love Me Tender"		
		American Bandstand, starring Dick Clark, debuts		

Did You Know?

In a contemporary review of Waiting for Godot, Time *magazine claimed that:* "With its lost . . . straw-clutching outcasts, its bullying and later blinded magnate, its endless rain of symbolic and allegorical smallshot, its scarred and almost sceneryless universe, Waiting for Godot *can be most variously interpreted—somewhat after the fashion of the blind men and the elephant."*

	Art and Architecture	Music	Literature	Popular Culture
1957	Chagall: *Self-Portrait*	Fortner: *Blood Wedding* (opera)	Fleming: *From Russia, with Love*	Movie: *The Seventh Seal*
	Levi: *Anna Magnani*	Britten: *The Prince of the Pagodas*	Dr. Seuss: *The Cat in the Hat*	Ford Fairlane 500 sells for $2,495
	Le Corbusier designs Tokyo Museum of Art	Stravinsky: *Agon*	Nobel Prize: Albert Camus	*Leave it to Beaver* premieres on CBS
		Gardner: *The Moon and Sixpence* (opera)		

Art and Architecture	Music	Literature	Popular Culture
	Bernstein: *West Side Story*	Shute: *On the Beach*	Movie: *The Bridge on the River Kwai*
	Wilson: *The Music Man*	Murdoch: *The Sandcastle*	Movie: *Twelve Angry Men*
	Elvis' hit: "All Shook Up"	Beckett: *Endgame*	Movie: *Love in the Afternoon*
	Wilson: "Seventy-Six Trombones"	O'Neill: *Long Day's Journey Into Night* (Pulitzer)	USSR launches Sputnicks I, II
	Patsy Cline's career begins when she wins Arthur Godfrey Talent Scout contest; her hits include "I Fall to Pieces," "Crazy," "She's Got You"	Vidal: *Visit to a Small Planet*	"Beatniks" become popular
		"Beat" writers—Alan Ginsberg, Jack Kerouac, Lawrence Ferlinghetti, etc.	Lucille Ball's television show attracts millions of viewers
		Camus: *The Guest*	

Did You Know?

In an assessment of Stravinsky's accomplishments, Time magazine noted that "He experimented with virtually every technique of twentieth-century music: tonal, polytonal, and twelve-tone serialism. He reinvented and personalized each form while adapting the melodic styles of earlier eras to the new times. In the end, his own musical voice always prevailed."

Art and Architecture	Music	Literature	Popular Culture
1958 Brooks: *Acanda*	78 rpm record discontinued	Nobel Prize: Boris Pasternak	Hula hoop debuts
Poliakoff: *Composition in Blue-Yellow-Red-Brown*	Hense: *Ondine* (ballet)	Pinter: *A Birthday Party*	Phone booth stuffing becomes a fad
Moore: *Reclining Figure*	Menotti: *Maria Golovin* (opera)	Hansberry: *A Raisin in the Sun*	Cha cha is the hot new dance
NY: Guggenheim Museum opens	Seville: "Chipmunk Song"	Capote: *Breakfast at Tiffany's*	Movie: *Touch of Evil*
Gropius: Pan American Building, NY	Wooley: "The Purple People Eater"	Pasternak: *Dr. Zhivago*	Movie: *Cat on a Hot Tin Roof*
van der Rohe: Seagram Building	Elvis' hits: "Jailhouse Rock" and "King Creole"	Uris: *Exodus*	Movie: *Gigi*
		MacLeish: *J. B.* (Pulitzer)	Elvis appears in three movies: *Loving You, Jailhouse Rock,* and *King Creole*

	Art and Architecture	Music	Literature	Popular Culture
		Rodgers and Hammerstein: *Flower Drum Song*	Achebe: *Things Fall Apart*	
		Ray Charles at Newport released		
1959	Inoue: *Fish*	Sinatra's *Come Dance with Me* album of the year	"Confessional Poets" John Berryman, Robert Lowell, Sylvia Plath, Theodore Roethke, Anne Sexton (through 1960s)	*Ben-Hur* top movie
	Hepworth: *Meridian*			Barbie dolls debut
	Bluhm: *Chicago*	Rodgers: *The Sound of Music*		Movie: *Anatomy of a Murder*
	Bill Maudlin wins Pulitzer for his cartoons	Styne: *Gypsy*	Bellow: *Henderson the Rain King*	Movie: *Hiroshima, mon amour*
	Nevelson: *Royal Tide IV*	Cowell: *Symphony No. 13*	Mailer: *Advertisements for Myself*	
	Wright: Solomon R. Guggenheim Museum, NY	*Fiorello!* (Pulitzer Prize)	Grass: *The Tin Drum*	
	Niemeyer designs cathedral in Brasilia	London: "He's Got the Whole World in His Hands"	Naipaul: *Mugel Street*	
		Modugno: "Volare"	Spark: *Memento Mori*	
			Packard: *The Status Seekers*	
			Drury: *Advise and Consent* (Pulitzer)	
			Tawfiq al-Hakim: *The Sultan's Dilemma*	
			Nobel Prize: Salvatore Quasimodo	
			Updike: *Poorhouse Fair*	
			Gibson: *The Miracle Worker*	
			Michener: *Hawaii*	
			Hart: *Act One*	
			Fleming: *Goldfinger*	

Art and Architecture	Music	Literature	Popular Culture

Art and Architecture	Music	Literature	Popular Culture
1960 Le Corbusier: Monastry La Tourette	Chubby Checker introduces the "twist"	Paperback book sales top 300 million	Chicago's last meat-packing house closes
Bratby: *Gloria with Sunflower*	Boulez: *Portrait of Mallarme*	Lee: *To Kill a Mockingbird* (Pulitzer)	Oral contraceptive Enovid 10
Yamasaki designs Pavilion of Science, Seattle	Bart: *Oliver!*	Bolt: *A Man for All Seasons*	Movie: *La Dolce Vita*
Moore: *Reclining Mother and Child*	Carter: *String Quartet No. 2* (Pulitzer)	Robert Frost recites "The Gift Outright" at Kennedy's inauguration	First Playboy Club opens
Louis: *Beth Aleph*	Hyland: "Itsy Bitsy Yellow Polka Dot Bikini"	Shirer: *The Rise and Fall of the Third Reich*	Movie: *Midnight Lace* starring Doris Day
	Dave Brubeck's "Take Five" hits top of the charts	Updike: *Rabbit, Run*	World population tops 3 billion
	Ray Charles' hit "Georgia on My Mind"	Sillitoe: *The Loneliness of the Long Distance Runner*	Movie: *Exodus*
		Hersey: *The Child Buyer*	Movie: *Psycho*
	"Easy Listening" bands Herb Alpert & the Tijuana Brass; Arthur Fielder & the Boston Pops; The Mamas and the Pappas; Peter, Paul & Mary are popular	Nobel Prize: St.-John Perse	Movie: *The Apartment*
		Duras: *Hiroshima, mon amour*	Twist becomes the popular dance
		Shono Junzo: *Still Life*	

	Art and Architecture	Music	Literature	Popular Culture
1961	"Pop Art," Roy Lichtenstein, Andy Warhol, George Segal, Claes Oldenburg China: Museum of Chinese Revolution opens	The Supremes sign with Motown Chubby Checker wins Grammy for "Let's Twist Again" Piston: *Symphony No. 7* (Pulitzer) Nono: *Intoleranza* Williams: "Moon River" Marcels: "Blue Moon" Vee: "Take Good Care of My Baby" Charles: "Hit the Road, Jack" Bob Dylan's debut album, *Bob Dylan*	J. D. Salinger: *Franny and Zooey* Joseph Heller: *Catch-22* Malamud: *A New Life* Steinbeck: *The Winter of Our Discontent* Stone: *The Agony and the Ecstasy* Robbins: *The Carpetbaggers* Heinlein: *Stranger in a Strange Land* Nobel Prize: Ivo Andric Naipaul: *A House for Mr. Bisawas*	The Peace Corps created Amnesty International founded Movie: *West Side Story* Movie: *Judgment at Nuremberg* Movie: *The Hustler* US: "Freedom Riders" civil rights workers attacked by whites Soviet astronauts orbit earth

Did You Know?

The 1969 film version of To Kill a Mockingbird *is a gem. Peck's brilliant performance as a Southern lawyer who defends a Black man (Brock Peters) won him an Oscar; Horton Foote's screenplay also copped an Oscar.*

	Art and Architecture	Music	Literature	Popular Culture
1962	Kokoschka: *Ringed with Vision* Saarinen: TWA Terminal, NY	Tippett: *King Priam* (opera) Britten: *War and Requiem*	K. A. Porter: *Ship of Fools* Steinbeck: *Travels with Charley*	ABC begins color telecasts Trans-Canada Highway

Did You Know?

West Indian novelist V. S. Naipaul (born in India) often writes about poverty in his adopted country. His novels are marked by great insight and delicate irony.

Art and Architecture	Music	Literature	Popular Culture
Bacon: *Red Figure* shows distorted human forms	Ward: *The Crucible* (Pulitzer)	Faulkner: *The Reivers* (Pulitzer)	90% of US households have at least one TV
Japanese architecture unites traditional forms with steel and concrete	Dylan: "Blowin' in the Wind"	Carson: *Silent Spring*	Tab-opening cans debut
	Laurindo Almeida records wildly popular *Viva Bossa Nova*, including "The Girl from Ipanema"	Nobel Prize: John Steinbeck	First Wal-Mart store
		Loesser and Burrows: *How to Succeed in Business without Really Trying* (Pulitzer)	Movie: *Dr. No*
	Orbison: "Working for the Man"	Albee: *Who's Afraid of Virginia Woolf?*	Motel 6, first roadside economy chain, with $6 rooms
		Roth: *Letting Go*	First Kmart store
		Jones: *The Thin Red Line*	Diet-Rite Cola introduced
		Williams: *The Night of the Iguana*	Movie: *Lawrence of Arabia*
		Lessing: *The Golden Notebooks*	Movie: *The Manchurian Candidate*
		Robbe-Grillet: *Snapshots*	Schulz: *Happiness is a Warm Puppy*
		Kesey: *One Flew Over the Cuckoo's Nest*	

Did You Know?

"The singer will have to go."—Eric Easton, manager of the Rolling Stones, on Mick Jagger.

1963	Lippold: *Orpheus and Apollo*	Beatles first big success	McCarthy: *The Group*	Weight Watchers founded
	Art Nouveau once again popular	Barbra Streisand wins Grammy for Album of the Year	Betty Friedan's *The Feminine Mystique* energizes women's movement	Alfred Hitchcock's *The Birds* hits the theaters
		Beatles: "I Want to Hold Your Hand"	West: *Shoes of the Fisherman*	Movie: *Dr. Strangelove*

Art and Architecture	Music	Literature	Popular Culture
Pop Art is newest style, represented by Andy Warhol, Robert Rauschenberg, Jasper Johns, etc.	Barber: *Piano Concerto No. 1* (Pulitzer)	Mitford: *The American Way of Death*	Movie: *Irma La Douce*
	Bill Monroe revitalizes bluegrass music when he appears at the University of Chicago Folk Festival	Grass: *Dog Years*	First class postal rate is 5¢
Warhol: *Marilyn Monroe Diptych*		Le Carre: *The Spy Who Came in From the Cold*	Movie: *Tom Jones*
Lichtenstein: *Whaam!*		Anna Akhmatova: *Requiem*	Mary Quant's bright, geometric designs and loose outlines spark the so-called Youthquake look of the 1960s
Ellsworth Kelly: *Yellow-Blue*	Patsy Cline killed in plane crash; posthumous hits include "Sweet Dreams of You," "Faded Love," and "Anytime"	Mahfouz: *God's World*	
Rudolph: Art and Architecture Building, Yale University, New Haven		Solzhenitsyn: *Matroyna's Home*	Dominos delivers its first pizza
		Malamud: *Idiots First*	
		Tuchman: *Guns of August* (Pulitzer)	
		Williams: *Pictures from Brueghel* (Pulitzer)	
		Nobel Prize: Giorgos Seferis	

Did You Know?

The United Artists executive who rejected Ronald Reagan as the lead for the 1963 film The Best Man did so by saying: "Reagan doesn't have that presidential look."

1964	NY: Gallery of Modern Art opens	Beatles debut on the *Ed Sullivan Show*	Saul Bellow: *Herzog*	Pop-Tarts toaster pastries introduced
	Jones: *Green Girl*	Britten: *Curlew River*	Miller: *After the Fall* and *Incident at Vichy*	Topless bathing suits become popular
	Picasso: *The Painter and his Model*	Stockhausen: *Plus/Minus*	Nobel Prize: Jean-Paul Sartre	G.I. Joe doll introduced
	Smith: *Cubi XVIII*			
	Rauschenberg: *Retroactive 1*	Herman: *Hello, Dolly*		Elizabeth Taylor divorces Eddie Fisher; ten days later, marries Richard Burton
		Bock: *Fiddler on the Roof*		

	Art and Architecture	Music	Literature	Popular Culture
	Segal: *Bus Riders*	Herman: "Hello, Dolly"		NY World's Fair opens
		Barry: "From Russia with Love"		Popular dances: The Watusi, Frug, Monkey, and Funky Chicken
				Discotheques ("Discos") are popular dance halls
				Go-go girls led dances
				NY: Verrazano-Narrows Bridge, world's longest suspension bridge, opens
				Movie: *A Hard Day's Night* (Beatles)
				Movie: *Goldfinger*
				Movie: *Zorba the Greek*
				"Psychedelia" mentioned in San Francisco
				Movie: *My Fair Lady*
				Movie: *Mary Poppins*
				Movie: *Topkapi*
1965	Op art becomes popular, based on optical illusions	The Grateful Dead rock group forms	Mailer: *An American Dream*	Diet Pepsi introduced
	Picasso: *Self-Portrait*	"A Taste of Honey" wins the Grammy	Nobel Prize: M. A. Sholokhov	Ralph Nader's *Unsafe at Any Speed*
	Rent Collection Yard shows misery of life in China	Williamson: *Julius Caesar Jones* (opera)	Moore: *The Green Berets*	Power failure blacks out northeast US and two Canadian provinces
		Bernstein: *Chichester Psalms*	Schleisinger: *The Thousand Days* (Pulitzer)	McDonald's goes public with its stock offering
		Blacher: *Tristan und Isolde*	Fleming: *Thunderball*	

Art and Architecture	Music	Literature	Popular Culture
	Miller: "King of the Road"	Berryman: *77 Dream Song* (Pulitzer)	Canada: Adopts maple leaf symbol for flag
	Beatles: "A Hard Day's Night"		Eight-track tape debuts
	Clark: "Downtown"		University of Michigan "teach-in" heralds the start of the student anti-Vietnam War movement
	Beatles: *Rubber Soul*		
	Jim Morrison carries The Doors to fame		
			Movie: *Help!* (Beatles)
			Movie: *The Sound of Music*
			Haight-Asbury becomes center of LSD and psychedelia movement

Did You Know?

Frank Stella used protractors to create the circles and squares of Tahkt-1-Sulayman. Abstract Expressionism inspired the large scale of his paintings, but his "hard edge" precise forms and vivid colors are in direct contrast to the Abstract Expressionists' painterly approach.

	Art and Architecture	Music	Literature	Popular Culture
1966	Sugai: *Mer soleil*	Frank Sinatra wins record of the year Grammy for "Strangers in the Night"	Malamud: *The Fixer*	US: First Medicare ID card presented to former president Harry Truman
	Egypt: Abu Simbel tomb moved to save it from the Nile River		Truman Capote: *In Cold Blood*	
	NY: Metropolitan Opera House opens at new Lincoln Center home	Leigh: *Man of La Mancha*	Porter: *Collected Stories* (Pulitzer)	*Mission Impossible* premieres on CBS
		Schuman: *The Witch of Endor*	Nobel Prize: S. J. Agnon, Nelly Sachs	Susann: *Valley of the Dolls*
	Oldenburg: *Soft Toilet*	Freedman: *Rose Latulippe*	Albee: *A Delicate Balance*	Walt Disney dies
		Barber: *Antony and Cleopatra*	Manchester: *The Death of a President*	Movie: *A Man for All Seasons*

	Art and Architecture	Music	Literature	Popular Culture
		Lane: *On a Clear Day You Can See Forever*		Movie: *Alfie*
				Movie: *Who's Afraid of Virginia Woolf?*
		Bassett: *Variations for Orchestra* (Pulitzer)		Movie: *Fahrenheit 451*
		Wesker: *The Kitchen*		Movie: *Torn Curtain*
		Motown in full swing: stars include The Supremes, The Four Tops, The Temptations, Stevie Wonder, Smokey Robinson and The Miracles		
		Sadler: "Ballad of the Green Berets"		
		August 28: The Beatles last concert		
1967	Treasures of Tutankhamen exhibit in Paris	Stright: *Toyon of Alaska*	Singer: *The Manor*	Twist, yogurt, miniskirts, turtlenecks, Afro hairstyles, and "big hair" catch on
	Chagall: *The Blue Village*	Levy: *Mourning Becomes Electra* (opera)	Levin: *Rosemary's Baby*	
			Uris: *Topaz*	Barbra Streisand sings in Central Park: 135,000 fans turn out
	Stella: *Tahkt-1-Sulayman*	Zuffre: *Hiroshima*	Pinter: *The Homecoming*	
	Hockney: *A Bigger Splash*	Kander and Ebb: *Cabaret*	Shaw: *The Man in the Glass Booth*	Movie: *Bonnie and Clyde*
		Carlos Santana firmly established as leader of Latin music	Marquez: *One Hundred Years of Solitude*	Movie: *In the Heat of the Night*
		Beatles: *Sergeant Pepper's Lonely Hearts Club Band* shows that rock is the medium of the moment	Stoppard: *Rosencrantz and Guildenstern are Dead*	Movie: *Guess Who's Coming to Dinner*
			Miller: *The Price*	
		Jimi Hendrix Experience forms; debut album *Are You Experienced*	Nobel Prize: Miguel Asturias	

	Art and Architecture	Music	Literature	Popular Culture
		"Queen of Soul" Aretha Franklin turns out hits		
		Rolling Stones appear on the *Ed Sullivan Show*		
		Rolling Stones: *Satanic Majesties Request*		
		Frank Zappa's debut album: *Freak Out!*		
1968	Temples on the Parthenon in Greece threatened by erosion	Jose Feliciano wins Grammy for Best New Artist	Mailer: *The Armies of the Night*	MPAA movie ratings begin
	Bonies: *Red-White Blue 68*	Rosen: *Concerto for Synket and Orchestra*	Updike: *Couples*	US: *60 Minutes* debuts
		Orr: *Full Circle*	Nobel Prize: Yasunari Rawabata	McDonalds introduces the Big Mac
		Boldemann: *The Hour of Folly*	Hailey: *Airport*	Ralph Lauren starts his fashion empire
		Stewart and Pascal: *George M!*	Braine: *The Crying Game*	Jackie Kennedy marries Aristotle Onassis
		Beatles: "Hey Jude"	Wolfe: *The Electric Kool-Aid Acid Test*	Movie: *Oliver!*
		Simon and Garfunkel: "Mrs. Robinson"	Sackler: *The Great White Hope* (Pulitzer)	Movie: *Funny Girl*
		The 5th Dimension: "Stoned Soul Picnic"	Simon: *Plaza Suite*	Movie: *The Odd Couple*
		Aretha Franklin, Jimi Hendrix top the pop charts	Spark: *The Prime of Miss Jean Brodie*	Movie: *The Lion in Winter*
			Brathwaite: *Masks*	Movie: *The Thomas Crown Affair*
				Movie: *In Cold Blood*
				Movie: *2001: Space Odyssey*
				The "midi-skirt" is a dismal flop; the "mini" holds sway

Art and Architecture	Music	Literature	Popular Culture

	Art and Architecture	Music	Literature	Popular Culture
1969	Judd: *Untitled* Close: *Frank*	Woodstock music festival—300,000 listen to music and wallow in mud Messiaen: *The Transfiguration* Searle: *Hamlet* (opera) Panderecki: *The Devils of Loudun* (opera) Musical: *1776* Menotti: *Triple Concerto* Tippett: *Knot Garden* Fela Kuti fuses Highlife African music with modern jazz, which takes Lagos by storm Raghi and Rado: "Hair" Sinatra records his signature song: "My Way"	Roth: *Portnoy's Complaint* Vonnegut: *Slaughterhouse-Five* Puzo: *The Godfather* Broadway: *Oh! Calcutta!* Nobel Prize: Samuel Beckett Vonnegut: *Slaughterhouse Five* Talese: *The Kingdom and the Power*	US: Stonewall Inn riot begins modern gay-rights movement PBS launches *Sesame Street* Movie: *Midnight Cowboy* Movie: *Easy Rider* Movie: *Bullitt* Movie: *MASH* Movie: *Butch Cassidy and the Sundance Kid* American astronaut Neil Armstrong is first person to walk on the moon
1970	Takeyama designs Tokyo's department store, Ichi-Ban-Kan Arbus: *Jewish Giant at Home with his Parents in the Bronx* (photograph)	The Carpenters win Best New Artist Grammy Janis Joplin dies of heroin overdose	Nobel Prize: Alexander Solzhenitsyn Bellow: *Mr. Sammler's Planet*	The "hippy" look is big One hundred percent polyester dresses sell for $16 at Mays Co.

Art and Architecture	Music	Literature	Popular Culture
Smithson: Spiral Jetty, Great Salt Lake, Utah	Henze: *El Cimarron*	Welty: *Losing Battles*	Movie: *Catch-22*
	Broadway Show: *Company*	Simon: *The Last of the Red Hot Lovers*	Movie: *True Grit*
	Broadway show: *Applause*	Walcott: *Dream on Monkey Mountain*	Movie: *Paint Your Wagon*
	James Brown's hits include *Sex Machine*	Yehoshua: *Three Days and a Child*	Movie: *Topaz*
	James Taylor: *Sweet Baby James*	Marquez: *Death Constant Beyond Love*	

Did You Know?

More than 6,000 tons of material had to be moved by tractors to create Spiral Jetty, an artificial spiral on the northern shore of Great Salt Lake.

| 1971 | Kennedy Center for the Performing Arts opens, Washington, DC

"Conceptual Art" becomes popular | Lily Tomlin is first woman to win a Grammy for Best Comedy Performance

Santana: *Abraxas*

King: *Tapestry* | Solzhenitsyn: *August 1914*

Plath: *The Bell Jar*

Nobel Prize: Pablo Neruda

Updike: *Rabbit Redux*

Forster: *Maurice* (published posthumously)

Wouk: *The Winds of War*

Zindel: *The Effect of Gamma Rays on Man-in-the-Moon Marigolds* | US: Cigarette commercials banned from TV

Eight-track cartridges sell for $4.95 each

Segal: *Love Story*

Movie: *Patton*

Movie: *A Clockwork Orange*

Movie: *The French Connection*

Charles Manson found guilty in Sharon Tate murder Amtrack begins service

Attica prison uprising

Movie: *Klute* |

Art and Architecture	Music	Literature	Popular Culture

Did You Know?

Duane Hanson's astonishingly realistic sculptures portray shoppers, tourists, and bums, among others. His sculptures show a startling combination of humor and pathos.

1972

	Shostakovich: *Symphony No. 15*	Bachmann: *Three Paths to the Lake*	First stand-alone video game, *Pong*
	Broadway: *Jesus Christ, Superstar*	Nobel Prize: Heinrich Boll	Lego and Slinky catch on
	Broadway: *Grease*	Solzhenitsyn: *August 1914*, published in US	Movie: *Cabaret*
	Programs of cultural exchange between Chinese and American musicians begin		Movie: *The Godfather*
			Movie: *Play It Again, Sam*

Did You Know?

Punk rock began in England in the 1970s, spurred by widespread unemployment and strikes.

1973

Hanson: *Janitor*	The Who's *Tommy* rock opera opens in London	Nobel Prize: Patrick White	Home Box Office starts
	Stevie Wonder wins Album of the Year Grammy for "Innervisions"	Vonnegut: *Breakfast of Champions*	Oregon is first state to decriminalize marijuana
		Pynchon: *Gravity's Rainbow*	Movie: *Lady Sings the Blues* (Diana Ross)
	Jackson Browne: *For Everyman*		Energy crisis created by Arab oil embargo
			McDonalds introduces the Egg McMuffin

Art and Architecture	Music	Literature	Popular Culture
			Movie: *Sleeper*
			Movie: *Last Tango in Paris*
1974 China: 7,500 life-sized terra-cotta statues unearthed Estes: *Woolworth's*	Reggae music flourishes, drawing from the Caribbean and Bob Marley Disco bands include The Bee Gees, Donna Summer, the O'Jays, K. C. and the Sunshine Band, Harold Melvin and the Blue Notes	White: *The Eye of the Storm* Le Carre: *Tinker, Tailor, Soldier, Spy* Bernstein and Woodward: *All the President's Men* Solzhenitsyn: *The Gulag Archipelago: 1918–1956* Nobel Prize: Eyvind Johnson, Harry Martinson	"Streaking" fad sweeps US US: Crack cocaine hits public consciousness Kidnapped heiress Patty Hearst joins her captors, the Symbionese Liberation Army AT&T, largest employer in US, bans discrimination against homosexuals

Did You Know?

The army of life-sized terra-cotta figures discovered near Xian in central China were each individually created, not cast from a mold. Originally, each figure had been brightly painted, but the colors had long since faded. Archeologists discovered that the army was commissioned about twenty-two centuries ago to guard the royal tomb of Qin Shi Huang Di, the first emperor to unify China. Huang Di thought on a grand scale: he was the ruler who began building the Great Wall.

Art and Architecture	Music	Literature	Popular Culture
1975 Interest in ancient art reflected in two-year US tour of *Treasures of Tutankamen* and *Pompeii 79AD*	*Jaws* soundtrack wins Grammy award *A Chorus Line* wins Tony as best musical Argento: *From the Diary of Virginia Woolf* (Pulitzer) Sarah Caldwell becomes first female conductor of NY's Metropolitan Opera Moore: *Wildfires and Field Songs*	Soyinka: *Death and the King's Horseman* Updike: *A Month of Sundays* Adams: *Watership Down* Shaffer: *Equus* wins major theater awards Albee: *Seascape* (Pulitzer)	Atari debuts home video games *Jaws* becomes a blockbuster movie NY: Steak and shrimp dinner special costs $6.45 Disco dancing, hot pants, punk look, wide neckties, preppy look catch on Patty Hearst caught by FBI

Art and Architecture	Music	Literature	Popular Culture
	Crumb: *Makrosmos II*	Athold Fugard's plays speak to South Africa's inhumanity to its Black citizens	Movie: *Nashville*
	Elvis declines; a parody of his former self		Movie: *The Sunshine Boys*
		Nobel Prize: Eugenio Montale	Air Force cargo jet carrying 243 Vietnamese orphans to US crashes on takeoff; more than 100 children die
	Punk rock bands include The Sex Pistols and The Clash	Christie: *Curtain*	
			Burma: Great Temples of Pagan destroyed by earthquake
			Postage increases 3¢ to 13¢ for a first-class letter

Did You Know?

In the novel Curtain, mystery writer Agatha Christie kills off her famous detective Hercule Poirot.

Art and Architecture	Music	Literature	Popular Culture
1976	Chicago wins Grammy for "If You Leave Me Now"	Bellow: *Humbolt's Gift* (Pulitzer)	Orient Express makes last Istanbul-Paris journey
	Floyd: *Bibly's Doll* (opera)	Ashbery: *Self-Portrait in a Convex Mirror* (Pulitzer)	VHS home video format
	Menotti: *The Hero* (opera)	Nobel Prize: Saul Bellow	First NYC marathon race
		Luce: *The Belle of Amherst*	*Charlie's Angels* premieres on ABC
		Stoppard: *Travesties* wins many theater prizes	Movie: *All the President's Men*
		Rabe: *Streamers*	Movie: *Rocky*
		Haley: *Roots*	Movie: *Taxi Driver*

	Art and Architecture	Music	Literature	Popular Culture
				World's first supersonic passenger service
				Israeli commandos rescue 103 hostages held at Uganda's Entebbe airport
				"Legionnaires' Disease" strikes for the first time
1977	Beal: *Hope, Faith, and Charity* Piano and Rogers: Centre Pompidou, Paris	Elvis Presley dies; the King has left the room Broadway show *Annie* wins major awards	Eberhart: *Collected Poems: 1930–1976* Stegner: *The Spectator Bird* Merrill: *Divine Comedies* (Pulitzer) Nobel Prize: Vicente Aleixandre Cheever: *Falconer* McCullough: *The Thorn Birds* Mamet: *American Buffalo* wins major awards Christofer: *The Shadow Box* (Pulitzer)	*Star Wars* debuts *Roots* miniseries draws millions of viewers Comedian Groucho Marx dies Disco dancing sweeps the country Movie: *Annie Hall* London Broil steak sells for 99¢ a pound Movie: *Saturday Night Fever* NY: Major blackout leaves 9 million people without power for up to a day; rampant looting and criminal activities US: Oil flows through Alaska pipeline Canada: French adopted as Quebec's official language Passenger service on the Concorde begins between NY and Paris, London

	Art and Architecture	Music	Literature	Popular Culture
1978		Penderecki: *Paradise Lost* (opera) *The Buddy Holly Story,* starring Gary Busey as Holly, sparks a new interest in Holly's songs and a Broadway show	Wouk: *War and Remembrance* Leonard: *Da* (Tony award) Nemerov: *Collected Poems* (Pulitzer) McPherson: *Elbow Room* (Pulitzer) Murdoch: *The Sea, The Sea* Tuchman: *A Distant Mirror: The Calamitous Fourteenth Century* Nobel Prize: Isaac Bashevis Singer	Movie: *Grease* Jim Jones's followers commit mass suicide in Jonestown, Guyana by drinking cyanide-spiked Kool-Aid The legal retirement age raised to 70 US: Nine Lives' Morris the cat dies at age 17 US: More than 120 million viewers watch the "Holocaust" miniseries Movie: *Interiors* Movie: *National Lampoon's Animal House* Movie: *The Deer Hunter* Celebrity nuptials: King Hussein of Jordan and Lisa Halaby David Berkowitz, "Son of Sam," receives life imprisonment for six murders Bakke "reverse discrimination" case resolved in Bakke's favor US: California voters approve Proposition 13 to cut property taxes fifty-seven percent

Art and Architecture	Music	Literature	Popular Culture

Did You Know?

When he was refused admission to the University of California medical school, Allan P. Bakke claimed the school's minority admissions plan made him a victim of "reverse discrimination." The US Supreme Court agreed with Bakke.

	Art and Architecture	Music	Literature	Popular Culture
1979		Sugarhill Gang's *Rapper's Delight:* First rap hit	Mariama Ba: *So Long a Letter*	Sony Walkman, personal portable cassette player
		Barber: *Third Essay for Orchestra*	Nobel Prize: Odysseus Elytis	*La Cage aux Folles,* first film with gay themes to attract wide audience
		Tippett: *The Ice Break* (opera)	Heller: *Good as Gold*	
		Schwantner: *Aftertones of Infinity* (Pulitzer)	Malamud: *Dubin's Lives*	*Deer Hunter* wins Academy award
		Beverly Sills retires as soprano; becomes director of NY City Opera	Golding: *Darkness Visible*	Hurricanes Frederick and David cause widespread damage in South
			V. S. Naipaul: *A Bend in the River*	
			Mailer: *The Executioner's Song*	
			Cheever: *The Stories of John Cheever* (Pulitzer)	
			Penn Warren: *Now and Then: Poems 1976–1978* (Pulitzer)	
			Shepard: *Buried Child* (Pulitzer/drama)	
			Pomerance: *The Elephant Man* (Tony award)	
			Styron: *Sophie's Choice*	
			Wharton: *Birdy*	
1980	Gauguin's *The Guitar Player* sells for over $500,000	John Lennon killed	Nobel Prize: Czeslaw Milosz	Pac-Man and other video games hit it big

Art and Architecture	Music	Literature	Popular Culture
Over a million visitors see the Picasso show at the Museum of Modern Art	Pat Benatar: Grammy for *Crimes of Passion*	Golding: *Rites of Passage*	Jean Harris shoots and kills her lover, Scarsdale Diet guru Dr. Hermann Tarnower
John's *Three Flags* sells for $1 million, a record for a living American painter	*Camelot* musical hits Broadway	Justice: *Selected Poems* (Pulitzer)	
	Sinatra once again captures the spirit of the times with hit song "New York, New York"	Wilson: *Talley's Folly* (Pulitzer)	Sir Anthony Blunt revealed as fourth man in spy scandal
Turner's *Juliet and Her Nurse* sells for $4 million, a world record		Le Carre: *Smiley's People*	Joy Adamson, English author of *Born Free*, murdered in Meru National Park, Africa
Christo: *Surrounded Islands*, Pink Fabric, Biscayne Bay, Greater Miami, Florida		Wolfe: *The Right Stuff*	
		Medoff: *Children of a Lesser God*	*Dallas* top TV show; everyone wonders who shot JR
Thiebaud: *Down 18th Street*		Shepard: *True West*	
		Harwood: *The Dresser*	*Kramer vs. Kramer* wins Academy Award
Mitchell: *The Goodbye Door*		Gordimer: *A Soldier's Embrace*	Movie: *The Amityville Horror*
		Mahasweta Devi: *Breast-Giver*	Movie: *Airplane!*
		Anita Desai: *Clear Light of Day*	Movie: *Ordinary People*
		Goodison: *Tamarind Season*	Movie: *American Gigolo*
			Movie: *The Empire Strikes Back*
			Movie: *Raging Bull*

Did You Know?

Rap's movement into the mainstream sparked a violent backlash, gangsta rap. Deliberately antisocial and violently crude bands such as Niggaz with Attitude and Snoop Doggy Dogg attracted a wide following.

| 1981 | Museum of Modern Art donates Picasso's *Guernica* to the Prado, Spain | *Cats* debuts on Broadway | Nobel Prize: Elias Canetti | US: First frequent flyer program |

Art and Architecture	Music	Literature	Popular Culture
National Gallery in Washington, DC, stages largest-ever exhibition of Rodin sculptures	Philip Glass: *The Panther* (opera)	Rushdie: *Midnight's Children*	US: John Hinckley shoots President Reagan, Jim Brady, and two others
	Floyd: *Willie Start* (opera)	Toole: *A Confederacy of Dunces* (Pulitzer)	Walter Cronkite retires from TV broadcasting
Canada: Toronto Art Gallery: exhibit on Turner	Stockhausen: *Donnerstag aus Licht*	Schuyler: *The Morning of the Poem* (Pulitzer)	England: *Brideshead Revisited* a hit
Pearlstein: *Two Models in Bamboo Chairs with Mirror*	Soviet conductor Maxim Shostakovich and his son defect to the West	Henley: *Crimes of the Heart* (Pulitzer; play)	*Ordinary People* gets Academy Award
	John Lennon and Yoko Ono win Grammy for *Double Fantasy*	Royal Shakespeare's *Nicholas Nickleby* plays to SRO crowds on Broadway	Top films: *Gallipoli; An Officer and a Gentleman; On Golden Pond; Raiders of the Lost Ark; Reds*
		Martin Cruz Smith: *Gorky Park*	Prince Charles and Princess Diana announce their engagement
		Silko: *Ceremony, Storyteller*	US: Concrete roof collapses in Kansas City's Hyatt Hotel, killing 111
			USA Today newspaper debuts
			US: IBM introduces first personal computer

Did You Know?

In a review of Garcia Marquez' One Hundred Years of Solitude, Time *magazine* said: "Marquez' work has survived export triumphantly. In a beautiful translation, surrealism and innocence blend to form a wholly individual style. Like rum calentano, the story goes down easily, leaving a rich, sweet burning flavor behind."

1982	Vietnam Memorial dedicated in Washington, DC	New concert halls in Toronto, Denmark, London	Nobel Prize: Gabriel Garcia Marquez	Movie: *E.T.*

Art and Architecture	Music	Literature	Popular Culture
Switzerland and England hold largest-ever exhibit of Jean Tinguely's sculptures	Beria: *La Vera Storia* (opera)		US Surgeon General C. Everett Koop denounces smoking
	Hermann: *Wuthering Heights* (opera)		Brainiff Airlines and Laker Airlines go bankrupt
I. M. Pei: Indiana University Art Museum, Bloomington, IN	Paulus: *The Postman Always Rings Twice* (opera)		World's Fair held in Knoxville, TN

Did You Know?

Picasso had directed that *Guernica* not be displayed in Spain until democracy was restored there.

	Art and Architecture	Music	Literature	Popular Culture
1983	Venturi, Rauch, and Scott Brown: Gordon Wu Hall, Butler College, Princeton University, Princeton, NJ	Def Leppard: *Pyromania*, "heavy metal" music	Nobel Prize: William Golding	CD introduces digital sound
			Walker: *The Color Purple* (Pulitzer)	US: Cell phone revolution begins
	Maya Lin: Vietnam War Memorial, Washington DC		Norma: *'Night, Mother* (Pulitzer)	Half the adults in America watch *The Day After,* a show about a nuclear attack
			Kinnell: *Selected Poems* (Pulitzer)	
	Michael Graves: Portland Public Services Building, Portland, OR		Le Carre: *The Little Drummer Girl*	US: *M*A*S*H* ends after 251 episodes
			Marquez: *A Chronicle of Death Foretold*	*Chorus Line* sets records for Broadway longevity
			Jhablava: *In Search of Love and Beauty*	Movie: *The Big Chill*
			Fo: *Mistero Buffo*	Movie: *Flashdance*
				Ecstasy replaces LSD as psychedelic drug
				US: Martin Luther King Jr.'s birthday becomes national holiday.

Art and Architecture	Music	Literature	Popular Culture

Did You Know?

There are more than 58,000 names inscribed on the black granite Vietnam Veterans' Memorial in Washington, DC.

	Art and Architecture	Music	Literature	Popular Culture
1984	Kiefer: *Departure from Egypt*	Rands: *Canti del sole* (Pulitzer) Sondheim: *Sunday in the Park with George* Band Aid's record *Do They Know It's Christmas?* to aid Ethiopian famine victims is worldwide hit Michael Jackson wins eighth Grammy for *Thriller; Fields* sells over 37 million copies	Ted Hughes becomes Poet Laureate of England Nobel Prize: Jaroslav Seifert Kennedy: *Ironweed* (Pulitzer) Heany: *Station Island* Oliver: *American Primitive* (Pulitzer) Mamet: *Glengarry Glen Ross* (Pulitzer) Duras: *L'Amant* Barnes: *Flaubert's Parrot* Kundera: *The Unbearable Lightness of Being* Updike: *The Witches of Eastwick*	Cabbage Patch dolls debut Movie: *Indiana Jones and the Temple of Doom* Michael Jackson makes nineteen-city tour Movie: *The Killing* Reebocks, Madonna look, Rayban sunglasses, and Yuppie look catch on Singer Marvin Gaye shot dead by his father Movie: *Beverly Hills Cop* Movie: *Ghostbusters* Movie: *Romancing the Stone*
1985	Christo wraps Pont Neuf in 40,000 yards of canvas	Sade wins Grammy as best new artist	Nobel Prize: Claude Simon Lurie: *Foreign Affairs* (Pulitzer)	Bill Gates, 30, world's youngest billionaire Nintendo introduced

Did You Know?

Speaking on his 100th birthday, ragtime composer Eubie Blake says, "If I'd known I was gonna live this long, I'd have taken better care of myself." He died five days later.

Art and Architecture	Music	Literature	Popular Culture
	Lionel Richie and Michael Jackson write *We Are the World* for U.S.A. for Africa Relief Fund	Kizer: *Yin* (Pulitzer) Irving: *Cider House Rules*	Film star Rock Hudson dies of AIDS Movie: *Rambo: First Blood Part II*
	Live Aid concerts raise over $60 million for African famine relief; performers Dire Straits, U2, David Bowie, Beach Boys, The Who, Madonna, Bob Dylan, Ultravox	Tyler: *The Accidental Tourist* Kramer: *The Normal Heart*	Movie: *Out of Africa* Movie: *Kiss of the Spider Woman* NY: Vigilante Bernhard Goetz charged only with illegal gun possession
	Broadway: *Big River* wins Tony		Movie: *Back to the Future*
	Albert: *River Run* (Pulitzer)		
	Xue Wei wins International Violin Competition		

KEY DOCUMENT

"You like me—right now! You *like* me!"—Sally Fields said, accepting the Oscar for *Places in the Heart*.

Art and Architecture	Music	Literature	Popular Culture
1986 US: Museum of Contemporary Art opens in LA France: Musee d'Orsay opens	*Phantom of the Opera* debuts on Broadway Birdwhistle: *The Mask of Orpheus* Osbourne: *Hells Angels* Menotti: *Goya* Meale: *Voss* Broadway: *Les Miserables* wins eight awards	Nobel Prize: Woye Soyinka McMurtry: *Lonesome Dove* (Pulitzer) Taylor: *The Flying Change* (Pulitzer) Ishiguro: *An Artist of the Floating World* Atwood: *The Handmaiden's Tale*	*Oprah Winfrey* show becomes highest-rated TV talk show

	Art and Architecture	Music	Literature	Popular Culture
			Le Carre: *The Perfect Spy* Fuentes: *The Old Gringo* Levi: *If Not Now, When?* Mo: *An Insular Possession* Ratushinskaya: *No, I'm Not Afraid* Seth: *The Golden Gate*	Parent unsuccessfuly sues Ozzy Osbourne, claiming his song "Suicide Solution" caused their child to kill himself England: Prince Andrew and Sarah Ferguson marry US: 25,000 AIDs cases diagnosed Movie: *The Name of the Rose* Movie: *Howard the Duck* Movie: *Mona Lisa* Movie: *Platoon* Movie: *The Color of Money* Movie: *Children of a Lesser God*
1987	Van Gogh's *Irises* sells for $49 million, *Sunflowers* for $37 million, *The Bridge of Trinquetaille* for $19 million, setting world records	Beastie Boys are first act ever censored on *American Bandstand* Amadeus String Quartet disbands Sondheim: *Into the Woods* Adams: *Nixon in China* (opera) Camps: *La Hacienda* (opera) Testi: *Ricardo III* (opera) Simon: "Graceland"	Poet Laureate of US: Richard Wilbur Nobel Prize: Joseph Brodsky Taylor: *Moon Tiger* (Pulitzer) Shipler: *Arab and Jew* (Pulitzer) Dove: *Thomas and Beulah* (Pulitzer) Wilson: *Fences* (Pulitzer) Tahar be Jelloun: *La Nuit Sacre*	Movie: *The Color Purple* (Whoopi Goldberg) US: Gary Hart drops out of the presidential race after his extramarital affair is revealed US: Baby M surrogate mother case ends with surrogate mother's defeat Movie: *Cry Freedom* Movie: *Dirty Dancing* Movie: *Empire of the Sun*

	Art and Architecture	Music	Literature	Popular Culture
		Trio album features three powerhouse country singers: Dolly Parton, Emmylou Harris, Linda Ronstadt	Moore: *The Colour of Blood* Achebe: *The Anthills of the Savannah* Grass: *The Rat* Wolfe: *Bonfire of the Vanities* Harling: *Steel Magnolias* Uhry: *Driving Miss Daisy* (Pulitzer)	Movie: *Fatal Attraction* Movie: *The Last Emperor* Movie: *Full Metal Jacket* Movie: *Wall Street* Movie: *Moonstruck*
1988	Picasso's *Acrobat and Young Harlequin* sold for $38 million Warhol's art collection sold for $25 million	Glass: *The Fall of the House of Usher* (opera) Howard: *Whit Sunday* (opera) Stockhausen: *Montag aus Licht* (opera) Maxwell-Davies: *Resurrection* (opera) Broadway: *Phantom of the Opera* debuts "Don't Worry, Be Happy" gets Grammy Grunge music develops; bands include Pearl Jam, Nirvana, Alice in Chains, Extreme, and Smashing Pumpkins	Poet Laureate of US: Howard Nemerov Nobel Prize: Nagib Mahfouz Morrison: *Beloved* (Pulitzer) Rhodes: *The Making of the Atomic Bomb* (Pulitzer) Allende: *Eva Luna* Marquez: *Love in the Time of Cholera* Ratushunskaya: *Pencil Letters* Tyler: *Breathing Lessons* (Pulitzer) Hwang: *M. Butterfly* Harris: *The Silence of the Lambs*	Prozac first marketed Muslims attack Salman Rushdie's novel *The Satanic Verses* for blasphemy; death contract on his life will be taken out US: TV evangelist Jimmy Swaggart admits visiting prostitute Crack cocaine epidemic grows Movie: *Beetlejuice* Movie: *Big* Movie: *Die Hard* Movie: *Good Morning, Vietnam*
1989	France: I. M. Pei's glass pyramid addition to Louvre sparks controversy	Baldad: *Cristobal Colon* (opera) Tippett: *New Year* (opera)	Haruki: *TV People* Broadway: *The Heidi Chronicles* (Tony)	England: Remnants of Globe Theater found Movie: *Batman*

	Art and Architecture	Music	Literature	Popular Culture
	Art prices hit stratosphere: Pontormo's *Duke of Cosimo de Medici* sells for $35.2 million	Broadway: *Aspects of Love* Broadway: *Miss Saigon* "Indie" new wave music; bands include The Stone Roses, Primal Scream, and Nude	Nobel Prize: Camilo Jose Cela Sheehan: *A Bright Shining Lie* (Pulitzer) Wilbur: *New and Collected Poems* (Pulitzer) Doctorow: *Billy Bathgate* Eco: *Foucault's Pendulum*	Movie: *Dead Poets Society* Movie: *Driving Miss Daisy* Movie: *Field of Dreams* Movie: *When Harry Met Sally* Movie: *My Left Foot*
1990	Mapplethorpe photographs incite controversy Zurah Tsereteli: *Good Defeats Evil* sculpture made from Soviet missile fragments Pritzker Prize: Aldo Rossi Tom Toles: Pulitzer Prize for Editorial Cartooning	Rap music hits the airwaves Broadway: *City of Angels* wins Best Musical Phil Collins: *Another Day in Paradise* wins Grammy Powell: *Duplicates: A Concerto for Two Pianos and Orchestra* (Pulitzer)	*Six Degrees of Separation* hits Broadway Nobel Prize: Octavio Paz Hijuelos: *The Mambo Kings Play Songs of Love* (Pulitzer) Simic: *The World Doesn't End* (Pulitzer) Wilson: *The Piano Lesson* (Pulitzer) Styron: *Darkness Visible* Updike: *Rabbit at Rest* Johnson: *The Middle Passage* Gerstler: *Bitter Angel*	US: President Bush announces that he does not like broccoli McDonalds opens twenty outlets in Moscow US: Americans with Disabilities Act England: Mysterious "crop circles" appear on corn fields Movie: *Presumed Innocent* Movie: *Wild at Heart* Movie: *Total Recall* *Dances with Wolves* wins Best Picture
1991	Pritzker Prize: Robert Venturi Jim Borgman: Pulitzer Prize for Editorial Cartooning	Sting: "Soul Cages" wins Grammy Broadway: *The Will Rogers Follies* wins Best Musical	Nobel Prize: Nadine Gordimer Rush: *Mating* Goldbarth: *Heaven and Earth*	Tamagotchi toys, Teenage Mutant Ninja Turtles, Beanie Babies catch on *Silence of the Lambs* wins Best Picture

	Art and Architecture	Music	Literature	Popular Culture
		Natalie Cole: *Unforgettable* wins Grammy		Movie: *City Slickers*
				Movie: *The Fisher King*
		Shulammit Ran: *Symphony* (Pulitzer)		
1992	Pritzker Prize: Alvaro Siza	US: Rap group Arrested Development wins Best New Artist Grammy	Morrison: *Jazz*	US: Presidential candidate Bill Clinton plays the sax on the *Arsenio Hall* show
	Signe Wilkinson: Pulitzer Prize for Editorial Cartooning		Ondaatje: *The English Patient*	
			McCullough: *Truman*	
		Broadway: *Crazy for You* wins Best Musical	King: *Dolores Clairborne*	US: Serial killer Jeffrey Dahmer sentenced to fifteen consecutive life prison terms
		Clapton: *Tears in Heaven* wins Grammy	Grishham: *The Pelican Brief*	
		Wayne Peterson: *The Face of the Night, The Heart of the Dark* (Pulitzer)	Nobel Prize: Derek Wallcott	World population: 5.2 billion
			McCarthy: *All the Pretty Horses*	Text-based Web browser available to the public; soon, Internet use explodes
			Carruth: *Collected Shorter Poems*	
			Smiley: *A Thousand Acres*	Prince and Princess of Wales separate
				Unforgiven wins Best Picture
				Movie: *Scent of a Woman*
				Movie: *Howard's End*
				Movie: *My Cousin Vinny*
1993	Pritzker Prize: Fumihiko Maki	Pop music superstars: Madonna, Prince, Michael Jackson	Nobel prize: Toni Morrison	Ruth Bader Ginsburg appointed to US Supreme Court
	Stephen R. Benson: Pulitzer Prize for Editorial Cartooning		Broadway: *Angels in America* tackles AIDS	
		Female singers such as Celine Dion score megahits	Proulx: *The Shipping News*	Movie: *A Few Good Men*
				Movie: *Alladin*

	Art and Architecture	Music	Literature	Popular Culture
		Broadway: *Kiss of the Spider Woman* wins Best Musical	Doty: *My Alexandria*	*Schindler's List* wins Best Picture
			Walker: *The Bridges of Madison County*	Movie: *Philadelphia*
		Whitney Houston: *I Will Always Love You* wins Grammy		Movie: *The Piano*
				Movie: *Dave*
		Christopher Rouse: *Trombone Concerto* (Pulitzer)		Movie: *Glengarry Glen Ross*
				Movie: *Groundhog Day*
				Movie: *The Crying Game*
1994	Pritzker Prize: Christian de Portzamparc	Sheryl Crow: *All I Wanna Do* wins Grammy	Munro: *The Albanian Virgin*	Football legend O. J. Simpson tried for murder of his wife; acquitted in 1995
	Michael P. Ramirez: Pulitzer Prize for Editorial Cartooning	Whitney Houston, Sade, Mariah Carey, the Judds, Sheryl Crow, Alanis Morissette have huge hits	Nobel Prize: Kenzaburo Oe	Jacqueline Kennedy Onassis dies of cancer
			Gaddis: *A Frolic of His Own*	
			Rudman: *Rider*	*Forrest Gump* wins Best Picture
		Broadway: *Passion* wins Best Musical	Grisham: *The Chamber*	Movie: *Blue Sky*
				Movie: *Ed Wood*
		Gunther Schuller: *Of Reminiscences and Reflections* (Pulitzer)		Movie: *Bullets Over Broadway*
1995	Pritzker Prize: Tadao Ando	Gould: *Stringmusic* (Pulitzer)	Nobel Prize: Seamus Heany	US: Million Man March draws thousands of Black men to Washington, DC
	Mike Luckovich: Pulitzer Prize for Editorial Cartooning	Hootie and the Blowfish win Grammy for Best New Artist	Roth: *Sabbath's Theater*	Snowboarding and inline skating catch on
			Matthews: *Time & Money*	
		Broadway: *Sunset Boulevard* wins Best Musical	Grisham: *The Rainmaker*	Swing dancing, Grunge look, baseball caps, backpacks, hiphop catch on
		Seal: *Kiss from a Rose* wins Grammy		

	Art and Architecture	Music	Literature	Popular Culture
				Braveheart wins Best Picture
				Movie: *Leaving Las Vegas*
				Movie: *Dead Man Walking*
				Movie: *The Usual Suspects*
				Self-help relationship books hit it big, as shown by Gray's *Men are From Mars, Women are From Venus*
1996	Pritzker Prize: Rafael Moneo Jim Morin: Pulitzer Prize for Editorial Cartooning	Bhangra, music of rural Punjab, becomes popular in England Broadway: *Rent* wins Best Musical Eric Clapton: *Change the World* wins Grammy George Walker: *Lilacs* (Pulitzer)	Nobel Prize: Wislawa Symborska Barrett: *Ship Fever and Other Stories* Haas: *Sun Under Wood* Grisham: *The Runaway Jury*	Prince Charles and Princess Diana agree to divorce Nike Air Jordans become a fad *The English Patient* wins Best Picture Movie: *Rush* Movie: *Fargo* Movie: *Jerry McGuire*
1997	Pritzker Prize: Sverre Fehn Walt Handelsman: Pulitzer Prize for Editorial Cartooning	Phenomenon of boy bands takes off *Titanic* wins Best Musical Colvin: *Sunny Came Home* wins Grammy Wynton Marsalis: *Blood on the Fields* (Pulitzer)	Nobel Prize: Dario Fo Frazier: *Cold Mountain* Wright: *Black Zodiac* Grisham: *The Partner* McCourt: *Angela's Ashes*	Princess Diana, 36, dies and funeral sparks worldwide public mourning Mother Theresa, 87, dies *Titanic* wins Best Picture Movie: *As Good as It Gets* Movie: *Good Will Hunting* Movie: *L. A. Confidential*

Art and Architecture	Music	Literature	Popular Culture

Did You Know?

The movie Titanic won 11 Academy Awards.

1998

Pritzker Prize: Renzo Piano

Stephen P. Breen: Pulitzer Prize for Editorial Cartooning

"Ol' Blue Eyes," Frank Sinatra, dies

Broadway: *The Lion King* wins Best Musical

Celine Dion: *My Heart Will Go On* wins Grammy

Aaron Jay Kernis: *String Quartet No. 2* (Pulitzer)

George Gershwin, Special Citation in Music

Backstreet Boys, Shania Twain, Will Smith, and 'N Sync have megahits

Nobel Prize: Jose Saramago

McDermott: *Charming Billy*

Ponsot: *The Bird Catcher*

Grisham: *The Street Lawyer*

Edson: *Wit* (Pulitzer)

Cunningham: *Hours* (Pulitzer)

Berg: *Lindbergh* (Pulitzer)

Shakespeare in Love wins Best Picture

FDA approves Viagra, male impotence drug

Movie: *Saving Private Ryan*

US: 20% of all homes have Internet access

US: Americans average 2,300 phone calls a year—each

Movie: *Life is Beautiful*

Movie: *Something About Mary*

E. R., Friends, Frasier, 60 Minutes, and *NYPD Blue* are hit TV shows

1999

Pritzker Prize: Norman Foster

David Horsey: Pulitzer Prize for Editorial Cartooning

"Techno" pop fully integrated into the mainstream; bands include Ultra Nate, Sash, The Prodigy, Bush

Broadway: *Fosse* wins Best Musical

Melinda Wagner: *Concerto for Flute, Strings, and Percussion* (Pulitzer)

Nobel Prize: Gunter Grass

Jhumpa Lahiri, Raj Kamal Jha, Pankaj Mishra, and Arundhati Roy are notable Indian writers popular in the West

US: Citadel graduates first woman

England: Prince Edward marries Sophie Rhys-Jones

John Kennedy, Jr., wife Carolyn Bessette Kennedy, and sister-in-law Lauren Bessette killed in plane crash off Martha's Vineyard, MA

	Art and Architecture	Music	Literature	Popular Culture
		Duke Ellington, Special Citation in Music		World population reaches 6 billion
				1 billion cups of Coca-Cola served per day
				Julia ("Butterfly") Hill finishes a 738-day treetop vigil to save a 600-year-old redwood in California
2000	Cézanne's *Still Life with Fruits and Ginger Pot,* sells for $18.1 million	Tito Puente, king of Latin music, dies	Stephen King publishes an e-book; Internet publishing takes off	Women's clothing gets smaller and smaller: microminis, handkerchief tops, sheer fabrics
			Harry Potter children's books become best-sellers and media event	US credit card holders owe $500 billion on their cards
			Lahiri: *Interpreter of Maladies* (Pulitzer)	Movie: *Mission Impossible II*
			Margulies: *Dinner with Friends* (Pulitzer)	Movie: *Chicken Run*
			Williams: *Repair* (Pulitzer)	

PART 2

POLITICS AND CIVILIZATION

Part 2 Politics and Civilization

PREHISTORIC DAYS TO −1 BCE

−3,000,000	Oldest known stone tools found in Africa
−500,000	Early hand axes Earliest known use of fire
−400,000	Earliest known shelter
−100,000	Middle East: Earliest known burials
−50,000	c. −53,000 Australia colonized c. −45,000 earliest cave art work
−5000 to −4001	−4241 First exactly dated year in history Mesopotamia: Earliest cities
−4000 to −3501	Babylon: Sumerians settle there Horses domesticated −3760 First year of Jewish calendar
−3500 to −3001	Sumerian civilization reaches height Egypt: First and Second dynasties; King Menes the Fighter unites Upper and Lower Egypt −3400 Bronze Age begins in Crete −3250 Wheel used in Mesopotamia
−3000 to −2501	China: Sage Kings −2815 to −2294 Egypt: Old Kingdom First city established at Troy Mesopotamia: Early dynastic period c. −2750 Gilgamesh, king of Uruk −2700 to −2675 Cheops, king of Fourth Egyptian dynasty Mesopotamia: Development of banking
−2500 to −2001	Palestine: Semitic Canaanite tribes settle China: Yao dynasty (to −2300) −2300 to −2205 China: Shun dynasty −2371 Sargon I of Akkad conquers Sumerians; creates an empire from Syria to Persia −2230 Akkadian Empire ends; rise of Sumerian Empire at Ur −2200 to −1760 China: Hsai dynasty −2200 to −1700 Egypt: Hyksos rule −2200 to −525 Egypt: Pharaohs rule −2100 to −1700 Egypt: Old Kingdom and Middle Kingdom

−2100 Earliest known legal texts, Ur-Nammu, King of Ur
−2006 Sumerian empire ends as Ur falls to Elamites from southwest Persia
India: Indus Valley civilization begins

−2000 to −1500   Egypt controls Crete and Aegean Islands
Hittites ravage Babylon
Babylonia: Hammurabi reunites kingdom
−1760 to −1122 China: Shang dynasty
−1750 to −550 Persian Empire
−1720 Hyksos (Palestinians) invade Egypt and occupy the Nile Delta
Syria: Hittites attack
Norway: Teutonic settlements
Egypt: Middle Kingdom ends
Babylonia: Empire declines under Hammurabi's son
−1650 to −1590 Minoan kingdom (Crete) at its height
−1575 to −1200 Egypt: New Kingdom begins
−1567 Egypt: New Kingdom expels invaders and extends empire to Nubia and Palestine
Egypt: Height of power under Eighteenth dynasty
−1555 to −1530 Egypt: Amenhotep I
−1530 to −1515 Egypt: Thutmose I
−1523 China: Shang dynasty established

−1500 to −1001   Mexico: Earliest settlement, Chiapa de Carzo
c. −1500 Fall of Indus Valley civilization
−1480 to −1450 Egypt: Thutmose III extends empire
−1420 to −1385 Egypt: Amenhotep III extends trade and culture
Malta: Phoenicians settle
c. −1375 Mycenaeans conquer Crete; Knossos destroyed
−1350 to −1200 Egypt: Nineteenth dynasty, ruled by Seti I, Ramses II, and Ramses III
c. −1250 Mycenaean refugees attack Egypt. Although defeated, some Philistines settle in Canaan
Moses leads Israelites from Egypt to Canaan
Mediterranean: Phoenicians become chief trading power
c. −1200 China: Cowry shells used as money
−1200 to −1090 Egypt: Twentieth dynasty
c. −1200 Greece: Fall of Mycenaean civilization in Crete; Dorians move into Greece
Israelites cross Jordan
−1193 Trojan War and fall of Troy
−1146 to −1123 Nebuchadnezzar I, king of Babylon
−1122 to −480 China: Chou (Zhou) dynasty founded
Ethiopia: Becomes independent force
Dorians conquer the Peloponnesus
−1090 to −945 Egypt: Twenty-first dynasty, civil war
−1010 to −925 David and Solomon establish Israel
−1002 to −1000 Israel: Saul becomes king, defeated by Philistines

−1000 to −901   Ionians establish twelve cities in Asia Minor
−1000 to −960 David becomes king of Judah and Israel
−960 to −925 Solomon becomes king; builds great temple

Did You Know?

According to legend, the Trojan War was sparked by the golden apple, inscribed "for the fairest" and thrown by Eris at a heavenly wedding. As a result of the toss, Helen of Troy (wife of King Menelaus of Sparta) went with Paris to Troy. To avenge Menelaus, Agamemnon headed an expedition, including Achilles, Patroclus, the two Ajaxes, and Nestor. When the Trojans refused to restore Helen to Menelaus, the Greeks invaded Troy with 1,000 ships. In the tenth year, Achilles withdrew from battle over his anger at Agamemnon, which furnished Homer the theme of the Iliad. The siege lasted 10 years. Troy was finally captured by treachery: a force of Greek warriors hid in a large wooden horse to get into the city. The Greeks sacked and burned Troy. Only a few Trojans escaped, including Aeneas, whose journey to what is now Italy was told by Virgil in the Aeneid. The Trojan War is believed to be based in the real war between the Greeks and the inhabitants of Troad or Troas in present-day Turkey.

    c. −950 Queen of Sheba and Solomon exchange gifts
    −945 to −745 Sheshonk I, Twenty-second dynasty (Egypt)
    −925 Hebrew kingdom becomes Israel and Judah
    Sheshonk I ravages Jerusalem

−900 to −801 China: Organized postal service for government use
    −883 to −859 Assurnasirpal II, king of Assyria
    −879 Samaria rebuilt as capital of Israel
    −831 Carthage established as trading center
    Dorians conquer Corinth

KEY DOCUMENT

No other Egyptian pharaoh can compare with Ramses II. By the time he died in −1225, Ramses II was more than 90 years old, had ruled for 66 years, fathered 111 sons and 67 daughters, built the exquisite temples of Abu Simbel, and added to those at Luxor and Karnak. The massive fallen statue of Ramses at Thebes probably inspired Percy Bysshe Shelley's sonnet of faded glory, "Ozymandias" (Ozymandias is the Greek version of one of Ramses' names):

> *"My name is Ozymandias, king of kings;*
> *Look on my works, ye mighty, and despair!"*
> *Nothing beside remains. Round the decay*
> *Of that colossal wreck, boundless and bare,*
> *The lone and level sands stretch far away.*

c. −814 Phoenicians from Tyre establish Carthage in Tunisia; Nubian kingdom of Kush in Sudan
−811 to −807 Queen Samuramat of Assyria
−800 to −730 Egypt: Twenty-third dynasty

−800 to −701   Etruscans move into Italy
Amaziah, king of Judah, killed in rebellion
−801 to −787 King Joas of Israel
−784 to −744 Jeroboam II, ruler of Israel
−753 Foundation of city of Rome
c. −750 England: Celts move in
c. −750 Africa: Kush (Nubia) rules Egypt for nearly 100 years
First Messenian War: Sparta gains power in Greece
Kingdom of Israel ends when Sargon II of Assyria conquers the Hittites
−735 Foundation of Rome by Romulus and Remus (legend)

KEY DOCUMENT

It is commonly believed that Rome was named for Romulus, who outwitted his brother Remus for control of the new settlement, but Plutarch argues that the name could have come from a woman: "At the taking of Troy, some few that escaped and met with shipping, put to sea, and driven by winds, were carried upon the coasts of Tuscany, and came to anchor off the mouth of the river Tiber, where their women, out of heart and weary with the sea, on its being proposed by one of the highest birth and best understanding amongst them, whose name was Roma, burnt the ships. With which act the men at first were angry . . . things in a short while succeeded far better than they could hope, in that they found the country very good, and the people courteous, they not only did the lady Roma other honors, but added also this, of calling after her name the city which she had been the occasion of their founding. . . ."

−722 to −705 Sargon II extends Assyrian Empire from Lebanon to Iran
−722 Samaria destroyed
−715 to −672 Numa Pompilius, second king of Rome

−700 to −601   −690 to −638 Manasseh, King of Judah
−689 Sennacherib of Assyria destroys Babylon
Second Messenian war
−671 Assyria briefly conquers Egypt
Assyrians destroy Memphis and Thebes
c. −650 Rise of kingdom of Medes in Persia
−638 to −608 Josiah, king of Judah
−614 to −612 Medes overthrows Assyria and destroys its capital, Nineveh
c. −610 Sparta dominates Peloponnesus and adopts a rigid constitution

Nebuchadnezzar II makes Judah a tributary; Babylonian captivity begins
Nebuchadnezzar II defeats Egyptians

–600 to –501   c. –592 Solon establishes constitution in Athens
Mexico: Mayan civilization
–587 Nebuchadnezzar II burns Jerusalem; many Jews taken to Babylon in
captivity
–578 to –534 Servius Tullius establishes class system in Rome
–559 to –529 Cyrus II establishes Persian Empire; frees Jews and aids their return
to Israel

KEY DOCUMENT

According to numerous historians, the Republican revolution began when Sextus Tarquin, son of the reigning monarch Tarquinius Superbus, raped the virtuous Lucretia, whom Romans idolized as the perfect wife and ideal woman. Livy explains how Roman men came to prove Lucretia as the ideal woman: "Sextus Tarquin, inflamed by the beauty and exemplary purity of Lucretia, formed the vile project of effecting her dishonor. [He] went in the frenzy of his passion with a naked sword to the sleeping Lucretia, and placing his left hand on her breast, said, "Silence, Lucretia! I am Sextus Tarquin, and I have a sword in my hand; if you utter a word, you shall die." When the woman, terrified out of her sleep, saw that no help was near, and instant death threatening her, Tarquin began to confess his passion, pleaded, used threats as well as entreaties, and employed every argument likely to influence a female heart . . . he threatened to disgrace her, declaring that he would lay the naked corpse of the slave by her dead body, so that it might be said that she had been slain in foul adultery. By this awful threat, his lust triumphed over her inflexible chastity, and Tarquin went off exulting in having successfully attacked her honor. Lucretia, overwhelmed with grief at such a frightful outrage, sent a messenger to her father at Rome and to her husband at Ardea, asking them to come to her. . . . Lucretia could not bear to live with her honor forsaken. "She had a knife concealed in her dress which she plunged into her heart, and fell dying on the floor. Her father and husband raised the death-cry." Incited by her body and spurred on by speeches advocating revolution, the crowd successfully overthrew Tarquinius Superbus, and established a republican government headed by two consuls.

---

c. –550 Etruscans dominate Italy and rule Rome
–546 to –511 Pisistratus and his sons rule Athens as tyrants
–530 Greece: Library established
–525 Cambyses, king of Persia, conquers Egypt
–522 to –485 Darius II reforms empire, including common currency and
taxation
–509 Tyranny in Athens overthrown; democracy begins

−500 to −451   −500 Persia: Pony Express
−500 to −429 Pericles of Athens
−490 Greece: First Persian invasion of Greece repelled by Athenians at Marathon
−499 Sardus burned by Athenians
−480 to −479 Xeres of Persia invades Greece; battles of Thermopylae (Persian victory),
Salamis, and Plataea (Greek victories), Persians retreat; Iona freed

Did You Know?

The Greeks gave democracy to the world. The center of democracy was Athens,
which had overthrown the aristocracy and established a constitution under the
reformer Solon (c. −638 to −559). The right to vote was by no means universal,
however: only freeborn male citizens (about 40,000 people out of a population
of 400,000) could vote. Women, slaves, freed slaves, and immigrants were
denied suffrage.

−480 In Sicily, Syracuse repels Carthaginian invasion
−479 Babylon destroyed
−478 Athens forms the Delian League, an anti-Persian alliance that becomes the nucleus
of the Athenian empire
−465 Democracy in Syracuse
−461 to −430 Pericles is the leading statesman in Athens
−454 Athens and Corinth War

−450 to −401   Beginning of Indian Empire
Wall of Jerusalem reputed to have been built
−449 Peace treaty between Persia and Greece
−431 Pericles' *Funeral Oration*
−431 to −421 First stage of the Peloponnesian War (Athens and Sparta); ends in Peace of
Nicias
−419 Rome: Coriolanus banished
−415 to −404 Second stage of the Peloponnesian War. Athenian expedition against
Syracuse and Sicily fails. Sparta invades and defeats Athens, destroying Athenian Navy
and the city's walls.
−404 Egypt regains independence from Persia
−403 Democracy restored in Athens
−403 China: Warring States epoch begins

−400 to −351   Mexico: Indian civilization ends
−390 Gauls sack Rome
−380 to −343 Egypt: Thirtieth dynasty
−371 Thebes defeats Sparta and becomes the dominant Greek city-state
−384 to −322 Demosthenes, Greek statesman and speaker
−357 Philip II of Macedon begins campaign to rule Greece
−356 to −323 Alexander the Great

–350 to –301	–350 Gauls settle in northern Italy –341 Persia reconquers Egypt –338 Philip II of Macedon defeats Greeks at Chaeronea; elected leader for war against Persia; Rome heads federation of central Italy

Did You Know?

Alexander the Great created the most magnificent empire the world has ever seen—as well as the shortest one. He became king of Macedonia in –336 at the age of 20; 2 years later, he conquered Persia. During the next 11 years, Alexander conquered an area the size of America—from the Indus River in the east to Greece and Egypt in the west. When his army refused to go on, Alexander retired to Babylon. He died a few years later at age 33. The empire he had forged was shattered as quickly as it had been created; within 13 years, the lands had been redistributed.

–336 Philip II of Macedon murdered, perhaps at the instigation of his wife; succeeded by Alexander the Great
–334 to –330 Alexander invades Persia and defeats King Darius III
–332 to –331 Alexander conquers Egypt and Tyre; founds Alexandria
–331 to –326 Alexander conquers Bactria (northern Afghanistan) and invades northwest India, but forced to turn back
–323 Egypt: New dynasty
–321 India: Chandragupta establishes Maurya dynasty in northern India; expels Greeks
–305 Alexander's generals divide his empire

–300 to –251	c. –280 Having defeated Etruscans and Samnites, Rome dominates all Italy except Greek cities in south –280 to –275 Pyrrhus, king of Epirus, attacks southern Italy and Sicily but is forced to withdraw; Rome dominates all Italy –275 Antiochus I defeats the Gauls –275 Babylon becomes Seleucia; end of history of Babylon –273 Asoka rules two-thirds of the Indian subcontinent. He becomes a Buddhist (–261) –264 to –241 Rome defeats Carthage in First Punic War; acquires Sicily as its first province

Did You Know?

The Great Wall of China, constructed by convict laborers under orders of Chinese Emperor Qin Shi Huahgdi, is probably the largest structure ever built. Although it stretches for nearly 1,500 miles, the wall cannot be seen from the moon, as has occasionally been asserted. The theory that the wall could be seen from space was exploded in 1969 by US astronaut Alan Bean, who reported that the wall couldn't be seen even a few thousand miles from Earth.

−250 to −201 −247 to −221 Egypt: Ptolemy III is king
−246 to −182 Carthaginian general Hannibal
−236 War between Sparta and Achaean League
−221 China: Ch'in (Qin) dynasty unites China
−218 to −202 Second Punic War; Hannibal of Carthage crosses Alps, defeats Romans, but finally defeated by Scipio Afranus in present-day Algeria
−215 China: Great Wall built to keep out invaders
−206 China: Han dynasty founded
−202 Carthage disarmed; Spain becomes a Roman province

KEY DOCUMENT
William Shakespeare's play *Julius Caesar* (1599) recounts the history of Caesar in glorious poetry. Shakespeare immortalizes the death of Caesar in his last words: "*Et tu, Brute?*— Then fall, Caesar!" (III, i)

−200 to −151 c. −200 Inscription engraved on Rosetta Stone
−163 Led by Judas Maccabeus, Jews revolt against Syria and form independent Judaea
−147 to −146 Rome sacks Corinth and rules Greece from Macedonia
Third Punic War; Rome destroys Carthage

−150 to −101 −133 Reforms of Gracchi brothers begin a 100-year challenge to Senate power in Rome
by −126 Parthian Empire established in Middle East, except Syria and Judaea
−121 Rome completes conquest of southern Gaul

Did You Know?

Cleopatra VII (c. −69 to −30), ill-fated queen of Egypt (−51 to −30), was 17 when she succeeded to the throne of Egypt with the provision that she marry her 12-year-old brother Ptolemy XI. Three years later, Ptolemy seized sole control and sent Cleopatra into exile. She raised an army but was not able to assert her claim until the arrival of Julius Caesar, who became her lover and supporter. In −47, Ptolemy was killed and Caesar proclaimed Cleopatra queen. Forced by custom to marry her 11-year-old brother Ptolemy XIII, Cleopatra then traveled to Rome and lived as Caesar's mistress. After Caesar's assassination, Cleopatra is said to have poisoned Ptolemy XIII, returned to Egypt, met and fallen in love with Mark Antony. In −36, Antony and Cleopatra reunited and married. At the naval battle at Actium in −31, Antony was deceived by a false report of Cleopatra's death and committed suicide. Hearing that Octavian, the victor, intended to exhibit her in triumph in Rome, Cleopatra committed suicide.

–100 to –51	–90 to –88 Social War, in which Italians rebel against Rome; Roman citizenship to all Italians
	by –87 China: Chinese Empire includes Korea and northern Vietnam
	–73 to –71 Spartacus, the famous slave and trained gladiator, leads a class rebellion against Rome in an attempted flight to freedom. He defeated numerous Roman battalions, but was finally defeated by Crassus, with the aid of Pompey.
	by –62 Pompey completes conquest of Syria and Judaea, which become Roman provinces
	–58 to –50 Julius Caesar conquers the rest of Gaul for Rome and invades Britain and Germany
–50 to –1	–49 to –45 First Roman Civil War; Caesar defeats Pompey and Senate and becomes dictator; assassinated March 15, –44
	–44 to –31 Second Roman Civil War. Mark Antony and Octavian, Caesar's heir, defeat Caesar's assassins (led by Brutus and Cassius) and divide Roman Empire. Mark Antony, aided by Cleopatra of Egypt, fights Octavian but is defeated at Battle of Actium (–31). Egypt becomes a Roman province.
	–27 Octavian (now Augustus) takes control of Roman Empire and establishes Julio-Claudian dynasty

Part 2 Politics and Civilization

1 TO 500

Did You Know?

Nero was a monster of cruelty. We might blame his rotten childhood—his family was rife with murder and incest—but ultimately the blame lies with the boy emperor himself. Ironically, up to year 59, he was a wise and virtuous leader: he forbade capital punishment, reduced taxes, and granted the Senate latitude. He became brutal when he was 22, starting with his command to kill his mother and wife and moving on to the persecution of the Christians. About the only thing we can't blame him for is the burning of Rome. In 64, two-thirds of Rome burned while Nero was at Antium. Far from celebrating the fire by playing his favorite instrument, the lyre, Nero rushed back to Rome to take charge of the fire fighting. His concern was no doubt heightened by the news that his new palace was afire.

201 to 250
212 Roman citizenship given to every freeborn subject in the empire
217 Caracalla assassinated; Heliogabalus becomes emperor
220 China: Han dynasty ends; country divided into three kingdoms
220 Goths invade Asia Minor and Balkan Peninsula
222 to 235 Emperor Alexander Severus
224 to 127 Artaxerxes I (Ardashir) founds Sassanid dynasty and reestablishes Persian Empire
225 India divides into several kingdoms
250 to 900 Mexico, Guatemala, Belize: Golden Age of the Maya

251 to 300
251 to 253 Emperor Gallus
257 Goths invade Black Sea region
257 Franks invade Spain; defeated at Milan (258)
268 to 270 Emperor Claudius II
269 Goths sack Athens, Sparta, Corinth
c. 300 Five German dukedoms: Saxons, Franks, Alemanni, Thuringians, and Goths
c. 300 Japan: first states
c. 300 Africa: Ghana becomes the first great West African trading empire

301 to 350
306 Constantine the Great proclaimed Roman emperor at York, England; he founds Constantinople (now Istanbul) on the site of Greek Byzantium
320 India: Chandragupta crowned first Gupta emperor of northern India
330 Seat of Roman Empire moved to Constantinople
350 Persians seize Armenia from Rome
c. 350 Africa: kingdom of Kush (Nubia) ends after armies from African kingdom of Axum destroy Meroe

351 to 400
360 England: Scots and Picts breach Hadrian's Wall and attack England
360 Europe: Huns invade
364 Roman Empire permanently divided; Rome is capital in west; Constantinople is capital in east (Byzantine Empire)
370 Theodosius drives Scots and Picts from Britain
375 Peru: Tiahuanaco Empire established
376 Russia: Huns invade

378 Visigoths kill Emperor Valens in battle
383 England: Romans retreat
383 Emperor Magnus Maximus conquers Spain and Gaul
392 Theodosius the Great becomes emperor of East and West
396 Alaric plunders Athens
398 Alaric sacks Balkans
400 Japan: First history written

401 to 450   401 Visigoths invade Italy
406 to 428 Gunderic, king of the Vandals
407 Angles and Saxons settle in England

Did You Know?

The time between 450 to 1400 is called the "Middle Ages" because it took place in the middle of the collapse of the ancient Roman Empire and the development of modern Europe. It is also called the "Medieval Age" from the a word meaning middle age in Latin, and the "Dark Ages" because the western Roman Empire was collapsing. Some historians say the Middle Ages began when the barbarian Odoacer overthrew the Roman emperor, which ended the western Roman Empire; others claim the era started earlier, when Alaric, king of the Visigoths, captured Rome. The ending is equally controversial: some historians claim the era ended with the fall of Constantinople; others claim the era ended with the beginning of the Reformation.

410 Alaric leads Visigoths on plunder of Rome; dies
410 England: Romans withdraw
416 Spain: Visigoths conquer Vandal kingdom
418 Franks settle in Gaul
418 to 415 Theodoric I, king of the Visigoths
425 Vandals settle in Roman kingdom, including Spain and Portugal
428 to 477 Gaiseric, king of the Vandals
429 Angles, Saxons, and Jutes expel Scots and Picts from southern England
429 Vandals expand to northern Africa
433 Attila leads Huns
436 Last Roman troops leave Britain
445 Attila murders his brother Bleda
447 Attila attacks the eastern Roman Empire for the second time; devastating the Balkans and driving south into Greece

451 to 500   451 to 453 Attila leads Huns into Italy; he was defeated by Romans and Visigoths at the Battle of the Catalaunian Plains. This is his sole defeat.
452 Italy: Venice established
453 to 466 Theodoric II, king of the Visigoths
455 Vandals sack Rome
455 to 467 India: Skandagupta, emperor of India

460 Franks capture Cologne
460 Vandals destroy Roman fleet
466 Theodoric murdered by his brother Euric, who seizes the throne

Did You Know?

The warrior Huns inspired almost unparalleled fear throughout Europe. Their ferocious charges and unpredictable retreats, brilliant strategy, and skilled horsemanship resulted in overwhelming victories. The most famous Hun is Attila, king of the Huns from 434 to 453. Known in the western world as the "Scourge of God," the great barbarian leader was described as a short, squat man with a large head, deep-set eyes, and a thin beard.

470 Huns leave Europe
470 Mexico: Mayan civilization flourishes
471 to 536 Theodoric the Great, king of the Ostrogoths
476 Odoacer overthrows western Roman Empire and becomes first king of Italy
477 to 484 Hunneric, king of the Vandals
479 to 502 China: Chi dynasty
481 Clovis becomes king of the Franks
c. 484 India: Gupta Empire overthrown
484 to 507 Alaric, king of the Visigoths
486 to 487 Franks (German tribe) under Clovis I control all France
493 Theodoric (Ostrogoth) murders Odoacer and becomes king of Italy
500 Thrasamund marries Theodoric's sister and gets Sicily as a dowry
c. 500 Peru: Moschica culture of Chimic Indians
c. 500 Peru: Pre-Inca culture, foundation of the Huari Empire

Part 2 Politics and Civilization
501 TO 1000

KEY DOCUMENT

Empress Theodora hailed from circus people: her father worked at the Hippodrome at Constantinople and was a bear keeper for the chariot races. She reigned first on stage and then from the throne. In *The Secret History,* Procopius reveals Theodora's behavior both on and off the stage: "Often, even in the theater, in the sight of all the people, she removed her costume and stood nude in their midst, except for a girdle about the groin: not that she was abashed at revealing that, too, to the audience, but because there was a law against appearing altogether naked on the stage, without at least this much of a fig-leaf." Yet she was a competent ruler, jointly with Justinian. Procopius claims that "neither did anything without the consent of the other. For some time it was generally supposed they were totally different in mind and action; but later it was revealed that their apparent disagreement had been arranged so that their subjects might not unanimously revolt against them, but instead be divided in opinion. . . ."

539 War between Persia and Byzantine Empire
c. 540 Africa: Nubia converted to Christianity
540 Sassania, under Khusrau I, sacks Anticho
550 Britain: Mercia, East Anglia, and Northumbria established

Did You Know?

According to legend, King Arthur was the son of Uther Pendragon, king of Britain. A wise and valiant leader, he gathered the Round Table of knights. With his queen, Guinevere, he maintained a magnificent court at Caerleon-upon-Usk (perhaps the legendary Camelot). Arthur extended his kingdom across Europe, until he was killed by his rebellious nephew, Mordred. Arthur was mysteriously carried away to the mythical island of Avalon to be healed of his "grievous wound."

Several early sources refer to a warrior-king named Arthur who lived around the middle of the fifth century. The most reliable source is On the Ruin and Conquest of Britain, *written in the 540s by a British priest named Gildas; the full legend was first set down in* Historia Regum Britanniae *(c. 1139).*

551 to 560	552 European silk industry begins
	553 Byzantine Empire takes Rome and Naples
	558 Chlothar I, son of Clovis, reunites kingdom of the Franks
561 to 570	567 Austrasia kingdom formed from Frankish kingdom (Lorraine, Belgium, France, Burgundy, Rhine)
	c. 570 Tibetan kingdom established
	570 Yemen: Persians overthrow Abyssinian rule
571 to 580	War between Byzantine Empire and Persia
581 to 590	China: Sui dynasty
591 to 600	600 Tibet becomes a unified state
601 to 650	607 China: First Japanese ambassadors
	614 Sassians capture Damascus and Jerusalem
	616 Egypt: Persians triumph
	618 China: Public officials selected on the basis of merit; system of centralized public examinations available to all
	618 China: Tang dynasty begins under Li Yuan
	620 Ireland: Northmen invade
	622 Emperor Heraclitus of Byzantium invades Sassania
	622 Asia: Muslims (Arab followers of Mohammad) begin Holy War against nonbelievers in Media
	632 Mohammad dies; caliphate established
	633 Persia: Arabs attack
	636 Japan: Rise of feudal nobility

637 Ctesiphon, capital of Sassania, falls to Muslim attack
641 Egypt: Cairo established
642 Muslim invasions end the Sassanian Empire
644 Korea: Chinese move in
by 650 Asia/Africa: Arabs led by Caliph Omar take Syria, Palestine, Egypt, and destroy Persian Empire

651 to 700   661 to 680 Asia/Africa: Arabs conquer North Africa and extend empire east to Afghanistan and Indus Valley
688 Korea: Civilization flourishes
697 Arabs destroy Carthage

701 to 750   711 Arabs invade Spain and southern France
715 Charles Martel ("the Hammer") becomes mayor of Frankish court
732 Charles Martel leads Franks to victory over Arabs at Battle of Poiters, halting Muslim advance into Europe
742 Charlemagne born

751 to 800   751 to 768 Pepin the Short (first Carolingian king)
768 to 814 Charlemagne, king of the Franks, conquers northern Italy, Germany, northeast Spain
771 Charlemagne becomes sole ruler of Frankish kingdom
786 Cynewulf, king of the West Saxons
787 Danes invade Britain
792 Britain: Viking era
795 Egypt: Revolts erupt
800 Charlemagne crowned first Holy Roman emperor by Pope Leo III
800 Northmen invade Germany
800 Northmen discover Faroe Islands
800 Peru: City of Machu Picchu

801 to 850   802 Vikings control Ireland

Did You Know?

Late in the tenth century, strange ships began appearing in the bays along the coasts of Europe. Pointed at each end so that they could go forward or backward without turning around, the ships had tall curved fronts, usually carved in the shapes of dragons. Each ship had a single square sail, often striped in brilliant colors. It took forty to sixty strong men to row these ships across the ocean. The invaders were Norsemen, or Northmen, because they came from the northern countries now called Denmark, Norway, and Sweden. Also called Vikings, these invaders were the most skilled and daring seamen of their day. At first, the Vikings attacked locally, in small groups. Later, they became bolder and attacked Russia, Britain, Ireland, France, Spain, Italy, and Africa. As many as 250 Viking ships attacked at one time.

808 Rise of Bulgarian Empire
810 Charlemagne and Byzantines recognize Venice as independent state
813 Charlemagne crowns his son Louis the Pious
814 Charlemagne dies
826 Crete: Arabs conquer island and extend influence
830 Great Moravian Empire established; Prince Moimir rules until 846
833 King Louis I deposed
834 King Louis I restored
834 Britain: Danes raid the country
841 Northmen sack Rouen and march to Paris
843 Treaty of Verdun, division of the Frankish Empire
845 China: Inflation and state bankruptcy
846 Arabs sack Rome; Vatican damaged
850 Earliest use of gunpowder
850 Tibet: Government collapses

Did You Know?

Alfred the Great of Wessex (871 to 899) is considered the first true king of England. He established the Saxon dynasty and became famous for his resistance to the Viking invasions. With some interruptions, the Saxon dynasty continued until the Norman conquest of 1066.

851 to 900
859 Northmen sack Mediterranean coast up to Asia Minor
860 Denmark: Gorm the Elder becomes king
860 Cambodia: Angkor Thom (later, Angkor) established
861 Northmen discover Iceland
862 Russia: Rurik establishes Novgorod
865 Russian Northmen attack Constantinople
868 Egypt: Tulunid dynasty
871 to 899 England: Alfred the Great
874 China: uprising against Tang dynasty
877 Egypt annexes Damascus
878 to 899 Alfred the Great of Wessex defeats Danes and rules southern England
878 Arabs conquer Sicily and make Palermo the capital
879 Nepal becomes independent from Tibet
887 Final division of France and Germany
893 to 927 Height of Bulgarian Empire under Simeon I
895 Japan: Fujiwaras establish dynasty
900 Mexico: Toltec civilization
by 900 Cambodia: Khmer Empire established, capital at Angkor
900 Mayans migrate to Yucatan peninsula
900 Vikings develop art of shipbuilding
900 Vikings discover Greenland

901 to 950   905 Egypt: Tulunid dynasty deposed
907 China: Collapse of Tang dynasty
907 to 960 China: Five Dynasties and Ten Kingdoms
909 Africa: Rise of Fatimid dynasty
916 Arabs expelled from central Italy
925 Aethelstan becomes king of Wessex and Mercia
927 Aethelstan defeats the Vikings
930 The Althing, world's first legislative assembly, founded by Norse settlers in Iceland
935 China: Central monarchy established
935 Arabs establish Algeria
936 China: Hou-Chin dynasty
950 Norway: Lapps settle

Did You Know?

The term "Holy Roman Empire" refers to the second medieval revival of the
Roman Empire in the west in the year 962. Although drained of most of its
power after 1250 and virtually all its power after 1648, the empire endured until
1806 when it was abolished by Emperor Francis II. Whatever the emperor's
power, the title Emperor of the Holy Roman Empire remained the most
prestigious moniker in Europe. Before 1356, the king of Germany was crowned
emperor by the Pope; thereafter, members of the electoral college chose the
Habsburg candidate.

951 to 1000   952 Scotland: Malcolm I, king
955 England: Edwy, Edmund's son, becomes king
959 England: Edgar the Peaceful becomes king
960 Poland: Mieczyslav I becomes first ruler
962 King of the Germans, Otto I the Great, conquers central Europe and is crowned
Holy Roman emperor
964 New Maya Empire
972 North Africa freed from Egypt
975 Edgar of Wessex crowned first king of England at Bath
979 England: Aethelred becomes king
980 Russia: St. Vladimir becomes prince of Kiev
c. 980 Viking raids throughout Britain
981 Bulgarian war
982 Greenland: Eric the Red establishes Viking colonies
986 Norse reach Greenland and North America
987 Hugh Capet crowned king of France at Noyon
988 Vikings attack Somerset and Devon
992 Boleslaus I becomes first king of Poland
996 Rome: Civil war
1000 Peru: Tiahuanaco civilization
1000 America: Leif Eriksson, son of Eric the Red, lands at Nova Scotia

Part 2 Politics and Civilization
1001 TO 1500

1001 to 1050   1000s Africa: Due to gold trade, kingdoms of Takrur and Gao flourish in West Africa; Bantus settle in southern Africa
North America: Blown off course, Vikings (under the leadership of Biarni Heriulfsson) sight land

KEY DOCUMENT

Here is an excerpt from *Biarni Goes in Quest of Greenland:*
> Biarni said, "I will take the ship to Greenland, if you will bear me company." They all replied that they would abide by his decision. Then said Biarni, "Our voyage must be regarded as foolhardy, seeing that no one of us has ever been in the Greenland Sea." Nevertheless, they put out to sea when they were equipped for the voyage, and sailed for three days, until the land was hidden by the water, and then the fair wind died out, and north winds arose, and fogs, and they knew not whither they were drifting. . . . Then they saw the sun again, and were able to determine the quarters of the heavens; they hoisted sail and before long they saw land. . . . [T]he land was level, and covered with woods, and that there were small hillocks upon it.

c. 1000 Pacific Islands: Maori people settle in New Zealand; Polynesians begin to build stone temples
1001 to 1022 Turkey: Basil II ("The Bulgar Slayer") restores eastern Roman Empire at Constantinople by defeating Bulgars and Armenians
1001 Hungary: Stephen crowned first king

Did You Know?

Today, more than 1,000 languages are spoken in Africa. Apart from Arabic (which is not confined to Africa), the most widely spoken African tongues are Swahili and Hausa, each with more than 10 million speakers. Although very few African languages have written literature, most have long-standing oral traditions.

1004 Italy: Arabs sack Pisa
1006 India: Mohammedans settle in northwestern region
1009 Jerusalem: Mohammedans sack Holy Sepulcher church
Germany: First Imperial Diet at Goslar

1011 South Wales: Ethelred invades; Danes take Canterbury
1012 England: Danes sack Canterbury
1013 England: Sweyn lands and is proclaimed king; Ethelred flees to Normandy

Did You Know?

The name Constantinople was officially changed to Istanbul in 1930.
Constantinople/Istanbul is historically important first as the capital of the
Byzantine Empire and later as the capital of the Ottoman Empire.

1014 England: Sweyn dies; Ethelred II becomes king
India: Rajendra I becomes ruler of Cholas, who dominate much of India
Ireland: Brian Boru, high king of all Ireland, defeats Vikings at Battle of Clontarf, but is
killed after victory
Rome: Henry crowned emperor
1015 Italy: Arabs conquer Sardinia
England: Canute invades; war between Danes and Saxons
1016 England: Ethelred II ("the Unready") dies; Canute takes throne

Did You Know?

Today, a diet is the legislative body of certain countries, such as Japan. In the
past, the term diet was also used to refer to the general assembly of the estates
of the Holy Roman Empire.

1016 to 1035 Europe: Reign of Canute, Viking king of England, Denmark, Norway, and
Sweden
1018 India: Mahmud of Ghazni pillages the sacred city of Muttra
Scotland: Southern and northern areas united

Did You Know?

Sardinia, the second largest island in the Mediterranean, is about 166 miles long.

1019 to 1054 Russia: Jaroslav the Wise, ruler of Kiev, unifies many Russian principalities
and builds cities, schools, and churches
1020 Italy: Rome, Florence, and Venice become city-states
1021 to 1035 Middle East: Reign of Fatimid caliph al-Zahir marks decline of Fatimid
power
1024 Afghanistan and Iran: Mahmud takes Somnath in Gujarat
1025 Poland: Boleslaw I becomes king and creates a powerful state

1028 Norway: Canute conquers Norway; son Sweyn becomes king
1030 Norway: Olaf killed at the battle of Stiklestad

Did You Know?

Mahmud of Ghazni (971 to 1030) made his kingdom the center of an empire including at its height Pakistan and most of Iran. The first to carry the banner of Islam into the heart of India, Mahmud was famous as a patron of the arts as well as a great warrior. He transformed Ghazni into a cultural center rivaling Baghdad.

1031 to 1060 France: Henry I crowned king
1033 Spain: Rise of Spanish Christian kingdom in Castile under Ferdinand I (1033 to 1065)
1034 Scotland: Malcolm II dies; grandson Duncan takes throne
1037 Spain: Castile and León unite
1040 Scotland: Macbeth murders King Duncan and seizes the throne
1042 Byzantine Emperor Constantine IX rules for the next decade
1044 Burma: Anawrata builds a large empire
c. 1043 to 1099 Spain: El Cid (Rodrigo Diaz), national hero

Did You Know?

El Cid Campeador ("The Lord Champion") became a Spanish legend and the embodiment of chivalry and virtue. Born of minor aristocracy, El Cid became a commander under the Castilian king in 1065. Exiled in 1081 after raiding Toledo, he then served the Muslim rulers of Saragossa seeking honor, glory, and booty. In 1094, El Cid achieved his goals when he took the Moorish kingdom of Valencia. El Cid's exploits are recorded in many poems, songs, and epics, including the famous Spanish epic El cantar de mio Cid *(The Song of the Cid).*

1046 Norway: King Harald Haardraada
Rome: Henry III crowned king
1047 to 1076 Denmark: King Sweyn II
1050 Egypt: Military dictatorship
England: Normans attack
c. 1050s Africa: Yoruba people of Ife flourish in Nigeria
1050s to 1146 Africa: Almoravids (Berber Muslims from western Sahara) take over Morocco, Algeria, and part of Spain; in 1076, they invade Ghana and establish a power base

1051 to 1100   1053 England: Henry IV crowned Holy Roman emperor
Italy: Normans conquer southern Italy
1054 Africa: Abdallah ben Yassim begins Muslim conquest of West Africa
Scotland: Macbeth defeated
1055 Asia: Seljuk Turks take Baghdad; sultanate established

1057 Scotland: Malcolm murders Macbeth; Lulach takes throne
1058 Scotland: Malcolm kills Lulach and seizes the throne
Europe: William of Normandy defeats Geoffrey of Anjou at Battle of Varaville

KEY DOCUMENT

Shakespeare's *Macbeth* (1606) is one of his greatest tragedies, a compelling and timeless tale of success, treachery, ambition, and the disintegration of a brave but flawed man. Shakespeare based the play on the historical Macbeth. In the play, Macbeth delivers one of the play's most famous speeches after he learns of his wife's death:

> *She should have died hereafter;*
> *There would have been time for such a word.*
> *Tomorrow, and tomorrow, and tomorrow*
> *Creeps in this petty pace from day to day,*
> *To the last syllable of recorded time:*
> *And all our yesterdays have lighted fools*
> *The way to dusty death. Out, out brief candle!*
> *Life's but a walking shadow, a poor player*
> *That struts and frets his hour upon the stage*
> *And then is heard no more. It is a tale*
> *Told by an idiot, full of sound and fury*
> *Signifying nothing. (V, v, 17–28)*

1061 Africa: Muslim Almoravid dynasty in North Africa; later, will conquer Spain
Europe: Malcolm of Scotland invades Northumbria
Europe: Normans conquer Messina
1062 Africa: Almoravids establish capital at Marrakech
1064 Europe: Hungarians take Belgrade
1065 Asia Minor: Muslim Seljuk Turks invade
1066 England: Normans conquer England by defeating the Anglo-Saxons at the Battle of Hastings; William I, the Conqueror, is the first Norman king of England

Did You Know?

The Domesday Book, a *statistical survey of England carried out under William the Conqueror's orders*, was an attempt to register the country's landed wealth. The book enabled William to strengthen his authority by exacting oaths of allegiance from tenants, nobles, and churchmen.

1068 to 1085 China: Emperor Shen Tsung makes radical reforms
1069 to 1072 Egypt: Widespread famine

1071 Middle East: Seljuks defeat Byzantine army at Battle of Manzikert
1072 Scotland: William invades

Did You Know?

The Seljuk Turks were a tribe of nomads who settled near Bokhara (now Uzbekistan) in the late 900s.

1075 Middle East: Seljuk leader Malik Sha conquers Syria and Palestine
1076 Africa: Berbers from Morocco sack Kumbi Saleh, beginning Ghana's decline
Europe: Gregory VII dethrones and excommunicates Henry IV
1077 Europe: Gregory VII absolves Henry IV
1080 Europe: Henry IV excommunicated again
1083 Europe: Henry attacks Rome, which he captures in 1084

Did You Know?

By dressing as a penitent and standing barefoot in the snow for three days outside the castle of Canossa where Pope Gregory was staying, Henry IV obtained readmission to the church.

1086 Spain: Mohammedan rule
1091 Europe: Treaty of Caën (William II and Robert of Normandy)
1094 Spain: El Cid takes Valencia from the Moors

Did You Know?

The Song Dynasty ruled in China from 960 to 1279.

1096 to 1097 Turkey and Middle East: First Crusade: Three armies of French and Normans reach Constantinople, defeat the Turks, and take Palestine from the Muslims
1099 Middle East: Crusaders take Jerusalem and establish a Latin kingdom there under Geoffrey of Bouillon

1101 to 1150 c. 1100 Africa: Ghana Empire declines
Africa: Katanga in Zaire likely established
Cambodia: Epidemics of malaria and plague and neglect of the irrigation system undermine imperial rule
Peru: Height of Chimu civilization at Chan Chan, on the northwest coast
South Pacific: Polynesian islands colonized

1100s Hawaii: Hawaiian Islands colonized
Peru: Rise of Incas
South Pacific: Polynesians settle Pitcairn Island
1100 Peru: Sinchi Roca civilization
US: Third Pueblo period in southwest; Anasazi people build cliff dwellings at Mesa Verde, Chaco Canyon, and Canyon de Chelly

Did You Know?

The Normans dramatically changed English life by introducing a social, economic, and political system called feudalism. Under this system, land was divided among nobles. They, in turn, were served by knights, who provided protection, and serfs, who farmed the land and herded the animals.

1100 to 1400s Africa: Shona create thriving state at Great Zimbabwe
1101 China: Emperor Hai-tsung takes the throne
1104 England: Henry IV abdicates
1106 England: Henry V takes the throne upon the death of his father, Henry IV
1108 to 1137 France: King Louis VI
1109 to 1113 Europe: Anglo-French war
1112 England: King Henry V excommunicated

Did You Know?

The Inca Empire grew to control 2,500 miles along the Andes in South America.

1113 to 1150 Cambodia: Peak of ancient Khmer Empire under Suryavarman II
1115 China: State of Chin established
Italy: Florence becomes a republic

Did You Know?

Thick stone walls and a cone-shaped tower are all that remain of the once-mighty empire of Great Zimbabwe. By 1400, more than 10,000 people lived in the region; by 1450, no one did. Scholars do not know why the Shona abandoned the site; possible theories include soil depletion and violent wars.

1120 Europe: Louis VI of France and Henry I of England make peace
1122 Middle East: Byzantines slaughter Patzinak Turks
1125 Africa: Almohads (Berber Muslims opposed to Almoravids) conquer Morocco
1126 to 1157 Spain: King Alfonso VII

1130 Africa: Almohad dynasty comes to power in Morocco
1139 England: Civil war erupts

Did You Know?

The crowning glory of the ancient Khmer Empire, the temple-tomb of Angkor Wat built during the regin of Suryavarman II was later hidden for centuries in the dense jungle. In 1860, French naturalist Henri Mouhot rediscovered the site. Angkor Wat is crowned by five lofty towers, with a central pinnacle soaring 213 feet. It is surrounded by a moat 623 feet wide at every point. The outer wall forms a rectangle 5,085 feet by 4,592 feet.

1143 Portugal: Alfonso I becomes king and makes Portugal independent of Spain
1145 to 1150 Spain: Almohads begin conquest of Moorish Spain
1146 to 1148 Middle East: Second Crusade, led by King Louis VII of France and Emperor Conrad VII, attacks Damascus but achieves little success

Did You Know?

The Maori came to New Zealand from the Polynesian Islands, the last wave arriving around 1350. The people were divided into tribes, called iwi, *descended from a common ancestor. Each tribe was made up of* hapu *(clans), comprised of family groups called* whanau.

1147 Almohads seize Marrakech and go on to conquer Spain, Algeria, and Tripoli
c. 1150 US: End of Hopewell culture
Pacific Islands: Maoris settle in the river mouth areas in New Zealand
1150s Africa: Zagwe dynasty rules in Ethiopian highlands

1151 to 1200
1151 Mexico: End of Toltec Empire
1152 England: Louis VII divorces Queen Eleanor; she marries Henry of Anjou, who becomes king of England

Did You Know?

Eleanor of Aquitaine (1122? to 1204) is one of the most interesting queens in history. For a fascinating film interpretation of her life, see The Lion in Winter, *the 1968 British film starring Katharine Hepburn as Eleanor and Peter O'Toole as Henry. This brilliant, fierce drama shows Henry deliberating over a successor on a fateful Christmas Eve. Oscars went to Hepburn, writer James Goldman, and composer John Barry. The film also marks the debuts of Anthony Hopkins and Timothy Dalton.*

1152 to 1190 Reign of powerful Holy Roman emperor Frederick I called Barbarossa ("Red Beard")

1154 to 1189 England: Henry II Plantagenet becomes king of England; he reforms law and government and starts Plantagenet rule (until 1485)

1155 Europe: Pope Hadrian IV gives Ireland to Henry II

1156 to 1185 Japan: Civil wars

1157 Finland: Eric of Sweden conquers Finland

1160 North Africa: Normans expelled

c. 1163 to 1227 Genghis Khan, founder of Mongol Empire

Did You Know?

In the twelfth century, Genghis Khan's soldiers sun-dried mare's milk to a powder to preserve it. At the start of each day's journey, they put some of the powder and water into a bottle and hung it on their saddles. By the end of the day, the milk and water had been mixed to a fine froth.

1163 England: Power struggle between Henry II and Thomas à Becket

1167 Middle East: Amalric, king of Jerusalem, captures Cairo

1168 Middle East: Arabs regain Cairo

1169 to 1174 Middle East: Saladin, vizier of Egypt; sultan from 1174

1170 England: Power struggle between Henry II and Archibishop Thomas à Becket ends in Becket's murder in Canterbury

1170s Mexico: Chichimec nomads overthrow Toltec capital at Tula

1171 Egypt: Saladin, Muslim warrior and commander in Egyptian army, overthrows Fatimid dynasty

1171 Europe: Henry II annexes Ireland

1172 Europe: Eleanor raises Aquitaine against Henry II; Henry and the Pope reconcile

1173 Egypt: Saladin declares himself sultan

1173 to 1185 England: Eleanor imprisoned

1173 to 1193 Saladin overcomes Palestine and Syria, taking Damascus

Did You Know?

The Aquitaine is a historic region in southwestern France. The last duke of Aquitaine was William X, whose daughter Eleanor inherited the land.

1174 Middle East: Saladin conquers Syria

1175 India: Muslim rulers established in central India

1177 Middle East: Baldwin IV defeats Saladin

1179 Middle East: Saladin attacks Tyre

c. 1180 Mexico: Toltecs driven out of Chichen Itza

1181 to c. 1219 Cambodia: During his reign, King Jayavaram VIII builds hospitals and rest houses along the roads that run through his kingdom.
1180s Decline of Chola kingdom
1184 Cyprus gains its freedom from Byzantium
Europe: Diet of Mainz; power of Emperor Frederick I peaks
1186 Japan: Kamakura era begins
1186 to 1187 India: Mohammed of Ghur deposes Ghaznavid ruler
1187 Middle East: Saladin, sultan of Turkish Syria and Egypt, retakes Jerusalem
India: Mohammed of Ghur conquers Punjab
1189 Middle East: Third Crusade, led by Emperor Frederick Barbarossa, Philip Agustus of France, and Richard I of England (Richard the Lionhearted), fails, but 1192 truce with Saladin allows Christians access to Jerusalem
1190 Asia: Mongol leader Temujin creates an empire
1191 Central America: Second era of Maya civilization

Did You Know?

In effect, the shogunate was a hereditary military dictatorship. From 1192 to 1867, Japan's shoguns ("supreme commanders") had great power. The Minamoto ruled until the 1300s, when the Ashikaga family took over. They held power until the 1600s.

1192 Japan: Minamoto Yoritomo becomes shogun after he wins long civil war
1193 Middle East: Muslims capture Bihar and Bengal
1194 Italy: Henry VI conquers Sicily and is crowned king of Sicily

KEY DOCUMENT

The Magna Carta, considered the basis of English constitutional liberties, contained the first detailed description of the relationship between the king and the barons, guaranteed feudal rights, and regularized the judicial system. It also protected commerce and established a system of standard weights and measures. Life, liberty, and property were guaranteed by these words:

No freeman shall be taken and imprisoned or exiled or in any way destroyed, nor shall we go upon him nor send upon him, except by the lawful judgment of his peers and by the law of the land.

1196 to 1203 Morocco: Marimind dynasty established at Fez
1199 France: King Richard I killed; King John takes the throne
c. 1200 Africa: Mali becomes second great West African trading empire
Mexico: Maya revolt
Morocco: Jews given special privileges
North America: Temple mounds built

Peru: Incas settle in Cuzco
US: Cahokia, city of temple mounds, at zenith

1201 to 1250   1202 to 1204 Egypt: Great famine
c. 1203 Japan: Hojo family rules after Minamoto Yoritomo's death
1204 Middle East: Fourth Crusade: Crusaders sack Constantinople; Byzantines flee
to Nicaea
Greece: Venice gains control of the Aegean Sea and the Ionian islands
1206 Asia: Temujin is proclaimed Genghis Khan, "Emperor within the Seas"
India: Former Turkestan slave Aibak founds new sultanate of Delhi

Did You Know?

*Genghis Khan's army, although not especially large for its day, was distinguished
by its superb horsemanship and expert archery.*

1206 to 1223 China: Mongol attacks begin as Genghis Khan leads Mongol warriors
through China and Persia to defeat the Russians
1211 China: Genghis Khan invades
1212 Almohads defeated by Christians at battle of Las Navas de Tolosa
China: Genghis Khan captures Beijing
Crete: conquered by Venice
Middle East: Children's Crusade: 50,000 children set off for Jerusalem
1215 England: King John sets royal seal on Magna Carta, accepting limits on royal
powers demanded by barons
1217 England: French leave the country
1218 Egypt: Ayyubid Empire breaks up, but Ayyubids rule Egypt to 1250
Persia: Genghis Khan conquers country

Did You Know?

*Eventually Genghis Khan's vast empire stretched from the China Sea to the
Dnepr River and from the Persian Gulf nearly to the Arctic Ocean.*

1218 to 1221 Fifth Crusade tries but fails to take Egypt
1219 to 1333 Japan: Hojo clan rules
c. 1220 Africa: City-state of Kilwa in Tanzania prospers
1223 Russia: Mongols invade
1225 England: Magna Carta reissued in definitive format
1227 Genghis Khan dies; empire divided among his sons
1228 to 1229 Middle East: Frederick II leads Sixth Crusade, recaptures Holy City;
Frederick crowns himself king of Jerusalem

c. 1230 Africa: Hafsid monarchy takes over from Almohads in Tunisia and acquires many trade routes across the Sahara Desert
1234 Mongols annex the Chin Empire

Did You Know?

The largest desert in the world, the Sahara is about 1,000 miles across and 3,200 miles long, with a total area of more than 3,500,000 square miles.

1235 Africa: Under King Sundiata Keita, Mali Empire grows very powerful
c. 1235 Africa: Great warrior leader Sun Diata establishes Mali Empire
1240 Africa: Ghana Empire incorporated into Mali Empire
Europe: Border created between England and Scotland
1240 to 1450 Russia: Mongol khanates of the Golden Horde rule central and southern regions
1242 Russia: Aleksander Nevskii successfully defends Novgorod against Teutonic attack
1244 Middle East: Muslims retake Jerusalem, which remains under Muslim rule until 1917
1248 Middle East: Louis IX leads Seventh Crusade; crusade fails and Louis is captured and ransomed
1250 Egypt: Last Ayyubid ruler in Egypt murdered; Mamluks, soldiers from central Asia employed by Ayyubids, establish military state
c. 1250s Africa: Kanem kingdom in Lake Chad region divides into rival factions; under the leadership of Mali's first ruler, Sundiata, the Mandinka people seize the gold trade
Mexico: Maya revival; new capital built at Mayapan
Peru: Chimu people expand their empire

1251 to 1300   1254 to 1273 Great Interregnum: Bitter struggle for imperial crown
1254? to 1324 Marco Polo, Italian traveler and writer
1256 Persia: Hulagu, grandson of Genghis Khan, founds Mongol kingdom of Persia
1260 to 1277 Egypt: Mamluk commander Baybars takes over as sultan
1260 to 1294 Asia: Kublai Khan (grandson of Genghis) completes Mongol conquest of China and establishes his capital at Beijing
1260 to 1368 China: Mongol dynasty rules
1261 Greek army from Nicaea reconquers Constantinople and overthrows Latin rule, restoring Byzantine Empire
1262 Europe: Teutonic Knights complete conquests south of Baltic Sea; bring German influence to Prussia; Iceland and Greenland come under Norwegian rule
1270 Middle East: Louis IX and Prince Edward lead Eighth Crusade to Tunis; Louis dies
1271 Venetian explorer Marco Polo sets out for China
1273 Austria: Rudolf of Habsburg elected emperor; dynasty rules until 1918
1274 Japan: Mongols invade but fail to gain a foothold
1276 to 1299 North America: Severe drought in southwest, in Mesa Verde area
1276 to 1284 Europe: Edward I conquers Wales and unites it with England
1281 Japan: Second Mongol invasion ends in disaster
c. 1283 Mexico: Mayapan, capital of the Itza, last site of the prehistoric Mayan civilization

1285 to 1307 Scotland: Edward I conquers Scotland
1288 India: Marco Polo arrives

Did You Know?

In 1273, the Golden Horde sacked Moscow and Kiev and continued westward into Poland, Hungary, and the Danube River valley. By 1241, the army had reached the coast of the Adriatic Sea, poised to invade western Europe. Europe was spared only by the death of the Great Khan Ogadai in 1241.

1290 to 1326 Turkey: Osman I establishes Ottoman dynasty
1290 India: Turkish leader Firuz establishes the Khalji dynasty in Delhi
1291 Middle East: Saracens (Muslims) capture Acre, last Christian stronghold in Palestine

Did You Know?

Through his writings, Italian traveler Marco Polo (1254? to 1324) gave Europeans their first authentic look at life in the Far East. The Travels of Marco Polo, *perhaps the most famous and important travel book in history, became the basis for some of the first accurate maps of Asia, helped spark Columbus's interest in Asia, and suggested the all-sea route that Vasco da Gama sailed in 1497 to 1498.*

1295 England: First representative parliament
1297 Europe: Battle of Cambuskenneth: Scottish patriot William Wallace defeats English army
1298 Europe: Edward I defeats Wallace and reconquers Scotland
c. 1300 Peru: Incas expand their empire throughout central Andes
Pacific Islands: Hawaiians become prosperous through agriculture; they develop a class structure
c. 1300 to 1500 Africa: Rise of Kongo kingdom on the lower Zaire (Congo) River

1301 to 1350
1301 Osma, founder of the Ottoman Turks, defeats the Byzantines
1305 Europe: English capture and execute William Wallace
1306 France: Philip IV expels the Jews
1312 to 1337 Mali: Greatest ruler, Mansa Musa, extends kingdom to Atlantic Ocean
1314 Scotland: Robert Bruce reestablishes Scottish independence by defeating English at Bannockburn
1317 France: Salic law passed; excludes women from inheriting the throne
1321 to 1413 India: Tughluq dynasty founded in Delhi
1324 Arabia: Emperor of Mali, Mansa Musa, goes on a pilgrimage to Mecca
c. 1325 Mexico: Aztecs establish city of Tenochtitlan (now Mexico City) on an island in Lake Texcoco
1327 England: Edward III becomes king
1328 France: Philip VI, first king of the House of Valois

1333 to 1336 Japan: General Ashikaga Takauji rebels against emperor and becomes first of the Ashikaga shoguns

1336 India: Hindu empire of Vijayanagar is center of resistance to Islam

---

KEY DOCUMENT

English poet Samuel Taylor Coleridge (1772 to 1834) based his poem "Kubla Khan" on a description he read of the great Mongol leader. The poem begins this way:

In Xanadu did Kubla Khan
A stately pleasure dome decree:
Where Alph, the sacred river, ran
Through caverns measureless to man
Down to a sunless sea.

1337 to 1453 Europe: The Hundred Years' War (England vs. France); Edward III of England wins naval battle of Sluis and land battle of Crecy

1338 to 1573 Japan: Ashikaga shoguns dominate

1347 to 1558 France: Calais surrenders to England

1350 Southeast Asia: Last Hindu Javanese kingdom of Majapahit spreads

c. 1350 Pacific Islands: Maoris flourish in the North Island, New Zealand; first terrace-type fortifications

Did You Know?

Braveheart (1995) is an epic tale of Scottish rebel warrior William Wallace, who sparks a grass-roots resistance to the tyranny of King Edward I. The movie tells a compelling story through a series of bloody and riveting battle scenes. Winner of Academy Awards for Best Picture, Director, Cinematography, Makeup, and Sound Effects, the movie stars Mel Gibson, Sophie Marceau, and Patrick McGoohan.

1351 to 1400   1354 Ottoman Turks establish toehold in Europe at Gallipoli

1358 The jacquerie, a revolt by French peasants, is suppressed by the regent Charles, son of John II

1360 Europe: Treaty of Bretigny ends the first stage of the Hundred Years' War; Edward III gives up his claim to the French throne

1368 Asia: Mongol leader Tamerlane begins his conquest of Asia

Did You Know?

On his pilgrimage to Mecca in 1324, Musa stopped first in Cairo. He entered the city in great style, with 500 slaves, and handed out so much gold that its value dropped for more than a decade.

1368 China: Mongols driven out; Zhu Yuanzhang founds Ming dynasty (to 1644)
1369 to 1405 Tamerlane of Samarkand establishes Mongol Empire over all central Asia; it falls apart after his death.
c. 1370 Mexico: Acampitchtli chosen king of the Aztecs

Did You Know?

The Hundred Years' War erupted over the English claim to the French throne: King Edward III of England maintained that King Philip IV of France was a usurper. Edward also feared that Philip would deprive him of the duchy of Guienne, which Edward held as a fief from Philip.

1371 to 1390 Scotland: Robert II, first Stuart king
1373 Europe: John of Gaunt, duke of Lancaster, son of Edward III, leads English invasion of France
1374 England: John of Gaunt returns to England to rule
1375 Europe: Truce of Bruges ends fighting between England and France
1376 England: "Good Parliament" introduces many governmental reforms
1380 Dmitri Donskoi defeats Golden Horde at Battle of Kulikovo, but Mongol domination continues until 1480
c. 1380 Africa: Foundation of Kongo kingdom in Congo river-mouth region of Zaire
1381 Peasants' Revolt in England during reign of weak King Richard II is crushed
1389 Christian Serbs defeated by Ottoman Turks at Kossovo in Serbia

Did You Know?

The Ming rulers extended the Chinese Empire into Korea and Mongolia on the north and Vietnam and Burma on the south, thereby achieving greater influence in Asia than any other native rulers of China.

c. 1390 Ottoman Turks complete conquest of Asia Minor
c. 1390s Peru: Viracocha becomes eighth Inca ruler
1392 to 1910 Korea: I Dynasty
1396 Europe: Ottoman Turks conquer Bulgaria
1398 India: Tamerlane sacks Delhi; 100,000 prisoners killed
1399 England: Henry of Bolingbroke lands in Yorkshire with forty men and soon has 60,000 supporters; Henry deposes Richard II and takes the name Henry IV, king of England (to 1413) (first of the house of Lancaster)
c. 1400 US: Pueblo people abandon northern sites and gather in large towns
1400s Mexico: Aztec and Maya empires grow

1401 to 1450   1400s Africa: Gold from mines in Zimbabwe is exported to Asia via Sofala on the east coast
c. 1400 Africa: Engaruka farmers in Tanzania

1401 Turkey: Tamerlane, conqueror from central Asia, sets fire to Damascus and Syria and sacks the Great Mosque; according to an eye witness, 30,000 women, children, priests, and refugees perish

Did You Know?

By the 1400s, there were seven Hausa city-states in Africa. Kano became a busy center of trade after its rulers built a road to the forest areas in the south. Hausa merchants dealt in many items, including gold dust and kola nuts.

1402 Turkey: Tamerlane's Mongols defeat Ottomans at battle of Ankyra
1402 to 1403 Richard III campaigns in Scotland and Wales by usurping King Henry IV and his son, later Henry V
1405 to 1433 Chinese Muslim, Zheng He, makes seven voyages westward to collect tribute for Ming emperors
1406 Italy: Florence conquers Pisa
1407 Italy: Casa di San Giorgio, one of the first public banks, founded in Genoa

Did You Know?

Far from trying to forget his brutality, Tamerlane had the unique dome of the Great Mosque copied at Samarkand for his own tomb, Gur Amir. The dome's unmistakable style spread to India after one of Tamerlane's descendants, Baber, overthrew the sultan of Delhi in 1526 and established the Mogul Empire. Shah Jahan, a member of Baber's dynasty, built the Taj Mahal, whose dome derives directly from the mosque that Tamerlane had destroyed nearly 250 years earlier.

1411 to 1442 India: Reign of Ahmad Shah of Gujarat, who builds capital city of Ahmadabad
1415 France: Henry V defeats French at Agincourt and captures Paris
1418 to 1460 Portugal's Prince Henry the Navigator sponsors exploration of Africa's coast
1419 to 1450 Korea: Prosperity under King Sejong
1420 Portuguese sailors explore west coast of Africa, reaching the Madeira Islands
1420 to 1421 China: Ming capital moves from Nanjing to Beijing
1420s Africa: Songhai people in Gao region, West Africa, begin raids on Mali Empire
1426 to 1440 Mexico: Aztecs at Tenochtitlan form Triple Alliance with neighboring cities of Texcoco and Tlacopan; Emperor Itzcoatl reorganizes state to increase his power
1427 Portuguese reach the Azores
1429 France: Joan of Arc leads French to Victory at Orléans
1430s Southeast Asia: Collapse of Khmer Empire
c. 1430 Africa: Sultans of Kilwa expand kingdom
1431 France: Joan of Arc convicted of witchcraft and burned at the stake
Thailand: Thai army sacks Angkor Wat; city abandoned; Cambodian court is moved south to Phnom Penh

1431 to 1433 Africa: Zheng He makes seventh and final voyage, sailing to Africa's east coast
1434 to 1464 Italy: Cosimo de Medici rules Republic of Florence as "first citizen"
1434 to 1468 Africa: Reign of Christian emperor Zera Yacub in Ethiopia; he expands church and promotes great monasteries
c. 1438 Peru: Inca emperor Viracocha dies; his successor and son, Pachacuti, expands Inca Empire north to Ecuador

Did You Know?

The Hundred Years' War cost thousands of lives and destroyed much land and property. In France, it helped establish a sense of nationalism and made possible the emergence of a centralized government and absolute monarchy.

1440s Peru: Incas build great fortress at Cuzco
1440 to 1468 Reign of Aztec emperor Montezuma I; conquers large areas of eastern Mexico, taking many prisoners
1447 Casimir IV of Poland unites Polish kingdom with Grand Duchy of Lithuania
1448 to 1488 Thailand: King Trailok brings about major legal reforms

Did You Know?

Henry IV (1399 to 1413), Henry V (1413 to 1422), and Henry VI (1422 to 1461) are the Lancastrian kings of England.

1449 to 1474 Japan: Rule of shogun Ashikaga Yoshimasa
1450 Italy: Mercenary leader Francesco Sforza seizes power in Milan
c. 1450 Africa: Building at Great Zimbabwe at its zenith

Did You Know?

Joan of Arc, the patron saint of France, united the country at a crucial hour and turned the Hundred Years' War in France's favor. At 13, Joan said St. Michael and other early martyrs were speaking to her. In 1429, Joan's "voices" told her to help the Dauphin, later Charles VII, king of France. After convincing Charles that she had a divine mission to save France, Joan led the French to victory over the English. Charles opposed any further action against the English, but Joan defied him and led a battle against the English again. She was captured and executed. Twenty-five years later, Joan was declared innocent; in 1920 she was canonized.

Did You Know?

Virachcoha's son, Inca Pachacuti, who ruled from 1438 to 1471, is ranked by some historians with the greatest conquerors and rulers of all time.

1451 to 1500   1453 Europe: Hundred Years' War ends with French defeat of English at Castillon
Middle East: Turks conquer Constantinople, signaling the end of the Byzantine Empire and the beginning of the Ottoman Empire
1455 England: War of the Roses, civil wars between rival noble factions of York and Lancaster, begins; the war ends in 1485 with the death of Richard III at the Battle of Bosworth
1456 Europe: Hungarians under nobleman John Hunyadi storm Belgrade and drive out Turks; Portuguese reach the Cape Verde Islands
1459 Ottoman Turks conquer Serbia
1462 Africa: Sonni 'Ali becomes ruler of the Songhai and builds an empire
Russia: Ivan the Great rules Russia until 1505 as first czar; ends payment of tribute to Mongols

Did You Know?

At the time of Inca Huayna Capac (c. 1493 to 1525), the Inca Empire was at its peak, stretching more than 2,500 miles north to south, about 500 miles east to west. About 3.5 million to 16 million Indians of different tribal backgrounds lived in this vast region.

1463 to 1479 War between Ottoman Turks and Venetians; Turks win
1464 Africa: Songhai king Sonni 'Ali conquers lands along the Niger River
1467 to 1477 Japan: Onin civil war; ends Ashikaga shogunate's authority

Did You Know?

Don't be fooled: the 1989 movie War of the Roses, *starring Danny DeVito, Michael Douglas, and Kathleen Turner, is a satiric commentary on yuppie materialism, not a reenactment of the English war of the same name.*

1469 to 1492 Italy: Lorenzo de Medici ("the Magnificent") rules Florence
1470s Peru: Collapse of Chimu culture
1471 to 1493 South America: Emperor Topa Inca expands Inca Empire into Bolivia, Chile, and Argentina
1473 Mexico: Tenochtitlan absorbs neighboring Aztec city, Tlatelolco
1478 Russia: Muscovy defeats Novgorod

Spain: The Inquisition persecutes Jews, Muslims, and heretics
1479 Europe: Spain is unified by marriage and joint rule of Fernando, king of Aragon, and Isabella, queen of Castile; Turks wrest control of southern Adriatic from the Venetians

Did You Know?

A wooden stool supported by an ancestral figure was the symbol of royal power in Songhai.

1480 Italy: Lodovico Sforza seizes power in Milan
Russia: Moscow becomes the most powerful Russian city
1482 Africa: Portuguese explore Congo River estuary
1486 to 1502 Mexico: Rule of Aztec emperor Ahuitzotl; Aztec Empire at height of power
1488 Japan: First major Ikko-ikki, or Uprising of Ikko Buddhists
1491 to 1547 England: Henry VIII

Did You Know?

The Aztecs established a powerful empire based on conquest, tribute, and the religious sacrifice of animals and people.

1492 Caribbean: Columbus becomes first European to encounter Caribbean islands, returns to Spain (1493); second voyage to Dominica, Jamaica, Puerto Rico (1493 to 1496); third voyage to Orinoco (1498); fourth voyage to Honduras and Panama (1502 to 1504)
India: Sikander Lodi, sultan of Delhi (1489 to 1517), annexes Bihar and moves capital to Agra
Spain: Ferdinand and Isabella conquer the Moors
1493 to 1528 Africa: Zenith of Songhai Empire under King Askia Muhammed
1494: At Sforza's invitation, Charles VIII of France invades Italy; Treaty of Tordesilla: Pope divides Americas between Spain and Portugal, but the treaty is ignored by other European countries

Did You Know?

Henry VIII is often remembered for his determination to sire a legitimate son, which resulted in six marriages. (He did succeed in having the son, Edward.) His wives were Catherine of Aragon, Anne Boleyn, Jane Seymour, Anne of Cleves, Catherine Howard, and Catherine Parr. Use the British rhyme to remember their fate: "divorced, beheaded, died; divorced, beheaded, survived."

1495 Europe: French capture Naples but are forced to leave by an alliance of Spain, England, Venice, and Milan

1496 Caribbean: Santo Domingo, first European town in the Americas

1497 Canada: John Cabot, employed by England, reaches and explores Canadian coast; discovers Newfoundland

Africa and Asia: Vasco da Gama leaves Lisbon, rounds Cape of Good Hope, South Africa, and reaches India (1498); discovery of sea route to India signals beginning of colonial and commercial European presence; establishes Portuguese colony in India (1502)

1499 Louis XII of France seizes Milan

c. 1500 Greenland: Norse colony extinct

Part 2 Politics and Civilization

1501 to 1800

1501 to 1510 1500s Africa: Songhai Empire has greatest expansion and power; trade encourages growth of Hausa states in West Africa
Canada: French exploration in Canada begins
1501 to 1502 Brazil: Amerigo Vespucci explores coast
Italy: France and Spain occupy Naples
US: First black slaves in Americas brought to Spanish colony of Santo Domingo
1501 to 1524 Middle East: Reign of Ismail, first Safavid shah of Persia
1502 to 1504 Columbus's fourth voyage; he reaches Honduras, Nicaragua, Costa Rica, Panama, Colombia
Europe: War between France and Spain

Did You Know?

The Aztec civilization reached its height under Montezuma II (1502 to 1520) but was conquered by the Spanish under Hernán Cortés in 1519 to 1521.

1503 France: Defeated in battles of Cerignola and Garigliano
Russia: Basil III rules Moscow (to 1533)
1505 Treaty of Blois: France recognizes Spanish control of Naples
1505 to 1507 Africa: Portuguese capture Sofala on east coast and establish Mozambique; begin to trade with Africans
1506 Columbus dies in poverty
1507 Africa: Nzinga Mbemba becomes king of Congo
1508 Europe: League of Cambrai: Emperor Maximilian, Louis XII, and Ferdinand V ally against Venice
1509 England: Henry VIII ascends the throne
Battle of Diu establishes Portuguese control of Indian Seas
1510 Europe: Pope Julius II and Venice form Holy League to drive Louis XII from Italy

Did You Know?

Exploration has always been sparked by curiosity, but by the 1400s to 1500s, the great spur was trade. Europeans relied heavily on spices to preserve and flavor meat. Spices came from the East and had to be carried overland through the Near East at great expense, so finding a shorter water route would be a great economic coup.

1511 to 1520   1511 Europe: Ferdinand V and Henry VIII join Holy League
c. 1511 South Pacific: Portuguese navigators begin to explore Pacific
1512 Europe: Swiss join Holy League and drive French out of Milan
Turkey: Sultan Selim I rules (to 1520)
1512 to 1520 Europe: Russia and Poland at war
1513 China: Portuguese reach Canton
Italy: Battle of Novara: France forced to retreat from Milan
US: Spanish explorer Vasco Balboa becomes first European to encounter Pacific Ocean;
Ponce de León explores Florida
1514 War between Turkey and Persia; Battle of Chaldiran: Persia defeated
1515 France: François I becomes king (to 1547)
Battle of Marignano; Francis I of France defeats Swiss and regains Milan
1516 France: Treaty of Noyon between France and Spain; French give up claim to Naples
Middle East: War between Ottoman Empire and Egypt; Turks capture Cairo; end of
Mamluk Empire
Spain: Charles I becomes king (to 1556)

KEY DOCUMENT

John Keats' 1816 poem "On First Looking into Chapman's Homer" is famous
for its beauty—as well as its mistake: Keats believed that Cortés, not Balboa,
was the first European explorer to reach the Pacific. This matters to history,
but not to poetry. Here is the sonnet:

> Much have I traveled in the realms of gold,
>   And many goodley states and kingdoms seem;
>   Round many western islands have I been
> Which bards in fealty to Apollo hold.
> Oft of one wide expanse had I been told
>   That deep-browed Homer ruled as his demesne;
>   Yet did I never breathe its pure serene
> Till I heard Chapman speak out loud and bold:
> Then I felt like some watcher of the skies
>   When a new planet swims into his ken;
> Or like stout Cortez when with eagle eyes
>   He stared at the Pacific—and all his men
> Looked at each other with wild surmise—
>   Silent, upon a peak in Darien.

1517 Middle East: Ottomans conquer Egypt; Syria and Egypt added to Ottoman
Empire
1519 Charles, archduke of Austria (and king of Spain) becomes Holy Roman emperor
Charles V, the most powerful ruler in Europe
1519 to 1521 Mexico: Spanish adventurer Hernán Cortés conquers Mexico for Spain;
destroys Aztec Empire.
Middle East: Turks conquer Egypt, control Arabia

Portuguese under Ferdinand Magellan first to sail around the world. Magellan is killed in the Philippines in 1521 by local people, but one of his ships, under Juan Sebastián del Cano, continues around the world and reaches Spain (1522)
1520 Africa: Portuguese mission to Ethiopia
China: Portuguese traders reach China
Europe: Field of Cloth of Gold: François I of France meets Henry VIII of England but fails to gain his support against Holy Roman Emperor Charles V
Turkey: Suleiman I ("the Magnificent") becomes sultan of Turkey; invades Hungary (1521); Rhodes (1522); attacks Austria (1529); annexes Hungary (1541); Tripoli (1551); makes peace with Persia (1553); destroys Spanish fleet (1560); dies (1566)

Did You Know?

The Mamluks were slaves converted to Islam who advanced themselves to high military positions in Egypt. There were two ruling dynasties: the Bahri (1250 to 1382), comprised of Turks and Mongols, and the Burji (1382 to 1517), comprised of Circassians.

1521 to 1530   1521 Europe: Diet of Worms: Martin Luther is condemned as a heretic and excommunicated; France and Spain war over Italy; Turks capture Belgrade; Mexico: Cortés conquers the Aztec capital

Did You Know?

On November 8, 1519, Hernán Cortés (or Cortez) and his small force, aided by about 600 native allies, entered the capital city of Tenochtitlan and established headquarters. Because of an Aztec myth about Quetzalcoatl, a king who foretold future rule by white men, Cortez was believed to be a god and received with great honor. Despite this friendly welcome, Cortés took Montezuma hostage and demanded a ransom in gold and gems. Meanwhile, the Aztecs revolted. When he tried to quell the riot, Montezuma was stoned to death. The Aztecs drove out the Spanish and their allies in the famous "Sad Night" (Noche Triste, June 30, 1520). On August 31, 1521, Cortés seized the capital and new leader, Guatemotzin. Cortés razed the capital and built Mexico City on the ruins.

1522 Italy: Battle of Biocca: Charles V defeats the French, driving them from Milan
1523 Sweden: Gustavus I elected
1524 France: Invades Italy and recaptures Milan
Germany: Peasants' Revolt
Verrazano, sailing under the French flag, explores the New England coast and New York bay
1525 Battle of Pavia; François defeated by Charles V of Spain and forced to agree to the Treaty of Madrid

Pacific Islands: Portuguese probably visit Caroline Islands, northeast of New Guinea, and nearby Palau Islands

Did You Know?

The Turks called Suleiman I Kanuni, "the Lawgiver," because of his reforms of justice and administration; to Westerners he was called "the Magnificent" because of the splendor of his court and his many great military victories.

1526 India: Barbur (descendant of Mongol ruler Genghis Khan and of Tamerlane), first Moghul emperor, invades India; Moghul Empire established
South Pacific: Portuguese land on Papua New Guinea
Spain: Treaty of Madrid; François I of France renounces treaty and war begins again
Turkey: Battle of Mohacs: Turks defeat and kill Louis II of Bohemia and Hungary

Did You Know?

Although it sounds especially unappetizing, the Diet of Worms isn't a new food fad; rather, it was a legislative assembly that convened at the town of Worms. The first governmental body to be called a "diet" originated in the Frankish tribal councils.

1527 Ethiopia: Muslims from Harar invade; emperor asks Portuguese for help
Italy: Troops of the Holy Roman Empire attack Rome, imprison Pope Clement VII; the end of the Italian Renaissance; Medici family expelled from Florence

Did You Know?

Although the heyday of the Mongol (Moghul) Empire ended in the 1300s after the death of Kublai Khan, it had a brief revival under Tamerlane (who died in 1405) and a final revival with Tamerlane's descendant, Barbur. After invading India in 1526, Barbur became master of the Punjab. He soon established a new empire in India, called the Moghul Empire for the Persian version of the word "Mongol." Even though Barbur died in 1530, his empire lasted until the mid-1700s, when the British took over the country.

1528 Africa: Askia Musa seizes the throne from his father Askia Muhammed; soon after the Songhai Empire weakens
Hungary: Ferdinand of Austria succeeds to the throne
1529 England: Sir Thomas More appointed Lord Chancellor; Henry VIII calls the "Reformation Parliament" and severs ties with the Church of Rome
Europe: Peace of Cambrai between France and Spain; France renounces claims to Italy
Vienna: Turks attack the city, but are unsuccessful

1530 Switzerland: Catholics and Protestants fight civil war; Catholics win

c. 1530 Beginning of trans-Atlantic slave trade organized by Portuguese

Did You Know?

Today, the population of Ethiopia is nearly 60 million. The official language is Amharic, although Tigriny and Orominga are also spoken. The life expectancy is 39.8 years for men; 42.0 for females.

1531 to 1540   1532 England: Sir Thomas More resigns over issue of Henry VIII's divorce

Hungary: Turks invade but are defeated

1533 England: Henry marries Anne Boleyn and is excommunicated by Pope Clement VII

Peru: Francisco Pizarro, Spanish soldier, conquers Inca Empire

Russia: Ivan IV ("Ivan the Terrible") takes the throne (to 1584)

Peace between Suleiman I and Ferdinand of Austria

Did You Know?

Anne of the Thousand Days (1969), starring Genevieve Bujold, Irene Papas, Anthony Quayle, and Richard Burton, is an accurate and engrossing film version of the story of Anne Boleyn and King Henry VIII. The scenery is gorgeous, too.

1534 England: Oath of Supremacy—Henry VIII declared supreme head of Church of England

Turks capture Baghdad and Mesopotamia

Did You Know?

According to legend, Pizarro drew a line in the sand with his sword and asked the men who sought fame and fortune to cross it. The "famous thirteen" men who did make it to Peru accomplished their aim. Pizarro sent a priest to exhort Emperor Atahuallpa and his 3,000 to 4,000-member entourage to accept Christianity and Charles V; when Atahuallpa refused and threw the Bible to the ground, Pizarro's men attacked. On August 29, 1533, Pizarro had Atahuallpa strangled and occupied the capital, Cuzco, without a struggle.

1535 Africa: Charles V conquers Tunis

Chile: Spanish explore (to 1537)

England: Sir Thomas More executed for failing to take the Oath of Supremacy
Europe: War between France and Spain; Milan becomes a Spanish possession
1536 England: Henry VIII executes second wife, Anne Boleyn, and marries Jane Seymour
France: Invades Savoy and Piedmont; forms alliance with Turkey
Mexico: Cortés explores Baja California
1537 England: Jane Seymour dies in childbirth; the child is the future Edward VI
1538 Europe: Treaty of Nice between France and Spain

Did You Know?

On May 2, 1536, Anne Boleyn was imprisoned in the Tower of London on charges of adultery with her brother, three gentlemen of the privy chamber, and a court musician. She was also charged with conspiring with these men to assassinate Henry VIII. All the prisoners were convicted; the musician was hanged and the others beheaded. The next day, Henry was engaged to Jane Seymour.

1539 Europe: Treaty of Frankfurt between Charles V and Protestant princes
1540 England: Henry VIII marries Anne of Cleves; soon after Henry divorces Anne and marries Catherine Howard
US: Hernando de Soto discovers Mississippi River; Spaniard Hernando de Alarcón explores Colorado River
1540 to 1542 US: Spanish explorer Francisco Vásquez de Coronado explores southwest
1540s California: Spanish arrive in the region

Did You Know?

Spanish conquistador Francisco Vásquez de Coronado (1515 to 1554) and his men were the first Europeans to see the Grand Canyon; they spent the winter in what is now Santa Fe, NM.

1541 to 1550   1541 Hungary: Turks conquer the country
US: Hernando de Soto explores Mississippi River
1541 to 1564 Leadership of Protestant reformer John Calvin in Geneva, Switzerland
1542 England: Catherine Howard executed
Ethiopia: With assistance of Portuguese, Ethiopians defeat Muslims
Scotland: Battle of Solway Moss: King James V killed
1542 to 1567 Scotland: Reign of Queen Mary
1543 England: Henry VIII marries Catherine Parr
Europe: Alliance between Henry VIII and Charles V against Scotland and France
1544 France: Henry VIII and Charles V invade France
Treaty of Crepy between France and Spain
1546 Burma: Tabinshwehti conquers Pegu from the Mons and assumes title of King of All Burma

1547 England: King Edward VI takes the throne (to 1553)
Europe: Battle of Muhlberg: Charles V defeats the Schmalkaldic League
France: King Henry II takes the throne (to 1559)
Russia: Ivan IV ("the Terrible") crowned czar, begins conquest of Astrakhan and Kazan (1552); battles boyars (nobles) for power (1564); kills his son (1580); dies; and is succeeded by his weak and feebleminded son Fydor I

Did You Know?

Mary, Queen of Scots (1542 to 1587), daughter of King James V of Scotland and his second wife Mary of Guise, became a queen when she was just 1 week old. Her reign was far from peaceful. Her third marriage in 1567 to a Protestant turned the nobles against her. In 1567, Mary was forced to abdicate in favor of her son; the following year, she sought refuge in the court of Queen Elizabeth I only to be imprisoned for life. When it was discovered that Mary's page had plotted to assassinate Elizabeth, Mary was hanged.

1548 Netherlands: Holy Roman emperor Charles V annexes the country
1549 to 1551 Japan: Jesuit St. Francis Xavier comes to Japan

Did You Know?

Ivan IV really earned his nickname "the Terrible": In a fit of rage, he killed his eldest son (who was just as cruel), and one of his seven wives died under suspicious circumstances.

1550 Europe: Fall of duke of Somerset; duke of Northumberland succeeds as Protector
1551 to 1560   1551 Europe: Treaty of Friedenwalde between Saxony and France
Thailand: Bayinnaung inherits the Burmese throne and rules Thailand until 1581

Did You Know?

After Bayinnaung's death, succession squabbles and foreign encroachment (Portuguese along the coast, Siamese from the east, and Maniupri from the west) brought the decline of the Toungoo dynasty. It survived until the mid-1700s, however, thanks to a stable administrative and legal system.

1551 to 1562 Europe: Turkey and Hungary at war
1552 Europe: Charles V and Henry II battle; France seizes Toul, Metz, and Verdun; Peace of Passau between Saxony and Holy Roman Empire
1553 England: Lady Jane Grey becomes queen; reigns for nine days; Mary I takes the throne (to 1558)

1554 Africa: Turks conquer coast of North Africa
England: Lady Jane Grey executed

Did You Know?

Queen Mary I was the daughter of Henry VIII and his first wife, Catherine of Aragon.

1555 Peace of Ausgburg; states are free to introduce the Reformation and Protestant states are given equal rights with Catholic states
1556 India: Akbar the Great defeats Hindus at battle of Panipat and becomes Moghul emperor of India; conquers Afghanistan (1581); continues wars of conquest (until 1605)
Spain: Charles V of Spain abdicates

Did You Know?

Lady Jane, the 1985 film starring Helena Bonham Carter, Cary Elwes, John Wood, and Patrick Stewart, is a gripping historical drama about Lady Jane Grey, the teenager who ruled for just nine days. The film is well-acted and not hard on the eyes. Don't confuse the movie with the Rolling Stones' 1966 hit song "Lady Jane."

1556 to 1598 Reign of Philip II of Spain, son of Charles V
1557 China: Portuguese settle in Macao
Europe: Battle of St. Quentin; Spain and England defeat France
1557 to 1582 Europe: Livonian War; Poland, Russia, Sweden, and Denmark war over Balkan territory; Russia invades Poland
1558 England: Loses Calais, last English possession in France; Mary I dies; Elizabeth I takes the throne
Scotland: Mary, Queen of Scots, marries François, Dauphin of France

Did You Know?

Elizabeth I was the daughter of Henry VIII and his second wife, Anne Boleyn.

1558 to 1603 Reign of Elizabeth I of England; she restores Protestantism, establishes state Church of England (Anglicanism)

1559 Europe: Peace of Cateau-Cambresis ends Franco-Spanish war and confirms Spanish domination of Italy
France: François II becomes king (until 1560)
1560s Africa: First Portuguese embassies in Timbuktu
England: Treaty of Berwick between Elizabeth I and Scottish reformers
Treaty of Edinburgh: England, France, and Scotland
France: Charles IX takes the throne (to 1574)

1561 to 1570   1561 France: Persecution of Huguenots stopped by Edict of Orléans; French religious wars begin again with massacre of Huguenots at Vassy; St. Bartholomew's Day Massacre: thousands of Huguenots murdered (1572); amnesty granted (1573); persecution continues periodically until 1570; Edict of Nantes (1598) gives Huguenots religious freedom (until 1685)
Scotland: Mary, Queen of Scots, returns to Scotland
1562 Sir John Hawkins starts English slave trade, taking cargoes of slaves from West Africa to the Americas
Turkey: Truce between Turkey and Ferdinand I, Holy Roman emperor
1564 Europe: Peace of Troyes between England and France
Russia: Reign of Terror begins
1565 Malta: Turks attack, but fail
South America: Portuguese attack French colony

Did You Know?

The Republic of Malta, a 124-square-mile island in the center of the Mediterranean Sea, has been ruled by Phoenicians, Romans, Arabs, Normans, and the Knights of Malta. It became independent in 1964 and a republic in 1974.

1566 to 1574 Turkey: Selim II becomes sultan
1567 Scotland: Lord Darnley, Mary, Queen of Scots' husband, murdered; Mary marries Bothwell, is imprisoned, and forced to abdicate; James VI, her son, becomes king
South America: Portuguese settle at Rio de Janeiro
1568 Netherlands: Protestant Netherlands revolts against Catholic Spain; Spain acknowledges their independence in 1648
Scotland: Mary, Queen of Scots, escapes to England and is imprisoned by Elizabeth I

Did You Know?

In the late 1500s, Queen Amina ruled the Hausa city-state of Zaire in present-day Nigeria. As a young princess, Amina had many suitors, but she wanted to rule in her own right and so refused to marry. In a world of male rulers, she came to be known as the "headdress among the turbans."

1568 to c. 1600 Japan: National unification begins when feudal lord Oda Nobunaga captures capital, Kyoto

Did You Know?

In 1570, the Ottoman Turks invaded Cyprus, then owned by Venice. Because owning Venice would enable the Turks to dominate the Mediterranean, Pope Pius V assembled a fleet of over 200 ships under the command of Don John of Austria. This fleet battled an equal number of Turkish ships off Lepanto, Greece, on October 7, 1571. The fight lasted only three hours; all but forty of the Turkish ships were smashed or captured while the Christians lost only twelve ships. The battle marked the end of Turkish sea aggression in Europe.

1569 Europe: Union of Lublin merges Lithuania and Poland
1570 Europe: Turks attack Cyprus and war with Venice; Turkish fleet defeated at Battle of Lepanto by Spanish and Italian fleets (1571); Peace of Constantinople (1572) ends Turkish attacks on Europe
Japan: Permits visits of foreign ships
Russia: Ivan IV ravages Novgorod
c. 1570 to c. 1610 Africa: Kanem-Bornu kingdom in western Central Africa at its most powerful; alliance with the Ottomans brings firearms, military training, and Arab camel troops

1571 to 1580   1571 Africa: Bornu Empire in Sudan reaches zenith (until 1603)
Greece: Don John of Austria smashes Ottoman fleet at battle of Lepanto
1572 France: Massacre of St. Bartholomew: 8,000 Protestants die in Paris; at least 20,000 Protestants killed throughout France in two days
1573 Venice: Abandons Cyprus and makes peace with Turkey

Did You Know?

Catherine de Médicis, widow of Henri II, completely controlled her son Charles IX, who was only 10 when he became king. But in 1572, Catherine felt that Charles was being unduly influenced by the Huguenot leader Admiral Gaspard de Coligny. When her plan to assassinate Coligny failed, Catherine planned a mass killing of Huguenots in Paris in reaction to the marriage of Henri of Navarre to Catherine's daughter Marguerite. Coligny was killed, although Catherine spared Henri of Navarre.

1573 to 1620 China: Under Emperor Wan Li, painting and porcelain-making flourish; imperial kilns at Jingde Zhen produce vast quantities of ware
1574 Turkey regains Tunis from Spain
1575 to 1586 Stephen Batory, prince of Transylvania in Romania, elected king of Poland
c. 1575 Africa: Portuguese begin to colonize Angola; more than a century of warfare follows
Holland: Leiden University established as a secular institution open to all faiths
1576 Canada: Martin Frobisher, English explorer, sets out to find northwest passage to China; reaches Canadian coast, and Frobisher Bay is named after him.
France: Protestantism forbidden

1577 India: Akbar the Great unifies northern region
English seaman Francis Drake sails around the world (to 1580)
Europe: Alliance between Netherlands and England
1578 Battle of Al Kasr Al-kabil: Muslims defeat Portuguese
Netherlands: Duke of Parma subdues southern provinces
1579 Netherlands: Northern provinces form Union of Utrecht

Did You Know?

The Netherlands, located in northwest Europe on the North Sea, was first conquered in 55 BCE by Julius Caesar. After Charlemagne's empire fell apart, the region was split, passed to Burgundy, and then to Charles V of Spain.

1580 England: Francis Drake returns to England after circumnavigating the globe; knighted by Queen Elizabeth I (1581)
Portugal: Spanish conquer the country

1581 to 1590   1581 Poland invades Russia
Union of Utrecht declares itself the Dutch Republic, independent of Spain; William of Orange elected ruler

Did You Know?

William III, also called William of Orange, was a brilliant international tactician; at home, unfortunately, he displayed no such skill. Parliament, to which he was often opposed, brought about the significant reforms of his reign, such as the Bill of Rights, the establishment of the Bank of England, and a free press.

1582 Russia, Poland, and Sweden make peace
1584 The Netherlands: Philip II of Spain has William of Orange assassinated
Russia: Fedor I crowned czar
US: Sir Walter Raleigh sends exploring party to Virginia, followed a year later by a colonizing expedition that fails

Did You Know?

The explorers' boats were small—about 70 feet long on average; even Columbus's flagship was only about 117 feet long.

1585 Europe: "War of the Three Henrys": Henri III of France, Henri of Navarre, and Henri of Guise
Netherlands: England sends troops to Dutch Republic

1586 England: Mary, Queen of Scots, plots against Queen Elizabeth I; Francis Drake sails to West Indies

1587 England: Mary, Queen of Scots, executed for treason by order of Queen Elizabeth I; England at war with Spain

Did You Know?

The quarrels between England and Spain went beyond religious issues: Spain rejected English claims to territory in the Americas and resented English privateers plundering Spanish ships.

1587 to 1629 Persia: Shah Abbas I ("the Great") consolidates and expands territories

1588 Europe: English defeat Spanish armada, marking emergence of England as great sea power

France: Henri of Guise murdered

1589 France: Henri III murdered; Protestant leader Henry, king of Navarre, recognized as Henry IV, first Bourbon king of France; he converts to Roman Catholicism in 1593 in an attempt to end religious wars

Portugal: Antonio of Crato marches on Lisbon but is defeated by Spanish

1590 France: Henry IV enters Paris; wars on Spain (1595); marries Marie de Medici (1600); and is assassinated (1610)

Japan: Unified under Hideyoshi

Turkey: Peace between Turkey and Persia

Did You Know?

During this time, the English were well prepared for invasions: They lit beacons to warn of the approaching Spanish armada and the message traveled across the country in only eighteen minutes. The heavily armed Spanish invaded with about 130 warships; fewer than 60 returned home. The English did not lose a single ship.

1590 to 1591 Africa: Spanish and Portuguese mercenaries destroy Songhai Empire

c. 1590 to 1605 Burma breaks up into small states

Did You Know?

The Moroccans easily crushed the Songhai army because they were armed with arquebuses, a type of early gun invented in Europe. Soldiers armed with guns could quickly destroy an army armed with swords, spears, and bows and arrows.

1591 to 1600   1592 Korea: Hideyoshi leads Japanese invasion (to 1598)

India: Akbar the Great conquers Sind

1593 to 1606 War between Austria and Turkey
1595 Africa: First Dutch settlements on Guinea coast
Russia and Sweden: Sweden gains Estonia in Treaty of Teusina
1596 Hungary: Battle of Keresztes gives Turkish victory
1597 Ireland: Hugh O'Neill foments rebellion; quelled 1601
c. 1598 to 1617 US: American Indian princess Pocahontas
1598 Europe: Treaty of Vervins between Spain and France; all conquests restored to France
France: Edict of Nantes, granting civil rights to French Protestants
Russia: Rurikovich dynasty ends with death of Fedor I; Boris Godunov named czar
1598 to 1613 Russia: Period of Chaos and two False Dimitris
c. 1598 Africa: First Dutch trading posts established on Guinea coast
1599 Ireland: Rebels defeat the earl of Essex; he returns to England in disgrace
Poland: Confederation of Vilna
1600 England: English East India Company established
Japan: Battle of Sekigahara; Tokugawa Ieyasu defeats rivals and takes power; the Tokugawa (Edo) period begins
1600s Africa: Kalonga kingdom, north of Zambezi River, becomes rich through ivory trade; Hausaland dominates trade routes to Sahara; Great Zimbabwe replaced by several regional capitals in Transvaal, Botswana, and Zimbabwe
Tonga: Tu'i Konokupolu dynasty replaces Tu'i Tonga

1601 to 1610   1601 England: Essex rebellion against Elizabeth I fails; Essex is executed
1602 Europe: Savoy attacks Geneva; Protestant cantons ally with France
1602 to 1618 Persia: Holy war between Turkey and Persia; Persia conquers Tabriz, Erivan, Shrivan, and Kars
1603 England: James I (King James VI of Scotland) inherits English throne
Dutch East India Company formed
Japan: Tokugawa Iyeyasu names himself shogun (ruler); moves capital to Edo (Tokyo)
Scotland: King James VI of Scotland becomes James I of England (to 1625)
US: Samuel de Champlain explores St. Lawrence River
1604 French East India Company formed
Russia: Time of Troubles begins; people begin to settle in Siberia
US: Samuel de Champlain explores Maine Coast

Did You Know?

The Hausa of Africa had a proverb: "Better to live at peace than at a palace."
Nonetheless, Hausa kingdoms often fought with one another, trying to increase
their land and wealth. No Hausa king or queen was ever strong enough to unite
all the Hausa states into one kingdom.

1605 England: Gunpowder Plot fails
Russia: Czar Fedor II deposed and murdered
1606 Australia: William Jansz sights the continent
England: King James charters the London and Plymouth companies

Europe: Treaty of Zsitva-Torok between Turks and Austrians; Austria gives up
Transylvania but no longer pays tribute to Turkey
Russia: Czar Basil Shuisky (to 1610); peasant uprisings
South Pacific: Luis Vaez de Torres from Spain sails around New Guinea and reaches
straits now named after him
1607 Canada: Henry Hudson explores Canada
Cuba: Havana named the capital
US: John Smith founds Jamestown, first permanent English settlement in America;
Pocahontas, daughter of Chief Powhatan, saves John Smith's life

Did You Know?

*The British holiday Guy Fawkes Day (November 5) commemorates a conspirator
in the Gunpowder Plot.*

1608 Canada: Samuel de Champlain establishes French colony of Quebec
1609 US: English navigator Henry Hudson explores Hudson River
Holland: Twelve-Year Truce; Spain acknowledges Holland's independence
1610 England: The Great Contract: James I gets an annual income of £200,000
France: Henri IV assassinated; Louis XIII becomes king of France (to 1643)
Russia: Czar Basil Shruisky deposed; throne offered to Wladyslaw, son of king of Poland

1611 to 1620   1611 Europe: Plantation of Ulster: English and Scottish Protestants settle in Ulster
1611 to 1632 Sweden: Reign of Gustavus Adolphus of Sweden
1613 Russia: Michael Romanov elected first Romanov czar

KEY DOCUMENT

Captain John Smith claimed that Pocahontas saved his life. As Smith reports:
    . . . having feasted him after their best barbarous manner they could, a
long consultation was held, but the conclusion was, two great stones were
brought before Powhatan; then as many as could, laid hands on him,
dragged him to them, and thereon laid his head and being ready with their
clubs to beat out his brains, Pocahontas, the King's dearest daughter, when
no entreaty could prevail, got his head in her arms and laid her own upon
his to save him from death, whereat the Emperor was contented he [Smith]
should live to make him hatchets, and her bells, beads, and copper, for they
thought him as well of all occupations as themselves.
Many historians doubt the story is true.

1614 England: James I dissolves the "Addled Parliament," which had failed to pass any
legislation
France: Estates General summoned to curb nobility

Japan: Shogun Iyeyasu deports all Christian priests and orders Japanese to give up Christianity

1615 China: Tribes in northern region form military organizations, later called Manchus

1616 English navigator William Baffin explores the bay that now bears his name

Did You Know?

Gustavus Adolphus of Sweden was nicknamed "Lion of the North" because of his skill as a warrior and home in Scandinavia.

1617 Ferdinand II becomes king of Bohemia

1618 Africa: French explorer Paul Imbert reaches Timbuktu

Europe: Start of the Thirty Years' War, the Protestant revolt against Catholic oppression; Denmark, Sweden, and France invade Germany in later phases of war

1619 Europe: Ferdinand II becomes Holy Roman emperor, and together with Bavaria and the Holy League goes to war with Bohemia

US: First representative assembly in America held in Jamestown; first African slaves brought to Jamestown

Did You Know?

The Thirty Years' War (1618 to 1648) began with an argument over who should become the next Holy Roman emperor. The war ended with the Peace of Westphalia, which gave France part of Alsace and Lorraine. Germany lay in ruins, with millions dead.

1619 to 1624   Dutch establish virtual monopoly of spice trade in Moluccas and other Indonesian islands

France: Richelieu chief minister

1620 Europe: Battle of the White Mountain: Frederick V defeated by Maximilan of Bavaria

US: *Mayflower* lands in Massachusetts; Mayflower Compact written, laying foundation for democracy in America

Did You Know?

Pocahontas (Native American name Matoaka), daughter of the ruling chief and founder of the Powhatan confederacy of the Algonquians, was captured by the British in 1612, taken to Jamestown, and baptized Rebecca. In 1614, she married John Rolfe, a colonist. Four years later she traveled to England and was received by the king and queen with great honor. Pocahontas died of an illness on the eve of her return to Virginia.

1620s Angola: Queen Nzinga of Ndongo fights Portuguese
Japan: National policy restricts contact with outside world

KEY DOCUMENT
Mayflower Compact (1620)
(from Book II, Chapter XI, William Bradford's *Of Plymouth Plantation*)

I shall return a little back, and begin with a combination [a form of union] made by them before they came ashore; being the first foundation of their government in this place. Occasioned partly by discontented and mutinous speeches that some of the strangers [nonchurch members] amongst them had let fall from them in the ship: That when they came ashore they would use their own liberty, for none had power to command them, the patent they had being for Virginia and not for New England, which belonged to another government, with which the Virginia Company had nothing to do. And partly that such an act by them done, this their condition considered, might be as firm as any patent, and in some respects more sure.

The form was as followeth:
IN THE NAME OF GOD, AMEN.

We whose names are underwritten, the loyal subjects of our dread Sovereign Lord King James, by the Grace of God of Great Britain, France, and Ireland King, Defender of the Faith, etc.

Having undertaken for the glory of God and advancement of the Christian Faith and Honour of our King and Country, a Voyage to plant the First Colony in the Northern Parts of Virginia, do by these presents solemnly and mutually in the presence of God and one of another, Covenant and Combine ourselves together in the Civil Body Politic, for our better ordering and preservation and furtherance of the ends aforesaid; and by virtue hereof enact, constitute and frame such just and equal Laws, Ordinances, Acts, and Constitutions and Offices, from time to time, as shall be thought most meet and convenient for the general good of the Colony, unto which we promise all due submission and obedience. In witness whereof we have hereunder subscribed our names at Cape Cod, the 11th of November, in the year of the reign of our Sovereign Lord King James, of England, France, and Ireland the eighteenth, and of Scotland the fifty-fourth. Anno Domini 1620.

1621 to 1630   1621 China: Nurhachi expels Ming and establishes Manchu capital
Europe: Ferdinand II of the Holy Roman Empire becomes king of Hungary
1622 England: James I dissolves Parliament for asserting the right to debate foreign issues
Europe: Spain and France at war
1623 Dutch massacre English at Amboina
1624 Europe: Alliance between James I and France
US: Virginia becomes a crown colony

1625 Caribbean: French settlements begin (St. Christopher)
England: Charles I becomes king (to 1649)
Europe: Christian IV, Protestant king of Denmark, enters war against Ferdinand II
US: Dutch found New Amsterdam (later New York).

Did You Know?

Virginia boasts many fascinating tourists sites, including Colonial Williamsburg, Arlington National Cemetery, Mt. Vernon, Yorktown, Monticello, Lexington, and Appomattox. Virginia's tourism Web site is http://www.virginia.org.

1626 Madagascar: First French settlements
1627 Bohemia: New constitution confirms hereditary Habsburg rule
Europe: Siege of La Rochelle: Richelieu attacks Huguenots at La Rochelle
Korea: Manchus overrun Korea, which later becomes vassal state
1628 England: Petition of Right; Parliament curtails king's powers
c. 1628 Burma: Breaks up into small states
1628 to 1658 India: Reign of Moghul emperor Shah Jahan

Did You Know?

Over 20,000 men worked for 22 years to build the Taj Mahal in Agra, a monument built by Shah Jahan to house the body of his beloved second wife, Mumtaz Mahal ("The Chosen of the Palace"). She died in childbirth in 1630 at the age of 39, after having born him fourteen children.

1629 England: Charles I dissolves Parliament and rules alone until 1640
Europe: Treaty of Lubeck between Ferdinand II and Christian IV
1630 Europe: England makes peace with Spain and France
Persia: Turks take Hamadan
US: About 16,000 English colonists settle in Massachusetts Bay

1631 to 1640   1631 Catholics sack Magdeburg
Europe: Battle of Leipzig: Swedish and Saxon forces defeat Tilly
1632 Europe: Battle of Lutzen: Swedish victory but Gustavus Adolphus II killed
US: Dutch West India Company founds New Netherlands; Lord Baltimore founds Maryland

Did You Know?

When Swedish king Gustavus Adolphus II entered the Thirty Years' War, some of his opponents called him the "Snow King" and jeered that he would melt in the warmer south. Gustavus proved a fierce warrior, however, killing the count of Tilly, a fierce Roman Catholic general. Gustavus died bravely, leading a cavalry charge.

1632 to 1654 Sweden: Reign of Queen Christina
1633 US: Colony of Connecticut founded
1634 Battle of Nordlingen: Imperial forces defeat Swedish
Europe: Treaty of Polianov between Poland and Russia
1635 France declares war on Spain
Treaty of Prague: Ferdinand II revokes Edict of Restitution and makes peace with Saxony
1638 Baghdad: Turks conquer Iraq
Japan: Shimbara uprising; slaughter of Japanese Christians eliminates Christianity from country
1640 England: "Long Parliament" begins
Portugal: Gains independence from Spain
Spain: Revolt in Catalonia

Did You Know?

By 1641, only the Dutch maintained a trading post in Japan; all the other Europeans had been driven out. Japan was virtually cut off from the rest of the world and remained that way until the US forced a trade agreement—at gunpoint—in 1854.

1641 to 1650   1641 Asia: Dutch capture Malacca on the Malay peninsula
England: Triennial Act requires Parliament to be summoned every three years
1642 Canada: Montreal founded
England: Civil War begins; Cavaliers, supporters of Charles I, against Roundheads, parliamentary forces; Oliver Cromwell defeats Royalists (1646); parliament demands reforms; Charles I offers concessions, brought to trial (1648), beheaded (1649); Cromwell becomes Lord Protector (1653)
1642 to 1644 South Pacific: Abel Tasman reaches Tasmania and New Zealand
1643 England: Solemn League and Covenant
Europe: Battle of Rocroi: France defeats Spain
Denmark and Sweden war for Baltic supremacy (to 1645)
US: Colony of Maryland established
1644 China: Ming dynasty ends in China; Qing (Manchus) come to power
England: Battle of Marston Moor: Oliver Cromwell defeats Prince Rupert

Did You Know?

During the English Civil War, the "Roundheads" were so-called because of their close-cropped hair; the Royalists were called "Cavaliers" from their superiority in cavalry.

1645 Africa: Capuchin monks voyage down Congo River
Greece: Turkey and Venice at war over Crete
Russia: Alexis I succeeds his father, Michael

1646: English colonize the Bahamas
England: Oliver Cromwell defeats Royalists; Charles surrenders to the Scots
1647 England: Scots surrender Charles I to Parliament; he escapes to the Isle of Wight and makes secret treaty with Scots
1648 England: Thirty Years' War ends with Treaty of Westphalia; Presbyterians expelled from Parliament
Europe: Dutch and Swiss republics independent
France: Revolt of the Fronde against Louis XIV (to 1649)
1649 England: Charles I executed; England proclaimed a republic; beginning of Commonwealth and Protectorate, known inclusively as the Interregnum (1649 to 1660)
Ireland: Oliver Cromwell tries to force Irish off their land
Russia: Serfdom fully established as law

Did You Know?

Oliver Cromwell (1599 to 1658), the most important leader of the English revolution, was the dictator of England from 1653 until his death. Cromwell was buried with honor in Westminster Abbey, but after the restoration of Charles II in 1660, his body was dug up and hanged, his head put on a pole mounted above Westminster Hall, and his body buried at the foot of the gallows.

1650 France: Second revolt of the Fronde suppressed
Scotland: Charles II lands in Scotland
1650s Africa: Portuguese clash with Muslims in Zambezi region

1651 to 1660   1651 England: Charles II invades; defeated at Battle of Worcester; escapes to France; first Navigation Act gives England foreign trade monopoly
1652 Africa: Anglo-Dutch War; Dutch found Cape Town in South Africa
Spain: End of Catalan revolt
1653 England: Cromwell dissolves Parliament, takes the title "Lord Protector," and rules as dictator

Did You Know?

The violent reactions Oliver Cromwell provoked in life and death have persisted in history. Royalists vilified him for killing the king; republicans cursed him for betraying the revolution. In the nineteenth century, historian Thomas Carlyle buffed Cromwell's image by portraying him sympathetically in his book On Heroes *(1841).*

1654 Brazil: Portuguese take Brazil from Dutch
1655 English capture Jamaica from Spanish
Sweden declares war on Poland
1656 Venetians win victory over Turks in Dardanelles
Russia, Denmark, and Holy Roman Empire declare war on Sweden
1657 to 1661 Portugal and Dutch Republic at war

1658 England: Cromwell dies; Puritan government collapses
Europe: Battle of the Dunes; England and France defeat Spain; England gains Dunkirk
1658 to 1707 India: Aurangzeb is last great Moghul emperor; after 1707, empire begins to break up

Did You Know?

Louis XIV of France summed up his position as absolute ruler with the now-famous phrase: "L'etat, c'est moi"—"I am the state."

1659 Peace of the Pyrenees ends Franco-Spanish War, confirms Spanish decline, and beginning of France's rise.
1660 Africa: Rise of Bambara kingdoms on upper Niger
England: Monarchy restored; Charles II agrees to respect the Magna Carta and Petition of Rights
Europe: Treaty of Oliva: Poland gives Livonia to Sweden
Scandinavia: Treaty of Copenhagen: Denmark surrenders territory to Sweden
1660s Africa: Mawlay-al-Rashid restores sultanate of Morocco

1661 to 1670   1661 China: Koxinga takes Formosa
England: Charles II crowned king of England
Europe: Treaty of Kardis: Russia and Sweden restore all conquests to each other
France: Louis XIV begins personal rule as absolute monarch; starts building Versailles
India: English acquire Bombay
1661 to 1722 China: Kangxi emperor extends territory and supports scholarship

Did You Know?

Formosa, now called Taiwan, consists of one large and several smaller islands about 100 miles off the southeast coast of mainland China.

1662 Portuguese give Tangier to England
1664 Thailand: Dutch force king of Thailand to give them monopoly in deerskin exports and seaborne trade with China
US: British take New Amsterdam from the Dutch, changing the name to New York
1665 England: Great Plague
Second Anglo-Dutch War (to 1667)
1666 England: Great Fire ravages London
1667 War of Devolution: France invades Spanish Netherlands
Russia: Treaty of Andrussovo: Russia gains Smolensk and eastern Ukraine from Poland
1668 Europe: Triple Alliance: Netherlands, England, and Sweden against France
Europe: Treaty of Lisbon: Spain recognizes Portugal's independence

Treaty of Aix-la-Chapelle ends War of Devolution; France keeps most conquests in Flanders
1669 Greece: Venice surrenders Crete to Turkey

KEY DOCUMENT

In his diary, Samuel Pepys records these observations on the Great Fire:

> So near the fire as we could see for smoke; and all over the Thames, with one's face in the wind, you were almost burned with a shower of firedrops. This is very true; so as houses were burned by these drops and flakes of fire, three or four, nay, five or six houses, one from another. When we could endure no more on the water, we went to a little alehouse on the Bankside, over against the Three Cranes, and there stayed till it was dark almost, and saw the fire grow; and, as it grew darker, appeared more and more, and in corners and upon steeples, and between churches and houses, as far as we could see up the hill of the city, in a most horrid malicious bloody flame, not like the fine flame of an ordinary fire.

1670s Africa: French settle in Senegal; Fulani pastoral people gain control of Bondu in southern Senegal
Russia: Peasant uprisings
1672 Europe: Treaty of Stockholm between Sweden and France
Netherlands: Third Anglo-Dutch War; William III reigns
Russia: Turkey and Poland war for control of Ukraine (until 1676)

1671 to 1680   1673 England: Test Act allows only members of Anglican Church to hold public office
US: French explorers Jacques Marquette and Louis Jolliet explore the Arkansas River
1674 Europe: Treaty of Westminster between England and Netherlands
Holy Roman Empire declares war on France in defense of Dutch
1675 Battle of Fehrbellin: Frederick William of Brandenburg defeats Swedish
US: King Philip's War in New England; Native Americans against settlers

Did You Know?

By the late 1600s, waves of land-hungry settlers kept pushing farther into New England's Indian territory. In 1662, King Philip (Native American name Metacom), vowed to resist further English expansion by organizing the Narraganset, Nipmuck, Abnaki, and Mohawk tribes. The war erupted when settlers executed three Wampanogs for the murder of an informer. The Native Americans were winning until 1676, when their crops were destroyed and the English started using converted Indians as scouts. Following Philip's death that summer, Native American resistance collapsed. The war was devastating: entire tribes were wiped out and more than 600 settlers died. After their victory, the settlers expanded without fear into former Indian territory in New England.

1676 Europe: Treaty of Zuranvo; Turkey gains Polish Ukraine
India: Sikh uprising (to 1678)
1677 to 1682 Russia and Turkey at war
1678 England: Popish Plot: Titus Oakes falsely alleges a Catholic plot to murder
Charles II
1679 England: Habeas Corpus Act guarantees protection from arbitrary arrest.
Parliament dismissed; Charles II rejects petitions for new parliament; petitioners become
known as *Whigs;* opponents (Loyalists) become known as *Tories*
1679 to 1680s Africa: Rise of Asante kingdom in West Africa
1680 France: Louis XIV establishes Chambers of Reunion to annex territory; France
occupies Strasbourg, Luxemburg, Lorraine
1680s Africa: Butua kingdom flourishes in Zimbabwe plains; Portuguese are driven into
Zambezi Valley and eastward

Did You Know?

Easter Island is famous for its tall stone statues in human form, which stand on
stone platforms called ahus. The ahus are situated on bluffs that command a
view of the sea. Each ahu supports four to six statues, although one ahu, known
as Tongariki, has fifteen statues. Within many of the ahus, vaults contain
individual or group burials.

South Pacific: Statue building ends on Easter Island; resources and population decline;
civil war erupts

1681 to 1690   1681 England: Whigs reintroduce Exclusion Bill; Charles II dissolves Parliament
Russia: Treaty of Radzin: Russian gains most of Turkish Ukraine
1681 to 1682 US: Frenchman La Salle explores Mississippi River from source to mouth,
and founds Louisiana
1682 Ethiopia: Yasus the Great (ruled 1682 to 1706) last strong ruler before long decline
in which Ethiopia breaks up into separate regions
Russia: Ivan V and Peter of Russia co-rulers
US: William Penn establishes Pennsylvania

Did You Know?

Peter the Great was determined to make Russia a great world power. To that
end, he fought constantly: only one year of his 43-year reign passed without war.
Everything went for the war effort: even the Moscow church bells were melted
down to make cannon balls.

1683 Europe: War of European powers against the Turks (to 1699); Vienna withstands
three-month Turkish siege; high point of Turkish advance in Europe
Formosa (Taiwan) becomes Chinese territory

1684 Pope Innocent XI forms Holy Roman League: Venice, Austria, and Poland against Turkey

1685 England: James II inherits throne; passes laws to grant rights to Catholics and dissolves many anti-Irish laws

France: Revocation of the Edict of Nantes; only Roman Catholicism allowed

1686 Africa: Louis XIV of France officially annexes Madagascar

League of Augsburg formed

US: Dominion of New England formed

1687 Battle of Mohacs: Turks defeated; Habsburg succession to Hungarian throne confirmed

1688 England: "Glorious Revolution"; James II flees to Ireland; William and Mary become joint rulers

1689 England: Bill of Rights passed

Europe: Grand Alliance of the League of Augsburg, England, and the Netherlands

Ireland: James II's rebellion fails

King William's War between the British and the French

Russia: Sophia forced off Russian throne; Peter the Great becomes Czar of Russia and attempts to westernize nation and build Russia as a military power; defeats Charles XII of Sweden at Poltava

Russia and China: Treaty of Nerchinsk

Did You Know?

The 1689 English Bill of Rights established a constitutional monarchy and barred Roman Catholics from the throne.

US: French and Indian War (to 1763): Campaigns in North America linked to series of wars between France and England for domination of Europe

1690 Europe: Turks retake Belgrade from Austrians

India: Job Charnock founds the city of Calcutta, on a swamp by the Hooghly River in Bengal

Ireland: William III defeats former King James II and Irish rebels at Battle of the Boyne

Did You Know?

By the end of the Salem witchcraft trials, nineteen people and three dogs were executed as witches. Eighteen of the people were hanged and one, Giles Corey, pressed to death. Corey refused to answer the indictment; thus, he could not be convicted and his land would be passed down intact to his sons.

1691 to 1700   1692 Scotland: Massacre of Glencoe

US: Salem witch trials

1694 England: William III becomes sole ruler
Russia: Ivan V and Peter of Russia rule
1696 Poland: Augustus II is elected leader
Russia: Ivan V dies; Peter the Great makes secret visits to western Europe

---

KEY DOCUMENT

Cotton Mather recorded the testimony at the witchcraft trials. Mather reported that Phoebe Chandler claimed "she heard a voice, that she took to be Martha Carrier's, and it seemed as if it was over her head. The voice told her she should within two or three days be poisoned. Accordingly, within such a little time, one half of her right hand became greatly swollen and very painful; as is also part of her face; whereof she can give no actual account how it came. It continued very bad for some days."

1697 Turkey: Battle of Zenta: Eugene of Savoy defeats Turks
US: King William's War ends
1698 Africa: Portuguese expelled from Mombasa on eastern coast
Canada: Father Hennepin reaches Niagara Falls
1699 Treaty of Karlowitz; Habsburgs gain almost all of Hungary
1700 Europe: Great Northern War (to 1721); rivalry between Russia and Sweden
Spain: Charles II names Philip of Anjou as heir
Russia: Calendar reformed

Did You Know?

The death of Charles II of Spain in 1700 provoked a crisis as Europe's rulers rallied behind the three claimants for the throne: Philip of Anjou, Archduke Charles of Austria, and Prince Elector Joseph Ferdinand. The Treaty of Utrecht settled the conflict; Philip was acknowledged as king of Spain.

1701 to 1710 1701 England: Act of Settlement establishes Protestant Hanoverian succession in England
Europe: Grand Alliance among England, Netherlands, Holy Roman emperor Leopold I, and German states against France
Poland: Charles XII of Sweden invades
War of Spanish Succession (to 1713)
1700s Caribbean: European settlers explore the Caribbean
South Pacific: First contact between Tahitians and Europeans; they meet in Opunohu Valley on Moorea Island
US: North American colonies begin to prosper
1701 Africa: Osei Tutu creates free Asante nation in West Africa
England: Act of Settlement restricts throne to Anglicans

US: Antoine de Cadillac establishes Detroit to control passage between Lakes Erie and Huron

1702 US: Queen Anne's War (1702 to 1713), second of the four North American wars waged between the British and the French; called the War of the Spanish Succession in England, it ends with the Peace of Utrecht (1714) and marks the rise of the British Empire

1703 Europe: Methuen Agreement, trade treaty between England and Portugal
Russia: St. Petersburg founded; becomes capital of Russia in 1713

1704 Europe: Battle of Blenheim
US: Massachusetts Bay colonists massacred by French and Indians at Deerfield

1705 Turks overthrown in Tunis
c. 1705 Africa: Bey Husain ibn Ali founds dynasty at Tunis in North Africa
France: Battle of Ramillies: Duke of Marlborough defeats French

Did You Know?

Printer, diplomat, author, philosopher, scientist, and statesman: Benjamin Franklin is ranked among America's greatest citizens. In 1731, he established the first public library in America; around 1744 he invented the Franklin stove, which generated greater heat using less fuel. But his greatest accomplishments are based on his diplomatic skill. Urging his colleagues to sign the Declaration of Independence, *Franklin said: "We must all hang together, or assuredly we shall all hang separately."*

1706 to 1790 Benjamin Franklin
1707 India: Death of Moghul emperor Aurangzeb, followed by breakup of empire
England: Great Britain formed: England, Wales, and Scotland joined by parliamentary Act of Union

1708 Russia: Charles XII invades the country
1709 Europe: Battle of Malplaquet; French defeated but more than 20,000 soldiers killed
Japan: Death of shogun Tsunayoshi
Middle East: Ghilzai people under Mir Vais defeat Persian army; Afghanistan no longer province of Persian Empire

1710 Africa: Dey becomes pasha in Algiers, controlling northern Algeria
Kuwait: Sheik Sabah bin Jaber leads his clan into Kuwait and within the next 20 years becomes unofficial ruler
Russia: Cyrillic alphabet reformed

Did You Know?

The Cyrillic alphabet, created in the ninth century for Eastern Orthodox Slavs, is based on Greek characters.

1711 to 1720   1711 US: Tuscarora War between settlers and Native Americans in North Carolina
1712 US: New York Slave Rebellion in which Native Americans and African slaves
united
1712 to 1786 Prussia: Frederick the Great
1713 British take Mauritius in the Indian Ocean
1714 England: King George I succeeds to throne
France captures Mauritius

Did You Know?

*In addition to ruling his empire quite ably and boosting Prussia's reputation
around the world, Frederick the Great found time to play the flute, complete
thirty volumes of writings, and patronize the arts and sciences.*

US: Treaty of Utrecht ends War of Spanish Succession; Iroquois recognized as British
subjects
1715 England: First Jacobite rising attempts to restore exiled Stuart dynasty to throne
US: Yamasee nation attacks South Carolina colony killing hundreds of English settlers
1716 Canada: French build strong fortress
Spain: Seizes Sardinia from Austria
Tibet: Manchu emperor Kangxi sends troops to expel Junkar people from Tibet
1716 to 1745 Japan: Shogun Tokugawa Yoshimune rules; great reformer
1717 South America: Spain establishes viceroyalty of New Granada
1718 Europe: Quadruple Alliance of Austria, Britain, France, and Netherlands against
Spain

Did You Know?

*Famous Texans include entertainer Carol Burnett, presidents Dwight D.
Eisenhower and Lyndon Johnson, governor Sam Houston, industrialist Howard
Hughes, singer Janis Joplin, politician Barbara Jordan, writer Katherine Anne
Porter, and athlete Mildred "Babe" Didrikson Zaharias.*

US: City of New Orleans established
1718 to 1720 US: Texas becomes Spanish possession
1720 England: South Sea Bubble—financial scandal
Japan: Shogun Yoshimune repeals the laws against European books and study
Russia: Peter the Great signs trade treaty with China
Tibet: Kangxi enthrones seventh Dalai Lama as tributary ruler
1720s Africa: Yoruba state of Oyo still dominates region west of the Niger River

1721 to 1730   1721 to 1742 England: Robert Walpole is first and longest-serving British prime minister
Russia: Treaty of Nystadt between Russia and Sweden confirms Russia as great world
power
1722 China: Death of Manchu emperor Kangxi

Did You Know?

The Yoruba, a Nigerian people, are known today for their literary and artistic accomplishments.

South Pacific: Dutch navigator Roggeveen reaches Samoa Islands and Easter Island in Pacific

1722 to 1723 Africa: Asante conquer kingdom of Bono-Mansu north of Akan region, West Africa

1722 to 1735 China: Rule of Manchu emperor Yongzheng; Treaty of Kiakhta signed with Russia to define Siberian-Mongolian border

1724 India: Asaf Jah, a minister of the Moghul emperor, retires to the Deccan; declared first Nizam of Hyderabad

India achieves independence from Moghuls

1724 to 1734 Africa: King Agaja of Dahomey in West Africa disrupts slave trade; it is reintroduced in 1740s

1725 Russia: Catherine I takes throne

Did You Know?

Shrewd and courageous, Catherine I (1682? to 1727) was a Lithuanian peasant who rose from being a servant to being the empress of Russia. When Peter the Great died without naming an heir, Catherine became empress because she had built up a strong network of support, having often interceded on the victim's behalf when Peter flew into one of his frequent rages.

c. 1725 Africa: Fulani Muslim cleric Alfa Ibrahim appointed "Commander of the Faithful" in Futa Jalon

1726 Uruguay: Spanish establish Montevideo to stop further Portuguese colonization south of Brazil

1727 Africa: Death of Mulai Ismail followed by 30 years of anarchy in Morocco

Brazil: Diamonds discovered in Minas Gerais area

Did You Know?

Diamond, a mineral form of carbon, is the hardest known substance. Because they are excellent conductors of heat, diamonds are cold to the touch. Remember this the next time you buy a diamond!

England: George II takes the throne

Europe: Spain wars with England and France (until 1729)

Russia: Peter II crowned emperor

1729 China: Yongzheng sets up Grand Council, informal military advisers
1730 India: Maratha government (to 1735)
Russia: Anna becomes empress

1731 to 1740   1730s Danish explorer Vitus Bering reaches strait between Asia and North America now named after him
1732 to 1799 George Washington
1732 US: Georgia established
1733 War of Polish Succession (to 1735)
1734 France invades Lorraine
1735 Nadir Shah, chief adviser and general to last Safavid ruler in Persia, defeats Turks in great battle at Baghavand and captures Tiflis
US: John Peter Zenger libel trial helps establish freedom of the press in North America

Did You Know?

*In his newspaper the New York Weekly Journal, Zenger printed his backers'
articles criticizing the colonial governor of New York. On November 17, 1734,
he was imprisoned on charges of seditious libel. His lawyer Andrew Hamilton
argued that the anti-administration charges were true and therefore not libelous.
Even though the judge didn't agree with the argument, the jury did and Zenger
was found not guilty. This ruling is the basis of today's libel laws.*

1736 China: Chi'en Lung becomes emperor (to 1795)
Iran: Nadir Shah becomes king
Russo-Turkey War
1736 to 1747 Afghanistan: Shah Nadir Shah takes country
1736 to 1796 China: Rule of Qianlong, population increases greatly; frequent rebellions crushed ruthlessly
1738 Treaty of Vienna resolves War of Polish Succession
1739 Europe: "War of Jenkins's Ear"—trade war between Great Britain and Spain due to British attempts to circumvent Peace of Utrecht
India: Nadir Shah sacks Delhi, seizing Moghul emperors' Peacock Throne and vast wealth
US: Slave revolts in South Carolina
1740 Prussia: Frederick II ("the Great") becomes ruler
Russia: Ivan VI crowned emperor
1740 to 1748 Wars of Austrian Succession
1740s Africa: The Lunda create prosperous new kingdom
India: Power of Hindu Marathas of central India expands into northern India

1741 to 1750   1741 US: Captain Vitus Bering, Dane employed by Russia, explores Alaska
1741 to 1761 Russia: Reign of Elizabeth I of Russia, daughter of Peter the Great; she establishes Russia's first university at Moscow

Did You Know?

Was Benedict Arnold a brilliant patriot or a despicable traitor? Actually, he was both. In the early years of the Revolutionary War, he served the American cause with distinction. Later, however, Arnold decided he would be financially better off serving the British and so passed secret information to them. Not surprisingly, Arnold settled in England after the war.

1741 to 1801 US: Benedict Arnold
1742 Peru: Atahualpa II (Juan Santos) leads Native Americans in a failed revolt against Spanish
1743 Europe: Battle of Dettingen, English defeat French
1743 to 1826 US: Thomas Jefferson
1744 to 1748 US: King George's War between the British and French
1745 Canada: British capture French fortress of Louisbourg
England: "The Forty-Five": Jacobite rebellion led by Charles Edward Stuart (the "Young Pretender")

Did You Know?

In 1745, Charles Edward, the Young Pretender, landed in Scotland with a handful of followers. He quickly raised an army of 2,000 and defeated a British army at Prestonpans, but England didn't support him. His army was crushed in Scotland in 1746. Charles fled to France and was not heard from again.

Scotland: Second Jacobite rebellion tries to put "Bonnie Prince Charles" on the throne of Scotland and England but fails
1746 Africa: Mazrui dynasty in Mombasa, East Africa, becomes independent from Oman
British defeat Scots under Stuart pretender Prince Charles at Culloden Moor
1747 Afghanistan: Nadir Shah assassinated
1748 King George's War ends
War of the Austrian Succession ended by Treaty of Aix-la-Chapelle
1750 Tibet: Chinese capture Lhasa and take Tibet

Did You Know?

Delhi, located in north India, is surrounded by a high stone wall and approached through seven arched gateways. The Chandni Chauk (Silver Street), once considered the most lavish street in the world, is the main thoroughfare.

1750 to 1779 India: Ahmad Shah Durrani, invades, seizes Lahore; plunders Delhi in 1755

1751 to 1760 1751 India: End of French plans for supremacy in southern India
Tibet: Chinese conquer country
1752 Burma: Mon rebellion topples the Toungoo dynasty
1753 Burma: Alaungpaya reunites Burma; founds last Burmese dynasty, the Kombaung (to 1885)
US: French occupy Ohio Valley
1755 to 1763 US: Seven Years' War (called French and Indian War in US)
1755 to 1804 Alexander Hamilton
1756 Europe: Convention of Westminster between Prussia and Hanover
Europe: Treaty of Versailles between Austria and France
French and Indian War begins (Seven Years' War in England), to 1763, in which Britain and Prussia defeat France, Spain, Austria, and Russia. France loses North American colonies; Spain cedes Florida to Britain in exchange for Cuba
India: More than 100 British prisoners die in "Black Hole of Calcutta"
US: Governor of Pennsylvania offers bounty of 130 Spanish dollars for "the scalp of every male Indian enemy above the age of twelve years produced as evidence of their being killed."
1757 India: Beginning of British Empire in India as Robert Clive, British commander, defeats Nawab of Bengal at Plassey
Russia: Allies with France and Austria
1758 Battle of Zorndorf: Prussians defeat Russians
1759 Brazil: Jesuits expelled
British capture Quebec from French
1760 Canada passes into British hands
England: King George III begins reign (to 1820)

Did You Know?

Afghanistan, a landlocked country in southwestern Asia, is slightly smaller than Texas. Since 1995, the country has been ruled by a fundamentalist Islamic militia called the Taliban and engaged in an ongoing civil war.

1761 to 1770 1761 Afghanistan: Afghan victory at Battle of Panipat between the Marathas and Ahmad Shah Durrani
1762 Cuba: British expedition seizes Havana from Spain
England: Declares war on Spain
Philippine Islands: British capture Manila from Spain
Russia: Catherine II ("the Great") becomes Czarina; Treaty of St. Petersburg between Russia and Prussia
1763 Brazil: Rio de Janeiro becomes capital
Europe: Treaty of Paris is signed, ending Seven Years' War in Europe
French and Indian War ends
India: Britain becomes dominant power
US: Pontiac Conspiracy: Native Americans rise against British
1764 to 1777 West Africa: Reign of Asante ruler Osei Kwadwo
1764 to 1795 Poland: Reign of King Stanislas Poniatowski, last king of Poland

1765 US: Stamp Act passed, taxing the colonies; delegates from nine colonies meet in New York to draft a declaration of rights and liberties
1766 England: Stamp Act repealed
US: Charles Mason and Jeremiah Dixon lay down Mason-Dixon Line

Did You Know?

The Mason-Dixon line, the popular name for the boundary between Maryland and Pennsylvania, was created to settle a dispute between the Calvert family of Maryland and the Penns of Pennsylvania. In 1829, the line, about 244 miles west of the Delaware River, came to designate the separation between the free states and the slave states during the Missouri Compromise.

1767 South Pacific: British Captain Samuel Wallis is first European to reach Tahiti; six months later, French navigator Bougainville visits islands
Thailand: Burmese invade, destroy the capital Ayudhya, and force Thais to accept Burmese overlordship; Burmese withdraw to repulse Chinese invasion of Burma
US: Townshend Acts impose tax on various imports into North America
1768 Egypt: Mamluk army officer Ali Bey makes himself ruler of Egypt
Russo-Turkish war
South Pacific: Captain James Cook begins 3-year exploration of Pacific
1768 to 1773 Africa: Scottish explorer James Bruce travels in Ethiopia
1769 to 1821 Napoleon Bonaparte
1770 Easter Island: Spanish sailors reach the area
US: Boston massacre; Townshend Acts repealed
1770s Africa: Tukolor kingdom gains power in former Songhai region of West Africa

Did You Know?

Napoleon Bonaparte, one of the greatest military commanders of all time, conquered much of Europe and modernized the nations he ruled. His downfall came in 1812 after his disastrous retreat from Moscow. In 1815, however, he made a dramatic comeback, escaping from Elba and marching on Paris. Back in town, he established a new, more democratic constitution. Defeated at Waterloo on June 18, 1815, he was exiled to Saint Helena, where he remained until his death from stomach cancer 6 years later.

1771 to 1780   1771 Crimea: Russia conquers the region
1772 Partition of Poland: in 1772, 1793, and 1795, Austria, Prussia, and Russia divide land and people of Poland, ending its independence
1772 to 1775 South Pacific: Captain Cook's second voyage to the Pacific

Did You Know?

Captain James Cook (1728 to 1779) is famous for his three great voyages of exploration in the South Pacific ocean and the North American coastal waters. He is also justly famous for the health of his crew: his insistence on good hygiene and a healthful diet greatly reduced the incidence of scurvy among his crew.

1773 Africa: Ali Bey dies a week after being wounded in a battle with rebels led by Abu'l-Dhahab
Russia: Peasant uprising (to 1775)
US: Boston Tea Party (taxation protest)
1774 India: Warren Hastings appointed first governor general (1774 to 1785)
Russo-Turkish War ends
US: First Continental Congress drafts *Declaration of Rights and Grievances*
1775 India: War between British and Marathas (to 1782)
US: American Revolution begins with battle of Lexington and Concord; Second Continental Congress; Paul Revere's famous ride; War of Independence starts; June 17, Battle of Bunker Hill
1776 South America: Spanish create viceroyalty of La Plata
US: *Declaration of Independence;* General George Washington crosses the Delaware Christmas night
1776 to 1779 South Pacific: Cook's third voyage; in Hawaii, he is killed by the islanders
1777 Africa: Sidi Mohammed, ruler of Morocco (1757 to 1790), abolishes Christian slavery
Brazil: Treaty of San Idelfonso defines Spanish and Portuguese possessions in Brazil
1778 Europe: France joins war against Britain; War of Bavarian Succession

Did You Know?

The Xhosa (also spelled Xosa and formerly known as Kaffir) are a cluster of tribes in South Africa. Their language contains three types of click sounds as well as tones to set apart words that would otherwise sound identical.

1779 Africa: Dutch farmers in Cape Colony clash with organized Xhosa resistance
Gibraltar: France and Spain attack the region without success
1780 to 1782 Peru: Revolt of Tupac Amaru, Inca descendant

1781 to 1790 1781 Africa: Militant Tijaniyya Islamic order set up in Algeria
Burma: Bodawpaya loses control of Siam but captures the Arakan, rich coastal province bordering Bengal
US: British Lord Cornwallis surrenders at Yorktown, ending American Revolution
1782 India: Treaty of Salbai ends war between British and Marathas
1782 to 1809 Thailand: Rama I reigns; establishes Chakri dynasty
1783 to 1788 Japan: Severe famine

Did You Know?

The Crimea, a Russian peninsula projecting into the Black Sea, is home to Yalta, the scene of the historic World War II Yalta Conference.

1783 Russia annexes Crimea
US: Treaty of Paris formalizes American independence and defines America's borders
1784 India: India Act gives Britain control of country
US and China begin to trade
1785 Africa: Omani rulers reassert influence in Zanzibar
Russians settle Aleutian Islands
1787 Africa: Nomad Tuaregs abolish Moroccan pashalik of Timbuktu; British annex Sierra Leone
France: Assembly of Notables dismissed after refusing to introduce reforms
Japan: Famine causes rice riots in Edo
Russo-Turkish War (until 1792)
US: Constitution created (signed in 1789)
c. 1788 Africa: Fulani cleric Usuman dan Fodio sparks holy war against a Hausa king

KEY DOCUMENT

The film *1776*, starring nearly all the original Broadway cast, dramatizes the first US Congress struggling for independence from Britain. Catch William Daniels, Ken Howard, Howard da Silva, Blythe Danner, and John Cullum strutting their stuff in this delightful musical. Filmed in 1972, the movie earned three stars.

1788 Australia: First British convicts shipped to Botany Bay
England: African Association founded in England to explore interior of Africa
Iran: Qajar dynasty makes Tehran the capital and rules until 1920s
1789 Brazil: Conspiracy of Tiradentes; revolt in Minas Gerais gold mines
Canada: Alexander Mackenzie explores Mackenzie River

Did You Know?

Australia remained a penal colony for the first half of the nineteenth century, during which time the continent was explored and separate colonies established. Immigration accelerated with the discovery of gold in 1851.

Did You Know?

The 1935 film Mutiny on the Bounty *is movie-making at its best, a stunning adaptation of the Nordhoff-Hall book about the mutiny against the tyrannical Captain Bligh (Charles Laughton) on a voyage to the South Seas. Laughton steals the show, but Clark Gable, Franchot Tone, and Spring Byington are also worth a look-see. The film won an Oscar for Best Picture. There's a 1962 remake starring Marlon Brando, too.*

France: Louis XVI convenes Estates General, which had not been called since 1613; fall of the Bastille; start of the French Revolution
South Pacific: Mutiny on the British ship *Bounty*
US: George Washington becomes first president; John Adams, vice president; Thomas Jefferson, secretary of state; Alexander Hamilton, secretary of treasury
1790 England: Captain Bligh of the *Bounty* returns to England
1790s Haiti: Toussaint L'Ouverture leads revolt against French rule

Did You Know?

Word of the French Revolution helped spark the slave rebellion in Haiti led by Pierre Dominique Toussaint-Breda (1743 to 1803), nicknamed "L'Ouverture" because he found openings (ouvertures, in French) in enemy lines. The revolution ended in 1793, when the French abolished slavery. Toussaint then switched to the French side and after a period of civil war, ruled the country as a self-proclaimed governor. In 1802, Napoleon seized Haiti and reinstituted slavery. Toussaint died in a French prison. In 1804, the Haitians gained their independence.

1791 to 1800   1791 Canada: Canada Act divides Canada into Upper and Lower Canada
France: New constitution
Haiti: Toussaint l'Ouverture leads slave revolt
US: First ten amendments (commonly called the Bill of Rights) adopted
1792 Denmark: Prohibits slave trade
France: Declared a republic
France declares war on Austria and Prussia
Middle East: Sheik Mohammed Ibn Abdul Wahhab, founder of Saudi Arabia, dies
Nepal: Chinese army invades Nepal after Gurkhas menace Tibetan borders
Russo-Turkish War ends (began 1787)
US: US Mint established
1793 Australia: First free British people settle "Down Under"
Caribbean: Trinidad captured from Spanish
France: Reign of Terror; Louis XVI and Marie Antoinette executed
India: Judicial system reorganized
1794 France: Reign of Terror ends with execution of Robespierre
Persia: Aga Mohammed founds Kajar dynasty and unites country

Did You Know?

Marie Antoinette (1755 to 1793), born in Vienna, was greatly disliked by the French because she was a foreigner. She made matters worse by her devotion to all things Austrian, her extravagance, and her profligate friends. Especially damaging was her connection with the so-called Diamond Necklace affair, a scandal involving the fraudulent purchase of some jewels in 1785. Her disregard for the common folk has lived on in her infamous phrase, "Let them eat cake," which most scholars doubt she ever said.

Poland: Tadeusz Kosciuszko heads failed revolution
US: Whiskey Rebellion in Pennsylvania as farmers object to liquor taxes
1795 Africa: British seize Cape Colony from Dutch for the first time
France: Directory rules (to 1799)
British seize Cape Colony from Dutch for the first time
Poland: Third partition
1795 to 1796 Scottish explorer Mungo Park travels through Gambia and reaches Niger
1796 Ceylon: British take the country from the Dutch
US: Washington's Farewell Address (September 17); John Adams elected president; Thomas Jefferson, vice president
1796 to 1799 China: Emperor Qianlong relinquishes power, but still directs government

Did You Know?

French historians coined the term "Industrial Revolution" in the 1830s to describe the change from a world in which farming was the most important occupation to one dominated by factories and machines. The flying shuttle started the revolution by enabling weavers to produce cloth more quickly and in greater widths. Because the new machines were too big to drive by hand, factories were built next to rivers that could supply power. By the early 1800s, nearly all spinning and weaving were being done in factories. Soon the once-bucolic countryside became cluttered with factories and towns.

1798 Napoleon extends French conquests to Rome and Egypt: Battle of the Pyramids, Battle of the Nile
1798 to 1799 Australia: Bass and Flinders navigate strait between mainland Australia and Tasmania
Ireland: Wolfe Tone organizes Irish revolt against English rule
1799 France: Napoleon overthrows Directory, establishes the Consulate, and becomes first consul

India: Ranjit Singh founds Sikh kingdom in Punjab; British control most of southern India

South Pacific: Major civil war in Tonga

Syria: Napoleon invades

1800 Europe: Napoleon conquers Italy, firmly establishes himself as first consul in France

Russia: Annexes Georgia

US: Federal government moves to Washington

Part 2 Politics and Civilization

1801 TO 2000

1801 to 1810   1801 Africa: Rise of the Zulus, Bantu people of southern Africa
England: Act of Union formally unites Great Britain and Ireland as United Kingdom
Europe: Treaty of Luneville between France and Austria results in breakup of Holy
Roman Empire; France gains left bank of Rhine and keeps most of Italy
Russia: Alexander I crowned emperor; conquest of Caucasus region begins
US: Thomas Jefferson becomes third US president
1801 to 1803 Australia: Matthew Flinders circumnavigates and names "Australia"
1802 Europe: Treaty of Amiens between Britain and France; Bonaparte becomes First
Consul for Life
1802 to 1820 Vietnam: Emperor Gia-Long unites Vietnam
1803 Europe: War between Britain and France
US: Louisiana Purchase

Did You Know?

*The Louisiana Purchase in 1803 was a real bargain: For $15 million, the US
doubled its domain, increasing its territory by 827,000 square miles, from the
Mississippi River to the Rockies and from the Gulf of Mexico to British
North America.*

1803 to 1805 India: Second Maratha War disrupts central India
1804 Africa: Fulani begin *jihad* (holy war) in northern Nigeria
Europe: Russia and Persia war over annexation of Georgia
Europe: Third Coalition formed by Britain, Russia, Austria, and Sweden against France
France: Napoleon transforms the Consulate of France into an empire, proclaims himself
emperor of France, and systematizes French law under Code Napoleon
Haiti: Wins independence from France; first black nation to gain freedom from
European colonial rule
Japan: Russian envoy visits Nagasaki to get commercial treaty but fails
Scotland: Robert Owen sets up a "utopian" community
US: Lewis and Clark's expedition beyond Mississippi River
Yugoslavia: Serbian nationalists revolt against Turks; suppressed in 1813

Did You Know?

*In 1804, Aaron Burr challenged statesman Alexander Hamilton to a duel.
Although he strongly disapproved of dueling, Hamilton felt obliged to accept. On
July 11, they met on the spot where Hamilton's eldest son had been killed in a
duel 3 years earlier. Burr mortally wounded Hamilton, who died the next day.*

1804 to 1868 Thailand: Mongkut (Phra Chom Klao), king of Siam, 1851 to 1868
1805 Egypt: Mohammed Ali appointed *pasha* (governor) of Egypt by Eelim III, sultan of Turkey
Europe: Battle of Ulm, French defeat Austrians
1805 to 1806 Africa: Mungo Park explores Niger River, West Africa
Europe: Britain, Austria, Russia, and Sweden form Third Coalition against France; Lord Nelson defeats the French and Spanish fleets in the Battle of Trafalgar; Napoleon victorious over Austrian and Russian forces at the Battle of Austerlitz
1805 to 1848 Egypt: Under Mohammed Ali's rule, Egypt breaks away from Ottoman Empire

Did You Know?

The massacres at Cairo in 1805 and 1811 destroyed the power of the Mamluks; the survivors fled to Nubia.

1806 Austria: Emperor Francis II becomes Francis I of Austria (to 1835)
Europe: Napoleon dissolves Holy Roman Empire; replaces it with Confederation of the Rhine
Europe: Battles of Jena and Auerstadt: French defeat Prussia
Holland: Louis Bonaparte, Napoleon's brother, becomes king
Russia gains a region of Bessarabia and a position in the Balkans
Turkey: Wars with Russia and Britain (until 1812)
1807 Africa: Asante invade Fante confederacy of states
England: Slave trade abolished but slavery continues until 1833
Portugal: French invade and capture Lisbon
Russia defeated by the French in the Battle of Friedland
US: Bans the importation of slaves
1807 to 1870 Robert E. Lee, American general

Did You Know?

The 1994 British flick The Madness of King George *describes how England's benevolent King George III (Nigel Hawthorne) suddenly takes ill and shows signs of mental instability, opening the way for court intrigue and the usurping of the throne by his ne'er-do-well son, the Prince of Wales (Rupert Everett). Supported by a first-rate cast, Hawthorne brilliantly recreates his stage performance, in this witty and absorbing movie. Helen Mirren, Ian Holm, Rupert Graves, John Wood, and Amanda Donohoe also star.*

1808 Africa: Fulani invade Bornu near Lake Chad
Battle of Vimero: British victory
Spain: French occupy the country; Joseph Bonaparte becomes king of Spain
Russia and Sweden war (until 1809)

1808 to 1814 Spain: Peninsular War
1809 Europe: Battle of Corunna: British defeated; Sir John Moore, British commander-in-chief, dies
Sweden: Gustavus IV takes the throne
1809 to 1865 Abraham Lincoln, American president
1810 Africa: Chaka, Zulu leader, organizes neighboring Mthethwa tribe and trains *impis* (warrior armies)
Holland: King Louis abdicates; France annexes Holland
Mexico: Miguel Hidalgo y Costilla begins the fight for Mexican independence from Spain
Portugal: British troops hold line of Torres Vedras against the French
Spain: Napoleon conquers Spain, replacing Ferdinand VII with Joseph Bonaparte
Pacific Islands: Kamehameha I becomes king of all Hawaii

1811 to 1820   1811 Egypt: Mohammed Ali massacres Mamluks (ruling family) in Cairo
England: Luddite riots against mechanization of textile industry; George III declared insane; Prince of Wales rules as regent
Paraguay gains independence
Portugal: French driven out
Venezuela achieves independence
1811 to 1818 Mohammed Ali overruns much of Arabian peninsula; ends first Saudi empire
1812 England: Repressive industrial revolution legislation introduced
Europe: Battle of Salamanca leads to British victory in Spain; Treaty of Orebro between Britain, Sweden, and Russia
Russia: Napoleon invades Russia; forced to retreat in winter, most of Napoleon's 600,000 men perish
Treaty of St. Petersburg between Sweden and Russia
Treaty of Bucharest ends Russo-Turkish War
US: War of 1812 (war with Britain over freedom of the seas for US vessels)
1813 Europe: Battle of Leipzig (Battle of the Nations); Austrian, Russian, and Prussian forces defeat France
Napoleon wins Battle of Dresden
Prussia: War of Liberation from France, led by King Frederick William III
Spain: Battle of Vittoria: Wellington drives French from Spain
Treaty of Kalisch between Russia and Prussia against France; coalition joined by Britain, Austria, and Sweden
1814 Africa: Netherlands cede South African colony to England
Europe: Congress of Vienna settles postwar Europe
France: Napoleon exiled to Elba, off Italian coast; Bourbon king Louis XVIII takes French throne; Treaty of Paris ends Napoleonic Wars
Japan: Kurozumi sect established, first modern Shinto sect
Sweden: Gains Norway in Treaty of Kiel
Treaty of Ghent ends War of 1812
1815 England: Corn Laws restrict corn imports
Europe: Austrian and Prussian monarchies restored; German Confederation replaces Confederation of the Rhine; Kingdom of Netherlands unites Belgium and Holland; Switzerland gains independence from France; Norway and Sweden joined under one ruler
Quadruple Alliance of Britain, Austria, Prussia, and Russia
France: Second Treaty of Paris restores France's boundaries to those of 1790
Holy Alliance of Russia, Prussia, and Austria

Java restored to Dutch by British
Napoleon returns: "Hundred Days" begin; Napoleon defeated by Wellington at Waterloo
and is banished to St. Helena in South Atlantic
South Pacific: Russia tries to land in Hawaii
Turkey: Serbs revolt in Balkans

Did You Know?

*America had few taxes in its early history. From 1791 to 1802, the government was
supported by internal taxes on distilled spirits, carriages, refined sugar, tobacco,
property sold at auction, corporate bonds, and slaves. The high costs of the War
of 1812 brought about the nation's first sales tax on gold, silverware, jewelry, and
watches. In 1817, however, Congress did away with all internal taxes, relying on
tariffs on imported goods to provide sufficient funds for running the government.*

1816 Argentina declares independence from Spain
India: Hindu College established
1817 to 1895 US: Frederick Douglass, abolitionist and former slave
1817 to 1819 India: Last Maratha War; Maratha defeated; British rule India except
Punjab, Sind, and Kashmir
1818 Africa: Chaka forms great Zulu Empire
Chile: Gains independence from Spain
Europe: Congress of Aix-la-Chapelle; France joins with the four Great Powers (Quintuple
Alliance)
North America: Border between Canada and US fixed along 49th parallel; both countries
occupy Oregon
1819 England: Peterloo Massacre

Did You Know?

*The Peterloo Massacre took place when soldiers fired on a political meeting in
Manchester, England, killing several people.*

Germany: Carlsbad Decrees suppress political activity
Kashmir: Conquered by Sikh leader Ramjit Singh
Singapore established by British
South America: Simón Bolívar liberates New Granada (now Colombia, Venezuela, and
Ecuador) as Spain loses hold on South American countries; named president of Colombia
Southeast Asia: Stamford Raffles establishes Singapore
South Pacific: Death of Kamehameha I of Hawaii; his heir, Kamehameha II, abolishes
system which restricted contact between men and women
US: Spain cedes Florida to US
1820 England: George IV crowned (reigns to 1830); Cato Street conspiracy to assassinate
cabinet ministers fails

Europe: Liberal revolutions in Spain, Portugal, and Italy.
Middle East: Peace treaty ends piracy and leads to 150 years of British supremacy in the Persian Gulf
Sudan: Egypt conquers region
US: Missouri Compromise: Missouri admitted as slave state but slavery barred in rest of Louisiana Purchase north of 36°30′ N
1820 to 1841 Vietnam: Emperor Minh Mang expels Christians
c. 1820 to 1913 US: Harriet Tubman, abolitionist
c. 1820 Development of North Pacific whaling industry
1820 to 1864 Africa: Fulani in Mali establish and rule Hamdallahi caliphate
1820 to 1891 US: William Tecumseh Sherman, American general

Did You Know?

Mali is located in West Africa.

1821 to 1830   1821 Honduras, Venezuela, Mexico, Peru, Guatemala, Panama, and Santo Domingo win independence from Spain
Mexico: Agustin de Iturbide declares himself emperor; disbands elected congress when they refuse to support him
Persia and Turkey at war
1821 to 1829 Greek War of Independence against Turks; in 1829, Turks recognize Greek independence
1822 Africa: Liberia established as home for freed slaves
Brazil becomes independent of Portugal under the rule of Emperor Pedro I (son of the Portuguese king)
Colombia and Ecuador liberated
Europe: Congress of Verona breaks down over England's refusal to intervene in Spain; ends congress system
1823 Honduras achieves independence from Mexico
Mexico: Dictator Iturbide abdicates
Spain: Revolution crushed
US: Monroe Doctrine warns European nations not to interfere in Western Hemisphere
1824 Africa: War between British and Ashanti in Gold Coast (Ghana)
England: Kamehameha II of Hawaii visits England and dies there

Did You Know?

The spread of industrialization from England to northern Europe created a solid middle class advocating liberal and nationalistic ideas, as well as a new urban radicalism sharpened by regular economic booms and busts. These movements culminated in the nationalistic and radical revolts of 1848.

France: Charles X crowned

Mexico becomes a republic 3 years after declaring independence from Spain

Peru: Bolívar liberates Peru and becomes its president

1824 to 1826 First Burmese War with Britain; Treaty of Yandabo leaves British in control of Arakan to the west and Tenasserim to the east

1825 Africa: Egyptians found city of Khartoum in Sudan

Bolivia: Wins independence from Spain

Greece: Egyptian forces under Ibrahim (son of Mohammed Ali) invade

Russia: Tsar Alexander I dies; Decemberist uprising fails; Nicholas is crowned emperor

South Pacific: Dutch annex Irian Jaya, western part of New Guinea

1825 to 1828 Persian-Russian War; Russia captures Tabriz

1825 to 1830 Javanese revolt against Dutch

1826 Erie Canal opens

1827 Battle of Navarino: French, Russian, and British forces destroy Egyptian fleet

Treaty of London: Britain, France, and Russia guarantee Greek independence

1828 Africa: Zulu ruler Chaka assassinated by his half-brother Dingane, who seizes throne

Africa: Basel mission to Ghana (then called Gold Coast), West Africa

Colombia divided into Venezuela, Ecuador, New Granada

India: Raja Ram Mohan Roy founds reforming Hindu society, Brahmo Samaj

Portugal: Miguelite Wars, regent Dom Miguel overthrows government; defeated in 1834

Russo-Turkish wars; Russia gains controls eastern coast of the Black Sea; Treaty of Adrianople

Uruguay: Wins independence from Spain

Did You Know?

The Zulu Empire survived until 1887, when it was annexed by the British.

1829 Greeks win independence from the Ottoman Empire

1830 Africa: French invade and occupy Algeria

Belgium: Wins independence from France

Ecuador: Wins independence from Spain

England: William IV becomes king (to 1837)

France: July Revolution; Charles X overthrown; Louis Philippe becomes king (to 1848)

Greece: Formally becomes independent

Poland: Russia crushes revolution

Samoa: Malietoa Vaiinupo of Savai'i becomes king of Samoa

Did You Know?

In the 1600s, an estimated 60 million buffalo roamed America; by the 1880s, only 300 buffalo remained. The animals had been hunted to the brink of extinction.

South Pacific: Tahitian Protestant missionaries arrive in Fiji
US: Indian Removal Act legislates the "relocating" of Native Americans living east of the Mississippi to "Indian Territory" reserved for them in the West

1831 to 1840   1831 Belgium: Separates from the Netherlands; Leopold I becomes king (to 1865)
Italy: Guiseppe Mazzini forms revolutionary Young Italy movement
Middle East: Egyptians conquer Syria
US: Nat Turner leads unsuccessful slave rebellion
1832 England: Reform Act extends vote to middle class
Middle East: War between Egypt and Turkey (1833); Turks defeated at Battle of Koniah
1832 to 1847 Africa: Abd-al-Kadir leads Arab resistance to France in Algeria
1833 England: Factory Act forbids employment of children younger than 9 in factories
Syria: Mohammed Ali gains Syria through Convention of Kutahia
Treaty of Unkiar Skelessi between Russia and Turkey
1834 Europe: Quadruple Alliance: Britain, France, Spain, and Portugal ally to safeguard governments in Spain and Portugal
Spain: Carlist Wars (to 1839); Pretender Don Carlos attempts to gain Spanish throne
1835 to 1863 Afghanistan: Dost Mohammed rules
Austria: Ferdinand I becomes emperor (to 1848)

Did You Know?

In the 1700s, Texas was part of the Spanish Empire, but after 1821 it came under Mexico's rule. Warfare between American settlers and Mexicans began in 1830 and flared into open revolt in 1836, when the Texans proclaimed their independence. Antonio de Santa Anna and his army of 5,000 Mexicans attacked San Antonio; the 150 Texans in the garrison retreated into the Alamo, a former mission used as a fort. They held out for eleven days before the Mexicans stormed the fort and killed all but six of the men. Santa Anna had these six put to death; only two women and two children survived. A few weeks later, General Sam Houston smashed the Mexicans at San Jacinto, captured Santa Anna, and forced Mexico to acknowledge Texas's independence.

1836 England: Chartist movement demands vote for all adult males
US: Mexicans attack the Alamo; entire garrison, including Davy Crockett and Jim Bowie, killed; Texas gains independence from Mexico
1836 to 1837 South Africa: The Great Trek of Boers (Dutch farmers) away from British in South Africa; Natal, Transvaal, and Orange Free State founded
1837 to 1901 England: Reign of Queen Victoria

Did You Know?

The Opium War erupted over the importation of drugs into China.

1837 to 1853 Japan: Shogunate of Tokugawa Ieyoshi
1838 South Africa: Battle of Blood River; Boers defeat Zulus in Natal
US: "Trail of Tears": Cherokee Indians forcibly removed from their homeland in Appalachian Mountains

Did You Know?

Imam Sayyid Said ruled Oman from 1806 to 1856.

1839 to 1842 China: First Opium War between Britain and China
1839 Canada: Rebellions break out
England: War with Afghanistan
Syria: Turks invade; Turks defeated at Battle of Nesib
1840 Africa: Imam Sayyid Said makes Zanzibar his capital
Beirut: British Navy attacks
Canada: Upper and Lower Canada united in self-governing union
England: Women denied seats at the World Anti-Slavery Convention in London.
New Zealand: British and Maoris sign Treaty of Waitangi; New Zealand becomes British crown colony
Treaty of London: Britain, France, Prussia, and Austria agree to limit Egyptian expansion

Did You Know?

In the mid-nineteenth century, America expanded westward, with both industry and population increasing.

US: Hawaiian kingdom recognized as an independent country
c. 1840 to 1904 US: Chief Joseph, leader of Nez Percé tribe

1841 to 1850   1841 Egypt: Mohammed Ali becomes hereditary ruler
Straits Convention: Dardanelles and Bosporus closed to foreign ships in peacetime
1842 Afghanistan: British withdraw troops
China: Opium War ended by Treaty of Nanking; Hong Kong ceded to Britain
South Africa: British and Boers at war; British victorious
South Pacific: France annexes Marquesas Islands and makes Tahiti protectorate
US and Canada: Boundary issue settled by Webster-Ashburton Treaty
1843 Africa: Britain takes Natal from Boers
India: British conquer region now known as Pakistan
1843 to 1856 Africa: Dr. David Livingstone crosses Africa; follows course of Zambezi River; reaches Victoria Falls
1844 Cambodia: Becomes a Thai protectorate
England: First effective Factory Act

1845 to 1849 India: Sikh Wars with Britain; Britain annexes Punjab

1845 Ireland: Failure of potato crop causes famine; 1 million people die by 1851

US: Texas joins the US

1846 England: Corn Laws repealed

Ireland: Anti-British sentiment grows

South Africa: War between Bantus (Kaffirs) and British; Bantus defeated; first act of segregation; Zulu reserves set up in Natal

War between Mexico and US (1846 to 1848); US wins; California and New Mexico ceded to US

1848 Europe: Revolutions in France, Austrian Empire, Italy, and Germany

Hawaii: King Kamehameha III gives his people shares in the islands

Karl Marx and Friedrich Engels: *The Communist Manifesto*

Persia: Accession of Nasir ud-Din, ablest of Kajar dynasty

KEY DOCUMENT

Marx and Engels' *Manifesto of the Communist Party* (commonly called *The Communist Manifesto*) ends with this cry to action: "The proletarians have nothing to lose but their chains. They have a world to win. Workingmen of all countries, unite."

US: Women's Rights Convention in Seneca Falls, NY; calls for equal rights for American women

US: Treaty of Guadalupe Hidalgo: US gains California, New Mexico

1849 Europe: Revolutions in Italy and Hungary crushed

US: California gold rush

1850 Britain transfers some powers to the four major Australian colonies; they achieve self-government

US: Congress compromises over expansion of slavery, fails to resolve tension between states

1850 to 1889 Brazil: Pedro II leads country to great economic success

1851 to 1860   1851 Australia: Gold discovered

China: Taiping rebellion begins

Thailand: Mongkut becomes king

1851 to 1868 Thailand: Mongkut opens country to foreign trade

1852 Burma: Second Anglo-Burma War; British victory

France: Louis Napoleon establishes Second Empire as Napoleon III, Emperor of the French (to 1870)

Did You Know?

In Thailand, Mongkut was known as King Rama IV.

Persia: Nasir-ud-Din (1848 to 1896) takes personal power; Vizier Mirza Taki reforms administration
South Africa: Britain recognizes Transvaal's independence

Did You Know?

Mongkut is the king immortalized in the musical The King and I. *The 1956 film version stars Yul Brynner as the king and Deborah Kerr as the widowed English schoolteacher who travels to Siam to teach his many children. Brynner won an Oscar recreating his Broadway role.*

1853 Japan: Commodore Perry reaches Tokyo
Turkey declares war on Russia
New Caledonia: France annexes the country
1853 to 1878 Burma: Reign of King Mindon Min
1854 South Africa: Orange Free State established
South Pacific: Eureka stockade; brief miners' revolt at Ballarat
Spain: Government overthrown by liberal revolution
US and Japan: Treaty of Kanagawa, first modern trade treaty between US and Japan
US: *People v. Hall* rules that Chinese cannot give testimony in court
1854 to 1856 Europe: Crimean War (Britain, France, and Turkey against Russia)

Did You Know?

Disease caused more deaths in the Crimean War than fighting. The poor medical care given to British soldiers led nursing pioneer Florence Nightingale to establish hospitals.

1855 Russia: Alexander II crowned emperor
1855 to 1868 Africa: Reign of Emperor Theodore of Ethiopia
1856 Middle East: Iran besieges Afghan city of Herat; British (who control Afghanistan) declare war on Iran
Treaty of Paris
US: Antislavery Republican Party formed
1857 India: Sepoy rebellion (Hindu and Muslim soldiers revolt against British); India placed under crown rule as a result
US: In *Dred Scott* decision, Supreme Court rules that slaves are not citizens

Did You Know?

Sepoys were native Indian soldiers.

1858 China: Treaties of Tientsin open eleven Chinese ports
East India Company abolished
India Bill: Transfers Indian government to England
Mexico: Reformer Benito Juarez is president
Russia: Gains Amur region from China
1859 Europe: France-Austria War
South Africa: Europeans discover Lake Tanganyika
US: John Brown raids Harper's Ferry; is captured and hanged
1860 Australia: R. O. Burke and W. J. Wills cross Australia from south to north
China: British and French occupy Beijing; end of Anglo-Chinese War
Italy: Parma, Modena, Tuscany, and Romagna unite with Piedmont; Italian patriot
Giuseppe Garibaldi and his "Thousand Redshirts" conquer Naples and Sicily
1860 to 1870 New Zealand: Second Maori War

KEY DOCUMENT

Abraham Lincoln delivered his famous "House Divided" antislavery speech at
the close of the Republican State Convention on June 16, 1858. Here is an excerpt:

> *In my opinion, it will not cease, until a crisis shall have been reached, and passed.
> "A house divided against itself cannot stand." I believe this government cannot
> endure, permanently half slave and half free. I do not expect the Union to be
> dissolved—I do not expect the house to fall—but I do expect it will cease to
> be divided. It will become all one thing, or all the other.*

1861 to 1870   1861 England: Queen Victoria's husband Prince Albert dies
Italy unified (except for Rome and Venice)
New Zealand: Gold discovered
Prussia: William I becomes king (to 1888)
Russia: Emancipation of serfs
US: Civil War begins when Confederates fire on Fort Sumter (April 12)

Did You Know?

*In terms of casualties, the Civil War was the most devastating war in American
history. By the end of the war, 359,528 Union soldiers and 200,000 Confederate
soldiers had died.*

1861 to 1865 US: Civil War: Mississippi, Florida, Alabama, Georgia, Louisiana, and Texas
secede; with South Carolina, they form the Confederate States of America, with Jefferson
Davis as president; Virginia, Arkansas, Tennessee, North Carolina secede and join
Confederacy; First Battle of Bull Run (Manassas); in addition to the slavery issue, the

Civil War arose out of the economic and political rivalry between the agrarian South and the industrial North
1862 Prussia: Bismarck becomes prime minister
Southeast Asia: French begin occupation; Cambodia becomes French protectorate
US: Land given to European immigrants to farm
US: Native Americans wars in western territories
US: California passes a "police tax" of $2.50 a month on every Chinese
US: Confederate general Robert E. Lee victorious at Second Battle of Bull Run (Manassas)

Did You Know?

In 1862, in order to support the Civil War effort, Congress enacted the nation's first income tax law. During the Civil War, a person earning from $600 to $10,000 per year paid tax at the rate of three percent. Those with incomes of more than $10,000 paid taxes at a higher rate. Additional sales and excise taxes were added, and an "inheritance" tax made its debut. In 1866, internal revenue collections reached their highest point in the nation's 90-year-history—more than $310 million, an amount not reached again until around 1911.

1862 to 1882 US: 200,000 Chinese immigrants
1863 Africa: Al-Hajj 'Umar takes Timbuktu
Japan: French and American warships bombard Shimonoseki
Mexico: French capture Mexico City; proclaim Archduke Maximilian of Austria emperor.
Poland: Insurrection against Russia fails
US: Union victory at Vicksburg marks turning point in Civil War

Did You Know?

Historian George Santayana coined the famous observation: "Those who cannot remember the past are condemned to repeat it."

1864 New Caledonia: First French convicts sent to region
US: Sherman's Atlanta campaign and "march to the sea" (May to September)
1865 New Zealand: Seat of government transferred from Auckland to Wellington
US: Civil War ends on April 9, when Lee surrenders to Grant at Appomattox; Lincoln fatally shot at Ford's Theater by John Wilkes Booth; Booth caught and dies of gunshot wounds; four co-conspirators hanged; Thirteenth Amendment to Constitution outlaws slavery; Central Pacific Railroad Company recruits Chinese workers for the first transcontinental railroad
1865 to 1868 Africa: Wars between Orange Free State and Moshweshwe's Basuto people
1865 to 1870 Paraguay: Attacks neighboring countries and is nearly destroyed
1866 Austro-Prussian War
German Confederation disbanded; Schleswig-Holstein annexed by Prussia

US: Fourteenth Amendment grants blacks full citizenship
1866 to 1877 US: Northern US Republicans force through radical reconstruction of southern states

---

KEY DOCUMENT

Grant's description of the surrender at Appomattox belies the bitterness:

What General Lee's feelings were I do not know. As he was a man of much dignity, with an impassable face, it was impossible to say. . . . [M]y own feelings, which had been quite jubilant on the receipt of his letter [of surrender], were sad and depressed. I felt like anything rather than rejoicing at the downfall of a foe who had fought so long and valiantly, and had suffered so much for a cause, though that cause was, I believe, one of the worst for which a people ever fought.

1867 Austria-Hungary dual monarchy established
Canada: Becomes a British dominion; John A. Macdonald becomes prime minister
England: Second Reform Act passed
Europe: North German Confederation formed
Germany: Karl Marx writes *Das Kapital*
Japan: Last Japanese shogun, Hitotsubashi, resigns; emperor regains position as actual head of the government.
Mexico: French leave Mexico; Maximilian executed
South Africa: Diamonds discovered at Kimberley
US: Buys Alaska from Russia for $7,200,000; 2,000 Chinese railroad workers stage one-week strike
1868 to 1963 US: W. E. B. Du Bois, American sociologist and cofounder of the NAACP
1868 Africa: British expedition to Ethiopia
Japan: Capital moves to Edo (renamed Tokyo); Meiji period begins
Spain: Revolution: Queen Isabella deposed, flees to France
US: Burlingame-Seward Treaty
1868 to 1878 Cuba and Spain at war
1868 to 1910 Thailand: Reign of Rama V, founder of modern Thailand
1869 South Pacific: Germany acquires land in Caroline Islands
Suez Canal opened
US: Transcontinental railroad completed; Wyoming grants women the vote
1869 to 1948 India: Mohandas Gandhi, Indian nationalist leader
1870 Franco-Prussian War (to 1871)

Did You Know?

Mohandas Gandhi became an international symbol of a free India. He lived a spiritual and ascetic life of prayer, fasting, and meditation. Refusing earthly possessions, he wore the loincloth of the lowliest Indian.

France: Revolt in Paris; Third Republic proclaimed
Ireland: Land Act provides compensation for eviction; fails to ease Irish problems
New Caledonia: Gold rush
1870 to 1888 Venezuela: Major reforms under Antonio Guzman

KEY DOCUMENT

In 1873, Joseph became chief of the Nez Percé tribe, succeeding his father. Ten years earlier, the tribe had signed a treaty giving the US government control of their land, but Chief Joseph felt the treaty was illegal and refused to recognize it. In 1877, Joseph led his people on a long march from their homeland in Oregon through Idaho and Montana toward Canada. Although the tribe fought valiantly, they were greatly outnumbered by government troops and forced to surrender on October 9. Chief Joseph's surrender speech, "I Will Fight No More Forever," has become symbolic of the Native American displacement:

Tell General Howard I know his heart. What he told me before, I have in my heart. I am tired of fighting. Our chiefs are killed. Looking Glass is dead. Toohoolhoolzote is dead. The old men are all dead. It is the young men who say yes or no. He who led the young men is dead. It is cold and we have no blankets. The little children are freezing to death. My people—some of them have run away to the hills and have no blankets and no food. No one knows where they are—perhaps freezing to death. I want to have time to look for my children and see how many of them I can find. Maybe I shall find them among the dead. Hear me, my chiefs, my heart is sick and sad. From where the sun now stands I will fight no more against the white man.

1871 to 1880   1871 France: Surrenders after brutal siege
German Empire founded after defeat of France in the Franco-Prussian War; William I proclaimed kaiser (emperor)
Italy: Unified, with Rome as capital
South Pacific: Cakobau, most important leader of Bau, one of Fiji Islands, establishes a national monarchy in Fiji
1872 Europe: League of Three Emperors
South Africa: England grants Cape Colony self-government
1873 Spain: First Republic (to 1874)
1873 to 1874 Africa: England and Ashante Kingdom war; British defeat Ashanti; beginnings of Mande state in old Mali
1874 Hawaii: Prince David Kalakaua becomes ruler of Hawaii (to 1891)
1874 to 1965 England: Winston Churchill, politician and prime minister
1875 Africa: Egyptian khedive Ismail Pasha attacks Ethiopia; invasion halted, but Egypt occupies the Red Sea and Somalia ports
Third Anglo-Burmese War
Turkey: Insurrection breaks out
1875 to 1888 Japan: Shogunate abolished; civil legal code drawn up

1876 Bulgaria: Anti-Turkish insurrection suppressed; thousands massacred
India: Famine in the Deccan, southern India; over 5 million die
Japan: Samurai class of professional warriors abolished
Korea: Japanese pressure forces Korea to open ports to trade
Mexico: Porfirio Díaz becomes dictator
US: Custer's last stand at the Battle of Little Big Horn; last major Native American victory

Did You Know?

The discovery of gold in the Black Hills of Montana led to an influx of white prospectors. The Sioux, under the leadership of Chiefs Sitting Bull, Crazy Horse, and Rain-in-the-Face, attacked the prospectors who had settled on their land. The US Army planned an attack against the hostile Indians, but on June 25, Custer disregarded plans and attacked at Little Big Horn. Unaware that he was greatly outnumbered—260 US soldiers against between 2,500 and 4,000 Sioux—Custer led his troops into a death trap. Custer and all his men were killed. The battle has come to be known as "Custer's Last Stand."

1876 to 1911 Mexico: Great expansion under President Díaz
1877 Japan: Satsuma rebellion; last stand of traditional samurai class is defeated
India: Queen Victoria of England declared empress of India
Russo-Turkish War (ends in 1878 with power of Turkey in Europe broken)
South Africa: Britain annexes Transvaal
1878 New Caledonia (southwest Pacific island): Rebellion against French
Treaty of San Stefano, signed by Russia and Turkey, guarantees independence of Montenegro, Serbia, Bulgaria, and Romania
Europe: Berlin Conference reverses Treaty of San Stefano
US: The Knights of Labor, a secret group formed in 1869, form the first successful national labor union
1878 to 1879 Second Afghan War: British invade Afghanistan to counter Russian influence
1879 Africa: Zulu War with British; British defeated at Isandhlwana but victorious at Ulundi Chancellor
Egypt: Britain and France control Egypt
Europe: Bismarck negotiates a military alliance between Germany and Austria-Hungary
Ireland: Charles Stewart Parnell forms the Irish Land League
South Pacific: Britain establishes a naval station in Samoa
1879 to 1884 War of the Pacific between Chile, Peru, and Bolivia
1880 Australia: Most famous bushranger (an outlaw living in the bush), Ned Kelly, is hanged; becomes a folk hero
France: Annexes Tahiti as a colony
US-China Treaty allows US to restrict immigration of Chinese labor
1880 to 1881 South Africa: First Boer War, Transvaal defeats Britain

1881 to 1890   1881 New Zealand and Maoris reach peace
Russia: Alexander II assassinated; Alexander III crowned emperor
US: President Garfield assassinated

1882 Egypt: Britain invades and conquers Egypt
Europe: Triple Alliance between Germany, Austria-Hungary, and Italy signed
Ireland: Terrorism erupts after land evictions
Sudan: Mohammed Ahmed of Dongola leads anti-Egypt revolt
US: Chinese Exclusion Act bans Chinese workers for 10 years

Did You Know?

Arabs called Mohammed Ahmed of Dongola al-Mahdi, "the guided one," the Muslim equivalent of "Messiah." In 1882, the Mahdi roused his people to rebel against British rule. The British sent Charles Gordon, former governor of Sudan, to oversee the withdrawal of the Egyptian garrisons. The Mahdi besieged Gordon in Khartoum. The city held out ten months before it fell in 1885; Gordon was killed, two days before relief arrived. The Mahdi died soon after.

1884 China: Dowager Empress Cixi sacks grand council
Europe: Berlin Conference decides "spheres of influence" in Africa and partition country
1885 Africa: The Mahdi, Muslim leader, takes Khartoum from Egypt; German East Africa established
India: National Congress formed; campaign for home rule
1885 to 86 Third Burmese War; Britain annexes Burma
New Guinea: Goldfields opened up in Papua
1886 Africa: Gold found in Transvaal
Burma: British rulers move capital city from Mandalay to Rangoon
Ireland: Irish Home Rule defeated
US: American Federation of Labor established; Samuel Gompers first president

Did You Know?

Today, Burma is called the Union of Myanmar.

1887 England: Queen Victoria's Golden Jubilee
Europe: Italy and Ethiopia at war
US: Interstate Commerce Act
1888 Brazil: Pedro II deposed by army revolt; Brazil becomes a republic; slaves freed
Germany: William II becomes emperor
1889 Africa: Treaty of Wichale; Italians claim it makes Ethiopia their protectorate
Brazil becomes a republic
France: Panama scandal
Japan: New Meiji constitution
South Pacific: Malietoa Laupepa, king of Samoa, is recognized by Britain, United States, and Germany
US: First Pan-American Conference held at Washington; Oklahoma land rush

1890 Japan: First general election
Germany: William II becomes kaiser; forces Bismarck to resign
US: Battle of Wounded Knee; US cavalry massacre almost 200 Sioux to complete the conquest of the West; Sherman Anti-Trust Act
Africa: Zanzibar (an island off east Africa) becomes a British protectorate

Did You Know?

The Panama scandal was a financial scandal caused by collapse of Panama Canal Company.

1891 to 1900
1891 Russia begins to build the Trans-Siberan Railway
1893 Africa: Ivory Coast becomes French protectorate
England: Labor Party established
New Zealand: Women get the vote

Did You Know?

The Spanish-American War was created by "yellow journalism" (slanted journalism) to further American interests. At the end of the war, the US received Guam and Puerto Rico and agreed to pay Spain $20 million for the Philippines. Cuba became independent from Spain.

1893 to 1976 China: Communist leader Mao Zedong
1894 Africa: French protectorate in Dahomey (Benin)
China: Sun Yat-sen founds revolutionary society
France: Captain Alfred Dreyfus convicted on false treason charge (pardoned in 1906)
Russia: Nicholas II crowned czar (to 1917); last Russian czar
US: Pullman strike, Chicago, led by socialist Eugene V. Debs
1894 to 95 Sino-Japanese War; Japanese win, occupy Korea
1895 Africa: War between Italy and Ethiopia; Italians defeated at Adwa the following year; Cecil Rhodes establishes Rhodesia
Bulgaria: Prime Minister Stambuloff assassinated
Cuba: Revolution (to 1898)
Treaty of Shimonoseki: Japan gains Formosa; China recognizes Korea's independence
1895 to 1896 Africa: Jameson raid into Transvaal
1896 Africa: France takes Madagascar
Africa: Ethiopian ruler Menelik crushes Italian army at Adowa; Treaty of Addis Ababa; Italy recognizes Ethiopia's independence
Kuwait: Sheikh Mubarak becomes ruler after killing his two brothers
Malay: British persuade Malay states to form federation
Thailand: Anglo-French agreements
Sudan: General Kitchener begins reconquest of region

US: Supreme Court's *Plessy v. Ferguson* decision
1897 Africa: Slavery banned in Zanzibar
China: Germans occupy Kiaochow
Greece and Turkey at war over Crete
New Zealand: Introduces eight-hour working day

Did You Know?

In 1894, French Army officer Alfred Dreyfus, Jewish by birth, was accused of giving military information to Germany. Found guilty, he was deported to Devil's Island for life. Two years later, Emile Zola published J'Accuse to argue Dreyfus's innocence. Sentenced to a year in jail, Zola fled to England. Major Huber Henry, one of Dreyfus's accusers, admitted forging documents to implicate Dreyfus and then killed himself. Dreyfus was retried and again found guilty, but his sentence was remitted. He was finally cleared in 1906. Dreyfus died in obscurity in 1935.

1898 China: Dowager Empress Cixi crushes attempts at reform; China cedes Port Arthur to Russia
New Zealand: Introduces old age pensions
Russia: Russian Social Democratic Labor Party established and hold first party congress in March; Vladimir Lenin one of the organizers
Sudan: Battle of Omdurman: British defeat Sudan; Fashoda Incident: British and French confrontation; French withdraw (1899)

Did You Know?

The Plessy v. Ferguson decision established the "separate but equal" doctrine.

US: Annexes Hawaii
1898 to 1899 Spanish-American War; Spain gives Cuba independence, US takes Puerto Rico, Guam, and Philippines as colonies
1899 Southeast Asia: France proclaims protectorate in Laos
US: Open-Door Policy with China
1899 to 1902 South Africa: Second Boer War between British and Boers (descendants of Dutch settlers of South Africa); British victorious in 1902
1900 Africa: Buganda ruled by the kabaka (king) with British advice; British conquer northern Nigeria
China: Boxer Rebellion erupts
Europe: Sigmund Freud's *The Interpretation of Dreams*
New Zealand: Annexes the Cook Islands
Russia annexes Manchuria
South Africa: British annex Orange Free State

South Pacific: Phosphate-rich Ocean Island annexed by British
US: Hurricane ravages Galveston, TX; 6,000 drown

1901 to 1910   1901 Australia: Commonwealth of Australia formed
China: Boxer Rebellion ends with Peace of Beijing
England: Queen Victoria dies; succeeded by son King Edward VII
Russia: Foundation of Russian Social Revolutionary Party (Bolsheviks); Russia occupies
Manchuria in northeastern China
South Pacific: Britain controls Tonga's external relations

Did You Know?

*The US had major investments in Cuba, especially in sugar production. When it
seemed that a revolution against Cuba's Spanish overlords would disrupt
business, American business interests decided to step in. The opportunity came
on February 9, 1898, when newspaper mogul William Randolph Hearst
published a private letter in which the Spanish minister to the US insulted
President McKinley. The president sent the USS Maine to Havana Harbor to
protect Americans in Cuba. Six days later, the Maine exploded, killing 266
crewmen. Amid the finger-pointing, the cry "Remember the Maine . . . to hell
with Spain!" helped propel the US into war with Spain. Secretary of State John
Hay called the ten-week exercise in Spanish humiliation a "splendid little war."*

US: J. P. Morgan forms U.S. Steel; as President McKinley begins second term, he is fatally
shot by anarchist Leon Czolgosz; Theodore Roosevelt sworn in as successor; acquires
rights to use Cuba's Guantanamo Bay indefinitely as a naval base

Did You Know?

*The "Boxers" (the fanatical "Society of Harmonious Fists" sect), determined to rid
China of foreign influence, attacked 3,000 European and Chinese Christians in
Beijing. The siege lasted fifty-five days before an international force of soldiers
came to the rescue. More than 200 Europeans and thousands of Chinese
Christians were murdered. As a result, the foreign powers imposed humiliating
punishments on the Chinese.*

1900 to 1901 Africa: Uprising in Asante, West Africa; Britain annexes Asante
1901 to 1909 US: President Theodore Roosevelt reforms business, railways, child labor,
and conservation
1902 Commercial treaties between China and Britain, US and Japan
Middle East: Ibn Saud captures Riyadh, beginning the creation of Saudi Arabia
South Africa: Treaty of Vereeniging ends Second Boer War; Britain wins; defeated Boers
remain bitter and determined to regain power
Trans-Pacific telephone cable connects Canada and Australia

US: Acquires control of Panama Canal zone; Chinese exclusion extended for another 10 years

1903 Africa: British take over Sokoto caliphate in Hausaland
Boundary dispute over Alaska between Canada and US settled
Europe: Assassination of Alexander, king of Serbia
Panama: Secedes from Colombia with US backing
Russia: Russian Social Democratic Labor Party splits into Bolshevik and Menshevik factions.
US: Alaska's boundary determined
1904 Africa: French create federation of French West Africa
Europe: Entente Cordiale between Britain and France
Fiji: Fijian delegates sit in legislative council for Fiji
Russo-Japanese War, competition for Korea and Manchuria (1904 to 1905)
South America: Final settlement between Bolivia and Chile after the War of the Pacific
Tibet: Open for trade
US: Chinese exclusion made indefinite
1904 to 1909 Bolivia: President Ismael Montes enacts social and political reforms
1905 Africa: Kaiser William II of Germany visits Tangier and provokes crisis with France;
Maji-Maji rebellion begins in Tanzania (German East Africa)
Canada: Provinces of Alberta and Saskatchewan formed
India: Partition of Bengal based on Hindu and Muslim populations
Japanese Navy fights and defeats Russian fleet in Tsushima strait
Norway breaks away from Sweden; elects King Haakon VII
Russia: Revolution breaks out after "Bloody Sunday" when troops fire at demonstrators in St. Petersburg; strikes and riots follow; sailors on battleship *Potemkin* mutiny; reforms, including first Duma (parliament), established by Czar Nicholas IIs "October Manifesto"
Russo-Japanese War ends; Japan wins
South Pacific: British New Guinea becomes the possession of Australia and is named Papua

US: Modern labor movement begins with the creation of the International Workers of the World (IWW), founded by Eugene V. Debs

1906 Africa: Tripartite Pact (Britain, France, Italy) seeks to preserve integrity of Ethiopia

Cuba: Occupied by US forces following a liberal revolt

India: Moslem League organized

Iran: Mozaffer ed-Din Shah grants first constitution

Russia: First Duma (representative body) meets but is dissolved

South Pacific: England and France rule over New Hebrides

US: San Francisco earthquake and fire; more than 500 dead; Alaska elects its first Congressional delegate; Theodore Roosevelt wins Nobel Peace Prize

1907 Africa: Government of Mozambique organized

Europe: Triple Entente among Britain, France, and Russia in opposition to Triple Alliance of Germany, Austria-Hungary, Italy

Korea: Emperor Kojong abdicates; succeeded by his son Sujong

New Zealand: Becomes a dominion

Philippines: First elections for national assembly

Russia: Second Duma dissolved; third Duma lasts until 1912

US: J. P. Morgan halts run on American banks; Oklahoma becomes forty-sixth state; Japanese immigration to US prohibited

KEY DOCUMENT

Theodore Roosevelt is the only twentieth-century president enshrined on Mount Rushmore in South Dakota. Asked to comment on his presidency, he said, "I believe in a strong executive; I believe in power, but I believe that responsibility should go with power, and that it is not well that the strong executive should be a perpetual executive. I have tried to do justly and to love mercy and to walk humbly with my God."

1908 Africa: Belgium takes over Congo Free State; changes name to Belgium Congo

Austria: Annexes Bosnia and Herzegovina

Bulgaria: Ferdinand I proclaimed emperor; declares independence from Turkey

China: Empress Dowager Cixi and Guangxu emperor die

Greece and Crete form union

Italy: Earthquake kills 150,000 in southern Italy and Sicily

Portugal: Carlos I assassinated

South Africa: Union of South Africa established as confederation of colonies; becomes British dominion in 1910

Turkey: Young Turks movement leads revolution against Abdul Hamid

1909 Africa: Liberia calls on US for financial assistance

New Zealand: Labor Party created

South Africa: Union of South Africa formed

Turkey: Sultan Abdul Hamid II overthrown

US: Robert E. Peary and Matthew Henson reach North Pole; National Association for the Advancement of Colored People (NAACP) founded by prominent black and white intellectuals and led by W. E. B. Du Bois

1910 Australia: First victory for Labor Party under Andrew Fisher in general election
China: Abolishes slavery
England: King George V succeeds to the throne (to 1936)
Japan: Annexes Korea
Mexico: Revolution begins
Portugal: Revolution ends with establishment of republic
Union of South Africa becomes independent dominion within British Empire

1911 to 1920   1911 China: Manchu dynasty overthrown; Sun Yat-sen elected president but warlords gain power
Denmark: Abolishes corporal punishment
England: Parliament Act reduces power of House of Lords
Italy: Defeats Turks and annexes Tripoli and Libya
Mexico: President Díaz overthrown; replaced by Francisco Madero
Morocco: Conflict between the France and Germany
New Zealand: Universal military training established
Russia: Premier Peter Stolypin is murdered; Grigori Rasputin gains influence over royal family

Did You Know?

The opulent Titanic was touted as being "unsinkable"—but sink it did, to become a symbol of the arrogance of the early twentieth century. The luxury liner, speeding to set a new record for crossing the North Atlantic, collided with an iceberg shortly before midnight on April 14; it broke apart and sank within two hours. As the orchestra played, about 1,500 of the more than 2,200 passengers and crew went down with the ship or plunged into the icy Atlantic. In 1996, scientists found the wreck and discovered that the iceberg damage amounted to no more than six small punctures, fatally located in the ship's starboard watertight holds.

US: Triangle Shirtwaist Company fire in New York; 146 killed
1912 Africa: New loans to Liberia coupled with US control over customs revenue; French make Morocco a protectorate at Treaty of Fez
Argentina: Secret ballot and universal suffrage
Europe: First Balkan War: Serbia, Bulgaria, and Greece attack Ottoman Empire
Italy: Tripoli ceded to Italy after Italo-Turkish War
Japan: Taisho period (until 1926)
Morocco: French protectorate established
Titanic sinks on her maiden voyage
US: Alaska granted territorial status; Arizona and New Mexico become states; anti-Indian racial riots on West Coast; Hindu immigrants expelled
1913 China recognizes Outer Mongolia's independence
Europe: Second Balkan War; Bulgaria attacks Serbia and Greece; London peace treaty partitions most of European Turkey among the victors
Ireland: Threat of civil war when Home Rule bill fails to pass House of Lords

Mexico: President Francisco Madero and vice president assassinated
New Zealand: Foundation of United Federation of Labor and Social Democratic Party
South Pacific: Wallis Islands become a French protectorate
Turkey: Young Turks form dictatorship
US: Sixteenth Amendment (income tax) and Seventeenth Amendment (popular election of US senators)

KEY DOCUMENT

"You will be home before the leaves have fallen from the trees," said Kaiser Wilhelm to the German troops in August 1914.

1913 to 1921 South Africa: Government introduces laws to reserve eighty-seven percent of land for whites
US: Woodrow Wilson is president
1914 Africa: Britain and France occupy German colonies in West Africa
Canada: Completion of Grand Trunk Pacific Railway
Europe: Assassination of Archduke Ferdinand sparks World War I; Austria declares war on Serbia, Germany on Russia and France, Britain on Germany
Mexico: US invades Mexico
Panama Canal opens

KEY DOCUMENT

When the US entered World War I, President Wilson called it "the war to end all wars" and said it would "make the world safe for democracy." Unfortunately, it did neither. Just 12 years after World War I ended, Europe was once again moving toward war.

1915 Europe: Germans start submarine campaign to blockade British Isles; German U-boats sink SS *Lusitania*
South Pacific: Britain annexes Gilbert and Ellice islands
Turkey: Soldiers kill 600,000 to 1 million Armenians
1916 Africa: Boer leader Jan Smuts leads an anti-German drive from Kenya into Tanzania
Africa: British and Belgian troops take Yaounde, the capital of German Cameroon
Europe: Battle of Verdun; Battle of the Somme
Ireland: Easter Rebellion against British government in Ireland
Mexico: US invades again
Middle East: Hussein proclaims himself King of the Arabs; Arab revolt against Ottoman Turks in Hijaz
Russia: Rasputin murdered

US: Buys Virgin Islands from Denmark for $25 million
1916 to 1918 Australia: Efforts to introduce national army conscription are defeated in referenda
1916 to 1922 Argentina: Hipolito Irigoyen elected president; institutes extensive reforms
1917 Africa: Ras Tafari (later Haile Selassie) becomes regent of Ethiopia; German forces in German East Africa withstand British and Portuguese at Mahiwa; Germans withdraw into Mozambique
Brazil: Declares war on Germany
China: Sun Yat-sen struggles for leadership of Chinese republic
Mexico: Revolution ends and a new constitution is written establishing an eight-hour work day; minimum wage; the right of peasants to own land; and denying foreigners the right to own land except under special situations
Middle East: British troops capture Baghdad and Jerusalem
Palestine: Balfour Declaration promises homeland for Jews in Palestine
Philippine Islands: Filipino National Guard organized
Russia: Czar abdicates; Russian Revolution begins; liberal revolution (February); Bolshevik revolution (October)
US: America enters World War I (April 6)

Did You Know?

World War I (1914 to 1918) pit the Central Powers (Austria-Hungary, Germany, Bulgaria, and Turkey) against the Allies (US, Britain, France, Russia, Belgium, Serbia, Greece, Romania, Montenegro, Portugal, Italy, Japan). About 10 million soldiers were killed, 20 million wounded.

1918 Europe: Battle of Marne; Armistice signed, ending World War I; German kaiser flees to Holland; Brest-Litovsk Treaty signed between Germany and Russia, taking Russia out of the war
Panama Canal completed, at a cost of $380 million and 10 years
Poland becomes independent
Russia: Nicholas II and family assassinated
Syria: Emir Faisal proclaims Syrian state; becomes king in 1920
Tonga: Salote becomes queen
Yugoslavia created
Venezuela: Oilfields opened
US: President Wilson's Fourteen Points for settling World War I
1918 to 1981 Anwar Sadat, Egyptian president
1919 Europe: Treaty of Versailles signed between Allies and Germany

Did You Know?

Describing the Eighteenth Amendment, President Herbert Hoover said: "Our country has deliberately undertaken a great social and economic experiment, noble in motive and far reaching in purpose."

Germany: Political power given to the democratic Weimar Republic
Hawaii: Dry dock completed at Pearl Harbor in US territory of Hawaii
India: British troops massacre over 300 civilians at Amritsar; Mahatma Gandhi initiates *satyagraha* ("truth force") campaigns, beginning his nonviolent resistance movement against British rule in India
Ireland: Sinn Fein declares Ireland a republic; 3 years of fighting follow
South Africa: African National Congress demonstrates against pass laws in Transvaal
US: Congress refuses to recognize League of Nations; Eighteenth Amendment ratified, prohibiting alcohol
1919 to 1930 Peru: Progress during Augusto Legu's presidency
1920 Africa: British and Indians settle Kenya
Australia: Federal Country Party formed
France: League of Nations formed in Paris

Did You Know?

The Treaty of Sèvres dissolved the Ottoman Empire.

India: Gandhi becomes leader in independence struggle
Italy: Italian Fascists under Mussolini actively combat Communists
Middle East: Palestine becomes British mandate
New Zealand: Given mandate over Samoa; joins League of Nations
Turkey: Signs Treaty of Sèvres, which confined it to Anatolian Plateau.
US: Nineteenth Amendment passed, granting women the vote
US: Soviet Russia issues Decree of Abortion; first nation to legalize the practice
USSR: Red Army takes Odessa

1921   Australia: Given mandate over German New Guinea
         Germany: Reparations Commission fixes German liability at 132 billion gold marks; German inflation begins

Did You Know?

The Immigration Quota Act severely limited immigration to no more than 3 percent annually of each nationality, based on the number of that nationality already residing in the US as of 1910.

Iran: Riza Shah Pahlevi marches his troops against Iran government
Panama: Costa Rica invades Panama
Russia: New Economic Plan is instituted

US: Immigration Quota Act; Sacco and Vanzetti convicted of armed robbery and murder; despite worldwide protests, they are executed in 1927; Tomb of the Unknown Soldier established, with burial of the unknown soldier; Arlington National Cemetery established in Washington, DC
1921 to 1925 Bolivia: Progressive government of President Juan Bautista Saavedra
1921 to 1926 Africa: Abd-el-Krim leads Berbers and Arabs against Europeans in North Africa

1922   Egypt: Under King Fuad, Egypt becomes independent from England
Greece: King Constantine abdicates; succeeded by George II
Italy: Mussolini becomes Italian prime minister and forms Fascist government; dictator from 1925
Ireland: Irish Free State, a self-governing dominion of the British Empire, officially proclaimed
Middle East: New borders between Iraq, Kuwait, and Saudi Arabia
Turkey: Kemal Atatürk, founder of modern Turkey, overthrows last sultan; Turkey becomes a republic
US: Rebecca Latimer Felton becomes first woman senator

Did You Know?

Germany experienced rampaging inflation in the 1920s. By the end of 1923 alone, $1 equaled 7,000 German marks.

1923   Ethiopia admitted to League of Nations
Germany: Nazi Party holds first Congress in Munich; Hitler's "Beer Hall Putsch" in Munich fails
Iran: Riza Shah Pahlevi becomes prime minister
Ireland: Civil war ends
Japan: Earthquake destroys one-third of Tokyo
Mexico: Rebel leader Pancho Villa assassinated in Parral, Mexico
Turkey: Mustafa Kemal becomes president of new republic
US: Widespread Ku Klux Klan violence

Did You Know?

The Locarno Agreements aimed to maintain peace and stability by defining Germany's western borders with France and Belgium.

1924   Chile: President Arturo Alessandri Palma overthrown but soon returned to power
China: Nationalist Party, Kuomintang, holds first national congress

Germany: Adolph Hitler's *Mein Kampf,* vol. 1
US: Dawes plan (German reconstruction); Teapot Dome scandal
USSR: Death of Lenin; Stalin wins power struggle, rules as Soviet dictator until his death in 1953

1925   Chile: Carlos Ibañez forces Chilean president Arturo Alessandri Palma out of power
Europe: Locarno Agreements between major European powers
Iran: Riza Shah Pahlevi becomes the shah of Iran
Saudi Arabia: Ibn Saud becomes king
Turkey abolishes polygamy
US: Scopes "Monkey Trial" pits creationists against evolutionists in Tennessee

1926   Cuba: Fidel Castro (1926–)
Japan: Emperor Yoshihito dies; successor Hirohito will rule for 63 years
Middle East: Abd al Aziz ibn Saud proclaimed leader and names the new nation Saudi Arabia
Nicaragua: US Marines quell revolt
Panama and US agree to protect Panama Canal in wartime
Poland: Jozef Pilsudski rises to power

Did You Know?

In the Teapot Dome scandal, Interior Secretary Albert B. Fall and oilmen Harry Sinclair and Edward L. Doheny were charged with conspiracy and bribery, involving fraudulent leases of naval oil reserves. In 1931, Fall was sentenced to 1 year in prison, but Doheny and Sinclair were acquitted of bribery.

1927   Australia: Canberra becomes federal capital
China: Kuomintang leader Chiang Kai-shek establishes government at Nanking; Communists challenge his rule
Germany: Economic system collapses on "Black Friday"
Russia: Trotsky expelled from Russian Communist Party
US: Teapot Dome scandal; Sacco and Vanzetti executed

Did You Know?

The Maginot Line was a fortification on the German border.

1928   China: Chiang Kai-shek elected president; unifies county
France: Kellogg-Briand Peace Pact, a universal renunciation of war, signed by sixty-five nations, including US
Germany: French begin to build the Maginot Line

Japanese troops murder military ruler of Manchuria
USSR: Stalin launches 5-year plan to expand Soviet industry

Did You Know?

Right before the stock market crash that plunged the world into the Great Depression, Yale economist Irving Fisher said: "Stocks have reached what looks like a permanently high plateau."

1929   Iraq: Premier Sir Abdul Muhsin commits suicide
New Zealand: Mau people of Samoa revolt against government
US: Stock market crash, setting off Great Depression and world economic crisis; losses were estimated at between $8 billion and $9 billion
USSR: Trotsky expelled from country; Joseph Stalin rules from 1929 to his death in 1953
Charles G. Dawes and J. Austen Chamberlain win the Nobel Peace Prize for the Dawes plan; Martin Luther King, Jr., civil rights leader (1929 to 1968)

KEY DOCUMENT

In *Hard Times: An Oral History of the Great Depression,* Studs Terkel collected the stories of men and women who lived through the crash. Here's an excerpt from one such story:

The Crash didn't happen in one day. There were a great many warnings. The country was crazy. Everybody was in the stock market, whether he could afford it or not. Shoeshine boys and waiters and capitalists. . . . A great many holding company pyramids were unsound, really fictitious values. It was a mad dream of get-rich-quick.

It wasn't only brokers involved in margin accounts. It was banks. They had a lot of stinking loans. The banks worked in as casual a way as the brokers did. And when they folded. . . .

I had a friend in Cincinnati who was young and attractive. He had a wife and children and he was insured for $100,000. Life was over as far as he was concerned. He took a dive, to take care of his wife and kids. There was a number who took the dive, to collect on insurance policies. It's unthinkable now. . . .

1930   Africa: Ras Tafari crowned emperor of Ethiopia; takes name Haile Selassie
Brazil: Getulio Vargas becomes president; assumes dictatorial powers in 1937
China: Japanese invade Manchuria
Constantinople renamed Istanbul
First Round Table Conference between British government and India

India: Mahatma Gandhi defies British laws and makes salt
South Africa: White women given the vote
1930 to 1932 Burma: Saya San Rebellion

1931

Australia: United Australia Party formed
China: Mukden Incident begins Japanese occupation of Manchuria
El Salvador: Arturo Araújo is elected president but overthrown by the military, led by Vice President General Martínez
Ethiopia: Haille Selassie I establishes a parliament and a judicial system but forbids all political parties
Spain: Alfonso XIII abdicates in favor of republic
Statute of Westminster makes dominions of British Empire self-governing
US: Scottsboro trial exposes Southern racism

Did You Know?

By the end of 1931, more than 12 million Americans were unemployed.

1932

Chile: Arturo Alessandri re-elected president
China: Japan controls Manchuria
El Salvador: Rebellion fails; over 30,000 killed
Germany: Nazis lead in German elections with 230 Reichstag seats
Iraq: Becomes independent
Thailand: Absolute rule of Thai king ends; he agrees to new constitution
US: Democrat Franklin D. Roosevelt elected president; Bruno Hauptmann kidnaps infant son of Charles Lindbergh and his wife Anne Morrow Lindbergh; 17,000 World War I veterans converge on Washington, DC, to demand bonus payments; the "Bonus Army" was dispersed in 1932
USSR: Famine: Between 1932 to 1933, 3 million people died
1932 to 1935 Bolivia and Paraguay: Chaco War

KEY DOCUMENT

Despair and panic gripped the US in the winter of 1932 to 1933. One of four workers could not find jobs; thirty-eight states had closed their banks. In Europe, fascism was on the rise. In his first inaugural speech, Franklin Delano Roosevelt gave the desperate country hope with these ringing words: "This great nation will endure as it has endured, will revive and will prosper. So, first of all, let me assert my firm belief that the only thing we have to fear is fear itself—nameless, unreasoning, unjustified terror which paralyzes needed efforts to convert retreat into advance."

1933   Australia: Controls large sector of Antarctica
Germany: Adolph Hitler appointed chancellor; Reichstag fire in Berlin; Nazi terror
begins
Iraq: King Faisal I dies; his son Ghazi rules
Peru: President Sanchez Cherro assassinated
US: Roosevelt launches New Deal to help rescue the US from Depression; Twenty-first
Amendment repeals Prohibition after 14 years of nationwide ban on liquor
USSR: Soviet Party purged

1934   Africa: British colonial government of Ghana suppresses radical African critics
Austria: Nazis assassinate Chancellor Dollfuss
Belgium: Leopold III succeeds to throne
China: Mao Zedong begins the Long March north with 100,000 soldiers
Cuba: Batista rules Cuba; US provides military training and supplies
Germany: Hitler elected fuhrer by German plebiscite; Mussolini meets Hitler
Middle East: Opening of British oil pipeline from Kirkuk (Iraq) to Tripoli (Syria)
USSR: Enters the League of Nations
USSR: Stalin begins purges of Communist Party
1934 to 1940 Spain: Civil war

1935   Germany: Nuremberg Laws deprive Jews of citizenship; Nazis repudiate Treaty of
Versailles and introduce compulsory military service
India: Government of India Act passed; provinces of British India granted autonomy
and self-government from 1937
Italy: Mussolini invades Ethiopia; League of Nations invokes sanctions
New Zealand: First Labor government elected; many reforms follow
US: Second phase of New Deal; Huey Long, autocratic and controversial Louisiana
political leader, assassinated
USSR: Seventh (and last) Comintern congress orders all Communists to join antifascists
1935 to 1936 Africa: Italians under Mussolini invade and annex Ethiopia

Did You Know?

*The second phase of the New Deal included the Social Security Act, equitable
taxation, and farm assistance.*

1936   England: Edward VIII takes the throne in January; abdicates in December
Ethiopia: War ends with Italy annexing the country
Germany: Invades Rhineland region on French-Belgian border
Japan: War with China, to continue through World War II
Philippines: Gain independence from US
Rome-Berlin Axis proclaimed (Japan to join in 1940); Germans occupy Rhineland
South Africa: Representation of Natives Act denies black South Africans any chance of
political equality

Syria: General strike in Syria; French grant Syria home rule
USSR: Major purge in the Communist Party; Trotsky exiled to Mexico
US: Bruno Hauptmann executed for Lindbergh kidnapping

Did You Know?

Between 1937 and 1938, 300,000 people died in the Rape of Nanking.

1937   Amelia Earhart disappears during around-the-world flight
Burma: Becomes self-governing
China: Japanese invade and seize Beijing, Shanghai, and Nanking
German zeppelin *Hindenburg* crashes, killing thirty-five
Ireland: Eamonn de Valera becomes prime minister

Did You Know?

*The crash of the Hindenburg, the first great tragedy to be recorded by the news
media, remains the most memorable aviation disaster of the first half of the
twentieth century. Scores of newsreel and still cameras captured the astonishing
sight of the 803-foot ship as it exploded and collapsed. Herbert Morrison captured
the drama on the radio, screaming "It's burst into flames!" and "Oh, the humanity!"
Amazingly, sixty-two of the ninety-seven people on board survived.*

Italy: Leaves League of Nations
New Zealand: National Party formed
Palestine: Conflict between Jews and Arabs
US: National Labor Relations Act; Roosevelt's attempt to "pack" the Supreme Court
with extra justices fails

KEY DOCUMENT

On September 30, 1938, British Prime Minister Neville Chamberlain said:
"This is the second time in our history that there has come down from Ger-
many to Downing Street peace with honor. I believe it is peace for our time."
He was wrong.

1938   Europe: Germany annexes Austria; Hitler now war minister
Munich Pact: Britain, France, and Italy let Germany partition Czechoslovakia
Mexico: Government takes over US and British oil companies in Mexico
US: Fair Labor Standards Act establishes minimum wage of 25¢ per hour and forty-four-hour work week.

Did You Know?

Thailand is the only country in Southeast Asia never taken over by a European power.

1939   Australia: Robert Menzies becomes prime minister
Europe: World War II begins when Germany invades Poland; Stalin and Hitler divide Poland between them (August 23)
Russo-Finnish War: Finns to lose one-tenth of territory in 1940 peace treaty
Siam: Renamed Thailand
Spain: Civil war ends with Francisco Franco as dictator
South Africa: Declares war on Germany at start of World War II

1940   Africa: British begin offensive in North Africa
England: Churchill becomes prime minister
Europe: Germany invades Norway, Denmark, Holland, Belgium, France: all capitulate; Battle of Britain
Mexico: Trotsky assassinated
US: Roosevelt elected to third term as president
USSR: Annexes Estonia, Latvia, and Lithuania

1941   Africa: German army under Rommel attacks British in North Africa; Rommel retreats; *Bismark* sunk
England: German air raids and U-boat attacks intensify against Britain
Ethiopia: Liberated from Italians by Ethiopians and British, and recognized as independent
Iran: Riza Shah forced to abdicate; his son Mohammed Riza Shah becomes shah and signs a peace treaty with Russia and England
Japan: Enters World War II on the German side
Russia: Germans invade
Southeast Asia: Japanese capture Hong Kong and overruns much of Southeast Asia
US: Manhattan Project (atomic bomb research) begins; Japanese attack Pearl Harbor; US enters World War II

1942   Egypt: British defeat German army at Battle of El Alamein
Japan: Invades Malaya, Burma, Dutch East Indies
South Pacific: Americans bomb Tokyo and win battles of Coral Sea and Midway
Germany: At Wannsee Conference, Nazis coordinate the "final solution to the Jewish question," the Holocaust; Germans reach Stalingrad
US: More than 120,000 Japanese and persons of Japanese ancestry living in western US moved to "relocation centers," some for the duration of the war (Executive Order 9066)

KEY DOCUMENT

President Franklin D. Roosevelt's speech asking Congress to declare war on Japan has become famous. The speech begins: "Yesterday, December 7, 1941—a day which will live in infamy—the United States of America was suddenly and deliberately attacked by naval and air forces of the empire of Japan." It ends:

> I believe that I interpret the will of the Congress and of the people when I assert that we will not only defend ourselves to the uttermost but will make it very certain that this form of treachery shall never again endanger us.
>
> Hostilities exist. There is no blinking at the fact that our people, our territory, and our interests are in grave danger.
>
> With confidence in our armed forces, with the unbounding determination of our people, we will gain the inevitable triumph. So help us God.
>
> I ask that the Congress declare that since the unprovoked and dastardly attack by Japan on Sunday, December 7, 1941, a state of war has existed between the United States and the Japanese empire.

1943   Africa: English reach Tripoli; Germans and Italians driven from North Africa
                  Europe: Casablanca Conference (Churchill and Roosevelt); Mussolini deposed; Germans withdraw from Caucasus; Americans retake Guadalcanal; massacre in Polish Warsaw ghetto

Did You Know?

Between 1938 and 1945, the Nazis killed 6 million Jews in the Holocaust. Another 9 to 10 million people—Gypsies, Slavs (Poles, Ukrainians, and Belarussians), homosexuals, and the disabled—were killed in the Holocaust as well.

Italy: Allies invade Sicily and advance up Italy; Italy surrenders and declares war on Germany
Lebanon: Becomes independent (from France)
South Pacific: Americans liberate Pacific Islands
US: Chinese Exclusion Repeal Act

Did You Know?

In the D-Day invasion, the US-led Allies hurled 175,000 men at the beaches of Normandy.

1944   El Salvador: General Martínez forced from power; military government continues
Europe: Allies land at Anzio; siege of Leningrad lifted; June 6: Allies invade Normandy
on D-Day; Dec. 16: Battle of the Bulge; first V-1 flying bomb hits London; Americans
capture Guam
Guatemala: First free presidential elections
Syria: Becomes independent (from France)

Did You Know?

*The Battle for Iwo Jima, a tiny volcanic island guarding the flight path to Japan,
was one of the fiercest in World War II. Nearly one-third of the 80,000 troops
who fought there were killed or wounded; about half of the 22,000 Japanese
defending the island died. James Bradley's* Flags of Our Fathers *(2000) traces the
battle and the subsequent lives of the six men who raised the flag over Iwo Jima
in the famous picture by Joe Rosenthal.*

1945   Europe: British offensive in Burma; Russians take Warsaw; Americans enter Manila;
February: Yalta Conference (Roosevelt, Churchill, Stalin) plans final defeat of Germany
(February 7); Hitler commits suicide (May 7); Germany surrenders (May 7); Potsdam
Conference (Truman, Churchill, Stalin) establishes basis of German reconstruction (July
to August)
Japan: US drops atomic bombs on Japanese cities of Hiroshima (August 6) and Nagasaki
(August 9); Japan formally surrenders after bombings of Hiroshima and Nagasaki
(September 2); end of World War II
Middle East: World Zionist Conference calls for Jewish state in Palestine
US: Franklin D. Roosevelt dies (April 12); Truman becomes president; United Nations
established in New York City

1946   Argentina: Juan Perón elected president
China: War between Communists and Nationalists
England: UN General Assembly opens in London; soon after, League of Nations
dissolved; Churchill's "Iron Curtain" speech marks beginning of Cold War
Europe: Verdict in Nuremberg war trial: twelve Nazi leaders (including one tried in
absentia) sentenced to hang; seven imprisoned; three acquitted; Goering commits suicide
a few hours before ten other Nazis are executed
Italy: Italy abolishes monarchy.
India: Muslims riot
Iran: Oil development agreement with Russia; Azerbaijan and Kurdistan republics
collapse, letting Iran control oilfields again
Kuwait: First oil exported
Vietnam: Chinese and British withdraw; French reestablish control over parts of
Vietnam, refusing to recognize Ho Chi Minh's government
US: Atomic Energy Commission formed

1947   Europe: Peace treaties for Italy, Romania, Bulgaria, Hungary, Finland
India: Gains independence, partitioned into India and Pakistan

Japan: New democratic constitution
Nigeria: Constitution gives limited native participation in provincial legislatures
US: Marshall Plan to help rebuild Europe; Roswell incident (alleged alien landing in New Mexico); Truman Doctrine: US government promises aid to any government resisting communism

Did You Know?

On August 14, 1947, the Muslim parts of India (on the east and west) became the independent country of Pakistan. The following day, the Hindu lands became the independent country of India.

1948   Burma and Ceylon become independent
Czechoslovakia: Communists seize power
Europe: Stalin and Tito break
Germany: Soviets blockade West Berlin; Berlin airlift begins to combat embargo
India: Mohandas K. Gandhi assassinated by Hindu fanatic (January 30).
Indonesia: United States of Indonesia established as Dutch and Indonesians settle conflict
Israel: Independent Jewish state of Israel proclaimed
Korea: Independent Republic of Korea proclaimed
Middle East: First Arab-Israeli War
Netherlands: Juliana succeeds to the throne
South Africa: Afrikaner National Party wins power
US: Alger Hiss, former U.S. State Department official, indicted on perjury charges after denying passing secret documents to communist spy ring; convicted in second trial (1950) and sentenced to 5-year prison term; Truman ends racial segregation in military; under Marshall Plan, US dispenses aid to Europe to help postwar recovery (1948 to 1951)

1949   Canada: Newfoundland becomes a province
China: Communists, under Mao Zedong, seize the country and proclaim it the Peoples Republic of China
England: Recognizes Irish independence
Germany: German Federal Republic (West Germany) established (September 21)
Israel: Cease-fire in Palestine; signs armistice with Egypt
Russians: Lift Berlin blockade
South Africa: Government institutionalizes apartheid
US: Harry Truman elected president; US and Western European nations set up North Atlantic Treaty Organization (NATO) for collective security

1950   India: Becomes a republic
Korean War begins when North Korean Communist forces invade South Korea
Middle East: Jordon annexes West Bank
Tibet: Chinese seize the country
Turkey: First free elections

US: McCarthyism begins; Senator Joe McCarthy claims 205 communists have infiltrated State Department; black Americans intensify campaign for civil rights; Korean War (1950 to 1953)

1951 England: Churchill forms his first peacetime government
Iran: Oil industry nationalized
Libya: Gains independence
Korea: North Korean army crosses 38th parallel and retakes Seoul; UN forces recapture Seoul; armistice negotiations fail; General Douglas MacArthur relieved of his command in Korea after advocating expanded US military effort there
US: Julius and Ethel Rosenberg sentenced to death for passing atomic secrets to Russians; Twenty-second Amendment takes effect, limiting the president to two terms in office

1952 China: Farmers organized into cooperatives
Cuba: Castro imprisoned after a failed uprising
Egypt: Becomes a republic
England: Queen Elizabeth succeeds to the throne
Hungary: Communist Party's general secretary Matyas Rakosi becomes prime minister
Poland: Adopts a constitution
Vietnam: Vietminh guerrilla forces control of the countryside
1952 to 1959 Africa: Mau-Mau guerrilla war against British in Kenya results in state of emergency

1953 China: Mao Zedong introduces first 5-year plan
Egypt: Military junta rules
Germany: East Berliners rise against Communist rule; quelled by tanks
Iran: US overthrows the Iran Mossadeq government
Korea: Korean War ends; armistice signed July 27
US: Dag Hammarskjold elected UN secretary-general; General Dwight D. Eisenhower becomes president; Julius and Ethel Rosenberg executed for passing atomic secrets to Russians
USSR: Stalin dies; Nikita Khrushchev takes power
Yugoslavia: Tito becomes president

1954 Egypt: Gamal Abdel Nasser becomes president and rules Egypt until 1970
Guatemala: Government overthrown in US-backed coup
Nigeria becomes a federation
Vietnam: Dien Bien Phu, French military, falls to Vietminh army
US: Supreme Court (in *Brown v. Board of Education of Topeka*) unanimously bans racial segregation in public schools; Senate censures Senator Joseph McCarthy for "communist" hunt
Africa: War for independence in Algeria; freedom won in 1962

1955 Ethiopia: New constitution
Argentina: Army seizes power from President Juan Perón
Cuba: Castro released from prison in Cuba; flees to Mexico
England: Winston Churchill resigns as prime minister; Anthony Eden succeeds him
Germany: Federal Republic of West Germany becomes sovereign state

Indonesia: Afro-Asian conference sparks nonalliance movement among third world countries that wish to stay neutral in Cold War
Middle East: Israel-Jordan border see increased air raids; Iran, Iraq, Britain, Turkey, and Palestine sign the Baghdad Pact
Japan: Fast economic growth
US: Rosa Parks refuses to sit at the back of the bus; Martin Luther King, Jr., leads black boycott of Montgomery, AL, bus system; desegregated service begins December 21, 1956
American Federation of Labor (AFL) and Congress of Industrial Organizations (CIO) merge
USSR: Nikolai A. Bulganin becomes Soviet premier, replacing Malenkov
Vietnam: Ngo Dinh Diem becomes prime minister
Poland: Warsaw Pact signed; East European mutual defense agreement

1956   Hungary: Revolt starts when Soviet troops and tanks crush anti-Communist rebellion
Middle East: Israel launches attack on Egypt's Sinai peninsula and drives toward Suez Canal; British and French invade Egypt at Port Said; cease-fire forced by US pressure, stops British, French, and Israeli advance

Did You Know?

On November 18, 1956, Soviet leader Nikita Khrushchev claimed: "Whether you like it or not, history is on our side. We will bury you."

Morocco: Gains independence
Poland: Workers' uprising against Communist rule in Poznan, Poland, is crushed; Communist Wladislaw Gomulka rules
Sudan: Gains independence
Tunisia: Gains independence
USSR: Nikita Khrushchev, head of the USSR Communist Party, takes control of the government

1957   Africa: Ghana is first country in sub-Saharan Africa to become independent
Canada: John George Diefenbaker elected prime minister
Jordan: King Hussein proclaims martial law after Israeli war
Nigeria: Internal self-governing status
Norway: Olaf V succeeds to throne
US: Little Rock, AK, school desegregated
Treaty of Rome ushers in the European Economic Community (EEC)

1958   Cuba: Fidel Castro becomes ruler of Cuba and declares war on Batista government
Europe: Common Market established
France: General Charles de Gaulle becomes premier; he remains in power until 1969
Iraq: Hashemite monarchy overthrown in a bloody coup
Mexico: Women allowed to vote in a presidential election for the first time
Middle East: Egypt and Syria merge into United Arab Republic

US: National Aeronautics and Space Administration (NASA) formed
USSR: Khrushchev becomes premier of Soviet Union

1959   Cuba: President Batista resigns and flees; Castro takes over
Tibet: Chinese forces conquer Tibet; Dalai Lama escapes to India
US: Alaska becomes forty-ninth state; Hawaii becomes fiftieth state; Vietnam War (1959 to 1975)

1960   Africa: Senegal, Ghana, Nigeria, Madagascar, and Zaire (former Belgian Congo) gain independence; civil war in Zaire

Did You Know?

Zaire was formerly known as the Belgian Congo.

Brazil: Brasília becomes capital
Cyprus: Gains independence from Britain
Japan: Socialist Party leader Inajiro Asanuma assassinated
Middle East: Organization of Petroleum Exporting Countries (OPEC) is formed by Iraq, Iran, Kuwait, Saudi Arabia, and Venezuela; Nazi murderer of Jews, Adolf Eichmann, captured by Israelis in Argentina
South Korea: President Synghman Rhee elected to a fourth term
South Vietnam: President Ngo Dinh Diem regains power
US: John F. Kennedy elected thirty-fifth president
USSR: Soviet Union shoots down an American U-2 spy plane

1961   Africa: Rwanda becomes a republic; Sierra Leone gains independence; United States of the Congo founded; northern part of British Cameroons joins Nigeria
Central America: Central American Common Market is formed providing a "free trade zone" in El Salvador, Guatemala, Honduras, Nicaragua, and Costa Rica
China: Famine spreads after 3 years of crop failure and floods
Cuba: Bay of Pigs invasion ends in disaster (April 17)
Germany: Berlin wall is built, dividing East and West Berlin (August 13)
Korea: South Korean military junta overthrows democratic government
Middle East: Kuwait gains independence; English troops stop Iraqi attempt to annex Kuwait
South Africa: Severs ties with British Commonwealth
US: Freedom Riders protest for civil rights; President Kennedy starts the Peace Corps; US ends diplomatic relations with Cuba
USSR: Fires 50-megaton hydrogen bomb, biggest explosion in history

1962   Africa: Burundi and Uganda become independent; Tanganyika becomes a republic
Caribbean: Jamaica, Trinidad and Tobago, and other countries in British West Indies become independent

Cuba: Cuban missile crisis brings US and USSR to brink of war (August to November)
India: Chinese Communist forces invade and then withdraw
Iran: Earthquake in Iran kills more than 12,000 people
Israel: Adolf Eichmann executed
South Pacific: Western Samoa gains independence

1963　　Africa: Organization of African Unity founded
Canada: Lester Bowles Pearson elected prime minister

Did You Know?

Martin Luther King, Jr. was greatly influenced by Henry David Thoreau's stance on civil disobedience and Gandhi's advocacy of nonviolence, known as ahimsa (Sanskrit for "noninjury").

England: Profumo scandal
Europe: France and West Germany sign treaty of cooperation, ending four centuries of conflict
Germany: President Kennedy's "Ich bin ein Berliner" speech
Iran: Women given the vote
Iraq: Ba'th Party executes Qassem and seizes power
Kenya: Becomes independent
Malaysia: Federation established

Did You Know?

Dr. King delivered his "I Have a Dream" speech from the steps of the Lincoln Memorial on the hundredth anniversary of the Emancipation Proclamation. King began speaking slowly that hot, sunny Wednesday afternoon, referring to the Declaration of Independence's recognition of the rights of all citizens, as well as President Abraham Lincoln's Emancipation Proclamation of 1863. "But one hundred years later," King said, "the Negro still is not free," but he still "had a dream": "It is a dream deeply rooted in the American dream. I have a dream that one day this nation will rise up and live out the true meaning of its creed, 'We hold these truths to be self-evident, that all men are created equal.' . . . So let freedom ring from the prodigious hilltops of New Hampshire; let freedom ring from the mighty mountains of New York. . . ." The marchers were electrified. King's speech and the march contributed support for civil rights reform, although resistance to the administration's bill was not overcome until well after Kennedy's assassination in November 1963. President Lyndon B. Johnson, Kennedy's successor, steered an enlarged version of the Kennedy bill through Congress in the spring of 1964, and on July 2 signed it into law.

Nigeria: Adopts republican government under President Nnamdi Azikiwe
US: Congress guarantees women equal pay for equal work; Kennedy orders black students admitted to University of Alabama; President John F. Kennedy assassinated in Dallas, TX (November 22); Lee Harvey Oswald, accused assassin, shot and killed by Jack Ruby, Dallas nightclub owner, two days later
Vietnam: South Vietnam government of Ngo Dinh Diem falls; Buddhist monks burn themselves in the streets to protest the corrupt government

---

KEY DOCUMENT

The Warren Commission was created to discover the truth concerning the assassination of President Kennedy. Here are some of their conclusions:

1. The shots which killed President Kennedy and wounded Governor Connally were fired from the sixth floor window at the southeast corner of the Texas School Book Depository. . . .

The shots which killed President Kennedy and wounded Governor Connally were fired by Lee Harvey Oswald. This conclusion is based upon the following:

The Commission has found no evidence that either Lee Harvey Oswald or Jack Ruby was part of any conspiracy, domestic or foreign, to assassinate President Kennedy. . . .

On the basis of the evidence before the Commission it concludes that Oswald acted alone. Therefore, to determine the motives for the assassination of President Kennedy, one must look to the assassin himself. Clues to Oswald's motives can be found in his family history, his education or lack of it, his acts, his writings, and the recollections of those who had close contacts with him throughout his life.

1964   Brazil: Military leaders seize power
Chile: US spends $20 million to back Eduardo Frei for president instead of Marxist candidate Allende (Salvador Allende Gossens)
Cyprus: UN forces intervene in war between Turkey and Greece
Middle East: Arab leaders set up Palestine Liberation Organization to unite Palestinian refugees
India: Prime Minister Nehru dies; Lal Bahadur Shastri becomes prime minister
Malta: Gains independence
Mozambique: Revolts against Portuguese rule
Russia: Leonid Brezhnev takes over from Khrushchev as ruler
South Africa: Nelson Mandela sentenced to life imprisonment
US: Civil Rights Act bans racial discrimination in federal funding and employment
Vietnam: War escalates as North Vietnamese attack US ship
South Africa: Zambia created from what was Northern Rhodesia

1965   Africa: White regime in Zimbabwe declares independence; civil war in Zaire ends
Cuba: Thousands of refugees airlifted from Cuba to US

The Gambia: Gains independence
India and Pakistan: Border disputes
Indonesia: General Suharto orders mass murder of Communists
Romania: Nicolae Ceausescu gains power
US: Blacks riot for 6 days in Watts section of Los Angeles leaving 34 dead, over 1,000 injured, nearly 4,000 arrested, and fire damage put at $175 million; North Carolina begins a busing program to integrate schools; Lyndon Johnson becomes thirty-sixth president; Medicare, senior citizens' government medical assistance program, begins; Malcolm X, black-nationalist leader, shot dead at Harlem rally in New York City
US and Canada: Power failure in Ontario plant blacks out parts of eight northeastern states of US and two provinces of southeastern Canada (November 9)
Vietnam: Generals Nguyen Ky and Nguyen Van Thieu gain control of the government in South Vietnam: protests against war intensify

KEY DOCUMENT

"We're going to bomb them back into the Stone Age"—General Curtis LeMay of the North Vietnamese, 1965.

1966   China: "Cultural Revolution"; demonstrations against Western influence
India: Indira Gandhi elected prime minister
Indonesia: General Suharto establishes dictatorship
Nigeria: Military dictatorship is established
Syria: Radical Marxists seize power
US: Supreme Court decides *Miranda v. Arizona*

1967   Africa: Biafra secedes from Nigeria; Biafran War
Greece: Military coup
Middle East: Six-Day War ends with Israel occupying Sinai Peninsula, Golan Heights, Gaza Strip, and east bank of Suez Canal (June 5)
US: Massive anti-Vietnam War demonstration in Washington, DC; Supreme Court legalizes abortion; Thurgood Marshall sworn in as first black US Supreme Court justice

1968   Canada: Pierre Elliott Trudeau elected prime minister
Czechoslovakia: Soviets invade; Warsaw Pact crushes liberal regime

Did You Know?

Civil war erupted in Nigeria when the eastern region, Biafra, declared its independence. The Ibo people in the region did not want to be ruled by people from the north. Despite the United Nations' attempts to stop the fighting, it continued until Biafra collapsed.

France: Paris erupts into student riots followed by general strike
Iraq: Iraqi Ba'th party holds power and establishes pan-Arab national command
Korea: North Korea seizes US Navy ship *Pueblo;* holds eighty-three on board as spies
US: Dr. Martin Luther King, Jr. assassinated (April 4); Robert Kennedy assassinated (June 5)
Vietnam: Tet offensive, turning point in Vietnam War
US: Yippies lead riots at the Democratic Convention in Chicago
US and USSR, England: Nuclear Non-Proliferation Treaty

Did You Know?

Before her victory, Margaret Thatcher said: "No woman in my time will be prime minister."

1969   Israel: Golda Meir becomes prime minister
Northern Ireland: Protestants and Catholics escalate fighting
South America: War between the Honduras and El Salvador
US: Senator Edward M. Kennedy pleads guilty to leaving scene of fatal accident at Chappaquiddick, MA, in which Mary Jo Kopechne was drowned; he gets a two-month suspended sentence

1970   Cambodia: Communist Khmer Rouge ousts Prince Norodom Shianouk; General Lon Nol takes over
Chile: Allende elected president
Egypt: President Nasser dies
Jordan: Assassination attempt on King Hussein
Nigeria: Civil war ends with capitulation of rebel Biafra
Rhodesia: Severs last tie with British Crown and declares itself a racially segregated republic
South Pacific: Tonga and Fiji gain independence from Britain
US: Death toll of American soldiers rises to 44,241

1971   US: UN seats Communist China and expels Nationalist China; *Pentagon Papers* published; 1,000 NY state troopers storm Attica prison; 43 inmates and guards die in riots
Vietnam: War spreads to Laos and Cambodia

Did You Know?

The Watergate scandal began when five men attempted to bug Democratic National Committee headquarters in the Washington, DC, Watergate complex.

1972   Bangladesh: (formerly East Pakistan) becomes a sovereign nation
Germany: Eleven Israeli athletes at Olympic Games in Munich are killed after eight members of an Arab terrorist group invade Olympic Village; five guerrillas and one policeman also killed
Ireland: "Bloody Sunday" in Londonderry, Northern Ireland: troops fire on civil rights marchers
US: Richard Nixon reelected president; Watergate scandal; Congress passes Equal Opportunity Act in response to growing women's movement
US and USSR: Strategic Arms Limitation Talks agreement (SALT I)

Did You Know?

The Yom Kippur War began on October 6 (Yom Kippur), the holiest day on the Jewish calendar, when Egyptian and Syrian forces attacked Israel. Both sides gained and lost territory by the time a truce was signed on October 22. Israel later withdrew from the east bank of the Suez Canal.

1973   Afghanistan: Mohammad Daoud Khan, king's cousin, overthrows monarchy
Chile: Marxist president Salvadore Allende killed in a military coup led by General Pinochet
Greece: Greek military junta abolishes monarchy and proclaims republic
Israel: Yom Kippur War; Egypt and Israel sign US-sponsored cease-fire accord
Uruguay: Military coup
US: Organization of Petroleum Exporting Countries embargo oil shipments because of US support to Israel; abortion legalized
Vietnam: US and North Vietnam sign a cease-fire agreement

1974   Africa: Nigeria becomes leading oil producer in Africa; revolutionary regime in Ethiopia; civil war spreads
Portugal: Military coup; Portuguese colonies gain independence after long struggle (1974 to 1975)
South Africa: Expelled from UN
US: President Nixon resigns before being impeached as a result of Watergate scandal

1975   Australia: Governor-general dismisses elected government, sparking political crisis
Cambodia: Khmer Rouge begins reign of terror; 2 million deaths by 1979
Honduras: Colonel Juan Alberto Melgar Castro leads government coup
Lebanon: Muslims and the Maronite-dominated Phalange faction battle
Mozambique: Becomes independent
South Pacific: Papua New Guinea gains independence from Australia
Spain: Juan Carlos sworn in as king, first in 44 years

1976   Africa: Schoolchildren spark uprisings in Soweto
China: Zhou Enlai and Mao Zedong die; Gang of Four discredited
Helsinki: Convention on human rights adopted

KEY DOCUMENT

Here is Richard Nixon's resignation speech:

Good evening.

This is the thirty-seventh time I have spoken to you from this office, where so many decisions have been made that shaped the history of this Nation. Each time I have done so to discuss with you some matter that I believe affected the national interest.

In all the decisions I have made in my public life, I have always tried to do what was best for the Nation. Throughout the long and difficult period of Watergate, I have felt it was my duty to persevere, to make every possible effort to complete the term of office to which you elected me. . . .

From the discussions I have had with Congressional and other leaders, I have concluded that because of the Watergate matter I might not have the support of the Congress that I would consider necessary to back the very difficult decisions and carry out the duties of this office in the way the interests of the Nation would require.

I have never been a quitter. To leave office before my term is completed is abhorrent to every instinct in my body. But as President, I must put the interest of America first. America needs a full-time President and a full-time Congress, particularly at this time with problems we face at home and abroad.

To continue to fight through the months ahead for my personal vindication would almost totally absorb the time and attention of both the President and the Congress in a period when our entire focus should be on the great issues of peace abroad and prosperity without inflation at home.

Therefore, I shall resign the Presidency effective at noon tomorrow. Vice President Ford will be sworn in as President at that hour in this office.

Middle East: Israeli airborne commandos attack Uganda's Entebbe Airport and free 103 hostages held by pro-Palestinian hijackers of Air France plane; one Israeli and several Ugandan soldiers killed in raid
Thailand: Military seizes the government in a bloody coup
Vietnam: North and South Vietnam reunited as a single country

1977   Canada: Quebec adopts French as official language
China: Deng Xiaoping, purged Chinese leader, restored to power as Gang of Four is expelled from Communist Party

Did You Know?

"There is no reason for any individual to have a computer in their home," the *president of Digital Equipment Corporation said in 1977.*

Czech Republic: Intellectuals sign Charter 77 stating that democratic freedoms are still denied

Israel: Menachem Begin elected prime minister

US: President Carter pardons Vietnam draft evaders

1978   Afghanistan: Dictator Mohammad Daoud Khan executed

Bolivia: President ousted

Cambodia: Vietnam invades and forces out Khmer Rouge

China and US: Diplomatic relations reestablished

Guyana: Mass murder-suicide in Jonestown

Honduras: General Policarpo Paz García ousts Colonel Melgar

Italy: Former Italian premier Aldo Moro kidnapped by left-wing terrorists and killed

Middle East: Egypt's President Sadat and Israeli Premier Begin sign "Framework for Peace"

Rhodesia: Prime Minister Ian D. Smith and three black leaders agree on transfer to black majority rule

US: In *Bakke* case, Supreme Court bars quota systems in college admissions but affirms constitutionality of programs giving advantage to minorities

1979   Afghanistan: Soviets invade

Africa: Emperor Bokassa of Central African Empire overthrown; new President David Dacko abolishes empire

Cambodia: Fall of Phnom Penh, Cambodian capital, and collapse of Pol Pot regime

El Salvador: President Carlos Romero overthrown in military coup

England: First female prime minister, Margaret Thatcher

Iran: Ayatollah Khomeini expels shah; adopts Islamic constitution; militants seize US Embassy in Teheran and hold hostages

Korea: President Park Chung Hee shot dead, allegedly by accident by his chief of intelligence

Nicaragua: Sandinista army overthrows dictator Anastasio Somoza and forms government

Nigeria: Alhaji Shehu Shagari elected president

Uganda: General Idi Amin flees country

US and USSR: Carter and Brezhnev sign SALT II agreement

1980   Afghanistan: Afghan rebels clash with Soviet troops in Hindu Kush mountains

Algeria: Severe earthquakes; 20,000 dead

Canada: Pierre Trudeau elected prime minister again

Honduras: Peace treaty with El Salvador

Iceland: Vigdis Finnbogadottir elected first female president

India: Indira Gandhi reelected prime minister, after having lost her seat in 1977; son Sanjay killed in a plane crash

Iraq: Saddam Hussein becomes president; Iran-Iraq war begins

Poland: Independent trade union Solidarity formed with Lech Walesa as chairman

Nicaragua: Anastasio Somoza Debayle, ousted Nicaragua ruler, and two aides assassinated in Asunción, Paraguay capital

US: Americans held hostage by Iran; airborne rescue raid fails disastrously (eight Americans killed, five wounded); Carter administration discredited; Ronald Reagan elected president in landslide victory against Jimmy Carter

USSR: Sends Nobel physicist and dissident Andrei Sakharov into internal exile
Zimbabwe: Gains independence

1981   Antigua, BWI: Barbuda: Gains independence
Bangladesh: President Ziaur Rahman assassinated
Belize: Formerly British Honduras, gains independence
Egypt: Anwar Sadat assassinated; Vice President Hosni Mubarak succeeds him
France: François Mitterand elected president
Iran: Releases fifty-two hostages
Israel: Annexes Golan Heights
Lebanon: Civil war rages
Norway: Gro Harlem Brundtland becomes first female prime minister
US: Ronald Reagan becomes fortieth American president; John Hinckley shoots and
wounds President Reagan and three others; Sandra Day O'Connor becomes first female
US Supreme Court justice

1982   Africa: Government of Chad overthrown
Falkland Islands: Argentine army driven out after British invasion
Guatemala: Rios Montt becomes president in military coup
Israel: Returns Sinai to Egypt (Camp David agreement)
Lebanon: Newly elected president Bashir Gemayel is assassinated; brother Amin
Gemayel is elected to replace him; Israeli forces invade

1983   Africa: Countries adopt International Monetary Fund (IMF) plans for managing their
economies
Ethiopia: Drought brings famine to millions
Grenada: US invades after a coup of pro-Cuban Marxists
US: Sally Ride becomes first American woman to fly in space, aboard the *Challenger*

1984   Canada: Brian Mulroney elected prime minister
India: Indira Gandhi assassinated; her son Rajiv Gandhi becomes prime minister
India: 6,000 die when deadly gas released from Union Carbide pesticide plant
Upper Volta: Renamed Burkina Faso ("republic of honest men")

1985   Honduras: José Azcona Hoyo elected president
Mexico: Mexico City struck by magnitude 7.8 earthquake, killing 20,000 people
Nigeria: Major General Babangida overthrows dictator Major General Buhari
US: First version of Gramm-Rudman-Hollings Act signed into law to control the
national deficit
USSR: Mikhail Gorbachev elected Soviet Communist Party leader; introduces
reforms

1986   Libya: US bombs the country
Philippines: President Marcos flees country after ballot scandal
Sweden: Olof Palme, leader of the Social Democratic Party, assassinated.
US: Nobel Peace Prize goes to Elie Wiesel, human rights advocate
USSR: Nuclear meltdown at Chernobyl in Ukraine; over 133,000 evacuated; fallout
affects all of Europe

1987   Earth: Five billionth inhabitant born
England: Margaret Thatcher elected for third term as prime minister
Lebanon: Syrian troops occupy the Muslim sector
Russia: Gorbachev introduces the term "glasnost"

1988   Afghanistan: Pakistan and Afghanistan sign Geneva Accords
Iran and Iraq: Declare cease-fire
Nicaragua: Contras and the Sandinista government reach a cease-fire agreement
US: Indicts Manuel Noriega on drug charges
Pakistan: Benazir Bhutto becomes the first female prime minister of a Muslim country
Russia: Gorbachev introduces "perestroika"
US and Canada: Comprehensive free trade agreement signed

Did You Know?

"That virus is a pussycat," claimed Dr. Peter Duesberg, a molecular biology professor at the University of California at Berkeley, describing the HIV virus on March 25, 1988.

1989   Cambodia: Vietnamese troops withdraw
China: Tanks drive pro-democracy protesters from Tiananmen Square, Beijing
Germany: Berlin wall dismantled
Honduras: Rafael Leonardo Callejas elected president
Japan: Prince Akihito succeeds to throne
US: Supertanker Exxon *Valdez* hits the rocks in Alaska, spilling 11 million gallons of crude oil into Prince William Sound; invades Panama and deposes ruler, General Noriega

KEY DOCUMENT

"Let me say directly to Fidel Castro: You're finished," postured Ronald Reagan on May 17, 1990. President Reagan was wrong.

1990   Africa: Fighting begins between the Rwandan Patriotic Front and the Rwandan government
Burma: First free military elections in 30 years, with opposition party winning a decisive victory; the military refuses to hand over power
Chile: Returns to democracy after 17 years under a dictator; Patricio Awlyn Azocar takes government
England: Prime Minister Margaret Thatcher resigns; succeeded by John Major
Germany: East and West Germany reunite, unified as one nation
Middle East: Iraq invades Kuwait; US and allies send forces to the Gulf region; Gulf War begins

Mozambique: Democracy emerges
Namibia: Gains independence
Rwanda: Strife between Rwandan Patriotic Front and Rwandan government
South Africa: Nelson Mandela is freed after 27 years in prison; Apartheid dismantled
US: Americans with Disabilities Act requires employers to take reasonable steps to make
the workplace accessible to disabled workers
USSR: Yeltsin elected president; Ukraine declares its sovereignty; Mikhail Gorbachev
wins Nobel for his role in the peace process
Yemen Arab Republic and the People's Democratic Republic of Yemen merge

1991   India: Rajiv Gandhi assassinated
Iraq: Accepts the terms of a cease-fire that ends Persian Gulf War
Middle East: US and UN forces defeat Iraq in Operation Desert Storm
Myanmar: Aung San Suu Kyi wins Nobel Peace Prize
Thailand: Prime Minister Choonhavan ousted in a bloodless coup
Europe: USSR ends with creation of Commonwealth of Independent States; Yeltsin takes
power; six Yugoslavian republics, including Slovenia and Croatia, declare independence

1992   Brazil: President Fernando Collor de Mello resigns
El Salvador: Peace accords signed between the National Republican Alliance and the
leftist rebels of Faribundo Marti National Liberation Front
Guatemala: Rigoberta Menchú wins Nobel Peace Prize
Japan: Top leader, Shin Kanemaru, resigns in scandal
Kenya: First multiparty elections
Somalia: UN intervenes in effort to combat famine
US: Palestinian leader Arafat and Israeli prime minister Rabin sign peace agreement
Yugoslavia: Breaks up and erupts into bloody civil war; 200,000 killed

1993   Africa: Eritrea breaks from Ethiopia; first successful secession in postcolonial Africa
Bosnia: US begins airlift of supplies to besieged Bosnia towns
Czech Republic: Václav Havel elected president
Middle East: Israel and PLO sign Middle East Peace Accord
Nigeria: Major General Babangida declares elections void and refuses to give up power
Sri Lanka: President assassinated
South Africa: F. W. de Klerk and Nelson Mandella win Nobel Peace Prize
US: Bill Clinton elected forty-second president
US: "Great Flood of 1993" leaves at least 50 dead, over 70,000 homeless, and $12 million
in property damage

1994   Israel: Yitzhak Rabin wins Nobel Peace Prize
Mexico: Zapatista uprising
Rwanda: Civil war; 800,000 deaths
South Africa: African National Congress (ANC) wins first multiracial election; Nelson
Mandella becomes first black president
US: Senate Whitewater hearings, involving Bill and Hillary Clinton, begin

1995   Bosnia: Fighting escalates in Bosnia and Croatia
Israel: Israelis and Palestinians agree on transferring West Bank to Arabs; Prime Minister
Yitzhak Rabin assassinated at peace rally

Japan: Earthquake kills more than 5,000
Poland: Joseph Rotblat wins Nobel Peace Prize
US: O. J. Simpson found not guilty of the murder of his wife Nicole Brown Simpson and waiter Ron Goldman; major terrorist bombing in Oklahoma City

1996 Afghanistan: Taliban Muslim fundamentalists capture Kabul
East Timor: Bishop Carlos Ximenes Belo and Jose Ramos-Horta win Nobel Peace Prize
Middle East: Iraqis strike at Kurdish enclave; US attacks Iraq's southern air defenses; Iraq halts attacks on US planes
Rwanda: Hundreds of thousands of Hutu refugees return to Rwanda
Sri Lanka: Seventy-three dead in suicide bombing
South Africa: New constitution

1997 England returns Hong Kong to China after 156 years of British rule
Egypt: Islamic militants kill sixty-two at Luxor tourist site
US: The International Campaign to Ban Landmines and its coordinator, Jody Williams, win Nobel Peace Prize

Did You Know?

Speaking before the world on January 26, 1998, President Clinton said: "I did not have sexual relations with that woman, Ms. Lewinsky."

1998 Africa: General Abubakar becomes the head of state
Europe: Europeans agree on single currency, the euro
Iran: Lifts death threat against Salman Rushdie
Ireland: Good Friday Accord, peace settlement; John Hume and David Trimble win Nobel Peace Prize
Kosovo: Serbs launch "ethnic cleansing" offensive
US: Theodore Kaczynski, the "Unabomber," sentenced to four life terms; White House sex scandal: President Clinton admits to affair with White House intern Monica Lewinsky; House of Representatives impeaches Clinton

1999 Doctors Without Borders wins Nobel Peace Prize
Ireland: New Northern Ireland self-rule for first time in 25 years
Japan: Worst nuclear accident on record; many people exposed to radiation
Jordan: King Hussein dies at age 63
Kosovo: UN intervenes; Serbs withdraw
Morocco: King Hassan II dies at age 70
Nigeria: General Olusegun Obasanjo elected president
Pakistan: Former prime minister Benazir Bhutto imprisoned for taking kickbacks while in office; government overthrown
Russia: Vladimir Putin becomes prime minister in fourth government shakeup in eighteen months
Serbia: Serbs sign agreement to pull troops out of Kosovo after eleven weeks of NATO air attacks

South Africa: Thabo Mbeki becomes president
US: Senate acquits President Clinton of impeachment charges; two Colorado students go
on shooting spree in Columbine High School, killing fifteen, including themselves
Yugoslavia: President Slobodan Milosevic charged with crimes against humanity

2000   Cuba: Elian Gonzalez, 6-year-old retrieved off Florida coast from failed attempt to sail to
US, returned to Cuba (June 29)
Israel: President Ezer Weizman resigns
Mexico: Major power shift occurs as Institutional Revolutionary Party (PRI) loses for the
first time in 77 years; Vincente Fox is president-elect
US: Approves normal trade rights for China; Supreme Court backs Boy Scouts ban of
gays from membership; first gay couple "married" under Vermont's civil union law

PART 3

PHILOSOPHY AND RELIGION

Part 3 Philosophy and Religion

PREHISTORIC DAYS TO −1 BCE

−4000 to −3501

−3500 to −3001

−3000 to −2501   Egypt: Pharaoh is god-king

−2500 to −2001   Egypt: Cult of Isis and Osiris
Crete: Snake and bull are religious symbols

−2000 to −1500   Crete: Religious dances

−1500 to −1001   Egypt: Amenhotep IV sets up sun god as sole god
Moses receives the Ten Commandments
c. 1400 *Rig Veda*, 1,028 Hindu hymns

Did You Know?

Ancient Egyptians originally believed that the earth rose as a hill from the ocean Nin. The sun god Ra dispersed the darkness. His offspring included Shu, god of air; and Tefnut, goddess of water. They had twins, the earth god Geb and the sky goddess Nut. Shu parted them to create heaven and earth. Each day, Nut gave birth to the sun. Khepri, a giant scarab beetle, crossed the sky as Ra. Each night it sank below the horizon as an old man. The fertility goddess Isis established marriage and taught agriculture, spinning, and weaving. Osiris, corn god, married his sister Isis when they were still in the womb, became king on earth, and abolished cannibalism. Murdered by his brother Set, he was restored to life by Isis and became supreme judge of the dead and ruler of the underworld.

−1000 to −901   Greek gods created (Zeus, Hera, and the rest of the gang)
Pantheistic religion develops in India; caste system

−900 to −801   Earliest Jewish prophets

−800 to −701   Woman is high priest in Thebes
Apollo worshipped at Delphi
Hebrew prophets Amos, Hosea, and Isaiah

−700 to −601   Greece: Worship of Apollo and Dionysus
Greece: Draco writes Athenian laws

KEY DOCUMENT

Two different versions of the Ten Commandments are given in Exodus 20:1–17 and Deuteronomy 5:6–21; the Exodus version gives a religious rather than humanitarian motive for observing the Sabbath and in prohibiting coveting, it classifies a man's wife with the rest of his possessions. Following is an abridged text of the Ten Commandments in Exodus 20:1–17:

I   I am the Lord your God, who brought you out of the land of Egypt, out of the house of bondage. You shall have no other gods before me.

II   You shall not make for yourself a graven image. You shall not bow down to them or serve them.

III   You shall not take the name of the Lord your God in vain.

IV   Remember the Sabbath day, and keep it holy.

V   Honor your father and mother.

VI   You shall not kill.

VI   You shall not commit adultery.

VIII   You shall not steal.

IX   You shall not bear false witness against your neighbor.

X   You shall not covet.

Most Protestant, Anglican, and Orthodox Christians follow Jewish tradition, which considers the Prologue ("I am the Lord . . .") the first commandment and makes the prohibition against idolatry the second. Roman Catholics and Lutherans combine the prologue and the first two Commandments and the last is divided into two that prohibit, individually, coveting a neighbor's wife and his property.

-630 to -553   Zoroaster establishes Persian religion
China: Philosopher Lao-tse

-600 to -501   *Old Testament* first written down in Hebrew
Athens: Solon's laws

Did You Know?

The doctrines preached by Zoroaster are preserved in the Gathas (psalms) which form part of the sacred scripture known as Avesta. The Gathas preach the monotheistic worship of Ahura Mazda (the "Lord Wisdom") and an ethical dualism opposing Truth (Asha) and Lie. All good comes from Ahura Mazda and his six assistant entities: Good Mind, Truth, Power, Devotion, Health, and Life. Persia was gradually converted to Islam after the Arab conquest in the seventh century. Zoroastrians, called Parsis, can be found today in India, chiefly around Bombay.

Did You Know?

Buddhists believe that life is misery and decay, with no ultimate reality. The cycle of endless birth and rebirth continues because of desire and attachment to the unreal "self." Right meditation and deeds will end the cycle and help the individual achieve "Nirvana," the Void, nothingness. Today, Buddhists live throughout Asia, from Sri Lanka to Japan, including several thousand followers in America.

Oracle at Delphi influential
−581 to −497 philosopher and mathematician Pythagoras
India: Jainism founded
−551 to −479 China: Philosopher Confucius
−553 to −483 Siddhartha (Gautama Buddha) establishes Buddhism
Buddha's "Inspiration"

KEY DOCUMENT

Written and assembled by the followers of Confucius, the Analects encapsulates the body of Confucius' philosophy. With its focus on individual and communal humanitarianism, this text has had a great impact on past and current Chinese culture. Here are some excerpts from Book Two:

1. The Master said, "He who exercises government by means of his virtue may be compared to the north polar star, which keeps its place and all the stars turn towards it."

3. The Master said, "If the people be led by the laws, and uniformity sought to be given them by punishments, they will try to avoid the punishment, but they have no sense of shame. If they be led by virtue, and uniformity sought to be given them by the rules of propriety, they will have the sense of shame, and moreover will become good."

10. The Master said, "See what a man does. Mark his motives. Examine in what things he rests. How can a man conceal his character?"

20. Chi K'ang [Tzu] asked how to cause the people to reverence their ruler, to be faithful to him, and to go on to nerve themselves to virtue. The Master said, "Let him preside over them with gravity; then they will reverence to him. Let him be filial and kind to all; then they will be faithful to him. Let him advance the good and teach the incompetent; then they will eagerly seek to be virtuous."

−500 to −451   −497 to −581 philosopher Pythagoras of Samos
−485 to −424 Greece: Herodotus, "Father of History"
−470 to −399 Socrates, Greek philosopher
−458 Ezra travels to Jerusalem to restore the laws of Moses

Did You Know?

Judaism stresses ethical behavior (and among the traditional, careful ritual observance) as true worship of God. Chief annual observances include Passover (celebrating the liberation of the Israelites from Egypt) and the ten days from Rosh Hashanah (New Year) to Yom Kippur (day of Atonement), a period of fasting and penitence.

−450 to −401	Torah becomes Jewish moral compass −427 to −347 Plato, Greek philosopher
−400 to −351	
−350 to −301	−340 to −271 Epicurus, Greek philosopher −301 Egypt rules Palestine

Did You Know?

Cats were sacred to ancient Egyptians. If convicted of killing a cat, a person was executed.

−300 to −251	−255 Greek *Old Testament*, "Septuagint"
−250 to −201	
−200 to −151	−168 Antiochus IV persecutes Jews; desecration of the Temple at Jerusalem −165 Judas Maccabaeus rededicates the Temple after expelling the Syrians c. −165 *Old Testament* "Book of Daniel"
−150 to −101	"Book of Maccabees"
−100 to −51	c. −98 to −55 Titus Lucretius Carus, Roman philosopher
−50 to −1	−4 Probable birth of Jesus Christ

Part 3 Philosophy and Religion

1 TO 500

1 to 50
27 Baptism of Jesus Christ
30 Probable date of crucifixion of Christ
40 Corinth: Earliest Christian churches

51 to 100
58 St. Paul's "Letters to the Corinthians"
64 Persecution of Christians
65 Gospel according to St. Mark
67 St. Peter killed
68 "History of the Jewish War"
85 Gospels according to St. Matthew and St. John
88 to 97 Pope Clement I
100 Buddhism reaches China

101 to 150
150 India: Earliest known Sanskrit inscriptions
c. 150 Mexico: Pyramid of the Sun built at Teotihuacan

151 to 200
189 to 199 Pope Victor I
c. 200 Neo-Platonism
c. 200 Bishop of Rome becomes Pope

201 to 250
222 to 230 Pope Urban I
c. 250 Increased persecution of Christians
Martyrs considered saints

251 to 300
c. 300 First religious plays

301 to 350

351 to 400

401 to 450
c. 400 to 600 *Suttee*, the custom of a widow throwing herself on her husband's funeral pyre, begins

Did You Know?

Suttee is based on the story of Sati. The wife of Shiva, one of the principal Hindu deities, Sati killed herself by walking into a fire when her husband and father quarreled. The widows, or satis, who immolated themselves on their husband's funeral pyre were promised 35 million years in Svarga, the Hindu paradise. Suttee was outlawed in 1829 by the British governor of India.

401 to 417 Pope Innocent I
411 St. Augustine's "The City of God"
432 Ireland: St. Patrick
440 to 461 Pope Leo I

451 to 500   478 Japan: first Shinto shrines
480 to 543 St. Benedict of Nursia
484 to 519 Pope excommunicates Patriarch Acacius of Constantinople, resulting in break between Eastern and Western churches
491 Armenian Church secedes from Rome and Byzantium
496 Gelasian Missal, book for Catholic Mass
499 Synod of Rome issues decree on papal elections
500 Incense first used in Christian church
500 First plans for the Vatican in Rome

Part 3 Philosophy and Religion
501 TO 1000

Did You Know?

The Koran, the religious scripture of Islam, is believed to be a word of Allah, the one true God according to the Muslim faith. Muslims believe that the Koran is a divine book revealed by their prophet, Mohammed, over the latter third of his life. These revelations first started coming to Mohammed when he was meditating outside his home in Mecca. Suddenly, the angel Gabriel appeared and commanded Mohammed to recite something. Gabriel said, "Recite the name of the Lord Who creates." This is the first line of the Koran: "In the Name of God, the Merciful, the Compassionate/Praise belongs to God, the Lord of All Being."

643 Jerusalem: Dome of the Rock
650 England: St. Martin's Church, Canterbury

651 to 700   673 to 735 The Venerable Bede, English monk and historian
673 First synod of the English church
674 England: Glass windows first used in churches
681 Gloucester Abbey
685 Winchester Cathedral
695 Persecution of Jews in Spain
697 Northern Ireland: Church submits to Roman Catholicism

KEY DOCUMENT

Much of what we know about England before 700 is based on a history written in Latin by Bede, a Benedictine monk. Often called "the father of English history," Bede was the most learned scholar of his day in all of western Europe. He wrote forty books, but his reputation rests on just one: *Historia Ecclesiastica Gentis Anglorum* or *A History of the English Church and People*. Here is an excerpt: "At the present time there are in Britain, in harmony with the five books of the divine law, five languages and four nations—English, British, Scots, and Picts. Each of these have their own language, but all are united in their study of God's truth by the fifth, Latin, which has become a common medium through the study of the scriptures. The original inhabitants of the island were Britons, from whom it takes its name, and who, according to tradition, crossed into Britain from Amorica [Brittany, France], and occupied the southern parts. When they had spread northward and possessed the greater part of the islands, it is said that some Picts from Scythia [southeastern Europe] put out to sea in a few long ships and were driven by storms around the coast of Britain, arriving at length on the north coast of Ireland. Here they found the nation of the Scots, from whom they asked permission to settle, but their request was refused."

---

701 to 750   Psalms translated into Anglo-Saxon
India: Cave temples
Tibet: Jokhang Temple
Arab desert castle at Mshatta
Christians use Easter eggs
702 North Africa: Berbers convert to Islam
705 Damascus: The Great Mosque
711 Spanish Jews begin cultural flowering
772 Pope Hadrian I appeals to Charlemagne for help against the Lombards
750 Four sects of Islam: Sunnites, Hafenites, Shafites, and Malikites

751 to 800   760 "The Book of Kells," Latin gospels written in Irish
765 Japan: Kasuga shrine established
775 Caliph Mahdi sanctions an inquisition
785 Cologne becomes an archbishopric

790 St. Albans Abbey established
800 Charlemagne adopts the "Filoque" at the Synod of Aix-la-Chapelle

801 to 850   828 Venice: St. Mark's established
830 Baghdad: Caliph establishes Academy of Translations
840 Doctrine of transubstantiation
845 Vivian Bible written
845 China: Buddhist persecution
850 German Jews develop the Yiddish language

Did You Know?

Originally, Yiddish was spoken mainly by Jewish people in Europe, but many Yiddish expressions have become part of the everyday language in large American cities. Here are some of the most common Yiddish words and expressions:

chutzpah	*(khoot'spah)*	*nerve, real gall*
kibitzer	*(kib' its er)*	*a spectator, especially someone at a card game who gives unwanted advice*
Mazel Tov	*(ma'zel tov)*	*good luck*
nebbish	*(neb'ish)*	*a drab, insignificant person*
mensch	*(mensh)*	*a decent, mature, sincere person*
nudnik	*(nood'nik)*	*a pest*
oy	*(oi)*	*an expression for pain or annoyance*
schlepp	*(shlep)*	*to lug something heavy around*
schlock	*(shlok)*	*a cheap, shoddy article*
schmooz	*(shmooz)*	*gossip*

851 to 900   879 The Pope and the Patriarch of Constantinople excommunicate each other
879 Egypt: Oldest mosque in Cairo, Ibn Tulun, built
895 Earliest surviving Hebrew manuscript of the *Old Testament*
900 Arabia: Abu Tanari compiles *Koran* commentaries

901 to 950   910 Benedictine Abbey at Cluny
913 From now on, Popes only use names of previous popes, adding Roman numerals
917 Bulgarian church breaks away from Rome and Constantinople
925 Easter plays begin
938 Milton Abbey, Dorset
942 Augsburg Cathedral

951 to 1000   960 Nayin Mosque, Persia
965 St. Dunstan enforces celibacy for English priests
966 Worcester Cathedral
966 Poles convert to Christianity
976 Venice: St. Mark's Cathedral started

980 Germany: Mainz Cathedral started
993 First saints canonized
997 St. Martin of Tours built
998 Feast of All Souls celebrated for the first time
999 First French pope, Pope Sylvester II
1000 Spain: Spiritual center of Judaism

Part 3 Philosophy and Religion
1001 TO 1500

1001 to 1050
1009 Europe: Prussian martyr Bruno of Querfurt
1012 Germany: First persecution of heretics
1012 to 1023 Pope Benedict VIII
c. 1016 Middle East: Caliph al-Hakim proclaims himself divine and establishes the Druse sect
1017 Middle East: Hamzah ibn Ali ibn Ahmad becomes vizier to Hakim, leader of the Druse sect

Did You Know?

The Druse (or Druze) are members of a Middle Eastern sect who live mainly in mountainous regions of Lebanon and southern Syria. The Druse believe that at various times God has been divinely incarnated in a living person; His final incarnation was in the person of al-Hakim (985 to 1021). Although an outgrowth of Islam, the Druse religion contains elements of Judaism and Christianity. Druse abstain from alcohol, tobacco, profanity, and obscenity.

1022 Europe: Synod of Pavia passes laws on celibacy (Pope Benedict VIII)
1038 Tibet: Buddhism firmly established
1049 to 1054 Europe: Pope Leo IX issues decrees against simony (purchase of church office)
1050 Russia: First monasteries built

Did You Know?

Isma'iliyah, a sect of the Shi'ah (one of the major branches of Islam), flourished from the 800s to 1200s. The Isma'ili doctrine stressed the dual nature of the Koran interpretation and made a distinction between the everyday Muslim and the initiated Isma'ili.

1051 to 1100
1052 England: Westminster Abbey established
1054 Split between Roman and Eastern churches
1059 Papal elections by cardinals only
1065 England: Westminster Abbey consecrated

305

1067 Italy: Monte Cassino monastery rebuilt
Jerusalem: Order of St. John established
1074 Europe: Married priests excommunicated

Did You Know?

During the Middle Ages, Europe was torn by a power struggle between the emperors of the Holy Roman Empire and the popes. The emperors claimed control over the Church's activities within their realms; the popes claimed complete spiritual authority over Europe. The conflict reached its climax in 1075 when Pope Gregory forbid Emperor Henry IV to control the election of bishops in Germany.

1076 Europe: Gregory VII dethrones and excommunicates Henry IV
1077 Europe: Gregory VII absolves Henry IV
1080 England: Henry IV again excommunicated
Italy: Order of St. John established
1083 Italy: Henry attacks Rome, which he captures in 1084
1085 Europe: Decree of the Emperor Henry IV Concerning a Truce of God
1086 Europe: Bruno of Cologne establishes Carthusian Order
1090 to 1153 Pope Bernard, Cistercian abbot of Clairvaux, encouraged mysticism and contemplation in opposition to the scholastic rationalism then popular
1092 Jewish bible commentator Ibn Ezra (1092 to 1167)
1093 Europe: Hugh le Gros establishes Benedictine monastery
1095 Europe: Pope Urban II consecrates the church of Cluny
1096 to 1097 Middle East: First Crusade: Three armies of French and Normans reach Constantinople, defeat the Turks, and seize Palestine from Muslims
1098 France: St. Robert founds the monastery at Citeaux; start of Cistercian order of monks
Middle East: Crusaders defeat the Saracens (Muslims) at Antioch
1099 Middle East: Crusaders take Jerusalem and establish a Latin kingdom there under Geoffrey of Bouillon

1101 to 1150   1100s England: Middle English supersedes Old English as the everyday language of the people
Spain: The Moors, who had tolerated Jewish communities, turn against them
1104 Middle East: Crusaders capture Acre
1111 to 1059 Arab theologian Al-Gazali
1113 Pope acknowledges establishment of Order of St. John
1114 England: Chichester Cathedral established
1115 to 1153 Career of Bernard of Clairvaux, whose abbey becomes most important monastery in Europe
1118 to 1170 Thomas à Becket of Canterbury
1119 Italy: Bologna University established
Jerusalem: Order of Knights Templars formed to fight the Crusades
1120 Scholastic philosophy develops

KEY DOCUMENT

Here is an except from Henry IV's Decree Concerning a Truce of God:

Whereas in our times the holy church has been afflicted beyond measure by tribulations through having to join in suffering so many oppressions and dangers, we have so striven to aid it, with God's help, that the peace, which we could not make lasting by reason of our sins, we should to some extent make binding by at least exempting certain days. . . . this decree of peace shall be observed. The purpose of it is that those who travel and those who remain at home may enjoy the greatest possible security, so that no one shall commit murder or arson, robbery or assault, no man shall injure another with a whip or a sword or any kind of weapon, and that no one, no matter on account of what wrong he shall be at feud, shall . . . presume to bear as weapons a shield, sword, or lance—or, in fact, the burden of any armor.

If, during the space for which the peace has been declared, it shall be necessary for any one to go to another place where that peace isn't observed, he may bear arms; provided, nevertheless, that he harm no one unless he is attacked and has to defend himself. Moreover, when he returns, he shall lay aside his weapons again. If it shall happen that a castle is being besieged, the besiegers shall cease from the attack during the days included in the peace, unless they are attacked by the besieged, and are obliged to beat them back.

1122 Concordat of Worms: Conference of German princes ends the disputes between the pope and emperor over appointing bishops

1123 Lateran Council suppresses simony and marriage of priests

1124 England: William of Malmesbury's historical record *On the Antiquity of the Church of Glastonbury*

Did You Know?

Horrified by the presence of the Seljuk Turks in Jerusalem, Pope Urban II called for a Crusade to free the Holy Land from the Saracens, as the Muslims were known. There were eight crusades in all, from 1096 to 1270.

1125 Japan: Tarnenari's Japanese history *O-Kagami*

1126 to 1198 Averroes, Islamic scholar

1128 Italy: Pope recognizes Order of Templars

Scotland: David I establishes Abbey of Holyrood

1130 to 1138 Anacletus II, antipope; distinguished scholar and diplomat

1132 to 1144 France: St. Denis Abbey, the first Gothic church, built by Abbot Suger in Paris

1133 Europe: Diocese of Carlisle established

1135 to 1204 Moses Maimonides, Jewish religious philosopher

1133 to 1212 Japan: Honen establishes Pure Land Sect

Did You Know?

At the Concordat of Worms, Henry V established a compromise on investiture
with the papacy, abandoning the antipope Gregory VIII; he was then reinstated
in the communion of the church but retained the right to appoint church
officials.

1137 Scotland: Bishopric of Aberdeen established
1138 Europe, Middle East: False Messiah appears in France and Persia
1139 Second Lateran Council ends schism in church
1140 Europe: Council of Sens condemns Abelard's heresies
c. 1140 *Decretum Gratiani*, collection of canon law

Did You Know?

Maimonides is ranked as the outstanding Jewish philosopher of the Middle Ages;
his contributions to the development of Judaism earned him the title "second
Moses." His greatest work in the field of Jewish law is the Mishneh Torah, a
fourteen-volume work. In addition, he created the Thirteen Articles of Faith,
which many Orthodox Jews still follow. Maimonides is also famous as a physician
and a writer on astronomy, logic, and mathematics.

1146 to 1148 Middle East: Second Crusade, led by King Louis VII of France and
Emperor Conrad VII, attacks Damascus but achieves little success
1147 Europe: Geoffrey of Monmouth's *Historia regum Britanniae*
1150 France: Paris University established
Wales: *Black Book of Carmarthen*, oldest Welsh manuscript

1151 to 1200   1151 Simon Darschan's Jewish commentaries on the Old Testament
1154 to 1159 Pope Hadrian IV, only English pope
1155 Carmelite Order established
1159 to 1181 Pope Alexander III
1161 Europe: Edward the Confessor canonized
1162 England: Thomas à Becket made archbishop
1163 Paris: Notre Dame built
1165 Europe: Charlemagne canonized

Did You Know?

In the 1700s, Charlemagne is reduced to "blessed" from "saint."

1167 England: Oxford University established

1169 Middle East: Averroes' commentaries on Aristotle

1170 England: Archbishop Thomas à Becket murdered at the cathedral in Canterbury

Europe: Pope Alexander III sets rules for canonization of saints

Middle East: *Mishneh Torah*, Maimonides' fourteen-volume work on Jewish law

1173 England: Thomas à Becket canonized

1180 England: Ranulf de Glanville reforms English judicial system

1181 England: First Carthusian monastery

1182 to 1226 St. Francis of Assisi

1182 France: Philip II banishes the Jews

1185 England: Knights Templars established in London

Did You Know?

After the destruction of Jerusalem in AD 70, most Jews were exiled from their homeland. The Diaspora (dispersion) took Jews all over the world. In Spain, the Jews were known as Sephardim; in Germany, Ashkenazim.

1189 Massacre of the Jews at the coronation of Richard I

Middle East: Third Crusade, led by Emperor Frederick Barbarossa, Philip Augustus of France, and Richard I of England (Richard the Lion Hearted), fails but 1192 truce with Saladin allows Christians access to Jerusalem

China: Chu-Hsi's *The Four Books* introduces neo-Confucianism

1190 Germany: Teutonic Order of knights, a military society, set up to defend Christian lands in Palestine and Syria

1191 Japan: Zen Buddhism introduced by the monk Eisai

1197 to 1276 India: Madhava, Indian thinker

1198 Europe: William of Newburgh's *Historia rerum Anglicarum*

1200 England: Cambridge University founded

Europe: Cabala develops (Jewish mysticism)

Middle East: Islam begins to replace Indian religions

c. 1200 Morocco: Jews given special privileges

Pacific Islands: Tui Tonga monarchy builds coral platform for ceremonial worship on island of Tonga

Did You Know?

Cabala (from the Hebrew word meaning "received tradition") revolves around Sefer ha-zohar ("The Book of Splendor"), commonly called the Zohar. The Zohar describes the Godhead as a dynamic flow or force comprised of many aspects. It provides a cosmic-symbolic interpretation of Judaism and the history of Israel in which the Torah and commandments and Israel's life in exile become symbols for events and processes in God. Study of the Cabala has recently become fashionable among entertainers and movie stars.

Did You Know?

Zen stresses personal instruction by a master rather than the study of scripture as the way to enlightenment.

1201 to 1250   1202 Italy: *Venerabilem* decree asserts superiority of papacy over empire
1204 Middle East: Fourth Crusade; Crusaders sack Constantinople; Latin empire set up; Byzantines flee to Nicaea
1209 Europe: St. Francis of Assisi founds Franciscan religious order
1212 Europe: Children's Crusade; 50,000 children from France and Germany set off for the Holy Land
c. 1214 to c. 1294 Europe: Francis Bacon, Franciscan philosopher
1215 Europe: Fourth Lateran Council forbids trial by ordeal
France: St. Dominic establishes the Dominican Order
1218 to 1221 Middle East: Fifth Crusade tries but fails to take Egypt

Did You Know?

The Children's Crusade was a disaster; the German group turned back and the French children were sold into slavery. This tragedy is said to be the origin of the story of the Pied Piper.

1222 England: St. George's Day (April 23) established as a national holiday
1222 to 1282 Japan: Nicherin, Japanese Buddhist monk, added nationalistic element to religion
c. 1225 to 1274 St. Thomas Aquinas, scholastic philosopher
1228 Italy: St. Francis canonized
1228 to 1229 Middle East: Frederick II leads Sixth Crusade, recaptures Holy City and crowns himself king of Jerusalem
1229 Inquisition in Toulouse prohibits laymen from reading the Bible
1232 Italy: Antony of Padua canonized
1233 Italy: "Great Halleluyah" penitential movement
1235 Europe: Elizabeth of Hungary canonized
1241 Italy: Pope Celestine IV reigns for seventeen days
1247 to 1328 Giovanni Monte Corvino establishes the first Christian mission in China
1248 Middle East: Louis IX leads Seventh Crusade. Attempt fails and Louis is captured and ransomed
1249 England: University College, Oxford, established

1251 to 1300   1252 Inquisition begins to use torture
1254 Paris: Robert de Sorbon, court chaplain, establishes the Paris School of Theology
1256 Pope Alexander IV establishes Augustinian Order of Hermits
1260 Europe: First flagellant movement in Germany and Italy

Did You Know?

The Paris School of Theology was later called the Sorbonne, after its founder.

1263 England: Balliol College, Oxford, established
1264 England: Roger Bacon's *De computo naturali;* Merton College, Oxford, established
Europe: St. Thomas Aquinas stated his belief in the power of reason in *Summa Contra Gentiles,* which gave strong Aristotelian basis to Catholic theology
c. 1265 to 1308 England: Duns Scotus, English philosopher and Franciscan monk

Did You Know?

Saint Thomas Aquinas, one of the leading Roman Catholic theologians, was heavyset and taciturn. Not surprisingly, his fellow schoolmates nicknamed him "dumb ox." Philosopher Albertus Magnus, Aquinas' early teacher, recognized his student's brilliance and said: "This ox will one day fill the world with his bellowing." Magnus was quite correct.

1266 England: Roger Bacon, *Opus maius*
1268 to 1271 Italy: Papacy is vacant for 3 years
1270 Middle East: Final Crusade
1272 Francis Bacon, *Compendium Studii Philosophiae,* attacking clerical indifference
1273 Europe: Thomas Aquinas's *Summa theologica*
1275 Jewish theologian Moses de Leon's *Zohar,* Jewish mysticism
1277 to 1292 England: Philosopher Roger Bacon exiled for heresy
1289 China: Friar John of Montecorvino becomes the first archbishop of Peking
1290 England: Edward I expels all Jews
1294 Italy: Pope Celestine V renounces the throne

Did You Know?

The term friar comes from a Latin word meaning "brother."

c. 1300 Pacific Islands: Stone temple complexes erected on Rarotonga, Cook Islands, and on Moorea Island in the Society Islands
Pacific Islands: Huge stone statues erected on Easter Island
US: Emerald Mound, ceremonial center for the Natchez people
c. 1300 to 1349 England: William of Ockham, last of the great Franciscan philosophers

1301 to 1350   1302 Papal Bull *Unam Sanctam* declares papal authority to be supreme

1303 King Philippe IV of France abducts Pope Boniface VIII, who dies while imprisoned in the Vatican

1305 Pope Clement V, French, installed in Avignon, beginning what Petrarch would call the "Babylonian Captivity"; Great Schism follows

1307 China: Archbishopric of Peking established

1309 Papacy moves to Avignon, where it remained for nearly 70 years

1312 Europe: Order of the Knights Templars abolished for malpractices

1314 Italy: Papacy stands empty for over 2 years

Paris: Grand Master of the Templars, Jacques de Molay, burned at the stake for alleged heresy

Did You Know?

Ayers Rock, close to the geographical center of Australia, is sacred to the country's Aborigines. The rock, 1,143 feet tall and 5.5 miles around, sits alone in the desert, the remnant of a vast sandstone formation that once covered the area.

1315 Africa: Philosopher Raymond Lully of Majorca is stoned to death for preaching against Islam

1316 Africa: The Pope sends eight Dominican friars to Ethiopia to find Christian emperor Prester John

c. 1320 to 1384 England: John Wycliffe and his followers, the Lollards, argued for a propertyless church and direct access to God

1322 Italy: Thomas Aquinas canonized

1330 Europe: Monastery of Ettal, Bavaria, established

1332 to 1406 Middle East: Ibn Khaldun, great Islamic social thinker

1335 Italy: Pope Benedict XII reforms monastic orders

1338 Declaration of Rense: Electors of the Holy Roman Empire declare their independence from the Pope.

Treaty of Coblenz: Alliance between England and the Holy Roman Empire

1340 Europe: Naval victory at Sluys gives English control of the English Channel

1341 to 1360 Africa: Sulaiman, King of Mali

1348 to 1349 Germany: Jews persecuted

Did You Know?

Flagellation (whipping), a form of penance for sins, was thought to reduce the punishment a person would be given in the next world. The custom became popular in Europe around the late 1200s to 1300s, when followers whipped themselves three times a day and toured the country proclaiming flagellation as the road to salvation.

1351 to 1400   1353 Statute of Praemunire: English parliament forbids appeals to the Pope
1356 The Golden Bull: New constitution for the Holy Roman Empire, providing for seven electors
1367 Italy: Pope Urban V returns to Rome, meets resistance; returns to Avignon 1370 and dies
1372 England: Oxford becomes the spiritual center of England
1376 England: John Wycliffe's *Civil Dominion* calls for church reforms
1377 Italy: Gregory XI goes to Rome, also meets resistance; dies there March 1378; end of "Babylonian Captivity"
1378 Papal Schism: Cardinals elect Urban VI (Roman); reject him in favor of Clement VII (Robert of Geneva); England sides with Urban; France sides with Clement
1382 England: Wycliffe expelled from Oxford
1398 Prague: Jan Hus lectures on theology at Prague University
c. 1400 Pacific Islands: Tonga people build major ceremonial center at Mu'a, on the largest island in the Tongatapu Group

Did You Know?

Westminster Abbey, built in stages between the eleventh and nineteenth centuries, includes not only the main church but also chapels, a cloister, chapter house, and towers. French influence is apparent in the nave's soaring height (102 feet). Since 1066, English monarchs have been crowned in the abbey and many are also buried there. The abbey also houses the tombs of famous scientists (Isaac Newton, Charles Darwin), writers (Geoffrey Chaucer, T. S. Eliot), and actors (Sir Laurence Olivier). Poet's Corner is a favorite stop for tourists with a literary bent.

1401 to 1450   1408 Europe: Cardinals of Rome and Avignon meet to end Great Schism
1409 Italy: Council of Pisa, called to resolve the Great Schism, deposes the rival popes and elects a third
1410 Europe: Archbishop of Prague excommunicates Jan Hus and his followers
1412 to 1431 Joan of Arc
1413 Spain: Joseph Albo defends the Jewish faith
1415 Jan Hus, Bohemian preacher and follower of Wycliffe, burned at stake as a heretic
1416 Jerome of Prague burned for heresy
1417 End of Great Schism in Catholic church; a single pope elected in Rome
1428 Europe: Joan of Arc leads French against English, captured by Burgundians (1430) and turned over to the English; burned at the stake as a witch after ecclesiastical trial (1431)
1434 Rome: After a revolt, Pope Eugene IV flees to Florence
1400 Florence: Platonic Academy established
1440 to 1518 India: Mystic Kabir, whose ideas were the forerunner to Sikhism
1448 Concordat of Vienna; Emperor gives up attempts to reform the Church
1450 Germany: Gutenberg prints *Constance Mass Book*
1453 Constantinople: Turks convert St. Sophia Bascilica into a mosque

1463 Italian humanist Pico della Mirandola (1463 to 1494) argued that human nature was not fixed and people did not have to inherit a place in the world; rather, people could create their own niche

1451 to 1500

1468 Europe: Bishopric of Vienna established

1478 Spanish Inquisition: Converted Jews and Muslims, as well as Catholic intellectuals, are persecuted

1483 to 1546 Martin Luther

1484 Europe: Papal Bull condemns witchcraft; inquisitors sent to Germany to try witches

Did You Know?

At this time, the Incas had a highly formalized religion. The supreme deity was Viracocha, creator and ruler of all living things. Other major deities included the gods of the sun, stars, and weather and the goddesses of the moon, earth, and sea. Live animals were sacrificed at important ceremonies; human sacrifices were also occasionally offered.

1487 *Malleus Maleficarum,* published by the Catholic church, describes witchcraft and encouraged its halt

1491 Africa: Ruler of Congo kingdom baptized as Christian by Portuguese

1492 Italy: Rodrigo Borgia elected Pope (Pope Alexander VI)

Spain: Torquemanda, inquisitor-general of the Spanish Inquisition, gives Spanish Jews three months to convert or leave the country

1494 Scotland: King's College, Aberdeen, established

1495 Portugal: Jews expelled

1497 England: Jesus College, Cambridge, established

Italy: Savonarola, Italian religious reformer, excommunicated for attempting to depose Pope Alexander VI

1498 Italy: Savonarola burned at stake

1499 Spain: Inquisitor-general Francisco Jiminez de Cisneros forces mass conversion of the Moors, setting off Moorish revolt in Granada

c. 1500 India: Guru Nanak establishes Sikhism

India: Mystical teacher Chaitanya of Bengal spreads the cult of devotion to the Hindu god Krishna

Spain: University of Valencia established

Did You Know?

Sikhism is a monotheistic religion synthesizing elements of Hinduism and Islam. It is centered in northern India.

Part 3 Philosophy and Religion
1501 TO 1800

1501 to 1510
1503 to 1513 Italy: Pope Julius II
1506 to 1626 Rome: St. Peter's Cathedral, designed and decorated by Bramante, Michelangelo, da Vinci, Raphael, and Bernini
1509 to 1564 John Calvin, French theologian who will introduce the Reformation to Switzerland
1510 Europe: Pope Julius II and Venice form Holy League to drive Louis XII from Italy

Did You Know?

With his colleague Louis Bourgeois, John Calvin composed the famous Geneva Psalter, which became the basis for much Protestant hymnody.

1511 to 1520
1511 Europe: Ferdinand V and Henry VIII join Holy League
1512 Europe: Swiss join Holy League and drive French from Milan
Persia: Shi'ism state religion
1515 to 1582 Spain: St. Theresa of Avila
1517 Germany: Martin Luther posts his 95 theses denouncing church abuses on church door in Wittenberg and starts the Reformation
1519 Spain: Charles I of Spain chosen Holy Roman Emperor I
Switzerland: Ulrich Zwingli leads the Reformation

Did You Know?

Luther's reform of the church gave birth to a movement called the Reformation and the Protestant denominations. (The word Protestant came from the word "to protest.") Soon, all of Europe was divided into religious camps. The Catholic Church held sway in Spain, Italy, and parts of France and Germany; Protestant groups dominated in Switzerland, England, Scotland, and parts of Germany and France. In some areas, religious differences escalated to wars. In France, for example, the conflict lasted for more than 50 years.

1521 to 1530
1521 Diet of Worms: Martin Luther condemned as a heretic and excommunicated
1523 to 1534 Pope Clement VII takes office
1527 Troops of Charles V, Holy Roman Emperor, sack Rome and capture Pope Clement VII
1527 to 1608 England: John Dee, alchemist and magician

1529 England: Henry VIII dismisses Lord Chancellor Thomas Wolsey for failing to obtain the Pope's consent for Henry's divorce from Catherine of Aragon
1530 Malta: Charles V establishes Knights of St. John

Did You Know?

In 1530, several Protestant German rulers met at Schmalkalden to consider an alliance against Emperor Charles V and his allies. The result was the Schmalkaldic League. In 1546, Charles fought the League, and defeated them a year later. Although the League was dismantled, Duke Maurice of Saxony persuaded Charles to give temporary freedom of worship pending a conference. The conference, held in 1555, resulted in a permanent settlement, the Peace of Augsburg.

1531 to 1540

1531 Germany: Schmalkaldic League formed
1532 Religious Peace of Nuremberg; Protestants allowed to practice their religion freely
France: Calvin starts Protestant movement
1534 England: Act of Supremacy makes the King the head of the Church of England; Henry VIII of England breaks with Roman Catholic Church
St. Ignatius Loyola founds the Society of Jesus (*Jesuits*) to help reform the Roman Catholic Church
1535 England: Reformation begins as Henry VIII makes himself head of English Church after being excommunicated by Pope; Sir Thomas More executed as traitor for refusal to acknowledge king's religious authority
1536 Danish and Norwegian Reformations
England: Thomas Cromwell suppresses monasteries
England: Pilgrimage of Grace, Catholic uprising in the north
Switzerland: John Calvin establishes Reformed and Presbyterian form of Protestantism; writes *Institutes of the Christian Religion*
1537 First Catholic hymnal
1539 to 1604 Poland: Faustus Socinus' argument that Christ was not divine inspires the Polish Unitarian movement, which denied the existence of the Holy Trinity
1540 Pope Paul III officially recognizes Jesuits

Did You Know?

The Jesuit motto Ad majorem Dei gloriam, "To the greater glory of God," shows their devotion to spread the church's teachings. But Jesuit devotion to the Pope has sparked opposition nearly everywhere; at one time or another, the order was expelled from every country in Europe.

1541 to 1550

1541 Scotland: John Knox leads Reformation in Scotland, establishes Presbyterian Church there (1560)
Switzerland: John Calvin founds "City of God" in Geneva

1545 Council of Trent to meet intermittently until 1563 to define Catholic dogma and doctrine, reiterate 1550 papal authority
1549 England: *Book of Common Prayer* introduces uniform Protestant service
Japan: St. Francis Xavier introduces Christianity
1550 to 1555 Pope Julius III

1551 to 1560 1551 Archbishop Cranmer publishes Forty-two Articles of religion
1553 England: Queen Mary I restores Roman Catholicism
1554 to 1600 England: Writer Richard Hooker

Did You Know?

Because she ordered the execution of nearly 300 Protestants, Queen Mary strengthened anti-Catholic sentiment in England and earned the nickname "Bloody Mary."

1555 Peace of Ausgburg: states are free to introduce the Reformation, and are given equal rights with Catholic states
England: Returns to Roman Catholicism; Protestants are persecuted; about 300 Protestants—including Archbishop Cranmer—burned at the stake
1557 to 1638 Dutch Calvinist Johannes Althusius
1557 Ethiopia: Jesuit missionaries arrive. They convert Emperor Za Dengel, but subsequent attempts to spread Catholicism provokes a revolt, which ends in Emperor's death
1558 England: John Knox's *The First Blast of the Trumpet Against the Monstrous Regiment of Women,* a polemic against government by women
1560 John Knox founds Presbyterian Church
Denmark: Lutheranism state religion

Did You Know?

Originally a Roman Catholic priest, John Knox became attracted to the preachings of the Protestant reformer George Wishart in 1543. After Wishart was executed for heresy, Knox preached in the castle and parish church. For his temerity, Knox was imprisoned for a year and a half in French galleys.

1560 to 1590 French Wars of Religion: Protestant minority in conflict with Catholic majority as leading nobles struggle for power under weak Valois kings

1561 to 1570 1562 to 1578 French religious wars between Catholics and Protestants; 1,200 French Huguenots slain at Massacre of Vassy in 1562
1563 England: Thirty-nine Articles, which completes the establishment of the Anglican Church; term "Puritan" first used in England
1566 to 1572 Pope Puis V (later canonized)
1570 England: Pope excommunicates Queen Elizabeth
Roger Ascham's *The Scholemaster,* education manual
Peace of St. Germain: Huguenots are given conditional freedom of worship

Did You Know?

In France, Protestants were called "Huguenots."

1571 to 1580   1571 to 1641 England: Thomas Mun, advocated governmental regulation of the
economy; called "Mercantilist"
1572 France: Massacre of St. Bartholomew; 8,000 Protestants die in Paris
1572 to 1585 Pope Gregory XIII
1574 Mexico: First auto-da-fé

Did You Know?

*The auto-da-fé, from a French word meaning "act of faith," was a public
execution for victims of the Inquisition. The first recorded auto-da-fé took place
in 1481 in Spain under the inquisitor general Tomas de Torquemada; the last was
held in 1808. Nearly 350,000 victims were killed; 32,000 burned to death. The
ceremony was generally held on a Sunday between Whitsunday and Advent or
on All Saints' Day, and was marked by great pomp and circumstance.*

1575 Holland: Leiden University established as a secular institution open to all faiths
Italy: Oratorian movement begun in Vincenza
1576 France: Protestantism forbidden
Jean Bodin's *La republique*, advocating constitutional monarchy
1579 St. John of the Cross' *Dark Night of the Soul*

1581 to 1590   1581 Scotland: James VI signs Second Confession of Faith
1582 China: Jesuit mission established
Europe: Calendar reformed by Pope Gregory XIII, accepted only by Roman Catholic
countries
1583 Scotland: University of Edinburgh established as secular institution

Did You Know?

*"The War of the Three Henrys" was the eighth in a series of religious wars in the
1500s. The war began when Henri III, under the influence of Henri Duke of
Guise, banned Protestantism. Henri won some battles but when Guise seized
Paris, he escaped to Blois. Henri III murdered Guise and so had to make peace
with Navarre and the Protestants. Henri III was advancing to retake Paris when
Jacques Clement, a fanatical monk, assassinated him. Henri of Navarre became
King Henri IV, but he had to become Roman Catholic before he could take the
throne. The religious wars ended with the Edict of Nantes in 1598.*

1585 England: Richard Hooker's *Of the Laws of Ecclesiastical Polity* (government system of the church)
Europe: "War of the Three Henrys": Henri III of France, Henri of Navarre, and Henri of Guise
1585 to 1590 Pope Sixtus V
1587 England: Mary, Queen of Scots, executed for treason by order of Queen Elizabeth I
Europe: Savoy and the Catholic cantons ally with Spain
1589 Russia: Boris Godunov asserts Moscow's religious independence from Constantinople

Did You Know?

Mary went to her death a Catholic martyr. Her famous motto: "In my end is my beginning" took on new meaning when her death led Catholic Spain to declare war on England.

1591 to 1600   1592 New edition of the *Vulgate* (Roman Catholic Bible) published
1592 to 1605 Pope Clement VIII
1594 Sweden: Diet of Uppsala upholds Martin Luther's doctrines
1596 to 1650 France: Rene Descartes, founder of modern philosophy
1598 Edict of Nantes: Henry VI, first Bourbon king of France, grants toleration to Protestants (will be revoked 1685)
1600 Giordano Bruno burned as a heretic
Sweden: Catholics persecuted

Did You Know?

Queen Elizabeth I ended much of the religious turmoil of Mary I's reign by reestablishing the monarchy's supremacy in the Church of England and restoring the Book of Common Prayer. Queen Elizabeth also instituted a policy of religious moderation, although the policy failed to please many devout Protestants and Catholics.

1601 to 1610   1602 to 1618 Persia: Holy War between Turkey and Persia
1603 Dutch Calvinist Johannes Althusius advocates republican government and asserts that voluntary agreement should be the basis of political association
1604 England: James I restores Recussancy Acts, with more persecution and the expulsion of priests; he also bans Jesuits
Japan: Tung-lin Academy revives Confucianism and attacks graft
Pope Clement VIII requests that English Catholics refrain from rebellion
1605 England: Gunpowder Plot fails; Sir Francis Bacon's *The Advancement of Learning*
Russia: Nikon reforms parish clergy
1605 to 1621 Italy: Pope V
1606 England: Laws passed against Roman Catholics

Did You Know?

The Gunpowder Plot, a failed attempt by Catholic extremists to blow up
Parliament and the king, extended anti-Catholic feeling. ·

1607 Confucianism begins to be main force in Tokugawa politics and society
1608 Germany: Frederick IV leads formation of Protestant Union
1609 Bohemia: Emperor Rudolf II allows freedom of worship
Europe: Maximillan of Bavaria forms Catholic League in opposition to the Protestant
Union

Did You Know?

The Bible, a collection of books developed over a period of more than 1,200
years, consists of two main parts, the Old Testament and the New Testament.
The Old Testament was originally written in Hebrew; the New Testament in
Greek. In 382, St. Jerome began to translate the Bible into Latin. His translation,
the Vulgate Version, remained the standard Bible in the West for centuries.
English reformer John Wycliffe and his followers produced the first English
translation of the Bible from Latin in the late fourteenth century. With the
Reformation and the invention of movable type, people began to clamor for a
book written in English.

Accepting this mandate, King James commissioned fifty-four scholars and
clergymen to compare all extant texts of the Bible and produce a definitive
English edition. They succeeded beyond anyone's expectations: The King James
Version has been called "the only classic ever created by a committee." From its
first appearance, the King James Version has been regarded as one of the great
works of English literature. Although other translations followed, none has had its
impact.

1611 to 1620   1611 England: King James Version of the Bible published
1612 Matthias becomes Holy Roman Emperor
Spain: Francisco Suarez's *On Laws* tries to refute James I of England's claim to rule by
divine right
1612 to 1639 Japan: Persecution of Christians
1614 to 1657 England: John Libume leads The Levelers, Puritan group that demanded
egalitarian and republican society
1615 England: John Donne becomes an Anglican priest
1571 to 1641 France: Jean-Baptiste Colbert, a Mercantilist, advocates governmental
regulation of economy
1620 US: *Mayflower* lands at Plymouth; about half the 102 passengers seek religious
freedom

KEY DOCUMENT

In his *History of Plymouth Plantation*, William Bradford describes the *Mayflower's* landing:

> . . . Being thus arrived in a good harbor, and brought safe to land, they fell upon their knees and blessed the God of Heaven who had brought them over the vast and furious ocean, and delivered them from all the perils and miseries thereof, again to set their feet upon firm and stable earth, their proper element . . . But I cannot but stay and make a pause, and stand half amazed at this poor people's present condition; so I think the reader will, too, when he well considers the same. Being thus passed the vast ocean, and a sea of troubles before in their preparation, they now had no friends to welcome them nor inns to entertain or refresh their weather-beaten bodies; no houses or much less towns to repair to, to seek for succor.

1621 to 1630   1621 England: John Donne appointed Dean of St. Paul's Cathedral; Robert Burton's *The Anatomy of Melancholy*
1622 Battles of Wimpfen and Rochst: Count Tilly defeats Protestants
Japan: Christian missionaries executed
1623 to 1644 Pope Urban VIII
1624 Herbert of Cherbury's *On Truth* attempts to establish belief in God based on rational inquiry rather than faith
1624 to 1642 France: Cardinal Richelieu, chief minister to Louis XIII
1625 Dutchman Hugo Grotius publishes *De Jure Belli ac Pacis;* becomes the basis of international law
France: Vincent de Paul establishes Order of Sisters of Mercy

Did You Know?

Richelieu was consecrated Bishop of Lucon in 1607 when he was only 22 years old.

1626 England: John Donne's *Five Sermons*
Germany: Battle of Desau: Ferdinand II victorious in wars against the Protestants
1627 Bohemia: Ferdinand II outlaws all religions but Roman Catholicism
1627 to 1704 France: Jacques Bossuet upholds Louis XIV's absolute monarchy against Protestants, arguing that any legally formed government is sacred
1628 France: Edict of La Rochelle withdraws some privileges from French Protestants, but still allows freedom of worship
Italy: Pope Gregory XV canonizes Ignatius Loyola
1628 to 1688 England: John Bunyan, religious writer
1629 Edict of Restitution allows Roman Catholic Church to recover property seized by Protestants

1631 to 1640   1632 to 1704 John Locke, English philosopher, established school of empiricism
1632 to 1677 Dutch philosopher Baruch (or Benedict) Spinoza
1632 to 1694 Germany: Samuel von Pufendorf, based philosophy on social nature of
human beings

Did You Know?

*Born of Spanish-Portuguese-Jewish parents in Amsterdam, Spinoza received a
traditional Jewish education. Spinoza's readings in Thomas Hobbes and Rene
Descartes alienated him from his heritage, however, and he withdrew from the
synagogue in 1656. Excommunicated and banished, Spinoza supported himself
by grinding lenses while he wrote his philosophical works. He refused a chair at
the University of Heidelberg and a pension from Louis XIV so he could maintain
his independence. Although his philosophy did not give rise to an organized
group, Spinoza has had the most persuasive influence of all modern philosophers
after Immanuel Kant.*

1633 Italy: Galileo forced to reject Copernicus' theories
US: John Cotton becomes religious leader
1634 US: Anne Hutchinson comes to America; sparks religious controversy
1636 Canada: Saint Isaac Jogues, French Jesuit missionary, goes to Canada as missionary
to the Huron
US: Puritan Roger Williams banished from Massachusetts, establishes Providence, RI;
proclaims religious freedom
1637 Japan: Thousands of Japanese Christians massacred; all foreign traders except the
Dutch expelled
Scotland: People riot over new liturgy
1638 Scottish Presbyterians sign the Solemn League and Covenant
William Chillingworth's *The Religion of Protestants a Safe Way to Salvation*
1639 First Bishops' War: Charles I versus Scottish church; ends with Pacification of Dunse
1640 Second Bishops' War; ends with Treaty of Ripon
Europe: Jesuits are leaders of education, with more than 500 colleges throughout Europe
US: *Bay Psalm Book,* oldest surviving book printed in America

1641 to 1650   1641 Ireland: Catholic revolt; 30,000 Protestants murdered
1642 France: Cornelis Jansen's *Augustinus* attacks Jesuits and proclaims strict
predestination

Did You Know?

*The Whole Booke of Psalmes Faithfully Translated into English Metre came off
the press of Stephan Daye in Cambridge, Massachusetts in 1640. A slender calf-
bound volume with sturdy brass clasps, the hymnal was a colonial best-seller.
Revised and enlarged, it went through fifty editions. For over a century New
England Puritans carried it with them to worship.*

KEY DOCUMENT

New England Puritans demanded a literal translation of the Bible rather than an elegant one. The following lines from the *Bay Psalm Book's* version of the Twenty-third Psalm illustrates this:

The Lord to mee a shepheard is,
want therefor shall not I.
Hee in the folds of tender-grasse,
doth cause mee downe to lie:
To waters calme me gently leads
Restore my soule doth hee:
He doth in paths of righteousness:
for his names sake leade mee.

Italy: Papal Bull reduces annual feast days and condemns Jansen's *Augustinus*
1643 England: John Milton's *The Doctrine and Discipline of Divorce;* George Fox, a shoemaker from Nottingham, begins touring the country and giving sermons arguing that ordained ministers are irrelevant to the individual seeking God
1644 England: John Milton's *Areopagitica* argues for freedom of the press; Roger Williams' *Queries of Highest Consideration,* on separation of church and state
France: Descartes's *Principles of Philosophy*
1645 Tibet: Dalai Lama's residence built in Lahsa
1646 England: George Fox has divine revelation that inspires him to preach a gospel of brotherly love
1647 England: Anglican professors fired from Oxford University

Did You Know?

The Society of Friends was given the name "Quakers" because of their agitated movements before moments of divine revelation.

1648 Peace of Westphalia extends Peace of Augsburg (1555) to Calvinists
England: Quakers follow George Fox, an English lay preacher of the doctrine of "Christ within," which later developed into the idea of the "inner light"
France: Montesquieu: *Spirit of Laws*
Sabbatai Tzevi establishes a Jewish sect
1649 Ireland: Cromwell harshly suppresses Catholics
Maryland Assembly passes acts of toleration
1650 France: Philosopher, scientist, and mathematician Rene Descartes dies
c. 1650 Africa: Ethiopia expels Portuguese missionaries and diplomats

1651 to 1660   1651 England: In *Leviathan,* Thomas Hobbes declares that human life is "solitary, poor, nasty, brutish, and short"

Did You Know?

Sabbatai Tzevi, one of the most spectacular false Jewish messiahs, sparked a mass movement that threatened rabbinical authority in Europe and the Near East; it was even rumored that Tzevi would seize the Turkish throne. In 1665, Tzevi publicly proclaimed that he was the messiah. The following year, however, when the Sultan of Adrianople threatened him with torture, Tzevi converted to Islam and his followers fell away.

1653 England: Quaker James Naylor seen by some as a new Messiah
1655 England: Under Cromwell, Jews allowed to return to England; Thomas Fuller's *Church History of Britain;* Thomas Hobbs' *De Corpore*
1656 France: Blaise Pascal's *Lettres provinciales* against Jesuits
Spinoza excommunicated
Switzerland: First Villmergen War between Protestants and Catholics
US: Quaker women preachers begin work in Maryland and in the Massachusetts Bay Colony

Did You Know?

Oliver Cromwell's primary success was in maintaining peace and stability and providing a measure of religious toleration.

1658 to 1707 Emperor Aurangzeb is the last great Moghul emperor; after 1707, empire begins to break up
1659 US: Boston magistrates persecute Quakers

Did You Know?

Aurangzeb persecuted the Hindus, which greatly accelerated the break-up of the Moghul Empire.

1661 to 1670   1661 England: Claredon Code: Cavalier Parliament passes a series of repressive laws against Nonconformists (to 1665); John Eliot translates the Bible into Algonquin; first American edition of the Bible
US: Quakers establish yearly meetings
1662 England: Act of Uniformity; Royal Society established
1663 to 1728 US: Cotton Mather, Puritan minister
1664 England: Conventicle Act forbids meetings of more than five people; aimed at Nonconformists
France: Trappist order established

1666 Armenia: First bible printed

England: Bunyan's *Grace Abounding to the Chief of Sinners*

Russia: Great Schism in church

1666 to 1709 Govind Singh, tenth guru of the Sikh religion, advocates armed resistance to Moghul persecution

1669 India: Emperor Aurangzeb forbids Hindu religion

William Penn's *No Cross, No Crown*

1670 Europe: Secret Treaty of Dover between Charles II of England and Louis XIV of France to restore Roman Catholicism to England

Did You Know?

Sir Isaac Newton's Law of Universal Gravity sparked philosopher John Locke to prove that humanity was also ruled by universal laws of equality and independence.

1671 to 1680

1671 England: John Bunyan's *A Confession of My Faith*

Italy: First Bible printed in Arabic

1673 England: Test Act deprives English Roman Catholics and Noncomformists of public office

1675 Dutch philosopher Spinoza's *Ethics*, which argues that free will is an illusion

US: Quakers begin to settle in America, especially in New Jersey and Pennsylvania

1676 Roger Williams' anti-Quaker tract

1677 US: Increase Mather's *The Troubles That Have Happened in New England*

1678 England: Bunyan's *The Pilgrim's Progress from This World to That Which is to Come;* Popish Plot: Titus Oakes falsely alleges Catholic plot to murder Charles II; Ralph Cudworth's *True Intellectual System;* Isaac Newton's *Principia*, fundamental to the development of mechanistic and optimistic philosophy of the eighteenth century

Scotland: First complete exposition of the Quaker doctrine of the "inner light" in Robert Barclay's *An Apology for the True Christian Divinity, as the Same is Held Forth and Preached by the People Called in Scorn Quakers*, considered the greater Quaker theological work

Did You Know?

The Pilgrim's Progress, the most popular allegory in English literature, centers on the metaphor that life is a journey. Many phrases from Pilgrim's Progress entered English, including "slough of despond," "house beautiful," and "vanity fair."

1681 to 1690

1681 US: Charles II issues charter to William Penn to establish Quaker colony in Pennsylvania

1682 England: John Bunyan's *The Holy War*

1684 France: Jews expelled from Bordeaux

Italy: Pope Innocent XI forms Holy Roman League: Venice, Austria, and Poland against Turkey

US: Approximately 7,000 Quakers had settled in Pennsylvania

Did You Know?

William Penn's "Holy Experiment" tested how far a state could be governed consistently with Quaker principles, especially pacifism and religious toleration.

1685 England: Writer John Dryden converts to Catholicism
France: Revocation of the Edict of Nantes of 1598; only Roman Catholicism allowed. Thousands of Protestants flee the country
1686 England: James II ignores Test Act: Roman Catholics appointed to office
1687 England: Declaration of Liberty of Conscience extends toleration to all religions
1688 England: James II issues Declaration of Indulgence, allowing Dissenters and Catholics to worship freely; sparks Glorious Revolution, in which William of Orange takes control of English throne; James II flees
US: Quakers protest publicly against slavery

Did You Know?

The Glorious Revolution was so named because unlike the revolution of 1640 to 1660, it was both bloodless and successful. A victory for Whig principles and Tory pragmatism, the Revolution left parliament sovereign and England prosperous.

1689 England: Toleration Act grants freedom of worship to Protestant dissenters
1690 England: Locke's *Essay, Letter Concerning Toleration,* and *Two Treatises of Government* justified the English Revolution of 1688, claiming that rulers' legitimacy depended on their protecting the citizens' rights
Ireland: William III defeats former King James II and Irish rebels at Battle of the Boyne, ensuring that England will stay Protestant

1691 to 1700   1691 to 1700 Innocent XII is Pope
1692 Edict of Toleration for Christians in China
US: Salem witchcraft trials
1693 US: Cotton Mather's *Wonders of the Invisible World* on witchcraft
1695 England: John Locke's *The Reasonableness of Christianity*

Did You Know?

Govind Singh introduced strict practices to the Sikhs, who pledge to wear a turban, to carry a knife, and never to cut their hair. The Sikhs came to dominate the Punjab.

1699 Govind Singh gives the surname "Singh" (meaning "lion") to the Sikhs
1700 to 1721 Clement XI is Pope

Did You Know?

Twenty years after the last execution in the Salem witchcraft trials, the government awarded compensation to the victims still living. However, the fever was far from over; certain farms belonging to the victims were left to ruin and for more than a century no one would buy them or live on them.

1701 to 1710   1701 England: Act of Settlement restricts throne to Anglicans
Father Francisco Ximenes translates *Popul Vah*, sacred book of Quiche Indians of Guatemala
1702 Constantinople: Armenian priest Mekhitar of Sebaste establishes Order of the Mekhitarists, Roman Catholic Armenian monks
US: Cotton Mather's *Magnalia Christi Americana*, religious history of America
1703 to 1758 US: Jonathan Edwards, Puritan minister who leads the religious fervor called the Great Awakening
c. 1705 Africa: Congo prophetess, Dona Beatrice, founds new religious cult and helps end civil war
France: Bernard de Mandeville's *The Grumbling Hive* argues that people are motivated by self-interest, but this leads to the general good; this idea influenced the laissez-faire economists
Joseph I, Holy Roman Emperor

Did You Know?

Hasidism (also spelled Chasidim) centers on its leader, the zaddik ("righteous one") revered as a mediator between the Hasidim and God and as a wise counselor. Some zaddikim were reputed to perform miracles.

1708 England: Earl of Shaftesbury's *Letter concerning Enthusiasm* helps popularize Deism, or Natural Religion, which criticized formal religion, intolerance, and extremism
1710 Bishop Berkely's *The Principles of Human Knowledge* argues for an extreme idealism, claiming that all we perceive is in the mind alone; as a result, to exist is merely to be perceived
Leibniz: *Theodicee* ("God created the best of all possible worlds")

Did You Know?

The Jansenists believed in predestination; all people are incapable of doing good without God's unsolicited grace. People are thus destined by God for salvation or damnation, and ultimately only a chosen few will receive salvation. Because this doctrine closely resembles Calvinism, the group was accused of being Protestants in disguise.

c. 1700 to 1760 Poland: Ba'al Shem Tov founds Hasidism, a mystical sect that stresses joy
of religious practice and expression while rejecting academic elitism

1711 to 1720   1711 Charles VI becomes Holy Roman Emperor (to 1740)
1712 Switzerland: Religious warfare
1712 to 1778 France: Jean Jacques Rousseau, philosopher
1713 Papal Bull Unigenitus condemns Jansenists

Part 3 Philosophy and Religion
1801 to 2000

1801 to 1810   1803 England: Jeremy Bentham's *Civil and Penal Legislation*
1804 France: Code Napoleon
1806 to 1873 John Stuart Mill, English philosopher-economist who emphasized reason and liberty
1807 US: US Evangelical Association holds first convention
1809 US: Sisters of Charity founded

1811 to 1820   1811 Wales: "Great Schism"; Two-thirds of Welsh Protestants leave Anglican Church
1812 England: Baptist Union formed
Prussia: Jews emancipated
1813 Methodist Missionary Society established
1814 India: First Anglican bishop arrives
Rome: Pope Pius VII restores the Inquisition
1816 American Bible Society established

1821 to 1830   1821 England: James Mills' *Elements of Political Economy*
South Pacific: Protestant missionaries arrive on Cook Islands
1825 England: A Quaker educator writes that "there does not appear any reason why the education of women should differ in its essentials from that of men."; Saint-Simon's *New Christianity,* sought to combine the ideals of Christianity with science to form a new religion of socialism
1827 Plymouth Brethren founded
1828 India: Ram Mohun Roy establishes Brahmo Samaj, dedicated to Hindu social and religious reforms
1829 England: Catholic Emancipation Act; Roman Catholics can hold public office; Mill's *Analysis of the Human Mind*
France: Guizot's *History of Civilization in France*
India: Suttee abolished

Did You Know?

Suttee *is the Indian custom of a widow immolating herself on her dead husband's funeral pyre.*

1830 Comte coins the terms "sociology" and "positivism" in *Course of Positive Philosophy*
US: Joseph Smith founds Mormonism

1831 to 1840   1831 Gregory XVI becomes pope
William Miller, founder of Modern Adventism, begins to predict the end of the world

329

1832 US: Church of Christ formally organized
1833 England: Oxford Movement (within Anglicanism)
1834 France: Lamennais's *Thoughts of a Believer*
South Pacific: French Catholic missionaries arrive in Mangareva in Tuamotu Islands
1836 US: Emerson's essay "Nature"
1836 to 1886 India: Ramakrishna leads reform movement
1837 US: Presbyterians split into "old" and "new" school
1838 Japan: Nakayama Miki founds faith-healing Tenri sect
1840 Hawaii: Kamehameha III begins constitutional monarchy in Hawaii; first written Hawaiian constitution

Did You Know?

Transcendentalism *proposed that spiritual exploration of one's soul in communion with nature led to the highest wisdom.*

1841 to 1850

1841 Feurerbach's *The Essence of Christianity*
1843 Kierkegaard's *Either/Or*
1844 World fails to end on October 22, as Protestant Adventists had predicted; many Adventists lose faith and return to their former churches. Those remaining split into three main bodies: the *Seventh-Day Adventists, Advent Christian Church,* and *The Church of God*
Iran: Baha'i faith founded, teaching that the revealed religions of the world are in agreement
1845 England: John Henry Newman becomes a Catholic
1846 France: Proudhon's *The Philosophy of Misery*
Pope Pius IX (to 1878)
US: Brigham Young leads Mormons to Great Salt Lake
1847 US: Mormons found Salt Lake City

Did You Know?

Baha'i's principles can be summarized this way:
1. The oneness of humankind, which will lead to world unity.
2. Independent investigation of truth.
3. The common foundation of all religions.
4. The essential harmony of science and religion.
5. Equality of men and women.
6. Elimination of prejudice of all kinds.
7. Universal compulsory education.
8. A spiritual solution to economic problems.
9. A universal auxiliary language.
10. Universal peace upheld by a world government.

1848 England: Macaulay's *History of England*
Marx and Engles: The *Manifesto of the Communist Party* (commonly called *The Communist Manifesto*)
John Thomas founds the Christadelphians, a pacifist millennial Adventist sect
1850 China: Taiping Rebellion, radical religious movement influenced by Protestant Christian teaching

1851 to 1860   1852 Africa: Tukolor leader al-Hajj 'Umar launches jihad along Senegal and upper Niger rivers to establish Islamic state
1853 Maurice's *Theological Essays*
1854 Thoreau's *Walden*
1855 Le Play's *European Workers*
1856 to 1939 Sigmund Freud, founder of psychoanalysis
1859 Darwin's *Origin of Species*
England: John Stuart Mill's essay "On Liberty"
France: Virgin Mary reputed to have appeared at Lourdes

Did You Know?

Darwin's Origin of Species *aroused the opposition of the Church of England because it contradicted Genesis and seemed to render the role of God in creation superfluous. By implying that humans stood at the top of evolutionary development, Darwin's theory reinforced contemporary ideas about the inevitability of social progress.*

1860 Middle East: Conflict between Maronites (Syrian Christians) and Druse; thousands of Maronites killed and others driven from their homes
US: Advent Christian Church organized in Salem, MA, preaching "conditional immortality," according to which the dead remain in an unconscious state until the resurrection, which would take place at the second coming after the millennium

1861 to 1870   1863 England: Mill's *Utilitarianism*
Seventh-Day Adventists formally organized; today, about 5.5 million members
1864 England: Cardinal Newman's *Apologia pro Vita Sua*
Italy: Pope Pius IX condemns liberalism, socialism, and rationalism
Lebanon: Christian governor-general appointed to mediate between Druse and Maronites; end of the political importance of Lebanese Druse
1865 to 1870 Korea: King Kojong persecutes Christians
1866 US: American Evangelical Alliance established
1869 Disestablishment Act: Irish Church ceases to exist (1871)
England: J. S. Mill: "On the Subjection of Women"
1870 US: Jehovah's Witnesses organized; members believe that soon the forces of good (led by Christ) will defeat the forces of evil (led by Satan) at the battle of Armageddon; thereafter, Christ will rule the world for a thousand years; the dead will rise again and everyone will have a second chance for salvation; perfect humanity will enjoy perfect life on earth
Italy: Vatican Council issues doctrine of papal infallibility

Did You Know?

Seventh-Day Adventists hold these beliefs:
1. Christ will return to earth soon, even though the exact time cannot be determined.
2. The Bible is the sole religious authority.
3. Grace alone is sufficient for salvation.
4. The wicked will be destroyed at the Second Coming.
5. The just (including the living and the resurrected dead) will be granted everlasting life.
Because they believe that the body is the temple of the Holy Spirit, Seventh-Day Adventists put great stress on health and avoid eating meat and using narcotics and stimulants. The Sabbath is observed on Saturday. Dancing and theatre-going are forbidden and baptism is by immersion.

1871 to 1880	1871 England: Darwin: *The Descent of Man*
	1875 US: Madame Blavatsky founds Theosophical Society; Mary Baker Eddy's *Science and Health*
	1878 Pope Leo XVII ends the practice of castrating boys for the papal choir

Did You Know?

In Parliament, John Stuart Mill was considered a radical because he supported public ownership of natural resources, equality for women, compulsory education, and birth control.

1881 to 1890	1881 Russia: Pogroms against Jews
	1883 England: Fabian Society established
	Germany: Nietzsche's *Thus Spake Zarathustra*
	1884 Prussia: Zionist Conference
	Russia: Kropotkin's *Words of a Rebel* stresses nonviolence

Did You Know?

Because Jehovah's Witnesses acknowledge allegiance only to the kingdom of Jesus Christ, they refuse to salute any flag, to vote, or to perform military service.

1885 US: Mormons split into polygamous and monogamous sects
1886 France: Drumont's *Le France Juive* popularizes antisemitism
Germany: Nietzsche's *Beyond Good and Evil*

Did You Know?

Christian Scientists reject medicine and see prayer as the only cure for illness.

1890 England: Frazer's *The Golden Bough*
England: Marshall's *Principles of Economics*
US: William James' *The Principles of Psychology*

1891 to 1900   1891 Pope Leo XIII issues "Rerum Novarum"
1896 Herzl: *Der Judenstaat,* foundation of Zionism
1897 France: Durkheim's *Suicide*
Switzerland: Zionist Congress
US: Ellis' *Studies in the Psychology of Sex*
US: James' *The Will to Believe*
1900 Japan: Shintoism reinstated in Japan as a counterweight to Buddhist influence
Germany: Freud's *The Interpretation of Dreams*

1901 to 1910   1901 India: Tagore establishes Santiniketan school
1901 to 1905 France: Separation of church and state
1902 Italy: Pareto's *The Socialist Systems*
US: The Pentecostal movement begins around this time
1903 Pope Pius X (to 1914)
1905 Germany: Freud: *Dora (Fragment of an Analysis of a Case of Hysteria)*
1907 Pope Pius X recognizes validity of civil marriages
France: Henri Bergson's *Creative Evolution*
1908 France: Georges Sorel's *Reflections on Violence*

1911

1912

1913

Did You Know?

The Druse adhere to seven cardinal principles:
1. Veracity in dealing with others.
2. Mutual protection and assistance.
3. Renunciation of other religions.
4. Belief in the divine incarnation of Hakim.
5. Contentment with the works of God.
6. Submission to God's will.
7. Separation from those in error and demons.

1914

1915

1916

1917   Russia: Lenin's *The State and Revolution*

1918   Middle East: Syrian and Lebanese Druse assist Arab leader Faisal, who, in turn, helps
             British capture Damascus
             Spengler's *The Decline of the West*

1919

1920

1921   Middle East: Syrian plateau region of Jabal ad-Duruz granted autonomy
             US: First radio broadcast of a religious service (KDKA, Pittsburgh); Church of God of the
             Abrahamic Faith unified (also called the Church of God General Conference); members
             believe that the dead are merely asleep; at the time of the second coming the righteous
             will be resurrected on earth and the wicked will be destroyed

1922   US: Evangelist Aimee Semple McPherson builds Angelus Temple in LA and preaches the
             religion of the foursquare gospel

1923   Hungary: Lukacs' *History and Class-consciousness*

1924

1925   Canada: United Church of Canada founded
             Middle East: Druse exiled to Palmyra, setting off Druse revolt
             US: Watson's *Behaviorism*

Did You Know?

The 1925 Druse revolt gave impetus to the independence struggles of Syria and
Lebanon.

1926   US: Aimee Semple McPherson mysteriously disappears; weeks later, she reappears,
             claiming to have been abducted and tortured

1927   Germany: Martin Heidegger develops philosophy of Existentialism

1928

1929   Lateran Treaty establishes independent Vatican City
South Africa: Word "apartheid" first used to describe racial segregation

1930   England: Keynes' *Treatise on Money*

1931

1932   Russia: Trotsky's *History of the Russian Revolution*

1933

1934

1935

1936   England: John Maynard Keynes' *The General Theory of Employment, Interest and Money* promotes demand-side economics

1937

1938

1939

1940

1941

1942   France: Merleau-Ponty's *The Structure of Behavior*
Oxfam founded to combat Third World poverty

1943   France: Sartre's *Being and Nothingness*

1944   England: Popper's *The Open Society and its Enemies*

1945

1946

1947   Germany: Adorno and Horkeimer's *Dialectics of Enlightenment*
Germany: Buber's *Paths to Utopia*
India: Religious massacres accompany partition of India and Pakistan into independent states

1948   World Council of Churches formed

1949

1950

1951

1952   Frantz Fanon's *Black Skin, White Masks*

1953

1954

1955

1956   US: Tillich's *Dynamics of Faith*

1957   United Church of Christ organized in Cleveland, OH, when the General Council of the
            Congregational Christian Churches and the Evangelical and Reformed Churches
            combined; first major union in American Protestantism to have different historical and
            cultural backgrounds and mixed forms of worship
            US: Chomsky's *Syntactical Structures*

1958   France: Levi-Strauss' *Structural Anthropology*

1959

1960   France: Sartre's *Critique of Dialectical Reason*
            US: Laing's *The Divided Self*

1961   Amnesty International established to promote human rights and protect the rights of
            political prisoners
            Ecumenical Movement for Christian unity begins

1962   Italy: Pope John XXIII opens Second Vatican Council, which changed the liturgy of the
            Mass, gave the laity a bigger role in the church, and encouraged a new spirit of
            ecumenism

1963   Italy: Pope John XXIII dies; succeeded June 21 by Cardinal Montini, who becomes Paul
            VI
            US: Supreme Court rules no locality may require recitation of Lord's Prayer or Bible
            verses in public schools

1964   Marcuse's *One-Dimensional Man*

1965

1966

1967   US: Legalizes abortion

1968   Poland: Wladyslaw Gomulka stirs up antisemitic feelings, and within the next 2 years
            most of Poland's 30,000 Jews are forced to leave

1969

1970   Canada: Greenpeace is established to protest nuclear testing in the Pacific

1971   Western religious groups that stress personal awareness include "Jesus Freaks" and "Divine Light Mission"

1972

1973

1974

1975   UN declares "International Year of the Woman"

1976   US: Sun Myung Moon and his Unification Church spark controversy

1977   US: First female Episcopal priest ordained

1978   Italy: Pope Paul VI, dead at 80, mourned (August 6); new Pope, John Paul I, 65, dies unexpectedly after 34 days in office. He is succeeded by Karol Cardinal Wojtyla of Poland as John Paul II

Did You Know?

Karol Wojtyla (Pope John Paul II) is the first non-Italian to be chosen as Pope since 1522.

1979   Mother Teresa awarded Nobel Peace Prize
Europe: Pope John Paul II visits Poland; first Pope to visit a Communist country
Iran: Muslim fundamentalists select Ayatollah Khomeni to lead them
Saudi Arabia: Terrorists seize Grand Mosque in Mecca; Saudi troops recapture it

1980   El Salvador: Archbishop Oscar Romero assassinated while celebrating mass; 39 others killed at his funeral
Alternative Service Book 1980, first authorized prayer book for Anglican church since 1662
US: Moral Majority forms

1981   China: New translation of the *Koran*
Ethiopia: Marxist leaders close Christian churches and Muslim mosques and persecute the religious
Iran: Baha'i community persecuted
South Africa: Presbyterian Church tells clergy they can marry people of different races, in defiance of apartheid laws
Unification Church of Sun Myung Moon loses libel action against the *Daily Mail,* English newspaper

1982   England: John Paul II is first Pope to visit
US: General Assembly of the United Presbyterian Church merges with Presbyterian Church, healing split that existed since Civil War
Unification Church of Sun Myung Moon holds mass wedding for 2,075 couples in Madison Square Garden

1983   Pope John Paul II visits Poland, his birth country

1984   US: Texas Board of Education repeals ban on teaching evolution as scientific fact

1985   Ireland: Crowds mob Statue of Virgin Mary in Cork, which is said to move back and forth

1986   Pope Paul II is first Pope in history to visit a synagogue; also leads 100 world religious leaders in prayers for peace
South Africa: Desmond Tutu becomes first black Archbishop of Cape Town; Dutch Reform Church opens membership to all races

1987   England: Anglican Church ordains first female deacons
India: Sikh high priests excommunicate Punjab's Chief Minister for defiance
US: Oral Roberts raises $4.5 million; Jim Bakker, head of "Praise the Lord" TV network, resigns after adultery charges

1988

1989   India: Fundamentalists attempt to demolish Islamic mosque site
Nobel Peace Prize: Tenzin Gyatso, the Dalai Lama (1935–)
US: Jim Bakker convicted of fraud; sentenced to 45 years in jail

1990

Did You Know?

The last of the three Fatima prophecies is a 62-line handwritten account by Lucia de Jesus dos Santos of what she saw as a 10-year old shepherd in a pasture near Fatima, Portugal, on July 13, 1917. The text describes a radiant Virgin Mary, a flaming sword, and a "bishop in white," presumed to be a Pope, who leads a sad procession of priests and nuns up a mountain through a half-ruined city strewn with corpses. One by one, the bishop and his followers are slain by soldiers with bullets and arrows as angels near a cross collect the martyrs' blood and sprinkle it on their heaven-bound souls. Five successive Popes had kept Lucia's tale locked in a safe, feeding fevered speculations that it predicted the end of the world. The secret spawned a cult that held the mother of Jesus as both savior and prophet of doom.

1991   US: Supreme Court reaffirms right to abortion (June 29)

1992

1993   First female minister ordained by Church of England (Anglican)

1994

1995

1996

1997

1998   Pope John Paul II visits Cuba
              Presbyterians keep ban on gay clergy
              Vatican regrets inaction during Holocaust

1999

2000   Vatican publishes "Third Secret," the last of the three Fatima prophecies
              Jehovah's Witnesses allows members to use previously prohibited parts or fractions of
              blood components

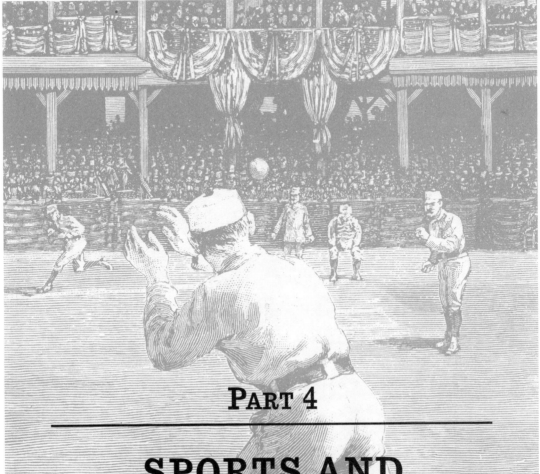

PART 4

SPORTS AND ENTERTAINMENT

Part 4   Sports and Entertainment

PREHISTORIC DAYS TO −1 BCE

−4000 to −3501

−3500 to −3001

−3000 to −2501   Egypt: Belt wrestling is a popular sport

Did You Know?

The bow first entered military history in 2340 BCE, when Sargon of Akkad in northern Babylonia conquered the Sumerians of southern Babylonia with an infantry made up mostly of archers. From that time on, many ancient peoples used archery in warfare in varying ways and with varying degrees of success.

There were archery contests in China more than 3,000 years ago. Egyptian pharaohs and Roman emperors often demonstrated their skill with the bow, and their soldiers probably had informal competitions of some sort, most likely linked with compulsory target practice.

−2500 to −2001   Egypt: Middle Kingdom tombs show depictions of belt-wrestling holds

−2000 to −1500   c. −1500 Just how far back in history organized athletic contests were first held is uncertain, but most scholars are certain they existed in Greece around this time
c. −1500 India: Loose wrestling flourishes

Did You Know?

The Mayans, who became a recognized political group in southern Mexico, Guatemala, and parts of Belize around −2000, played a number of ball games. Players bounced a solid rubber ball off their padded hips and elbows. They played for keeps—losing teams were sometimes sacrificed to the gods.

−1500 to −1001   c. −1425 Egypt: Tomb painting shows Nubian soldiers in wrestling motif
c. 1190 Earliest record of a fencing match found in a relief carving in the temple of Madīnat Habu near Luxor in Upper Egypt; the inscription reads: "on guard and admire what my valiant hand shall do."

343

−1000 to −901

−900 to −801

Did You Know?

Ancient Greece and contemporary America enjoyed some curious parallels, especially in the realm of sports. As is true today, success in athletic events was a passport to fame. The Olympics—held every four years from −776 to 393 at Olympia in the western Peloponnesus—were the most prestigious games. Some athletes were even exempt from paying taxes! The events included running, wrestling, boxing, the long jump, discus throwing, javelin throwing, and horse and chariot races.

−800 to −701   −776 Greece: First recorded Olympic Games. Four major sporting festivals held: Olympic Games (at Olympia), Pythian Games (at Delphi), Nemean Games (at Nemea), and Isthmian Games (at Corinth).
−724 Greece: Two-legged race (*diaulous*) included in games
−708 Greece: Wrestling and pentathlon included in games
−776 to AD 217 Records of Champions at Olympia's Greek games

−700 to −601   −700 China: Wrestling mentioned in documents
−688 Greece: Boxing introduced to games
−680 Greece: Chariot race added to games
−648 Greece: "Pancratium," no-holds-barred wrestling added to games. Only biting and eye-gouging forbidden.
−632 Greece: Events for boys added to games

−600 to −501   −582 Greece: Four-year game cycle introduced at Delphi
c. −564 Greece: Arrachion of Phigalea killed while defending his wrestling title

−500 to −451   Greece: Ball games played
−472 Greece: Games are spread over four days; fifth day devoted to closing ceremonies and banquet for champions

c. −500   Rome: Over 150 holidays for games, including chariot racing at the Hippodrome, horse racing at the Circus Maximus (with room for over 250,000 spectators), and an amphitheater with accommodation for 50,000 in which animals and humans were maimed and slaughtered.

Did You Know?

Most gladiators fought to the death. Not surprisingly, few gladiators were volunteers—most were prisoners of war, slaves, or condemned criminals. The spectacles were finally banned in 404.

Did You Know?

According to one story, the modern marathon was inspired by a professional courier named Pheidippides, who is said to have carried the news of the Athenians' victory over the Persians at Marathon in 490 BCE from the battlefield to Athens. He ran the twenty-two miles without stopping. On arriving in the city, he gasped, "Rejoice, we conquer!" and dropped dead, possibly from heat exhaustion.

−450 to −401

−400 to −351

−350 to −301

−300 to −251   Greece and Rome: Dice, ball games, board games
                       −264 Rome: First gladiators

−250 to −201

−200 to −151

−150 to −101

−100 to −51

−50 to −1   −23 Japan: First recorded wrestling match

Part 4 Sports and Entertainment

1 TO 500

1 to 50	Roman historian Tacitus reports battles in Pompeii's amphitheater between the hometown crowd and visitors from Nuceria. Insults escalated to battles with stones and weapons. The carnage was so great that Nero forbade similar gatherings for a decade.
51 to 100	
101 to 150	
151 to 200	
201 to 250	
251 to 300	
301 to 350	Constantine outlaws public gladiator contests
351 to 400	Theodosius forbids Olympic Games
401 to 450	
451 to 500	

Part 4 Sports and Entertainment
501 TO 1000

501 to 550   c. 550 India: Chess develops

551 to 560

561 to 570

571 to 580

581 to 590

591 to 600

601 to 650

651 to 700

701 to 750   710 to 1185 Japan: Sumo wrestling is under royal patronage; is a popular spectator sport

751 to 800   c. 800 Islamic rulers of Persia begin importing Turkic soldiers from central Asia whose traditional sport was wrestling. Eventually these Turks became masters of the entire Muslim dominion and spread their style of loose wrestling (*koresh*) with them wherever they went

801 to 850

851 to 900

901 to 950

951 to 1000   Iceland: Records of *glima* belt wrestling

Part 4 Sports and Entertainment
1001 TO 1500

Although there is very little documentation about sports during this period, various proclamations and laws forbidding sports and games indicates that they were very popular indeed!

1001 to 1050   1135 India: Someshwar writes about *bhrashram* (weight lifting), *bhramanshram* (walking) and *mall-Stambha* (wrestling)

1051 to 1100

1101 to 1150

1151 to 1200   1174 England: First horse races

1201 to 1250   England: Public wrestling matches gain in popularity

1251 to 1300

1301 to 1350   1337 Germany: Playing cards become more popular than dice

1351 to 1400

1401 to 1450   1402 England: Famous wrestling match between England and France

1451 to 1500   England: Everyday people played football; prizefights, bearbaiting, and cockfighting drew large crowds
Germany: Guild of fencing masters established; most famous is the Association of St. Marcus of Löwenberg
1452 France: Some scholars date the origin of billiards here
1462 Europe: Paul Kal wrestling text

Part 4 Sports and Entertainment
1501 TO 1800

1501 to 1510 c. 1500 England: King James IV as first recorded golf player in English; golf suppressed by government because it interfered with archery, necessary for defense
Europe: Rise of Christianity halts boxing
Italy: Longer, lighter rapier transforms fencing into a sport based on speed and skill
1500 England: First annual horse races at Chester
1501 Europe: Card games all the rage
1501 to 1576 Italy: First practical guide for gamblers, Geronimo Cardano's *Book of Games and Chance;* the advice Cardano offers on cards and dice is still valid

Did You Know?

Horse racing has been called "the sport of kings" or "the king of sports."

1511 to 1520 1511 Scotland: Oldest known curling stone found, bearing the date 1511
England: Henry VIII bans lawn bowling among the lower classes and levies fee of 100 pounds on any private bowling green; this ensures that only the wealthy can play
1512 England: Nobles race horses for cash prizes
Europe: Albrecht Dürer's *Fechtbuch* (wrestling manual)
1520 England: Henry VIII and Francis I have private wrestling match at the Field of Cloth of Gold
c. 1520 England: Henry VIII imports horses from Italy and Spain and establishes royal studs at several locations
England: Record of payments for the king's "golf clubbis and ballis."

Did You Know?

The balls used in lawn bowling are not quite round so they curve when thrown slowly. The game is scored like horseshoes. Aren't you glad you asked?

1521 to 1530 1526 Europe: Card game piquet first played
India: Moghul dynasties sponsor regular wrestling festivals
1527 India: Playing cards are circular, hand-painted, and lacquered; the Mir of Surkk ("King of Sun") is one of only two court cards in the ninety-eight-card pack

1531 to 1540   1533 to 1603 England: Students over 16 at Oxford University forbidden to play football; first two offenses punishable by fines and imprisonment; the third offense, expulsion
1539 Europe: Fabian von Auerswald's *Ringer-knust* (wrestling manual)

Did You Know?

Curling is like bowling on ice. Four-player teams slide large, round stones down the ice. A player's teammates use brooms to sweep the ice before the stone. By putting a spin on a stone, expert curlers can make it "curl" (curve) a long way to place it behind blocking stones.

1540 Henry VIII brings fencing back into favor by licensing a Corporation of Masters of Defence and granting them monopoly of teaching fencing in king's realm
c. 1540 England: Billiards, related to *shovilla bourde* (shuffleboard), is a popular game during this time
France: Clement Marot mentions billiards in one of his poems, but nothing certain is known about the game's origin

1541 to 1550   1547 Guy Chabot, Baron de Jarnac, defeats La Chataigneraie in fencing match with stroke thereafter known as "coup de Jarnac"
1550 England: First written reference to cricket (in Edward VI's wardrobe records)
Italy: Billiards first played
c. 1550 England: Bearbaiting a big draw
France: King Henry III installs early billiards table in his chateau at Blois
Europe: Golf becomes a well-known sport, played by kings

Did You Know?

La Chataigneraie was so certain of winning his fencing match against Guy Chabot that he had a banquet prepared before the match to celebrate his victory. When Chabot attacked with a secret stroke and cut his opponent inside his knee, La Chataigneraie was so mortified that he refused all help and died of blood loss.

1551 to 1560   1552 Scotland: St. Andrew's Golf Club founded; Mary, Queen of Scots, was likely the first female golfer. She was charged with playing golf only a few days after the murder of her husband Darnley.
1560 Pieter Breughel (Flemish painter) paints a busy Dutch curling scene, complete with brooms

1561 to 1570   1561 Spain: Modern chess develops

1571 to 1580   1576 England: In captivity, Mary, Queen of Scots, complains that her billiard table has been removed

1581 to 1590   1590 England: A form of badminton, a popular children's game

Did You Know?

The sport of badminton evolved from the ancient game of battledore and shuttlecock, played by adults and children for at least 2,000 years in ancient Greece, China, Japan, and India. (The battledore is a paddle and the shuttlecock is a small feathered cork, now usually called a "bird.")

1591 to 1600   1591 England: Edmund Spenser makes reference to billiards in *Mother Hubberds Tale*
1598 England: George Chapman creates a character who says, "Go, Aspasia, send for some ladies who could play with you at chess, at billiards, and at other games."
1600 England: Football, prizefighting, and cockfighting still very popular sports

Did You Know?

In butt shooting, archers aimed at targets mounted on earthen butts at ranges of 100 to 140 yards. In clout shooting, the target was a piece of canvas with a wooden peg in its center. Roving, the predecessor of modern field archery, grew out of hunting with bow and arrow. Archers are presented with targets of various shapes and sizes, and they shoot at unknown ranges over rough ground.

c. 1600 England: Three kinds of archery shooting popular: butt shooting, clout shooting, and roving
Europe: Wrestling taught as a martial skill to the knights of the Holy Roman Empire
Japan: Public professional sumo wrestling matches very popular
Spain: Specialized school of rapier fencing develops
US: Native Americans play many versions of what we now call lacrosse. French explorers thought the stick resembled a bishop's crozier—*la crosse* in French—giving the sport its name.

1601 to 1610   1603 to 1625 England: James I sponsors horse races, as he had done in his native Scotland

Did You Know?

Cherokees called lacrosse "the little brother of war" because it was considered excellent military training. An entire village or tribe—hundreds or even thousands of players—made up a team. The goals were often miles apart, and a game might last as long as three days. Because most players couldn't get anywhere near the ball, they concentrated on using the stick to injure opponents.

1603 England: James I appoints a royal golf club maker and forbids the purchase of golf balls from Holland (on which the Scots were spending "no small quantitie" of gold and silver)

1604 England: James I brings *paille-maille* (croquet) equipment as well as golf clubs to his new court.

1608 England: James I may have introduced golf to Blackheath; Blackheath Golf Club may have been founded in this year

Did You Know?

Golf's origin is controversial; it could have originated in Holland or Scotland. Scotland appears to have the stronger claim, based on the often-quoted statute of Parliament of King James II that decreed that both "Fute-ball and Golfe be utterly cryed downe." (1457)

1611 to 1620 1618 England: Puritans object to people playing sports; leads to decline in participation

Europe: Era of feudal wrestling ends with outbreak of Thirty Years' War

1620 England: Oliver Cromwell denounces cricket

US: According to legend, Pilgrims see Native Americans playing a form of soccer; Native Americans called it *Pasuckquakkohowog*, which means "they gather to play football"

1620 to 1706 England: In his diary, John Evelyn notes the billiard tables in the country mansions he visits

1620s Europe: Many wrestling manuals published

1621 to 1630 1623 England: In Shakespeare's *Antony and Cleopatra*, a character says, "Let us to billiards . . ."

1625 to 1645 England: Charles I had a stud of 139 horses

1626 France: Anyone who kills an opponent in a duel is condemned to death

1630 England: Sir John Suckling, English poet, invents cribbage (then spelled "Cribbidge")

1630s Europe: *Battledore* (a form of badminton) is popular with wealthy people; two players use bats to hit a shuttlecock back and forth as many times as possible without letting it hit the ground

Did You Know?

In the card game cribbage, the object is to form counting combinations that are scored by moving pegs on a special cribbage board. The dealer scores an extra hand (the crib) from discards. The most popular of all card games, it has changed little since it was created. The only big change in the rules concerns the number of cards dealt—now it is six instead of five.

1631 to 1640   1632 Japan: Akashi Shiganosuke declared first *Yokozuna,* or "grand champion" sumo wrestler
US: Lawn bowling played at Williamsburg, VA
1633 England: Diarist Samuel Pepys mentions that King Charles II used tennis as a diet aid; it was successful, as he lost 4½ pounds.
1635 England: Poet Francis Quarles's *Emblemes* contains an engraving of two angels playing a game like billiards
1637 England: Samuel Johnson includes an entry to billiards in his *Dictionary.*

KEY DOCUMENT
In a May 1633 entry, diarist Samuel Pepys describes a notable foot race:
    The foot race was between Lee, the Duke of Richmond's footman and tyler [sic], a famous runner. And Lee hath beat him, though the King and Duke of York and almost all men bet 3 to 4 to 1 upon this tyler's [sic] head.

1641 to 1650   1643 to 1715 France: Gambling on horse races is common
c. 1650 England: Charles II and his courtiers play croquet at St. James's Park
France: Fencing changes dramatically: elaborate clothing calls for a short sword rather than a long, trailing rapier

1651 to 1660   1651 France: Formal horse race, the result of a bet between two noblemen
1655 US: First known turf race in New York
1660 England: Puritan Revolution stops all sports in England

Did You Know?
For many years, the chariot races in Homer's Iliad *were regarded as the first recorded instance of horse racing, but subsequent discoveries of inscribed tablets in Asia Minor indicate that Assyrian kings had elaborate stables under professional horse trainers centuries before the Trojan War.*

    1660 to 1685 England: Charles II, known as "the father of the British turf," races horses and offers prizes to winners; he establishes Newmarket as headquarters for racing

1661 to 1670   1665 US: Richard Nicolls, first governor of New York, called "father of the American turf" for his support of horse racing; first racetrack laid out on Hempstead Plain, NY; beginning of course racing in America
1666 England: Cricket Club established at St. Albans

1671 to 1680   1673 England: Ancient Scorton Arrow Contest, first recorded archery contest
1674 England: Charles Cotton's *Compleat Gamester* contains first description of billiards in English; Charles Cotton devotes a section of *Compleat Gamester* to whist (early form of bridge): "Ruff and Honours [alias slamm] and Whist are games so commonly known in England in all parts thereof, that every child almost of eight years old hath a competent knowledg [sic] in that recreation."
Europe: Nicholaes Petter's *Worstel-konst* (wrestling manual)
1675 England: Billiards very popular; rule book for billiards published; its writer claimed that there were "few Towns of note therein which hath not a publick Billiard-Table."
1679 France: Dueling forbidden

Did You Know?

The beginning of organized horse racing can be traced to many areas at the same time, including China, Persia, North Africa, the Near East, and Arabia.

1681 to 1690   1681 England: Boxing bout mentioned in London newspaper

1691 to 1700   1694 France: Engraving shows Duchess of Burgundy playing billiards with a mace
1697 England: First recorded cricket match, played in Sussex
1698 England: Regularly scheduled boxing matches at Royal Theatre in London

1701 to 1710   1702 England: Queen Anne gives nod to horse racing; racing for money awards begins
1707 England: Cricket mentioned in book as favorite pastime; Queen Anne is shown on playing cards as the queen of clubs
Germany: Billiards played in Berlin coffeehouses

Did You Know?

When billiards first started, only three balls were used: two white cue balls, one for each player, and a red ball. Points were scored in several different ways.

1711 to 1720   1711 England: Ascot races established
1713 Europe: Sir Thomas Parkyn's *Progmnasmata* (wrestling manual)
1714 US: Lawn bowling played in Boston
1715 England: Prize established for yearly rowing race down Thames River
1719 England: First official cricket match

England: James Figg opens boxing academy in London; he becomes first boxing champion in England
England: First recorded cricket match between two counties
1720 Ireland: First yacht club established

1721 to 1730   1727 England: *Cheny's Horse Matches*, match books from different racing centers
1729 to 1750 England: Jack Broughton, "father of English boxing," writes first formal rules for the sport and invents the first boxing gloves, known as "mufflers"
1730 England: Figg retires from boxing, undefeated

Did You Know?

Athletic authors are not as rare as you might think. Sophocles was a great wrestler, Rudyard Kipling golfed, and Ernest Hemingway boxed. Ezra Pound studied jiu-jitsu. Lord Byron, wanting to emulate the legendary Leander, swam the Hellespont.

1731 to 1740   1732 US: Ninepins played for the first time in New York; lawn bowling played at Battery Park, NY
1734 US: First recorded horse race in America (Charleston, SC)
1740 US: Battledore shuttlecock played in colonial America

1741 to 1750   1742 England: Edmund Hoyle's *Short Treatise on Whist*, first book devoted to the game, becomes a bestseller
1743 England: Boxing with fixed rules, gloves, and roped-off ring commonplace
1744 England: First recorded cricket match
Scotland: "Several Gentlemen of Honour skillful in the ancient and healthfull exercise of Golf" petition the Edinburgh city council for a golf club for annual competitions; the magistrates agree; called the Silver Club
1745 Scotland: First golf tournament at Silver Club
1748 England: Court rules that cricket is a legal sport
1750 England: Jockey Club established in London
France: Master swordsman La Boessiere "invents" fencing mask, leading to more complex swordplay

Did You Know?

Although fencing masks were used by the ancient Egyptians, they were unknown in Europe until the French "reinvented" them.

c. 1750 French: The model for the jack of spades is thought to be Ogier the Dane, the fictional hero of medieval French literature

1751 to 1760

1751 England: Rules set for King's Plate horse races
1753 England: Jockey Club establishes permanent racetrack
1754 Scotland: The Royal and Ancient Golf Club of St. Andrews established
1758 France: First successful lottery, run by famous womanizer Giovanni Giacomo Casanova, raised 2 million francs
1759 France: Lotteries established as an effective fund-raiser and fashionable amusement
London: Belgian musician Joseph Merlin invents roller skates to impress guests at a masked ball; billiard cues with flat ends become fashionable

Did You Know?

Casanova promised the government that he would use a lottery to help raise money for a new military academy without costing the impoverished French government a cent. And so he did.

1761 to 1770

1771 to 1780

1773 England: *Cheny's Horse Matches* becomes *Racing Calendar* (records horse races of past years)
1774 England: Cricket rules written down; first written mention of baseball and "rounders," suggesting a difference between the two games
1774 to 1793 France: Louis XVI organizes a jockey club, racing rules are printed
1776 England: St. Legere, classic horse race
Norway: Military ski competitions
US: Soldiers play baseball at Valley Forge; lawn bowling no longer popular, perhaps because it was so closely linked with England
1777 England: Hambeldon Club continues its mastery of cricket
US: Boxing champion Bill Richmond taken to England to display his pugilistic skill; known as the "Black Terror," Richmond knocked out his first English opponent in just twenty-five seconds

Did You Know?

From Edmund Hoyle's famous book of game rules has come the phrase "according to Hoyle," referring to something done correctly, "by the book."

1779 England: Twelfth Earl of Derby establishes racing Derby at Epson Racetrack; First running of the Oaks (horse racing)

1780 England: First running of the Derby (horse racing)

KEY DOCUMENT

In her novel *Northanger Abbey*, Jane Austen said of her heroine, ". . . it was not very wonderful that Catherine should prefer cricket, base-ball, riding on horseback, and running about the country, at the age of fourteen, to books."

1781 to 1790

1785 England: Rozier and Romain killed trying to cross the English Channel by balloon; first casualties of flight

1786 Paccard and Balmat are the first to climb Mont Blanc, starting mountain climbing sport

1786 US: golf club established in Charleston, SC

1787 England: Marylebone Cricket Club established; Royal Toxopholite Society (archery) formed under the patronage of the Prince of Wales (later George IV)

US: Princeton professors ban baseball from campus

1788 England: "Gentleman Jack" Jackson, famous aristocrat and boxer

Europe: Playing cards often carry moral, educational, or political messages

1790s France: Napoleon establishes regional horse races for money prizes, with a runoff for a "Grand Prix" at Paris

Cue replaces the mace in billiard game

Did You Know?

Toxopholite *is from the Greek for "bow lover."*

1791 to 1800

1791 England: *English Stud Book* first published (horse racing)

1792 David Mendoza becomes champion boxer

c. 1795 Billiard cues with oblique cut at small end or slightly rounded on one side become fashionable

1796 *An Historical View of the United States* notes that the game "bat and ball" (baseball) is commonly played

1800 Bill Richmond, a former black slave, becomes popular boxer

c. 1800 England: Captain Barclay, famous English pedestrian (professional runner), walks 1,000 miles in 1,000 consecutive hours before thousands of fans
Billiard cue beveled all around its face
1800s India and South Africa: British army officers play table tennis, using cigar box lids as paddles and rounded wine corks as balls; rows of books set up across the middle of a table form the net.

Part 4 Sports and Entertainment
1801 TO 2000

1801 to 1810
1802 England: Horse racing introduced to Goodwood
1803 US: Fencing popular in colonies, especially Virginia
1805 England: Boxing champ Bill Richmond KO'd by Tom Cribb
Switzerland: Annual wrestling tournaments called *schwingen* ("swinging") belt
1806 France: Captain Mingaud invents leather billiard cue tip
1807 Canada: Royal Montreal Curling Club established
England: First Ascot Gold Cup
1808 US: Although pool is still a rich man's sport, it was spreading to America: eight pool tables in coffeehouses and hotels by this date
1809 England: Tom Molineaux, former slave, boxes in England
1810 England: First public billiards rooms (Covent Garden)

1811 to 1820
1812 England: Annual sports day held at Royal Military Academy at Sandhurst
1814 England: Pugilistic Society founded
1816 First boxing match in which Jack Broughton's rules are followed
1818 US: Earliest-known reference to bowling was made by Washington Irving in "Rip Van Winkle"; game is played with nine pins, not ten; First professional horse racing
1820s Europe: Billiards teacher Jack Carr hawks "twisting chalk" at an exorbitant price, throwing in a free lesson on how to make it work
US: Soccer is a popular but casual school sport

KEY DOCUMENT

Here's the reference to bowling in Washington Irving's "Rip Van Winkle":
On entering the amphitheater, new objects of wonder presented themselves. On a level spot in the centre was a company of odd-looking personages playing at nine-pins. They were dressed in quaint, outlandish fashion: some wore short doublets [jackets], others jerkins, with long knives at their belts, and most had enormous breeches, of a similar style with that of the guide's.

1821 to 1830
1823 England: Royal Thames Yacht Club established; Rugby football originates at Rugby School
1824 US: About twenty-four pool tables in the country; roller skating becomes popular
1828 US: Titian Ramsey Peale establishes the United Bowmen of Philadelphia archery group
1830s England: Cross-country running begins with a game called "hare and hounds" or "the paper chase"; runners left a paper trail, which a second set of runners then followed in pursuit

France: Doctor develops a version of croquet as exercise for his patients; he names it "croquet," from the French word for a *crooked stick,* and it was widely played at spas in the South of France; English visitors bring it home

1831 to 1840   1831 Ivory chess set from the twelfth century is found on the Isle of Lewis in the Outer Hebrides; now known as the "Lewis chessmen," they probably come from Iceland or Norway

Did You Know?

By the mid-nineteenth century, there were several different versions of billiards. In France, the most popular version was carom billiards, *played with three or four balls on a pocketless table. In England, the most popular version also had three balls, but was played on a table with six pockets. There were two ways of scoring: by pocketing a ball (other than the cue ball) or by hitting both of the other balls with the cue ball. This game is the ancestor of modern pocket billiards and English snooker.*

1832 US: Orchard Lake Curling Club (Michigan) established
1833 France: Society established to administer major horse racing tracks and training centers
1834 US: Castle Garden Boat Club, first amateur rowing club
1836 England: First cricket match
1837 England: Regular swimming competitions held in London, organized by the National Swimming Society in England; six pools in the city; Crick Run, held at Rugby School, is first formal cross-country race
1838 England: Pugilistic Society develops London Prize Ring Rules
Scotland: Grand Caledonian Curling Club (later the Royal Caledonian Curling Club) established; standardized rules for international play
1839 US: Misconception that Abner Doubleday invented baseball, but game had been around for at least a century
1840 India: Sadika becomes champion wrestler

Did You Know?

By the mid-1800s, the boxing rules called for a ring twenty-four feet square, enclosed by two ropes. A knockdown marked the end of a round. After a thirty-second break, the fighters were given eight seconds to "come to scratch," unaided, in the center of the ring.

US: Yale University holds informal football scrimmages, but it will take more than 25 years for the game to become part of college sports; ninepins becomes popular
1840s Europe: Wrestling tournaments begin
Scotland: Lawn bowling flourishes; Scots develop rules that are still used today

US: Billiards linked to gambling; modern fencing brought to US from Germany; bowling banned in several states because of link to organized crime; promoters add tenth pin to get around the ban; heat racing (form of horse racing) very popular until Civil War

1841 to 1850　　1841 US: Tom Hyer becomes American heavyweight boxing champion; first sports story sent over telegraph
1842 US: Baseball played in New York City
1843 Switzerland: Skiing develops as a sport
1844 England: Swimming already established as popular competitive sport
Canada: Canadians play lacrosse against Native American teams
1845 France: Early wrestling bouts linked with weight-lifting exhibitions
US: Knickerbocker Base Ball Club formed; Alexander Cartwright and Daniel L. "Doc" Adams write baseball's first formal rules
1846 US: First real baseball game: Knickerbockers lose 23 to 1 to the New York Club
1850 England: Scale of weights for horse racing published
US: New version of battledore shuttlecock; Michael Phelan, owner of a New York billiard parlor, publicizes billiards; bowling is very popular; indoor lanes built around the country
c. 1850 US: Lacrosse rarely played any more

Did You Know?

The sport badminton got its name from the Duke of Beaufort's estate at Badminton in Gloucestershire, England, where it was played in the middle of the nineteenth century.

1851 to 1860　　1852 Canada: Branch of the Royal Caledonian Curling Club established
1854 US: Brooklyn Eckford (baseball) club formed
1855 France: Wrestling becomes popular in Paris
1856 Canada: Montreal Lacrosse Club develops first written rules for lacrosse
US: Longest bare-knuckle boxing match in history: James Kelly vs. Jack Smith; 186 rounds lasting 6 hours, 15 minutes
US: Chicago baseball unions organized
1858 US: National Association of Base Ball Players (NABBP) formed; within 2 years, more than sixty teams belonged to the association
1859 Canada: English cricket team visits Canada and US
1860 England: British Open Golf Championship established; boxing match between Tommy Sayers of England and John Heenan of US goes forty-two rounds before the police intervene
US: Native American, calling himself "Deerfoot," is track sensation
US: First recorded baseball game in Sam Francisco
1860s India: British play a form of badminton called *poona*
US: Onondaga Indians revive lacrosse
England: New water sports develop, including water football (or soccer), water rugby, water handball, and water polo

1861 to 1870   1861 England: *Routlege's Handbook of Croquet* sparks interest in the sport
1862 US: Croquet equipment advertised in *New York Clipper;* first organized American soccer club, the Oenidas of Boston; William H. Cammeyer builds the first enclosed field in Brooklyn; team used the field free but spectator paid 10¢ admission fee
1863 England: Football association formed; Charles Wreford Brown coins the name "soccer"

Did You Know?

Baseball was the first really popular spectator sport in America.

US: James Plimpton invents modern four-wheel roller skates
1865 England: Canoeing becomes a sport; Queensberry Rules for boxing first outlined
US: Soccer becomes an organized college sport
1867 Canada: George Beers, "father of lacrosse," revises the rules; National Lacrosse Association established
England: Lacrosse comes to England when Caughnawaga Indian lacrosse team plays a match for Queen Victoria
US: Grand National Curling Club of America established; ice hockey rules written; first intercollegiate soccer match: Princeton vs. Rutgers; Rutgers won 6 to 4
1866 England: Amateur Athletic Club formed

Did You Know?

In water polo, players rode on floating barrels, painted to look like horses, and struck the ball with a stick. Due to underwater fights for the ball, players often passed out for lack of air.

US: Fencing becomes part of university athletic program; John Wesley Hyatt creates the composition billiard ball, replacing ivory balls
1868 Europe: Exbroyat of Lyon credited with reorganizing European loose wrestling into a professional sport, which he named "Roman" or "Greco-Roman" to link to classical games
France: First Tour de France bicycle race; 100 contestants rode "boneshaker" bicycles lacking tires (pneumatic tires not invented until 1888)
US: Non-Native Americans begin playing lacrosse again; The Cincinnati Red Stockings baseball club formed; introduce uniforms
1869 US: The first formal intercollegiate football game held between Princeton and Rutgers teams; Rutgers won
1870s Constantinople: *Khedive,* similar to bridge, a popular card game
Europe: Lacrosse spreads to Scotland, Wales, Ireland, Australia, New Zealand, and South Africa

In 1868, a New York paper editorialized, "Never in the history of outdoor sports in this country had any game achieved so sudden a popularity with both sexes, but especially with the ladies, as Croquet has."

US: Lacrosse teams organized in New York City; attempt to introduce wrestling to America fails; badminton played in New York; players wore formal dress; three-ball carom billiards becomes popular due to increasing skill of professional players
1870 to 1886 England: Jockey Fred Archer achieved 2,748 wins

1871 to 1880   1871 England: Rugby football association formed
US: National Association of Professional Base Ball Players (NAPBBP) established
1872 US: About half the oarsmen in a regatta banned because they aren't amateurs; first American ski club established
First international soccer game: England vs. Scotland

Tiddlywinks, an international game, has a language all its own. Players flick the winks (playing pieces) by pressing down on the counter's edge with a larger counter called a squidger. Avid players have their own squidgers specially made to their personal design.

1873 England: Lawn tennis introduced, under the name "Sphairistike"
1874 US: Tennis brought to America
1875 Captain Matthew Webb becomes the first person on record to swim the English Channel, twenty-one hours, forty-five minutes
India: Snooker invented by British Army officers bored with playing billiards
US: First Kentucky Derby; National Bowling Association formed
1876 England: National cross-country championship established

As he swam the English Channel, Webb sang, sipped coffee and beer, ate steaks, was stung by a jellyfish, and had to fight his way through a nasty storm. It took Webb twenty-one hours and forty-five minutes to swim the English Channel.

US: National League of Professional Baseball Clubs, first true major league; Christian Schepflin brings lawn bowling back to US; first completed, allowed forward pass in football in Yale-Princeton game (November 30); "dead man's hand" poker hand (two black aces, two black eights, and queen of hearts) named when Wild Bill Hickok (1837 to 1876) is shot in the back while holding those cards; first tennis tournament

Did You Know?

Wild Bill Hickok, a frontier scout, town marshall, and gunfighter, was killed by an old enemy who had lost $500 to Wild Bill at a poker game the previous day.

1876 to 1880 US: Immigrants bring soccer with them and the sport gains popularity among noncollege players
1877 England: Bath Badminton Club develops the first written rules
US: First intercollegiate lacrosse game—New York University vs. Manhattan College; sport spreads to other universities
Scotland: Introduction of goalposts and rule changes make water polo less dangerous
1878 A book called *The Witchery of Archery* makes archery a popular sport
US: The first badminton club in the US, the Badminton Club of the City of New York, formed; New Yorker William C. Vosburgh introduces cross-country racing
1879 US: National Archery Association formed; the National Croquet Association (NCA) established; US Amateur Lacrosse Association established
1880 England: British factory workers begin to play soccer; Amateur Swimming Association of Great Britain established
US: First real championship boxing match: English champ Joe Goss vs. Irish Paddy Ryan; Ryan knocked out Goss in the eighty-seventh round; cross-country running introduced at Harvard as an autumn training event for track and field distance runners; other colleges quickly follow suit; "catch-as-catch-can" wrestling gains popularity; bingo develops
1880s Canada: University of McGill students draw up first ice hockey rules
England: Card game "biritch" renamed "bridge"
Europe: Water polo spread across the continent

Did You Know?

James Creighton gets the nod as the first professional baseball player.

1881 to 1890   1881 American Association of Base Ball Clubs organized
1882 Japan: Jigoro Kano creates Kodokan Judo
US: Ryan vs. John L. Sullivan boxing match; Sullivan wins; the National Croquet Association (NCA) holds first national tournament; Intercollegiate Lacrosse Association formed
1883 US: Eight-inch balkline introduced in billiards
1884 England: First major women's tennis tournament; winner gets a silver hair brush
US: 14.2-inch balkline billiards established; American Football Association established in

Newark, NJ, to unify and standardize soccer; ball-bearing wheels added to roller skates
1885 US: John L. Sullivan is world heavyweight champion under the Marquis of Queensberry rules
US and Canada: First "international" soccer games outside England
1886 England: Lawn Tennis Association formed
US: Amateur golf championship first played

Did You Know?

Fencing is one of only four sports that have been on every modern Olympic program since 1896.

1887 US: National Cross-Country Association established; Princeton claims credit for first football team widely known by a nickname, the Tigers; nickname comes from the team's black-and-orange striped uniforms
1888 US: Amateur Athletic Union of the United States formed to regulate amateur wrestling; it is the largest athletic governing body in the world; Jacob Schaefer Sr. wins championship billiards match; first water polo team, Boston; lawn tennis association formed
1889 France: German, Russian, Turkish, and Indian wrestlers compete at Paris Exposition
Scotland: Scottish Rounders Association established
US: Walter Camp becomes "father of American football"
1890 Water polo becomes first team sport added to Olympics
US: First intercollegiate cross-country meet (City College of New York, Cornell University, and University of Pennsylvania participate)
1890s England: Lacrosse becomes a woman's sport (game based on field hockey); table tennis, called "whiff whaff" and "gossima," develops
India: Ghukam, Gama become champion wrestlers
US: Johns Hopkins University is major hockey center; Parker Brothers manufactures indoor tennis kit

Did You Know?

James Gibb gets the nod for naming "ping pong," the name coming from the sounds of the ball hitting the paddle and the table.

1891 to 1900 1891 Monaco: Charles de Ville Wells breaks the bank at Monte Carlo playing roulette; the gambler's exploits are later celebrated in the song "The Man Who Broke the Bank at Monte Carlo"
US: James Naismith invents basketball, using half-bushel peach baskets in place of hoops; several year later, some unnamed genius cut the bottom from the baskets to make actual

hoops; Amateur Fencers League of America (now the US Fencing Association) formed; "Gentleman Jim" Corbett defeats John L. Sullivan to win heavyweight boxing title
1892 England: English Lacrosse Union established; lacrosse very popular
Europe: First Greco-Roman amateur wrestling championships
US: National fencing championships begin

Did You Know?

When he invented paddle tennis, Frank Beal halved the tennis court, replaced the tennis ball with a sponge rubber ball, and used a wooden paddle instead of a tennis racket.

1893 Canada: Baron Stanley of Preston, governor general of Canada, announces he will award a "cup" to the team that wins Canada's amateur ice hockey championship
England: Badminton Association of England founded as the first national governing body for the sport
US: Lacrosse comes to Johns Hopkins University and catches on fast; Vanderbilt University is first college to have a men's basketball team; card game "bridge" played at the Whist Club of New York
1894 England: Yale sends a track team to compete against Oxford
US: Lord Brougham apologizes for failing to turn up the trump card with the excuse that he had forgotten he was not playing bridge, "the finest card game ever introduced"; William G. Morgan, YMCA instructor in Holyoke, MA, invents volleyball by combining basketball, baseball, tennis, and handball
1895 US: American Bowling Congress formed; first professional football game (PA); first US Open Golf Championship

Did You Know?

The first Stanley Cup, won by the Montreal Amateur Athletic Association, cost $48.50. Today, the Stanley Cup is awarded yearly to the team that wins the best-of-seven series in the National Hockey League playoffs.

1896 Greece: First modern Olympic Games held in Athens, leads to start of many national and international sports organizations; wrestling included in the modern Olympics; men's foil and saber events part of Olympic contests
Switzerland: First alpine skiing school
US: First volleyball game played Springfield College (July 7, 1896)
1897 US: 18.1-inch balkline introduced in billiards
1898 International cross-country racing begins with competition between England and France.
US: First pocket billiards championship; the game was then called "61 pool"; Frank Beal, a kid himself, creates paddle tennis to teach tennis to children; Intercollegiate Cross-Country Association established

Did You Know?

Today, more than 46 million Americans play volleyball; worldwide, 800 million people play volleyball at least once a week.

1899 England: First all-England badminton championship
India: Several sources claim that auction bridge was invented by F. Roe and two other members of the Indian Civil Service
Belgium: Camille Jenatzy first man to travel 100 kmh (62 mph); his top speed, 105.87 kmh.
1900 Archery added to Olympic Games (dropped in 1920); fencing epee added to Olympic Games
England: James Gibb brings home hollow celluloid balls and begins playing indoor tennis with friends, using the new balls; Hackenschmidt becomes known as "world's best" wrestler
US: Eight ball, most popular form of pool, created; Baltimore becomes major lacrosse center

Did You Know?

In eight-ball pool, one player or team shoots the low balls, those numbered 1 through 7, which are represented by solid colors, and the other shoots the high balls, or "stripes." After a player has made all seven of his or her balls, the player can sink the eight ball to win the game. A player can also win by sinking the eight ball on the break, or lose by sinking the eight ball out of turn.

1901   England: Boxing acknowledged as a legal sport
US: Constance M. K. Applebee of England brings field hockey to American women; John Jacques registers the name "Ping-Pong" and sells American rights to Parker Brothers, who come out with a new kit under that name; Ping-Pong craze sweeps the country; first bowling tournament (Chicago)

1902   England: Amateur Fencing Association formed; E. C. Goode covers his wooden Ping-Pong paddle with pebbled rubber, which allows him to put spin on the ball; Ping-Pong Association established, but doesn't last
US: First Rose Bowl; 18.2-inch balkline introduced in billiards; Philadelphia Athletics claim first professional football championship

1903   US: Modern World Series born; Boston Red Sox win the first World Series against Pittsburgh Pirates; Lou Gehrig, baseball player
France: Maurice Vignaux wins billiards championship; first formal Tour de France, 23-day, 2,500-bicycle race
England: English Lawn Bowling Association (EBA) established; Henry Chadwick, first reporter to cover baseball, asserts in *Spalding's Baseball Guide* that baseball came from rounders

1904   France: Federation Internationale de Football Association (FIFA) established to regulate soccer
US: Basketball demonstrated at Olympics (St. Louis); lacrosse becomes Olympic sport in 1904; soccer played at Olympics

1905   England: First mention of auction bridge (in a letter to the London *Times*)
US: Intercollegiate Lacrosse League formed; Ty Cobb begins major league baseball career (playing with Detroit Tigers)

1906   France: 18-year-old American, Willie Hoppe, wins upset victory against champion billiards player Maurice Vignaux; Fédération des Salles des Armes et Sociétés d'Escrime formed (fencing)
US: Amateur Athletic Union (AAU) established for water polo

1907   US: Commission investigating the origins of baseball, "the great American pastime," decides erroneously that Abner Doubleday invented the sport; Australian swimmer Annette Kellerman performs "water ballet" at New York Hippodrome
First international cross-country meet

1908   Auction bridge very popular
England: Distance of the modern marathon set when 385 yards added so race goes from Windsor Castle to Edward VII's seat in the White City stadium
US: Spitballs ruled illegal in baseball; Badminton Health Club in Boston was formed; by 1925 includes more than 300 members; Jack Johnson becomes first black world heavyweight boxing champ

1909

1910   Straight pool, also known as 14.1 pocket billiards, develops; still a major championship sport

1911   Canada: Riot at a lacrosse game begins movement that supplants hockey as Canada's national game

1912   Cross-country on the Olympic program in 1912, 1920, and 1924 (dropped after that because it was considered unsuitable for summer competition)
US: Hawaiian Duke Kahanamoku wins Olympic 100-meter race (again in 1920); water polo becomes very rough; dropped from Amateur Athletic Union; Jim Thorpe is outstanding player at Stockholm Olympics, but is stripped of his medals when officials learn that he played semipro baseball in 1911

1913   France: The Fédération Internationale d'Escrime established to standardize fencing rules; now it is the governing body for international fencing, including the Olympics
US: Notre Dame football unveils the forward pass; numbers on players' uniforms; football teams of University of Chicago and Wisconsin

1914   US: Babe Zaharias (1914 to 1956) is one of the greatest female athletes of the century; water polo teams agree to follow international rules and championship games resume;

George Herman ("Babe") Ruth joins the Red Sox as a 19-year-old left-hand pitcher; Jack Dempsey starts boxing career; Yale Bowl opens; 80,000 capacity

1915 US: American Lawn Bowls Association (ALBA) established; Katherine "Kay" Curtis performs underwater swimming stunts

1916 Europe: First American soccer team plays in Europe
Philippines: Set and spike added to volleyball
US: "Roque" version of croquet becomes popular form of sport; American Roque League established; synchronized swimming added to University of Wisconsin's physical education program for women; at colleges, time is first recorded during wrestling matches; women's International Bowling Congress formed; oldest and largest women's sports organization in the world

1917 US: Volleyball changed from 21 to 15 points

1918 US: First national lawn bowling championship tournament

1919 US: Infamous "Black Sox" baseball scandal

1920 France: Water skiing invented
US: William T. "Big Bill" Tilden becomes first American to win Wimbledon, the first of his three Wimbledon titles; American Professional Football Association, first US professional football league, organized, with Jim Thorpe as president (renamed the National Football League in 1922); John Kelly banned from Henley Regatta because he was a bricklayer, not a gentleman; Babe Ruth sold to the New York Yankees; thoroughbred Man O' War, aka "Big Red," beats Triple Crown winner Sir Barton in Ontario, Canada, in one of history's most celebrated horse matches; Man O' War was then retired to stud, after having won twenty of twenty-one contests; nine ball originates as a gambling game; volleyball allows three hits per side and back row attack

c. 1920 Europe: Ping-Pong catches on
US: Lawn croquet reborn among wealthy; New York Celtics (white players) and New York Renaissance (black players) dominate basketball; plastic billiard balls made from cast resin used

1921 Charley Paddock sets world record in 100-meter dash at 10.4 seconds
Cuba: Jose Raoul wins world chess championship
England: Table Tennis Association established
US: Boxing match broadcast marks first radio sports coverage; paddle tennis spreads from Michigan to New York City; first radio coverage of major league baseball game, station KDKA, Pittsburgh

1922 US: Annie Oakley breaks women's trap shooting record, hitting 98 out of 100 targets; Johnny Weissmuller breaks the 1-minute mark in the 100-meter swim; first city-wide paddle ball tournament (New York City); first YMCA national volleyball championships (Brooklyn; twenty-seven teams from eleven states represented)

1923   France: First twenty-four-hour Grand Prix auto race at Le Mans
England: Henry Sullivan swims English Channel in twenty-eight hours
US: Yankee Stadium opens in New York City; American Paddle Tennis Association (now
the US Paddle Tennis Association) established; World's first indoor soccer league; Curtis
establishes water ballet at University of Chicago

Did You Know?

There have been many controversial World Series, but the most infamous was
certainly the thrown World Series of 1919. Even though the White Sox were
favored 5 to 1, about $2 million had been bet on the Cincinnati Reds to win.
Sensing a sure thing, Jack Doyle, head of a New York City betting ring, rigged the
series. Even though the series seemed respectable, with the Reds winning it five
games to three, sportswriter Hugh Fullerton suggested that something was not
quite right. Charles Cominsky, the White Sox' owner, offered a cash reward to
anyone who could prove a fix. It took almost a year for three men—Lefty
Williams, Eddie Cicotte, and J. Jackson—to sign confessions admitting the series
had been fixed and they were in on it. Just before the trial was scheduled to
start, the confessions mysteriously vanished from the office of the Illinois State
Attorney. When the case was finally tried, the three men denied having made any
confessions and having been involved in any way in the rigging scheme because
there was no proof against them.

1924   France: First winter Olympic Games at Chamonix; Finnish runner Paavo Nurmi wins
four gold medals at Olympics; Johnny Weissmuller wins the 100-meter swim in the
Olympic record time of 59 seconds
US: Rogers Hornsby bats .424, an all-time season record; Hornsby is baseball's batting
leader from 1920 to 1925
Women's foil competition added to Olympic program
Cushioned cork-center baseball debuts

Did You Know?

Weissmuller set world records in sixty-seven different events, from 50 yards
to 880 yards, before trading swimming for swinging through trees and even
greater fame as Hollywood's most durable Tarzan. Records and the ages of
leading swimmers are shrinking fast: the women's record in the 1,500 meters
freestyle is now less than the men's mark of 15 years ago.

1925

1926   England: Midland and East Anglian Bowling Association forms and makes a big change:
any field can be used as a playing area

Did You Know?

Harpo Marx, George S. Kaufman, Moss Hart, Sam Goldwyn, Howard Hawks, Darryl Zanuck, and Richard Rodgers are all members of the Croquet Hall of Fame.

Germany: International Table Tennis Federation established
US: Bobby Jones wins British Open; Gertrude Ederle becomes first woman to swim the English Channel, a feat that earned her a New York City tickertape parade; Gene Tunney beats the favored Jack Dempsey for the world heavyweight boxing crown in a unanimous ten-round decision

1927   Canada: First national curling championship held
England: First world Ping-Pong championship tournament
Norway: Sonja Henie ice-skating star
Segrave sets world land speed record (auto) at 203.79 mph in Golden Arrow
US: Babe Ruth hits sixty home runs for NY Yankees; Harlem Globetrotters organized

Did You Know?

Babe Ruth's 1927 record would not be broken for 34 years.

1928   Richard E. Byrd starts expedition to Antarctic; returns in 1930
England: Donald Healey wins Britain's first National Rally in a Triumph Super Seven
Holland: Women's events are featured for the first time at the Amsterdam summer Olympic Games; lacrosse is a demonstration sport at the Olympics
US: Lizzie Murphy (National League All Stars) is first woman on a major league team in an exhibition on game; Johnny Weissmuller picked up two more gold medals at the Amsterdam Olympics; United States Volleyball Association (USVBA, now USA Volleyball) formed; college-style wrestling adopted as national style

1929   US: Daytona Beach: Major Seagrave shatters auto speed record at 231.3 miles an hour (372.1 km) in 450-horse power Golden Arrow; Navy Lieutenant Apollo Soucek sets airplane altitude record at 39,190 feet; Intercollegiate Lacrosse League becomes US Intercollegiate Lacrosse Association

1930   US: Sonja Henie, James Cagney, Pat O'Brien, Harold Lloyd, Bette Davis, Boris Karloff, and Ginger Rodgers popularize badminton; first two-man beach volleyball game
Uruguay: Thirteen nations (including US) compete in first FIFA World Cup competition

1930s   Japan: Judo becomes a popular sport
US: Charles Darrow, an out-of-work heating engineer, invents Monopoly; initially, Parker Brothers turned down the game; 5 years later, after Parker Brothers had 5,000 sets made

privately and sold them, Parker Brothers realized the gold mine the game represented; lawn bowling booms when greens created at public parks across the country; James R. Smith develops new water polo ball that leads to a faster, higher-scoring game; American Ping-Pong Association established
Canada: Indoor version of lacrosse ("box lacrosse" or "boxla") develops
Switzerland: Northern face of the Matterhorn first scaled

1931   France: Fédération Internationale de Tir l'Arc (FITA), founded in Paris to standardize rules for international archery; holds world's first championship tournament
US: US Women's Lacrosse Association established

Did You Know?

Babe Didrikson Zaharias is considered the greatest woman athlete of the twentieth century. She began her career in the 1920s as a basketball star, set Olympic records in track and field, and then became a champion professional golfer. She also excelled at swimming, ice skating, baseball, and football.

1932   US: Winter Olympic Games are held in Lake Placid, NY; basketball becomes an official Olympic sport; soccer cut from Olympics over the definition of "amateur"; Olympic Village first introduced at Los Angeles

1933   US: US Amateur Table Tennis Association and the National Table Tennis Association established; National Collegiate Athletic Association (NCAA) official rulebook

1934   International Badminton Federation established (first world championship tournament planned for 1939, but didn't take place until 1949)
US: Sixty "Modern Mermaids" perform at Century of Progress World's Fair in Chicago, attracting national and international publicity

1935   US: American Badminton Association (ABA) established; all three Ping-Pong associations merge into the US Table Tennis Association; Santa Anita Handicap horse race begins (purse over $100,000)

1936   Electrical epee introduced; scores fencing hits automatically
Germany: African-American Jesse Owens wins Olympic gold before Hitler, exposing the fallacy of the Nazi Aryan race theory; tradition of carrying a flaming torch from Greece to the site of the Olympic games begins; Olympic medalist Sonja Henie is first woman to gain commercial success as a skater
US: Jim Brown born; will lead the National Football League in rushing for 8 of his 9 years playing; Baseball Hall of Fame at Cooperstown, NY, established

1937   US: National Mah-Jongg League established; Joe Louis is world heavyweight boxing champion from 1937 to 1942; in a rematch with German Max Schmeling, Louis knocked out the German belief in Aryan superiority; first national badminton championship tournament; paddle tennis court increased from 39 by 18 feet to 44 by 20 feet for adults (traditional dimensions kept for kids); US Volleyball Association is official national governing body

Did You Know?

Mah-jongg is a Western version of a Chinese game, similar to dominoes but engraved with Chinese symbols and characters. A full set of tiles contains 136 or 144 pieces, and is similar to rummy in that it is both an offensive and defensive game. Scholars believe the game originated in the 1800s.

1938 Don Budge becomes first amateur tennis player to win the "grand slam" (the four top singles championships of the time) in one year
Russia: Wrestling variation called *sambo* approved as a sport

1939 US: Lou Gehrig plays his last game, ending his consecutive game streak at 2,130; first recorded synchronized swimming competition (Chicago Teacher's College vs. Wright Junior College of Iowa); Billy Rose's Aquacade, featuring Olympic swimmers Eleanor Holm and Johnny Weismuller, boosts synchronized swimming; national Field Archery Association formed

1940 US: Central Association of the Amateur Athletic Union (AAU) stages the first multiteam synchronized swimming competition in Wilmette, IL

1941 US: Joe DiMaggio has fifty-six-game hitting streak; Lou Gehrig dies of amyotrophic lateral sclerosis (ALS); ALS becomes known as Lou Gehrig's disease; aquacade, starring Esther Williams, headlines San Francisco World's Fair

1942 US: Badminton match televised; top fourteen male and female players on the East Coast compete for the CBS Silver Bowl

1943 England: National Rounders Association established; however, rounders remains primarily a kid's game
US: Billie Jean King born; will be a major figure in women's tennis for 20 years

1944

1945 US: Badminton hits the flicks with MGM's movie *Badminton* (later named "MGM Movie Short of the Year" for 1945)
England: Midland and East Anglian Bowling Association renamed English Bowling Federation
Judo gains popularity around the world
US: Lawn bowling declines; paddle tennis spreads to California from New York City area
Europe: Central Europeans dominate international Ping-Pong tournaments

1946

Did You Know?

Branch Rickey, owner of the Brooklyn Dodgers, had looked long and hard to find a black ballplayer to become the first man to desegregate professional baseball. In 1945, he found his man: Jackie Robinson, the 26-year-old former star athlete for UCLA. Rickey prepared Robinson for the hatred that would come his way with a warmup season on the Dodgers' farm team in Montreal. Robinson was booed in Baltimore and a rival team let out a black cat as he walked to bat, but Robinson still led the league in hitting. Montreal won the pennant and Robinson moved to the majors. Robinson quickly won over his teammates with his skill and dignity, then the local fans, and finally the nation. His courage—and Rickey's vision—helped jumpstart the civil rights movement in America. It gathered steam with President Truman's 1948 order to integrate the Armed Forces and the 1954 Supreme Court decision against school segregation, Brown v. Board of Education.

1947   US: Jackie Robinson breaks baseball's color barrier when he joins the Brooklyn Dodgers; named Rookie of the Year; Little League World Series begins; US Women's Curling Association established

1948   US: Citation wins the Belmont Stakes to become racing's eighth Triple Crown winner; the Billiard Congress of America organized; first two-man volleyball beach tournament held

1949   Czech Republic: World Volleyball Championships

1950   Brazil: Biggest upset in international soccer history: Joe Gaetjens scores to lift the US over England 1 to 0 at the World Cup
Egypt: Hassan Abdel Rehim sets the record for a Channel swim: 10 hours 50 minutes
US: NY Yankee Joe Dimaggio and Red Sox Ted Williams become the first $100,000 baseball players; Joe Alston becomes first and only badminton athlete to hit the cover of *Sports Illustrated*

Did You Know?

In 1950, 400 American sportswriters and broadcasters selected Jim Thorpe as the greatest all-around athlete and football player of the first half of the twentieth century. A Sauk and Fox Indian, Thorpe was born in Oklahoma in 1888. At the 1912 Olympic Games in Stockholm, Thorpe won gold medals in both the pentathlon and the decathlon. A year later, the International Olympic Committee stripped Thorpe of his medals when they learned he had forfeited his amateur status by accepting money in 1911 to play baseball in North Carolina. Many people feel that Thorpe had been treated unfairly. In 1982, the International Olympic Committee agreed to restore Thorpe's amateur status and return his medals.

1950s	England: Queen Elizabeth keeps racing pigeons on her Sandringham estate US: Water polo becomes popular as a women's sport
1951	International Judo Federation established Synchronized swimming demonstrated at first Pan-American Games US: Leroy Robert ("Satchel") Paige, one of the greatest baseball pitchers of all time, signed with the St. Louis Browns; Sugar Ray Robinson wins five middleweight boxing championships (1951 to 1960)
1952	Japan: Horoi Satoh creates foam rubber Ping-Pong paddle; coating makes the game faster Finland: Synchronized swimming performed at Helsinki Olympics US: Rocky Marciano wins world heavyweight boxing championship from "Jersey" Joe Walcott

Did You Know?

With a strong wind, racing pigeons have been clocked at speeds of up to 110 mph in races. They can range from 100 miles to 1,000 miles.

1953	Asian players begin their dominance in international Ping-Pong tournaments Edmund Hillary and Tenzing Norgay reach the peak of Mount Everest, 29,028 feet high in the Himalayas US: Maureen Connolly wins Women's Grand Slam—all four major tennis championships; Ben Hogan wins Masters, US Open, and British Open championships; NY Yankees win fifth consecutive World Series, beating Brooklyn Dodgers
1954	Roger Bannister breaks the 4-minute mile, running 3:59.4 Fédération Internationale de Natation Amateur (FINA), which rules worldwide aquatic sports, adds synchronized swimming US: Arnold Palmer wins amateur championship in US Golf Association; New York Yankees win World Series
1955	First formal international synchronized swimming competition, Pan-American Games
1956	New York Yankee Don Larsen throws the only perfect game in World Series history First world championship judo competitions held
1957	US: Althea Gibson becomes the first African-American to win at Wimbledon and then first to win US Grand Slam event
1958	US: Brooklyn Dodgers and NY Giants move to West Coast; first world curling championship tournament; first NCAA Soccer Championship Tournament (Storrs, CT)
1959	US: Major changes made to paddle tennis (punctured tennis ball replaced the sponge rubber ball, the overhead serve was banned, and the size of the court was increased to 50

by 20 feet for adults); Vince Lombardi takes over hapless Green Bay Packers football team and makes them a powerhouse; results in surge of popularity for football; Wilt Chamberlain begins his professional basketball career with Philadelphia Warriors

1960   England: Neale Fraser wins in men's singles at Wimbledon
        Italy: Summer Olympic Games at Rome attract 5,396 contestants
        US: Pittsburgh Pirates win the World Series; runner Wilma Rudolph is first American woman to win three gold medals in a single Olympics

1961   England: Rodney George "Rod" Laver, 22 (Australia) wins at Wimbledon
        US: Roger Maris hits sixty-first homerun (October 1); Minnesota Twins play their first season; New York Yankees win the World Series; Wayne Gretskey born; considered the greatest player in the National Hockey League; pool gets biggest boost from the movie *The Hustler*, starring Paul Newman and Jackie Gleason, Piper Laurie, and George C. Scott; first women's water polo championship games

Did You Know?

Newman is outstanding in The Hustler *as a disenchanted drifter and pool hall hustler who challenges legendary Minnesota Fats (Gleason). The sequel,* The Color of Money, *released in 1986, shows Newman's Fast Eddie Felson finding a younger, greener version of himself in small-time pool hotshot Tom Cruise. Newman got a long-awaited Academy Award for his achievement in this film.*

1962   Brazil retains the World Cup in football (soccer)
        US: Sonny Liston world heavyweight boxing champ; Jack William Nicklaus wins US Golf Open; New York Yankees win World Series; Wilt Chamberlain of Philadelphia Warriors scores 100 points in a 169 to 147 win against the New York Knicks
        International Amateur Athletic Federation (IAAF) becomes governing body for cross-country

1963   US: First instant replay; used in Army-Navy football game; Michael Jordan born; often called the greatest all-around player in basketball history; adult-sized paddle tennis court adopted for children's play

1964   England: Roy Emerson wins men's singles at Wimbledon
        Peru: Worst soccer disaster on record; more than 300 soccer fans killed and over 500 injured during riot and panic following unpopular ruling by referee in Peru vs. Argentina soccer game
        US: Cassius Clay wins world heavyweight boxing championship (February 25) and declares himself "the greatest"; Clay will take the name Muhammad Ali; St. Louis Cardinals win World Series

1965   Japan: Tokyo Olympic Games; first Olympic Games in Asia; volleyball introduced to Olympic Games in Tokyo

US: Los Angeles Dodgers win the World Series; California Beach Volleyball Association (CBVA) formed; Satchel Paige, at the self-professed age of 59, pitches three shutout baseball innings for Kansas City Athletics

1966   US: Bill Russell becomes Boston Celtics basketball coach; first black coach of major US team

Did You Know?

As a Boston Celtics basketball player, Bill Russell led the team to eight straight NBA championships from 1959 to 1966 and was voted the league's most valuable player five times.

1967   Canada: Judy Devlin Hashman wins more than fifty major badminton championships from 1954 through 1967, including twelve US national titles and ten All-England championships; International Lacrosse Federation established
US: First Super Bowl: Green Bay beats Kansas City 35 to 10; two new professional soccer leagues: United Soccer Association and National Professional Soccer League; leagues merge to form North American Soccer League

Did You Know?

Although most cross-country competitors also run distance events in track and field, the two are separate sports. The cross-country season is still the fall and events are run through open country, often over rather crude trails, not on roads or tracks (although major races often begin and end on a track inside a stadium).

First women's world cross-country championship meet

1968   Mexico City: Bob Beamon breaks the long jump record; Tommie Smith and John Carlos give black power salute at Olympics, unleashing controversy
US: Peggy Fleming wins the Olympic gold medal in figure skating; Mickey Mantle hits his 536th—and last—home run; 15-year-old Cathy Rigby earns the highest Olympic score at that time for an American woman; holds eight gold medals in world gymnastic competitions

1969

1970

c. 1970   US: Six-wicket croquet makes a comeback; renewed interest in lawn bowling, especially in California and Florida; roller skates with plastic wheels first marketed

1971   Brazil: Soccer star Pele (Edson Arantes do Nascimento) retires from international competition after Brazil tied Yugoslavia 2 to 2 before 150,000 at Rio de Janiero's Maracana Stadium
China: American table-tennis team is invited to compete in China, a sign of improving relations between China and US
Scotland: Sixty-six killed in crush at Glasgow Rangers home stadium
US: Janet Guthrie finishes first overall at Bridgehampton Raceway (with co-driver Kent Fellows)

1972   Archery restored as Olympic sport
Badminton staged as a demonstration sport at the Olympics
Munich: Eleven Israeli athletes massacred by Palestinian guerrillas at the Summer Olympics; Mark Spitz wins seven Olympic medals for swimming

1973   Synchronized swimming included in first World Aquatic Championships, along with swimming, diving, and water polo
US: Billie Jean King defeats Bobby Riggs in a televised "Battle of the Sexes" tennis match; Secretariat wins the Triple Crown (racing); Kyle Rote, Jr. became the first rookie and first American to win the NASL (soccer), scoring title with thirty points

1974   England: Rone Jerome scores 1,961 points in a single play of Scrabble; letters are facing up to help players get the best score
US: Hank Aaron surpasses Babe Ruth's all-time home run record at 715; When he is hired by the Cleveland Indians, Frank Robinson becomes first black to manage a major league baseball team

1975   Japan: Junko Taebi becomes first woman to climb Mount Everest; thirty-sixth person to reach summit
Janet Guthrie wins the Vanderbilt Cup and the Bridgehampton 400 at Bridgehampton Raceway, NY; New York Cosmos signed Pele for $4.5 million; twice as much Monopoly money is printed as real money

Did You Know?

Mexican-born golfer Lee Trevino is one of the few people in the world to have been struck by lightning and survived. During the 1975 Western Open tournament, a bolt of lightning lifted him nearly eighteen inches in the air, knocked him unconscious, and scorched his left shoulder.

1976   Gymnast Nadia Comaneci scores the first perfect 10 at the Olympics
National Wrestling Hall of Fame dedicated
Women's basketball added to Olympic games
US: Jimmy Connors wins US Open men's singles tennis championship; Bjorn Borg captures Wimbledon's men's singles; Chris Everet wins Wimbledon and US Open; Henry ("Hank") Aaron retires from baseball, holding the US major league record of 755 career home runs

1977   Brazil: Pele retires from soccer
                 US: Janet Guthrie becomes the first woman to compete in the Indianapolis 500; US
                 Water Polo, Inc. becomes polo's governing body

Did You Know?

*Janet Guthrie also made a name for herself in endurance races, including
Bridgehampton Raceway's Bridgehampton 400. In trials, she averaged 172 mph,
with a top speed of 190 mph.*

1978   First national paddle tennis championships
                 Cuba: Chicago Sting play Cuban national soccer team in an exhibition in Havana; first
                 time since 1959 that an American professional sports team had visited Cuba
                 US: Leon Spinks wins world heavyweight boxing championship; Muhammad Ali beats
                 Spinks seven months later to regain the title; Norwegian Grete Waitz' win in the New
                 York Marathon spurs Olympic officials to add a woman's marathon in 1984

1979   England: Czech player Martina Navratilova wins Wimbledon
                 Montreal Canadiens defeat NY Rangers to win fourth consecutive Stanley Cup
                 US: United States Synchronized Swimming, Inc. established; at age 16 years and 8
                 months, Tracy Austin becomes youngest woman to win US Open tennis match;
                 Pittsburgh Steelers defeat Dallas Cowboys to win football's Super Bowl; Pittsburgh Pirates
                 defeat Baltimore Orioles to win World Series; Seattle SuperSonics win NBA
                 championship; John McEnroe wins US Men's Open singles

Did You Know?

*The US Open, which offers $200,000 in prize money, is the highest paying
tournament on the tour. The Grand Prix Finals tournament has a total purse of
$350,000.*

1980   US: NCAA begins Division III annual lacrosse championship tournament; Grete Waitz
                 (Norway) breaks 2.5-hour barrier in women's marathon during New York Marathon;
                 Pittsburgh Steelers beat LA Rams to win football's Super Bowl; Mary Decker first woman
                 to run a mile under 4.5 minutes; Thirteenth Winter Olympics at Lake Placid, NY; speed
                 skater Eric Heiden wins five gold medals; Philadelphia Phillies defeat Kansas Royals to
                 win World Series; Severiano Ballesteros (Spain) becomes youngest winner of golf's US
                 Masters; Ann Meyers is first woman to sign for NBA although she doesn't make a team;
                 Roberto Duran beats Sugar Ray Leonard for Welterweight title, but loses rematch; Bjorn
                 Borg wins at Wimbledon (tennis)
                 USSR: Over fifty nations boycott twenty-second Olympics in Moscow

1980s   Badminton becomes a professional sport when the IBF established the World Grand Prix
                 Circuit

1981   New Zealand: Jeff Grant earns 4,454 points for a complete game of Scrabble; the letters
                 were facing up to work out the best score; South African international rugby team tours;
                 many people protest and 1,000 are arrested
                 US: National lacrosse championship tournament for women; Oakland Raiders beat
                 Philadelphia Eagles to win Super Bowl; Stephen Ptacek makes first solar-powered flight
                 across the English Channel; Major League baseball players strike from June 12 to August
                 9; Muhammad Ali retires from boxing; Los Angeles Dodgers defeat NY Yankees to win
                 World Series; Boston Celtics win NBA (basketball); NY Islanders win hockey's Stanley
                 Cup

1982   England: Dr. Saladin Koshnaw earns 392 on a single Scrabble play for *caziques* (Indian
                 chiefs); letters were not exposed during play.
                 Russia: About 340 people die at Lenin Stadium when exiting soccer fans collide with
                 returning fans after final goal was scored
                 US: San Francisco 49ers beat Cincinnati Bengals to win Super Bowl

1983   Association of Volleyball Professionals (AVP) formed

1984   England: Diane Dennis earns 792 on a complete Scrabble game; letters were not exposed
                 during play
                 Mary Lou Retton wins USA's first all-around Olympic gold medal; first female athlete on
                 Wheaties cereal box
                 US: Synchronized swimming joins Olympic Games at LA, with solo and duet
                 competition; US wins first medals in volleyball at the Olympics in LA (men win gold;
                 women, silver)

1985   Belgium: British soccer fans storm Italian supporters before European Champion's Cup
                 final; wall collapses and 39 persons were crushed to death; more than 400 people injured
                 England: 56 burned to death and over 200 injured when fire engulfed main grandstand
                 at Bradford's soccer stadium
                 US: Division III lacrosse championship for women established; Kansas City Royals win
                 World's Series
                 USSR: Gary Kasparov defeats Anatoly Karpov; at age 22, becomes world's youngest chess
                 champion

1986   US: Major Indoor Lacrosse League (MILL) established; California and Florida produce
                 top water polo teams; Women's Professional Volleyball Association (WPVA) formed;
                 Nancy Lieberman averages eleven minutes per game for the United States Basketball
                 League, becoming the first woman to play in men's professional basketball; Harlem
                 Globetrotters hire their first female player, Lynette Woodward; Mike Tyson defeats
                 Trevor Berbick to become world heavyweight champion; Mets win World Series; Boston
                 Celtics win NBA championship

1987   US: American Croquet Association (ACA) established; USBA recognized as national
                 governing body for the sport of badminton; Minnesota Twins win World Series; Los
                 Angeles Lakers win NBA championship

1988	Nepal: Eighty soccer fans in Katmandu seeking cover during a violent hail storm at the national stadium trampled to death in a stampede because stadium doors were locked
	Korea: US men's volleyball team win gold Olympic medal
	Ping-Pong becomes an Olympic sport, with singles and doubles competition for both men and women

Did You Know?

According to a study by the Billiards and Bowling Institute of America, 42.4 million Americans played billiards at least once in 1995, an increase of 20.4 percent over 1986. Even more significant, the number of "frequent" players— those who played twenty-five or more times a year, was at 11.3 million, up 21.3 percent. Females represented 36.4 percent of the players compared to fewer than 20 percent in 1986.

	Switzerland: US earns right to host World Cup during the FIFA Congress
	US: Washington Redskins win Super Bowl; Claudell Washington hits 10,000th home run in Yankee history
1989	England: Britain's worst soccer disaster: 94 killed and 170 injured at Hillsborough stadium when soccer fans collapse a stadium barrier
	US: Badminton makes its USOC event debut at the US Olympic Festival in Oklahoma City, OK; Paul Caligiuri's thirty-five-yard shot clinches US 1 to 0 soccer victory over Trinidad and Tobago; San Francisco 49ers win Super Bowl; Pete Rose banned from baseball for life for betting on games
1990	Cuba: Javier Sotomayer is first high jumper to clear 8 feet
	US: Cincinnati Reds win World Series; Detroit Pistons win NBA championship; San Francisco 49ers win Super Bowl; World Volleyball League created
1991	China: US Women's National (soccer) Team wins first FIFA Women's World Championship with a 2 to 1 win over Norway
	US: National Collegiate Lacrosse League established
1992	Spain: Badminton makes first appearance as an Olympic event, singles and doubles competition for men and women
	US: Professional basketball players take part in Olympics; US "Dream Team," made up primarily of NBA stars, totally dominated competition
1993	US: Arthur Ashe dies of AIDS
1994	US: Football legend O. J. Simpson tried for murder; acquitted in 1995; Tonya Harding attacks fellow Olympic figure skater Nancy Kerrigan; Major League baseball players strike; baseball owners end season and cancel World Series; US Table Tennis Association renamed USA Table Tennis; More than 3.5 million fans at World Cup matches; Olympic diver Greg Louganis reveals that he has AIDS

1995   Argentina: Badminton first featured at the Pan American Games
                    France: Racing car in Grand Prix hurtled into grandstand, killing eighty-two spectators
                    US: Baseball great Cal Ripkin breaks Lou Gerhig's "Iron Man" streak of 2,131 games

Did You Know?

Over 1 million Americans play badminton recreationally at least twenty-five times a year, according to a recent study.

1996   Guatemala City: 84 killed and 147 injured by stampeding soccer fans before a World Cup
                    qualifying match
                    Nepal: Eight climbers perish in an attempt to scale Mount Everest
                    US: National Woman's Basketball Association formed; American female basketball players
                    win championship at the Atlanta Olympic Games; women's soccer team earns gold medal
                    at the Summer Olympic Games in Atlanta; two-person beach volleyball debuts at
                    Olympics; women's epee added to Olympic program

1997   US: Tiger Woods breaks multiple records in Masters golf tournament; National Lacrosse
                    League (NLL) established; soon after merges with Major Indoor Lacrosse League

1998   Japan: US women's hockey team wins over Canada, for their first victory; Austria's
                    Hermann Maier wins gold medal in men's super giant slalom, US's Tara Lipinski, age 15,
                    wins gold medal for figure skating
                    US: Mark McGwire slams seventy home runs; Denver Broncos upset the Green Bay
                    Packers 31 to 24, in their first Super Bowl win in four tries; Chicago Bulls guard Michael
                    Jordan named MVP in NBA finals for a sixth time
                    Japan: Curling became a full-fledged Olympic sport at the 1998 Winter Games in
                    Nagano

1999   International Olympic Committee expels six members as bribery scandal widens
                    First nonstop balloon flight around world completed in twenty days
                    US: Joe DiMaggio dies at age 84; pro golfer Payne Stewart and five others killed in plane
                    crash; women's soccer team tops China for World Cup; Michael Jordan retires from the
                    Chicago Bulls

2000   US: Juan Montoya wins Indianapolis 500 race; lawn mower racing becomes a fad sport

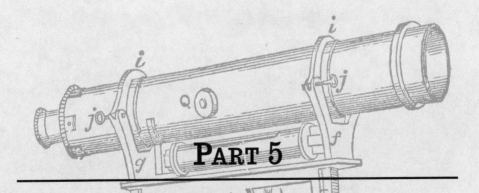

PART 5

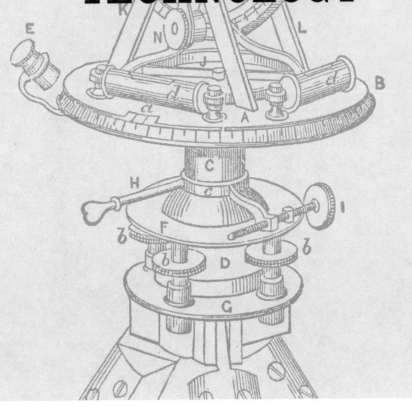

NATURE, SCIENCE, HEALTH, AND TECHNOLOGY

Part 5 Nature, Science, Health, and Technology

−35,000	Early counting devices
−25,000	Some scientists believe that the bow and arrow are invented
−20,000	Spear and harpoon invented
−10,000	Farming begins
−7,000	Turkey: Cloth is woven First boats China: Rice cultivated in Yangtze Valley
−5,000	Peru: Llama and alpaca domesticated Mexico: Avocados and cotton cultivated Egypt: Wheat and barley first cultivated
−4000 to −3501	Egypt: Calendar based on the sun and moon Abacus invented India: Date palms cultivated Crete: Olives cultivated
−3500 to −3001	Egypt and Sumer: Copper alloys used, gold and silver smelted Egypt: Earliest numbers −3372 First year in Mayan calendar China: Copper and silk manufactured Candles used Sumer: Dental cavities filled

Did You Know?

Nine medical treatises survive from ancient Egypt. One, the oldest surviving book of surgery in the world, details nearly fifty different operations. Among them is trepanning, boring a hole in the skull to relieve pressure on the brain. Although much of the book contains medical advice based on superstition, it also contains drugs whose efficacy have been proven, including castor oil and sodium bicarbonate.

−3000 to −2501	Europe: Weaving loom Egypt, Babylonia, India, China: Astronomical observations made Peru: Cotton cultivated

−2500 to −2001   Egypt: Papyrus first used
Mesopotamia: Potter's wheels, kilns first used
China: Lunar year of 360 days becomes variable moon-sun cycle
Egypt: First mummies
Babylon: Chickens domesticated
Tibet: Yak domesticated
Africa: Yam cultivated

−2000 to −1500   Egypt: Contraceptives, made of dung, first used
Babylonia: Geometry, signs of the zodiac
Egypt: Pythagorean numbers
Egypt: Code of Hammurabi has medical guidelines (including fees)
Crete: Decimal system
Korea: Rice cultivated
China: First zoo

Did You Know?

A "magic square" is a pattern of consecutive numbers in which every row adds up to the same total. Here's an example where every row, column, and both diagonals add up to fifteen:

4	9	2
3	5	7
8	1	6

−1500 to −1001   India and Egypt: Leprosy reported
Egypt: Complex clocks used
Possible first "Suez Canal"
China: "Magic squares" math formulas
Syria and Palestine: Iron Age
China: Decimals used

−1000 to −901   China: Complex math, including root multiplication, geometry, equations
China: Natural gas used

−900 to −801

−800 to −701   Greece: Skilled battlefield surgery
India: Medical training with real models
Babylonia and China: Planetary movement tracked

−700 to −601   Assyria: Water clocks
Iron soldering invented

Did You Know?

At its height (c. –1085 to –450), mummification took about seventy days to complete. First, the deceased's internal organs were removed through a four-inch cut on the left hip. They were cleaned in wine and spices. The brain was then removed through the nose. The cleaned body and organs were packed in natron (natural rock salt) and baking soda. The body was packed with sawdust, mud, or linen and the organs were individually wrapped and replaced in the body. Finally, each limb was wrapped in layers of resin-coated linen, usually over 1.5 miles of cloth.

–600 to –501	Rome: First stone bridge
	Phoenicians circumnavigate Africa
	"Thales Proposition": Among oldest mathematical theories
	Greece: Alcmaeon of Croton differentiates between veins and arteries
	China: Houses are fumigated to rid them of pests
–500 to –451	India: First cataract operations
	Greece: Discovery of Eustachian tubes (ears)
	Greece: Hippocrates, "Father of Medicine"
	India: Steel made
–450 to –401	–410 Italy: Forerunner of the catapult developed
–400 to –351	
–350 to –301	–323 Euclid: "Elements" (geometry)
	China: Bellows invented
–300 to –251	–295 Euclid: "Optica"
	–287 to –212 Greek mathematician Archimedes
	Tunisia: Convex lenses
	China: Cast iron
–250 to –201	–276 to –194 Eratosthenes claims earth moves around the sun
	–239 Egypt: Leap year added to calendar

Did You Know?

Pythagoras (c. –582 to –507), the Greek philosopher and mathematician, did not invent the theorem named after him. The theorem—which states that in any right-angled triangle, the sum of the squares on the two shorter sides equals the square of the hypotenuse—was used by ancient Egyptian surveyors. It was also known to the Babylonians at least 1,000 years earlier.

−200 to −151	−159 Rome: First water clock
	China: Place-value notation (mathematics)
	China: Paper invented, used for clothing, personal hygiene, packing material
−150 to −101	China: Collar harness for horses
	China: Negative numbers used
−100 to −51	Syria: Glass blowing
−50 to −1	

Part 5 Nature, Science, Health, and Technology

1 to 500

1 to 50	China: Cast iron suspension bridges Wheelbarrow invented
51 to 100	
101 to 150	Ptolemy writes the key text on astronomy that will be used during the Middle Ages
151 to 200	151 to 219 China: Zang writes a massive compendium of medical knowledge China: Ephedrine used to treat asthma 164 to 180 Rome: Great Plague c. 170 Ptolemy's maps of countries c. 180 Galen writes the standard medieval medical book c. 190 Galen uses plants as medicine c. 200 China: Silkworms imported from Korea

Did You Know?

The Maya were superb astronomers with advanced knowledge of mathematics; they also devised an accurate calendar.

201 to 250	209 China: Porcelain invented c. 250 First algebra books

Did You Know?

Looking for the Fountain of Youth or the Midas Touch? Then the alchemists are for you. The fundamental concept of alchemy stemmed from the Aristotelian doctrine that all things tend to reach perfection. Since some metals were less "perfect" than others, it seemed reasonable to assume that gold had been formed from metals deep within the earth. Thus, the alchemists sought to create or discover a substance, the so-called "philosopher's stone," so much more perfect than gold that it could be used to bring the baser metals up to the perfection of gold. Some scientists believed that dissolved gold was the elixir of life, too. At first, the alchemists' efforts were practical, but by the fourth century, astrology, magic, and ritual took over.

251 to 300	c. 271 China: First compass
301 to 350	
351 to 400	Hypatia: Only known female philosopher and mathematician from this period
401 to 450	409 China: Umbrella invented c. 410 Alchemy begins 425 Constantinople University established

501 to 550
c. 542 Plague begins in Constantinople and spreads across Europe
543 World-wide earthquakes
547 England: Plague outbreak
US: Anasazi, ancestors of the Pueblos, farmed in Colorado

Did You Know?

During the Middle Ages, the term "plague" was applied to any epidemic, including smallpox, dysentery, and measles. Today, however, we use the term to refer to a specific infection transmitted by rat fleas. There are three main types of plague: bubonic plague (fatal in thirty to seventy-five percent of all cases), pneumonic plague (fatal ninety-five percent), and septicemic plague (invariably fatal). Bubonic plague, the variety that swept through the Middle Ages, is characterized by huge swellings ("buboes") in the lymph nodes, reaching the size of eggs. The term "Black Death" came from septicemic plague, in which the victims turn deep purple and die several hours later. The number of deaths was staggering, reaching two-thirds to three-fourths of the population in various parts of Europe.

551 to 560

561 to 570

571 to 580
577 China: Matches invented

581 to 590
590 Plague in Rome

591 to 600
595 India: First decimal use documented
600 Smallpox spreads from India via China to southern Europe
600 Persia: First windmills built

Did You Know?

Chinese science and technology were by far the most active of the time. Chinese attitudes toward medicine were especially advanced; medical treatment was regarded as a necessity and so administered to all by the state. China also led the world in astronomy, chemistry, and mathematics.

601 to 650

615 China: Petroleum used
635 China: Value of π (pi) given as 3.1415927
650 India: Development of first surgical instruments

651 to 700

701 to 750

720 Abu Masa Dshaffar: Famous Arab chemist credited with inventing nitric acid, sulfuric acid, nitrate of silver
735 Venerable Bede: English historian and theologian, introduces counting of dates before the birth of Christ
740 Asia Minor: Earthquake
750 Arab Spain: Medicine, astronomy, mathematics, and chemistry flourish
Germany: St. Vitus' dance epidemic

751 to 800

780 Charlemagne establishes his foot as the unit of length
782 Arabia: Scientist Jabir distinguishes between chemistry and alchemy

Did You Know?

The twelve-inch foot was not universally accepted; as late as the 1600s, the Dutch foot was divided into eleven inches rather than twelve. The English king Henry established the yard in the twelfth century as the distance from the tip of his nose to the tip of his outstretched thumb; in 1305, Edward I redefined it as three feet. The Romans invented the mile, which they defined as a thousand paces, in which each pace was two steps or five feet long, making a total of 5,000 feet.

801 to 850

810 Persian mathematician al-Khowarizmi creates the term "algebra"
813 Baghdad: School of astronomy
814 Arabs adopt Indian numerals, including zero
825 Italy: Pavia becomes center of science
830 Al-Khowarizmi's *Al-jabar wa'l muqabalah*, known in the West as *Algebra*, provides ways to solve equations of the first and second degree with positive roots

851 to 900

880 Arab chemists and physicians distill wine
900 Arabia: Physician Rhases defines plague, consumption, smallpox, and rabies as infectious
900 Medical school established at Salero

901 to 950

930 Spain: Cordoba becomes the center of Arab learning in Spain

951 to 1000

977 Baghdad: Hospital established
984 China: Canal lock invented to reduce amount of theft on docks
1000 India: Mathematician Sridhara realizes the importance of zero
1000 Germany: Arabs and Jews become court physicians

Part 5 Nature, Science, Health, and Technology

1001 TO 1500

1001 to 1050
c. 1000 Peru: Sweet potatoes and corn cultivated
China: Coal is burned for fuel
c. 1030 China: Spinning wheels are used
1050 Spain: Arabs introduce decimal system into Spain

Did You Know?

The decimal system shows positional notation for numbers, based on ten and the power of ten. Except for computer work, the universally adopted system of mathematical notation today is the decimal system.

1051 to 1100
1066 Constantine the African (c. 1020 to 1087) introduces Greek medicine to Western world
1070 China: Shen Kua lays the foundations of earth science; first reference to a magnetic compass used for navigation
c. 1075 Persia: Omar Khayyam solves cubic equations by geometry
1080 Spain: Toledan table of stars' positions
c. 1100 China: Illustrated botanical texts, having medical as well as botanical importance
China: Multicolor printing used to make paper money harder to counterfeit
Italy: Brandy distilled

Did You Know?

Perhaps the most famous brandy is cognac, named after a town in France. The amber-hued drink is made by distilling white wine, which is then aged in an oak cask. Other notable brandies include kirsch (made from cherries) and slivovitz (made from plums).

1101 to 1150
1126 to 1198 Middle East: Averroes (Ibn Rushd), leader of Arabic science, writes major encyclopedia of his day
1135 to 1204 Middle East: Maimonides writes on medicine, especially psychosomatic ailments
1140 England: Norman king Roger II rules that people must have a government medical license to practice medicine
c. 1150 China: First rockets developed
France: Coal used at Liege for iron-smelting

1151 to 1200

1155 China: Oldest-known printed map
c. 1170 to c. 1240 Italy: Leonardo Fibonacci, greatest medieval mathematician
c. 1175 Europe: Old London Bridge and Avignon bridges built
1189 France: First paper mill erected
1199 China: Oldest-known drawing of a fishing reel
c. 1200 Alcohol used for medical purposes
Italy: Leonardo Fibonacci writes first algebra textbook
1200 China: Sign for zero devised

1201 to 1250

1202 Europe: Arabic numbers introduced in Europe
c. 1202 Italy: Fibonacci introduces the number sequences that bear his name

Did You Know?

Fibonacci invented the number sequence that bears his name to solve a puzzle about the breeding rate of rabbits. Each number in the series—which begins 1, 1, 2, 3, 5, 8, 13, 21, 34—is, after the first two figures, merely the sum of the previous two numbers. However, this seemingly-simple sequence has profound links to other math concepts and nature. For example, if you count the clockwise and counterclockwise spirals of seeds on the head of a sunflower, the figures will be consecutive Fibonacci numbers.

c. 1214 to 1294 Europe: Roger Bacon experiments in astronomy and medicine; used corrective lenses
1220 France: Window at Chartes Cathedral shows earliest-known Western wheelbarrow
1221 China: Bombs created that produce shrapnel and cause great damage
1230 China: Kites used to send messages during battle
1232 Asia: Earliest known use of rockets (war between Mongols and Chinese)
1250 Jordanus Rufus: Veterinary manual
c. 1250 England: John of Halifax (Sacrobosco) introduces decimal system
Hawaiian Islands: Beginnings of intensive valley irrigation

1251 to 1300

1270 Europe: Witelo's *Perspectiva*, discussion of optics
1272 Middle East: Nasir al-Din al Tusi's astronomical tables
1290 Europe: William of Saint-Cloud measures sun's angles
South America: Cable bridges built across the Andes
1298 Marco Polo describes coal and asbestos for the first time
c. 1300 Eyeglasses commonly used
Pacific Islands: Huge stone statues erected on Easter Island
Syria: Alum discovered

1301 to 1350

1303 China: Chu Shih-Chieh publishes first record of Pascal's Triangle
1304 Germany: Theodoric of Friebourg's *De iride* explains rainbow formation
1310 Europe: Mechanical clocks built
1317 Europe: Pope John XXII issues proclamation against alchemy
1327 China: Grand Canal completed (1,100 miles long)

1340 Europe: First blast furnace developed near Belgium
1348 Plague decimates Europe
1350 France: Jean Buridan develops the idea of impetus

Did You Know?

One of the largest outbreaks of the plague began in Sicily, October 1347. It reached France the following year and raged in Paris until 1349. England was hit between August 1348 until early 1350. Recurrences took place in 1360 and 1369. The worst hit cities were Avignon fifty percent (25,000 people), Paris fifty percent (50,000 people), and London thirty-three percent (18,000 people). Over 200,000 villages were wiped out in Europe.

1351 to 1400   1360 Europe: Guy de Chauliac's *Chirurgia magna* describes how to treat hernias and broken bones
1370 Steel crossbow used
1373 First recorded canal lock in the West
1391 Germany: Paper mill established
1394 to 1449 Middle East: Ulugh-Beg makes astronomical tables
1394 to 1460 Europe: Henry the Navigator encourages the study of navigation
1391 England: Chaucer's *A Treatise on the Astrolabe* shows how to build one and use it to figure a star's position
1400s Africa: Coffee made into a drink in Ethiopia
Oil used as paint base
Pacific Islands: Widespread cultivation of taro (edible, starchy, tuberous rootstock) in Hawaiian islands

Did You Know?

Taro, a large herb, is grown in tropical regions for its large, starchy tubers. Taro is poisonous if eaten raw. Poi, a popular dish in Hawaii, is made from boiled taro that is pounded and fermented into a sticky paste.

1401 to 1450   1401 to 1464 Nicolas of Cusa wrote that the earth, not the heavens, revolved daily
1408 Holland: Windmill used
1416 Dutch using drift nets over 350 feet long
c. 1420 Russia: Observatory built
c. 1422 to 1491 England: William Caxton, first English printer
1434 Italy: Drawings of perspective
1439 Europe: Prince Henry the Navigator establishes naval institute at Sagres

1451 to 1500   1450 Germany: Johann Gutenberg (c. 1390 to 1468) invents printing with movable type and prints first Bible
1452 France: University of Paris requires a student to read first six books of Euclid to get a degree

1452 to 1519 Leonardo da Vinci, painter, sculpture, architect, and scientist; conceived the helicopter, mobile canal cutter, optical systems, and several kinds of pumps; most of his inventions were never built, as mechanics had yet to catch up with his creativity

Did You Know?

The Morgan Library in New York City has a Gutenberg Bible on display.

1466 *Carracks*, earliest form of modern sailing ships
1471 Germany: Observatory built at Nuremberg
1472 First scientific study of a comet
1473 to 1543 Polish astronomer Copernicus

Did You Know?

Nicolaus Copernicus is best known for his theory that the earth rotates once daily on its axis and revolves around the stationary sun. Copernicus also argued that the planets also circle the sun and that the earth precesses (wobbles) on its axis. By the late seventeenth century, most major thinkers in England, France, Denmark, and the Netherlands were Copernicans; philosophers in other European countries, however, resisted Copernicus' theories for at least another 100 years.

c. 1475 Europe: First rifles made
1476 England: William Caxton set up the first movable-type press in England

Did You Know?

During his career, William Caxton printed nearly 100 publications, about 20 of which he also translated into English from French and Dutch. His most notable books include Geoffrey Chaucer's The Canterbury Tales and Troilus and Criseyde and the preface to Thomas Malory's Le Morte d'Arthur.

1478 *Treviso Arithmetic*, first popular printed mathematics textbook
1480 Mexico: Twenty-ton Aztec Stone Calendar (also known as the Sun Stone)
Italy: Da Vinci describes a workable parachute
1481 Europe: First lock on canal built
1482 Translation of Euclid's *Elements*. One of first important math books
1483 *Alfonsine Tables:* Astronomical tables
1484 First algebra book to use negative numbers as exponents

1487 to 1488 Bartholomew Diaz sails around Cape of Good Hope, South Africa
1489 The plus (+) and minus (−) signs come into use
1490 Italy: da Vinci notes capillary action
1491 Algorithm used for long division
1492 Dot used to show division by ten; precursor of the decimal point
Martin Behaim makes first globe map of Earth; Americas and Pacific Ocean not included
Italy: Da Vinci draws his flying machine
1493 US: Columbus discovers that Native Americans use tobacco as medicine

Did You Know?

Tobacco, which belongs to the potato family, is used for smoking, snuffing, and chewing. Native to South America, Mexico, and the West Indies, tobacco was first described by Linnaeus in 1753.

1493 to 1541 Paracelsus: Determined that disease was caused by something outside the body—"bacteria"—not an imbalance from within
1494 Italy: Luca Pacioli's *Summa de Arthmetica Geometria Proportioni et Proportionalita*, one of the most influential mathematics books of the day; da Vinci draws a pendulum clock
1495 Europe: Syphilis epidemic spreads among French soldiers
1496 Italy: da Vinci designs roller bearings and a rolling mill
1497 First written description of surgical treatment for gunshot wounds
1500 China: Wan Hu constructs a flying machine by tying nearly fifty rockets to a chair; the device explodes and kills Wan
Germany: Peter Henlein invents "Nuremberg Egg" (pocket watch)
Italy: da Vinci draws a wheel-lock musket, first known appearance of a gun in the West; systematic dissection of human cadavers in Padua medical schools
Switzerland: First recorded Cesarean section performed on living woman

Did You Know?

In Copernicus' day, people firmly believed that the earth was the center of the universe, surrounded by the moon and beyond that, the visible planets, and fixed stars. The heavens were considered perfect and eternal; earth, a place of corruption and decay.

Part 5 Nature, Science, Health, and Technology

1501 TO 1800

1501 to 1510
1500 Brazil: Pedro Alvarez Cabral explores the region
1501 to 1502 Brazil: Amerigo Vespucci explores coast of Brazil
1502 to 1504 Columbus' fourth voyage; he reaches Honduras, Nicaragua, Costa Rica, Panama, and Colombia
1503 Raw sugar refined
1507 First world map to show South America separate from Asia

Did You Know?

Amerigo Vespucci (1454 to 1512) was the first explorer to reach the North American mainland. He gained a measure of immortality when the German geographer and cartographer Martin Waldseemuller, who translated Vespucci's narrative in 1507, suggested that the new continent be named "America" in homage to its first European explorer. Applied first to the southern continent, the name caught on for North America as well in 1507 after Waldseemuller used it on a map.

1511 to 1520
1513 US: Ponce de León explores Florida; Balboa becomes the first European to encounter the Pacific Ocean
1514 Dutch mathematician Vander Hoecke first to use plus sign (+) and (−) with today's meaning
1515 Germany: Johannes Schoner constructs first globe that shows the Americas
c. 1515 Italy: Scipione del Ferro discovers algebraic method for solving one form of cubic equations
1517 Girolamo Fracastoro explains fossils are the remains of actual creatures
1518 Smallpox epidemic in Hispaniola islands
England: Royal College of Physicians established
1519 Magellan begins his voyage around the world
1519 to 1521 Mexico: Spanish adventurer Hernando Cortés conquers Mexico for Spain

1521 to 1530
1522 One ship from Magellan's expedition completes the first circumnavigation of the world
England: First book on arithmetic published

Did You Know?

Portuguese explorer Ferdinand Magellan (1480 to 1521) was the first European to cross the Pacific Ocean and the first person to circumnavigate the globe. On November 28, 1520, Magellan and his three ships reached the ocean, which he named "Pacific" because of its calmness.

1525 Diego Ribeiro, official mapmaker for Spain, makes first scientific charts showing the Pacific Ocean
Germany: Christoff Rudolff introduces version of modern sign for square root
Peru: Smallpox reaches the Inca empire, killing Inca ruler Huayna Capac
1526 Papua New Guinea: Portuguese explorer Jorge de Menezes navigates the region
1528 First hand grenades: Earthenware pots stuffed with explosives
1530 Girolamo Fracastoro coins the term "syphilis" and describes its symptoms
Europe: Matches being used, almost a thousand years after their invention in China

Did You Know?

When the Spanish arrived in Peru, they discovered the potato, an ancient
Inca food.

1531 to 1540 1532 Peru: After a long and bloody war, Atahualpa claims the throne; the conflict weakens the empire just as Pizarro (Spanish conquistador) arrives
1533 Germany: Major study of trigonometry, including law of sines
Peru: Francisco Pizarro, Spanish soldier, conquers the Inca empire of Peru

Did You Know?

Trigonometry is the branch of mathematics that deals with the relationships
between the sides and angles of triangles.

1535 Canada: French navigator Jacques Cartier explores the St. Lawrence River
Chile: Spanish explore the country (to 1537)
Diving bells invented
Galapagos Islands: Spanish captain Diego de Rivadeneira explores the region
1536 Italy: Tartaglia solves two types of cubic equations
1537 Science of ballistics starts
1540 US: Spaniard Hernando de Alarcón explores Colorado River

Did You Know?

Chile, located on the south Pacific coast of South America, is slightly larger than
Texas. The country became independent in 1818. Today, almost 15 million
people live in Chile.

1541 to 1550 1541 Amazon River: Spanish explorer Francisco Orellana navigates the region
Niccolo Tartaglia and Antonio Maria Fiore engage in famous mathematics duel, solving each others' set of cubic equations

US: Hernando de Soto explores Mississippi River

1543 Nicolaus Copernicus: *On the Revolution of Heavenly Bodies,* his theory that the earth revolves around the sun

Flemish scientist Andreas Vesalius writes first accurate work on human anatomy, *De Humani Corporis Fabrica*

1544 Germany: First major compendium on world geography

1545 Italy: Cardano's mathematical work *Ars Magna,* first book of modern mathematics

1548 to 1620 Flemish mathematician Simon Stevin

1552 Italy: Bartolemeo Eustachio describes the adrenal glands, structure of the teeth, and Eustachian tubes (named after him); work isn't published until 1714

Did You Know?

In early times, events as big and destructive as earthquakes weren't easy to explain. According to ancient Japanese folklore, quakes were caused by a giant catfish named Namazu, who lived under the earth and periodically shook the ground.

1551 to 1560   1556 January 23, Shaanxi (Shensi) Province, China: Most deadly earthquake in history; 830,000 killed

1557 England: Equal sign (=) introduced in a slightly different form; plus (+) and (−) signs introduced into English

First known reference to platinum

1564 Graphite is discovered

Did You Know?

Kepler's first law states that the planets orbit the sun in elliptical paths, with the sun at one focus of the ellipse. The second law states that the closer a planet comes to the sun, the faster it moves. The third law states that the ratio of the cube of a planet's mean distance from the sun is the square of its orbital period.

1561 to 1570   1564 to 1642 Italy: Galileo, who will create a furor when he asserts that the earth is not the center of the universe and in fact revolves around the sun

1567 South America: Portuguese settle at Rio de Janeiro

1571 to 1580   1571 to 1630 Johannes Kepler, German astronomer

1572 Italy: Bombelli uses complex numbers to solve equations

1573 Tycho Brahe describes supernova of 1572

1576 Canada: Martin Frobisher, English explorer, sets out to find a northwest passage to China; he reaches Canadian coast, and Frobisher Bay is named after him

1577 Denmark: Tycho Brahe proves that comets come from space and are not weather events as previously believed

1577 to 1580 Francis Drake sails around the world
1578 to 1657 England: William Harvey, physician
1579 First glass eyes

Did You Know?

Comets, from the Latin for "hairy stars," are now thought to be "snowballs" of ice and dust.

1581 to 1590 1582 Gregorian calendar first used in Roman Catholic countries; it was not used in England until 1752; Russia, 1918

Did You Know?

On Pope Gregory's orders, October 5, 1582 became October 15, to correct the error in the Julian calendar, which provided for a year that was eleven minutes and fourteen seconds longer than the actual year. To prevent the error from recurring, the Pope decreed that century years which could not be divided by 400 would not be leap years.

1585 Flemish mathematician Simon Stevinus' *De Thiende* (*The Tenth*) popularizes the decimal point
1586 England: William Lee invents the first knitting machine
Francis Drake sails to West Indies
Simon Stevinus proves Galileo's belief that two different weights dropped at the same time from the same height will reach the ground at the same time; he also shows that the pressure of a liquid on a given surface depends on the height of the liquid and the area of the surface
1589 Galileo experiments with falling objects
Germany: David Fabricus discovers a star that gradually disappears; in 1638, scientists discover this is the first known variable star
c. 1590 Holland: Compound microscope developed

Did You Know?

In 1589, Italian physicist and astronomer Galileo Galilei (1564 to 1642) is rumored to have shown his students the error in Aristotle's belief that the speed of fall is proportional to weight by dropping two objects of different weights simultaneously from the Leaning Tower of Pisa. Needless to say, he was right . . . so his contract wasn't renewed.

1591 to 1600   1591 Letters used to represent variables in mathematical equations

1592 Galileo invents the thermometer

Korea: Astronomers observe a nova in the constellation Cetus and track it for over a year

1593 China: First description of a modern abacus

1596 China: Written description of more than 1,000 plants and animals along with 8,000 medicinal uses for them

Korea: First ironclad warship developed

1596 to 1650 France: Rene Descartes will stress reason over dogma

Did You Know?

At first, Descartes doubted all knowledge, even of self, but concluded because he could think, he must exist: "Cogito, ergo sum" ("I think, therefore I am").

1598 Tycho Brahe describes his astronomical experiments

1600 Adriaen Ahthoniszoon and his son calculate pi as 3.1415929 (correct value is 3.1415927)

England: William Gilbert suggests that the earth is a giant magnet, which is why magnetic compasses indicate north

1601 to 1610   1601 Johannes Kepler becomes imperial mathematician and court astronomer to Rudolf II, Holy Roman Emperor

Tycho Brahe dies, still believing that the earth does not move, although he did think the other planets revolve around the sun

Brahe's *Astronomiae Instaurate Progymnasmata* published posthumously; describes 777 stars and a 1572 supernova

1603 Germany: First attempt at complete celestial atlas; Johann Bayer creates a method for describing locations of stars and names them with Greek letters

US: Samuel de Champlain explores St. Lawrence River

1604 Italy: Galileo announces his discovery that a body falling freely will increase its distance as the square of time

US: Samuel de Champlain explores Maine Coast

1606 Australia: William Jansz sights the continent

Did You Know?

If you're stopping in Maine, don't miss Acadia National Park, Mt. Desert Island, and Allagash National Wilderness Waterway. Tourist information is available on the Web at www.state.me.us.

South Pacific: Luis Vaez de Torres from Spain sails around New Guinea and reaches the straits now named after him

1607 Canada: Henry Hudson explores Canada

Cuba: Havana named the capital

US: John Smith founds Jamestown, the first permanent English settlement in America
1608 Holland: Dutch scientist Hans Lippershey invents telescope
1609 Canada: First attempt to use the tides of the Bay of Fundy as a power source
Italy: Galileo builds his first telescope; magnification of about 30
Germany: Johannes Kepler publishes first two laws of planetary motion
US: English navigator Henry Hudson explores Hudson River
1610 First chemistry book
Using a telescope, Galileo discovers Jupiter's moons, phases of Venus, and (although he does not know what they are) the rings of Saturn

Did You Know?

Sunspots tend to occur in pairs, with the two spots having magnetic fields that point in opposite directions, one into and one out of the sun.

1611 to 1620   1611 France: First lighthouse with a revolving beacon
Orion nebula discovered
Several astronomers simultaneously discover sunspots
1612 Germany: First mention of Andromeda galaxy
Kepler becomes the mathematician to the states of upper Austria
1614 First study of metabolism
Scotland: John Napier discovers logarithms
1615 to 1616 Cape Horn: Dutch navigator Willem C. Schouten explores the region

Did You Know?

During this time, it was believed that illness was caused by an imbalance among the four humors: blood, black bile, yellow bile, and phlegm.

1616 English navigator William Baffin explores the bay that now bears his name
England: Sir William Harvey discovers blood circulation
1617 England: Henry Briggs describes common logarithms
Scotland: John Napier describes a device for multiplying that comes to be known as Napier's rods or Napier's bones

Did You Know?

On November 10, 1619, Rene Descartes had a dream in which he was told that he should work out the unity of the sciences on a rational basis.

1618 Africa: French explorer Paul Imbert reaches Timbuktu
Italy: Francesco Maria Grimaldi discovers diffraction of light waves, but his work is ignored until 1803
Kepler proposes last of three laws of planetary motion
1619 Switzerland: Johann Cysat discovers the Orion nebula
1620 Cornelis Drebbel builds first navigable submarine
The word "gas" is coined to describe substances like air

1621 to 1630   c. 1621 England: Oughtred invents slide rule
1623 Switzerland: Gaspard Bauhin uses binomial names for the genus and species
1628 William Harvey publishes his work on the circulation of blood

Did You Know?

Harvey discovered that blood circulates around the body in a closed system of tubes, called arteries and veins. The most difficult part was discovering what connected these vessels—capillaries—which Harvey discovered before he ever saw them.

1631 to 1640   1631 France: Vernier scale created
Two multiplication signs introduced: × and ·
The symbols < (less than) and > (greater than) introduced
1632 Italy: Galileo put under house arrest
1633 Inquisition forces Galileo to recant his belief in Copernican theory

Did You Know?

According to legend, at the end of his recantation, Galileo whispered: "E pur se muove" ("Nevertheless, it moves").

1634 US: Frenchman Jean Nicolet explores Lake Michigan
1637 France: Rene Decartes publishes drawings of specimens he observed under a microscope; publishes first account of analytic geometry
Russia: Explorers cross Siberia and reach Pacific Ocean
1639 The division sign [÷] introduced
France: Desargues introduces projective geometry

Did You Know?

Siberia is a vast region marked by extremes in climate, with very long cold winters and short hot summers. Temperatures of 93°F in the summer and −93°F in the winter have been recorded at Verkhoyansk in the north.

1640 France: Blaise Pascal proves Pascal's theorem, also called "mystic hexagram"
Italy: Torricelli applies Galileo's laws of motion to fluids; Torricelli considered father of hydrodynamics

Did You Know?

Is blood thicker than water? Yes—about twice as thick, thanks to all the cells that float in it.

1641 to 1650

1642 Australia: Dutch navigator Abel Tasman explores Australia and Van Diemen's Land (now Tasmania)
France: Blaise Pascal invents the "pascaline," the first calculating machine, capable of addition and subtraction
New Zealand: Abel Janszoon Tasman sees the region and names it
1643 Italy: Evangelista Torricelli invents the mercury barometer, thereby producing first vacuum known to science
1645 England: Daniel Whistler gives the first medical description of rickets in his thesis at the University of Leiden; rickets is a nutritional disorder characterized by skeletal deformities.
1645 Germany: Athanasius Kirchner, a Jesuit, builds a magic lantern (a device for projecting images mounted on slides or film)
1647 Barbados: First recorded cases of yellow fever in the Americas
First map of the observable side of the moon

Did You Know?

The torr, a unit of measurement used by physicists working in near vacuum conditions, is named after Torricelli.

1648 Jan Baptista van Helmont shows plants do not obtain large amounts of material for growth from soil
Semjon Deshnjov's exploration proves that America and Asia are not connected
1649 Pierre Gassendi states that matter is made from atoms

1651 to 1660

1652 Sweden: Olof Rudbeck demonstrates the lymphatic vessels
1654 Robert Bissaker develops the first slide rule in which slide works between parts of a fixed stock
France: Blaise Pascal and Pierre de Fermat develop theory of probability
Italy: Grand Duke of Tuscany invents the sealed thermometer
1656 Christian Huggens discovers Saturn's rings
1658 England: Robert Hooke invents balance spring for watches
Holland: Jan Swammerdam describes red blood cells
1659 England: Thomas Willis describes typhoid fever

1660 Barometer first used to forecast weather
Italy: Marcello Malpighi correctly describes the lungs

1661 to 1670   1662 Boyle's Law: For gas kept at a constant temperature, pressure and volume vary inversely
1663 French: Blaise Pascal proposes Pascal's Law: Pressure in fluid is transmitted equally in all directions
1664 to 1665 England: Great Plague of London; 70,000 to 75,000 people die out of a population of 460,000
1664 Isaac Newton's experiments with gravity

Did You Know?

Sir Isaac Newton, a Cambridge University professor, was the foremost scientist in the 1600s. Before he was 26 years old, Newton made three far-reaching discoveries: the theory of gravitation, the nature of light, and calculus.

1665 England: Robert Hooke identifies cells
Nervous system described
1666 England: Sir Isaac Newton describes his invention of calculus but does not publish it
1667 England: Robert Boyle shows that animals can be kept alive on artificial respiration; Margaret Cavendish becomes the first female member of the Royal Society; the next woman wasn't admitted until 1945
France: Jean-Baptiste Denis tries first blood transfusions; when unsuccessful, he is tried and acquitted for murder and all blood transfusions are banned in France
Russia: Caucasia: Earthquake kills about 80,000 people

Did You Know?

Margaret Cavendish, Duchess of Newcastle, was called "Mad Madge" for her interest in science, thought most unseemly in a woman.

1668 Italy: Francesco Redi attempts to prove that rotting meat cannot spontaneously turn into flies
1669 Denmark: Nicolaus Steno correctly explains the origin of fossils
Richard Lower describes the heart as a muscle
1670 Boyle discovers hydrogen, although not named until much later
Thomas Willis rediscovers the connection between sugar in the urine and diabetes mellitus

1671 to 1680   1671 Giovanni Cassini correctly determines the distances of the planets from the sun
1673 Leeuwenhoeck publishes his first article in the *Philosophical Transactions of the Royal Society of London*

US: Frenchmen Jacques Marquette and Louis Jolliet explore the Arkansas River
1675 Denmark: Ole Christensen Romer becomes the first to measure the speed of light, although his number is later shown to be slow

Did You Know?

Faults, breaks in the earth's crust, occur where the plates meet. Most earthquakes take place along these faults. The San Andreas fault in California, for example, is a 700-mile hotbed where the North American plate, which moves southeast, meets the Pacific plate, which moves northwest.

1676 England: Richard Hooke discovers what is now known as Hooke's Law: The amount a spring stretches varies directly with its tension
1677 Leeuwenhoeck discovers protists (protozoa); also confirms the discovery of sperm and links them to reproduction
1678 Joseph Moxon describes a hidden fire in heated lime that appears upon the addition of water
Denmark: Christiaan Huygens develops the wave theory of light; not published until 1690
1679 Germany: Leibniz perfects binary system of notation, which will eventually be used by all computers

Did You Know?

The speed of light is 186,000 miles per second. It takes the sun's light approximately eight minutes to reach earth.

1681 to 1690   1681 The Canal du Midi is finished after eight years of work
1682 England: Edmond Halley describes the comet now known by his name; in 1705, he correctly predicts that it will return in 1758
US: Frenchman Sieur de La Salle explores Mississippi River
1683 Leeuwenhoek is the first to observe bacteria; will be over 100 years before other scientists see it
1684 Germany: Leibniz's independent discovery of calculus
1687 Sir Isaac Newton publishes *Philosophiae Naturalis Principia Mathematica*, containing his laws of motion and theory of gravity

Did You Know?

The law of gravity states that the gravitational force between any two objects is proportional to the product of their masses and inversely proportional to the square of the distance between them.

1691 to 1700   1691 England: First textbook showing complete bones in the human body
1698 England: Thomas Savery patents "Miner's Friend," first practical steam engine
1699 Australia: William Dampier sails along continent's northwest coast

1701 to 1710   1701 Constantinople: Giacomo Pylarini inoculates children with smallpox; Pylarini considered by some to be the first immunologist
England: Jethro Tull invents "seed drill," device for planting seeds
1702 Boric acid discovered
1705 France: Raymond Vieussens gives first accurate description of heart's left ventricle
1706 First textbook to use the Greek letter π for the ratio of the circumference of a circle to its diameter
1707 Italy: Giovanni Maria Lancisi offers first essay on cardiac pathology
1709 Daniel Gabriel Fahrenheit invents alcohol thermometer
1710 Three-color printing invented

Did You Know?

In the US, temperature is usually measured in degrees Fahrenheit: water freezes at 32°F and boils at 212°F. The basis of the Fahrenheit scale is 0°F, the coldest temperature that its originator, D. G. Fahrenheit, could obtain in the laboratory.

1711 to 1720   1712 England: Thomas Newcomen invents steam pump for use in mines
1713 England: John Needham, an English biologist who would "prove" abiogenesis works, is born
1714 Daniel Gabriel Fahrenheit invents mercury thermometer and a scale that will be named after him
1717 Value of π found to 72 places
1718 England: Halley discovers that stars move with respect to each other

Did You Know?

Abiogenesis *is spontaneous generation, the production of living organisms from inanimate matter.*

1721 to 1730   1721 US: Zabdiel Boylston inoculates children against smallpox during Boston epidemic
1722 Dutch navigator Jacob Roggeveen lands at Samoa and Easter Island
1724 Russia: Peter the Great establishes Russian Academy of Sciences
1727 Iran: 77,000 victims killed in deadly earthquake (November 18)
1728 France: Pierre Fauchard describes how to fill a tooth cavity with tin, lead, or gold
US: Alaska: Vitus Bering explores the strait that bears his name
1729 Sir Isaac Newton's *Principia* translated from Latin into English
Lazzaro Spallanzani, who would attempt to prove that abiogenesis doesn't work, is born
Stephen Gray discovers that electricity can be transmitted from one object to another

1731 to 1740   1733 England: John Kay invents flying shuttle loom
Sweden: Anders Celsius publishes his conclusions about the aurora borealis

Did You Know?

Along with the flying shuttle loom, the steam engine and improvements in making iron were key to the start to the Industrial Revolution.

1735 England: John Harrison builds his first marine chronometer; his fourth one is the most famous
Peru: French scientist La Codamine goes to Peru to measure one degree on the surface of the earth
Sweden: Linnaeus introduces system for classifying plants and animals
1736 Peru: Natural rubber discovered in rainforests
First successful operation for appendicitis
US: William Douglass describes scarlet fever

1741 to 1750   1742 England: Benjamin Huntsman introduces crucible process for molten steel
Sweden: Anders Celsius creates the temperature scale that bears his name

Did You Know?

On the Celsius scale, water freezes at 0°C and boils at 100°C. Very low temperatures are measured on the Kelvin scale, named for Baron Kelvin. It is also called the absolute scale because absolute zero 0°K is the temperature at which no body can give up heat.

1743 US: American Philosophical Society established, America's first scientific society
1744 US: Ben Franklin invents the stove that bears his name
1746 Netherlands: Method invented for storing static electricity, which becomes known as the Leyden jar
1747 Germany: Andreas Marggraf discovers sugar in beets, which starts Europe's sugar-beet industry
1748 Europe: John Needham and Comte de Buffon conduct a famous experiment that seems to prove spontaneous generation
1749 US: Franklin installs a lightning rod on his house

1751 to 1760   1751 England: Benjamin Huntsman invents crucible process for casting steel
1751 to 1772 France: *Encyclopedie* communicates scientific ideas to wider audience
1752 England: Georgian calendar adopted; William Smellie's *Treatise on Midwifery* is first scientific approach to obstetrics
France: de Reaumur discovers the role of gastric juices
US: Benjamin Franklin's famous kite experiment; he invents the lightening conductor
1753 George Richmann is killed performing Franklin's kite experiment

1755 Africa: Sailors bring smallpox to Cape Town, South Africa. It spreads rapidly inland, killing many Khoisan hunters and herders
Germany: Immanuel Kant proposes that many nebulas are composed of millions of stars and that solar systems are formed when giant clouds of dust condense
Portugal: Severe earthquake levels Lisbon, felt in southern France and North Africa; 70,000 killed
Scotland: Joseph Black discovers carbon dioxide

Did You Know?

Franklin's kite experiment demonstrated that lightning is a form of electricity.

1756 British engineer John Smeaton rediscovers hydraulic cement through repeated testing of mortar in both fresh and salt water
1758 England: Ribbing machine invented to make stockings
1759 John Harrison completes chronometer Number Four, the first practical tool for finding longitude at sea

Did You Know?

To convert a temperature from Fahrenheit to Celsius, subtract 32 from the temperature and multiply the result by 5; then divide the product by 9. The formula is $C = \frac{5}{9}(F - 32)$. To convert Celsius to Fahrenheit, multiply the temperature by 1.8 (or $\frac{9}{5}$) then add 32. The formula is $F = \frac{9}{5}(C + 32)$.

1761 to 1770   1761 Russia: Mikhail Lomonosov discovers the atmosphere of Venus
1763 England: Josiah Wedgwood patents the cream-colored earthenware that bears his name
France: Monge invents descriptive geometry, the mathematical techniques become basis for mechanical drawing
1764 England: James Hargreaves creates spinning jenny, mechanical spinning wheel
Scotland: James Watt invents the condenser

Did You Know?

Venus' atmosphere is mainly carbon dioxide. Venus is hot—470°C—and has a surface pressure 90 times that of Earth's.

1765 Scotland: James Watt invents the steam engine.
1766 Henry Cavendish discovers that hydrogen is lighter than air

1767 Italy: Lazzaro Pallanzani helps disprove John Needham's theory of spontaneous generation

1768 English navigator James Cook explores east coast of Australia; lands in New Zealand

Johann Lambert proves that π is an irrational number

1769 England: Sir William Arkwright patents a spinning machine; early step in the Industrial Revolution

New Zealand: English navigator James Cook explores the region

1770 James Cook explores Botany Bay

Did You Know?

The watt, an electrical unit, was named after Scottish inventor James Watt (1736 to 1819).

1771 to 1780

1771 Carl Scheele discovers oxygen

1772 Joseph Priestley discovers that burning hydrogen produces water

Scotland: Daniel Rutherford discovers nitrogen

1773 Antarctica: James Cook crosses Antarctic Circle and circumnavigates region

1774 Joseph Priestley discovers oxygen, 2 years after Scheele, but is the first to publish his work

1775 England: Percival Pott observes that chimney sweeps develop cancer as a result of their contact with soot, the first recognition of environmental factors on cancer

Priestley discovers hydrochloric and sulfuric acids

US: David Bushnell invents the Turtle, a hand-operated one-person submarine

1777 France: Nicholas Desmarest proposes that rock basalt starts as lava

1778 England: Joseph Bramah builds a better toilet

France: Lavoisier discovers that air is mostly nitrogen and oxygen

Franz Mesmer uses hypnotism

1779 Bry Higgin issued a patent for hydraulic cement (stucco) for exterior plastering use

France: Velocipedes, type of early bicycle, used in Paris

Holland: Jan Ingenhousz discovers that plants release oxygen when exposed to sun and consume carbon dioxide, the first step in understanding photosynthesis

1780 James Watt invents a paper copier

Steel pen points begin to replace quill feathers

1781 to 1790

1781 William Herschel discovers the planet Uranus

England: Richard Arkwright founds the modern factory system

Did You Know?

Uranus has a diameter of 32,188 miles, compared to Earth's 7,926 miles. It takes Uranus 84 years to orbit the sun. The atmosphere is mainly methane gas, which gives the planet its blue-green appearance.

1783 England: Cavendish announces that water is composed of hydrogen and oxygen; Lavoisier names the new gas *hydrogen*

Europe: L. S. Lenormand is the first westerner to use a parachute; names it

Iceland: Volcanic eruption kills 10,000; leads Ben Franklin to surmise that dust and gasses from a volcanic eruption lower temperatures by screening out radiation

Spain: Tungsten discovered

Threshing machine invented

Watt uses steam to heat his office, the first use of steam heat

1784 US: Franklin introduces bifocal eyeglasses

1785 England: Edmund Cartwright invents a power loom

Herschel demonstrates that the Milky Way is a disk group of many stars, one of which is the sun

William Withering uses digitalis to treat heart disease

Did You Know?

The Milky Way looks "milky" as a result of the combined light of stars too far to be seen individually by the unaided eye, although many of the stars can be seen through a telescope.

1786 Benjamin Rush suggests that some illnesses are psychosomatic

England/Germany: First experiments with gas lighting

1787 France: Jacques Charles discovers "Charles Law" describing the relationship between the volume and temperature of a gas

Lavoisier's work on chemical nomenclature

Did You Know?

In the law of conservation of matter, in chemical change, matter is neither created nor destroyed.

1788 Laplace's *Laws of the Planetary System*

1789 Canada: Alexander Mackenzie explores the river that bears his name

Lavoisier states the law of conservation of matter

1790 Aloisio Galvani experiments on electrical stimulation of muscles

William Herschel discovers planetary nebulas

Lavoisier formulates table of thirty-one chemical elements

Joseph Michel and Jacques Etienne Montgolfier became the first humans to fly with their invention of the hot air balloon

US: George Washington's dentist invents the dental drill

1791 to 1880 1791 England: William George discovers titanium; John Mercer invents a process for treating cotton cloth called *mercerizing*
France: Metric system proposed; Phillippe Pinel advocates a more humane treatment of the mentally ill
Italy: Luigi Galvani discovers that when two different metals touch a frog's muscle, they produce an electric current
Germany: Richer shows that acids and bases always neutralize each other in the same proportion

Did You Know?

A cotton gin separates cotton fibers from seeds.

1792 Scotland: William Murdock uses coal gas for lighting
1793 US: Eli Whitney invents the cotton gin, spurring the growth of the cotton industry
1794 John Dalton: First account of color blindness
France: Volta demonstrates that the electric force Galvani found can be obtained whenever two different metals are placed in a conducting fluid
1795 Africa: Scottish explorer Mungo Park begins exploring the Niger river
J. F. Blumenbach writes *The Human Species,* laying the foundation of anthropology
England: Lime juice made mandatory treatment for scurvy, giving rise to the nickname "limey" for British sailors
France: Adopts metric system
1796 England: Edward Jenner gives smallpox vaccinations; James Parker patents a natural hydraulic cement, called Parker's Cement or Roman Cement
1797 Scotland: Sir James Hall shows that melted rocks form crystals upon cooling
1798 England: Henry Cavendish determines gravitational constant and mass of Earth

Did You Know?

How does the American system of measurement compare to the metric system?
  1 inch = 2.54 centimeters (cm)
  1 foot = 30.48 cm
  1 yard = 91.44 cm
  1 mile = 1,609.34 meters (m)

Benjamin Thompson shows that heat is a form of motion
France: Pierre-Simon Laplace predicts the existence of black holes
1799 Germany: Gauss proves fundamental theorem of algebra: Every polynomial equation has a solution
Italy: Ruffini offers first proof that not all polynomial equations of fifth degree can be solved by algebra

Did You Know?

In 1795, Nicholas-Jacques Conte of France discovered the process of mixing graphite with clay. This mixture was then placed in a kiln fire and the strips cut and placed into wood. The pencil's strength depended on the amount of graphite located in the mixture. The more graphite that was used, the softer the pencil that would result. This mixture of graphite and clay is still used in our "lead" pencils.

1800 England: Chlorine used to purify water
India: Jute is cultivated
Italy: Alessandro Volta invents electric cell
William Herschel discovers infrared rays

Part 5: Nature, Science, Health, and Technology

1801 TO 2000

1801	England: Thomas Young develops wave theory of light
	France: Jacquard uses punch cards to control operation of mechanical loom; precursor of cards used in early data-storage systems
	Germany: Johann Ritter discovers ultraviolet light
	Italy: Guiseppe Piazzi discovers the first-known asteroid, Ceres
1802	France: Jean Baptiste de Lamarck coins the term "biology"
1803	England: John Dalton introduces atomic theory of matter
	US: Robert Fulton propels a boat by steam power
1804	England: First oil lamp designed by Frenchman Aimé Argand; Richard Trevithick builds first successful steam locomotive
	France: Nicolas Appert develops canning as a means of preserving food
	US: Meriwether Lewis and William Clark explore northwestern US
1805	Morphine isolated
1806	England: Sir Francis Beauford designs scale (zero to twelve) to indicate wind strength; Sir Humphry Davy discovers potassium and sodium
	Europe: Gas lighting introduced to many cities
1807	England: Geological Society of London founded
	US: Robert Fulton invents first commercially successful steamboat, the *Clermont*
1808	John Dalton states atomic theory
	Joseph-Louis Gay-Lussac discovers Law of Combining Volumes

Did You Know?

Lussac's Law of Combining Volumes states: "When measured at the same temperature and pressure, volumes of gaseous reactants and products of chemical reactions are always in simple ratios of whole numbers."

	Pompeii excavations begin
	Charles Darwin: English naturalist (1809 to 1882)
1810	Italy: Avogadro's Law

| 1811 | P. T. Barnum's famous Siamese twins, Chang and Eng, are born
US: Largest series of earthquakes known to have occurred in North America; earthquake reverses the course of the Mississippi River |
|---|---|
| 1812 | Germany: Friedrich Mohr classifies hardness of metals on Mohr Scale |

Did You Know?

Dalton's atomic theory stated that the same elements have the same atoms. Further, he correctly concluded that a compound is made up of atoms of elements combined in fixed proportions.

| 1814 | Sweden: Chemist Jöns Jacob Berzelius suggests using letters as symbols for the elements
George Stephenson builds first practical steam locomotive |
|---|---|
| 1815 | England: Doctors must be licensed to practice medicine; first geological map of London
John McAdam invents "macadam" road paving |

Did You Know?

Avogadro's Law proposes that equal volumes of gas at the same temperature and pressure contain the same number of molecules.

| 1816 | France: Joseph Niepce experiments with photography
Scotland: Sir David Brewster invents kaleidoscope
Single wire telegraph invented
Stethoscope invented |
|---|---|
| 1818 | James Blundell gives a woman blood transfusion from her husband—the woman lived, but other blood transfusions fail; no one knows why |

Did You Know?

We now know that a person with type O blood is a "universal donor" because his or her blood can be used by anyone. A person with type AB is the "universal recipient," since he or she can use A, B, and O blood.

1819	Denmark: Hans C. Oersted discovers electromagnetism
1820	England: Faraday discovers fundamentals of electromagnetic rotation
France: Andre-Marie Ampere formulates first laws of electromagnetism

1821	Antarctica: Nathaniel Palmer and Fabian Gottlieb von Bellingshausen explore the region John Tickell and Abraham Chambers issued more patents for hydraulic cement
1822	England: Babbage designs and builds prototype of "difference engine" for calculating logarithms France: Projective geometry developed; Andre Ampere founds and names the science of electrodynamics; Joseph Niepce produces earliest form of the photograph
1823	Scotland: Charles Macintosh patents waterproof fabric US: Cyrus P. Dalkin invents carbon copies, although the idea doesn't catch on for 50 years
1824	England: Joseph Aspdin patents what he called Portland cement, since it resembled the stone quarried on the Isle of Portland off the British coast France: Gay-Lussac discovers chemical isomers, chemicals with same formula but different structures New way to burn coal more efficiently developed
1825	England: First passenger-carrying railroad in England Hans Christian Oersted discovers aluminum US: Erie Canal creates the first great demand for cement in the US
1826	England: Friction match invented
1827	Brownian motion recognized, proving that molecules exist Georg Ohm: Ohm's Law, relating current, voltage, and resistance
1828	First comprehensive list of atomic weights Germany: Friedrich Wohler shows that life is basically the same as other matter
1829	US: William Austin Burt invents an early typewriter

Did You Know?

In 1828, when his pants did not come back from the cleaners in time for the show, circus performer Nelson Howard did his bareback riding act in his long underwear. When Julius Leotard, a popular French acrobat, wore his long underwear in his act soon after, they became known as leotards.

1830	Scotland: Sir Charles Lyell publishes *Principles of Geology;* convinces geologists that the earth is at least several hundred million years old First passenger steam railways open
1831	Michael Faraday and Joseph Henry independently discover principle of dynamo, first electric generators Ross determines position of magnetic North Pole

South Pacific: Charles Darwin sets out on five-year voyage to Pacific for scientific research
US and Germany: Chloroform invented; used as anesthetic

1833 England: Charles Babbage invents "analytical engine," precursor of computer; never goes beyond design stage

1834 US: Cyrus McCormick patents reaper

1835 Samuel Colt: Colt pistol, the first repeating firearm, patented
Elements of Botany, first botanical textbook
England: William Henry Fox Talbot invents photographic negative using silver chloride, essentially how black and white photographs are made today
US: One of the first sewing machines produced

1837 France: Louis Braille invents Braille
US: Samuel F. B. Morse invents the telegraph

1838 Germany: Friedrich Bessel determines distance to star other than the sun
US: Samuel F. B. Morse invents Morse Code

Did You Know?

Morse code consists of a combination of dots and dashes representing the letters of the alphabet and numbers. The letter A, for example, is a dot and a dash. The duration of one dash equals that of three dots.

1839 France: Louis Daguerre creates a process for making photographs, which come to be called "daguerreotypes"
Germany: Cell theory of life developed
Germany and Switzerland: Christian Schwann discovers ozone
Scotland: Bicycle invented
Switzerland: First electric clock
US: Charles Goodyear discovers how to make rubber resistant to heat and cold, a process called "vulcanization"

1840 Samuel F. B. Morse patents Morse Code

Did You Know?

On May 24, 1844, Samuel F. B. Morse transmitted the first telegraphic message: "What hath God wrought?"

1842　　England: Lawes patents superphosphates, first manufactured fertilizer
Germany: von Mayer states the law of conservation of energy
US: Physician Crawford Long uses ether as surgical anesthesia

1843　　James Joule: The joule, a measurement unit, invented

1844　　Samuel F. B. Morse patents telegraph; it revolutionizes communication

1845　　Ireland: Potato blight leads to great famine

Did You Know?

In the eighteenth and nineteenth centuries, the average Irish citizen planted potatoes; each ate about ten pounds of potatoes a day—and little else. Potatoes are nourishing: on this diet, the Irish population nearly tripled from the middle of the eighteenth century to just about the middle of the nineteenth century. But depending on only one food was dangerous. When the potato blight hit Ireland in 1845, the results were devastating. The potato famine meant more than starvation: It meant no seed potatoes to use to grow the next year's crop. It meant that the pig or cow that would have been sold to pay the rent had to be slaughtered, because there was nothing to fatten it on. No pig or cow meant no rent. No rent meant eviction. As a result, homelessness and disease followed on the heels of hunger. Almost a million Irish people died as a result of the potato blight; another million moved to America.

1846　　Germany: Johann Galle discovers the planet Neptune
Italy: Nitroglycerin discovered
W. T. Morton uses ether as anesthetic
US: Smithsonian Institute founded in Washington, DC; Elias Howe patents sewing machine and invents rotary printing press

1847　　Hungary: Ignaz Semmelweis demands asepsis by showing how childbed fever could be prevented if doctors washed their hands often
US: Alexander Graham Bell: inventor (1847 to 1922); Thomas Alva Edison: inventor (1847 to 1931)
England: George Boole creates Boolean Algebra
St. Lawrence Seaway opened

Did You Know?

According to most accounts, Thomas Alva Edison's formal education lasted only three months; he quit school after a teacher pronounced him "addled." His mother, a former teacher, home-schooled Edison for awhile, but his interest in chemistry soon sparked a rigorous course of independent study.

1850   Canada: Toronto streets lit by gas streetlights
Germany: Rudolf Clausius states the second law of thermodynamics: Energy in a closed
system tends to degrade into heat

1851   France: Jean-Bernard-Leon Foucault proves rotation of earth
Telegraph used to direct trains
Scotland: William Thompson, (later Lord Kelvin) proposes the concept of absolute zero
US: Isaac Singer invents continuous-stitch sewing machine

Did You Know?

Absolute zero is the lowest possible temperature, −460°F or −273°C.

1852   US: Otis invents first elevator incorporating a safety device that prevents the cage from
falling if cable breaks

1853   Hypodermic syringes used for injections

1854   England: George Boole creates symbolic logic, *Laws of Thought*
First "hard" vacuum created in a glass tube

Did You Know?

*The invention of the vacuum led to the discovery of x-rays and the electron. This
made radio, television, computers, and other electronic devices possible.*

1855   England: Alexander Parkes patents first plastic, later named "celluloid"
Florence Nightingale nurses wounded in Crimea

1856   Cocaine extracted from cocoa beans
England: Henry Bessemer develops a way of making inexpensive steel (Bessemer
process)
France: Louis Pasteur discovers microorganisms cause fermentation
Germany: First skeleton of Neanderthal found

1858   England: Charles Darwin and Alfred Wallace announce theory of evolution by natural
selection
Eraser is fitted to the end of a pencil
Italy: Atomic weights and chemical formulas standardized

1859   Charles Darwin: *On the Origins of Species*
             Germany: Spectroscope used to identify elements from light
             US: Edwin Drake drills first oil well, in Titusville, PA

1861   Australia: Australians Robert Burke and William Wills explore the continent
             Louis Pasteur's theory of germs

1862   Australia: English explorer John McDouall Stuart crosses the continent
             Gatling invents first form of machine gun

1863   England: First underground railroad, London

1864   France: Louis Pasteur proves that abiogenesis doesn't work
             US: George Perkins Marsh's *Man and Nature,* first conservation textbook

1865   Austria: Gregor Mendel's Law of Heredity
             England: James Clerk Maxwell creates theories on electricity and magnetism
             Germany: Line geometry created
             Joseph Lister begins antiseptic surgery
             US: Massachusetts Institute of Technology founded

1866   England: Robert Whitehead invents naval torpedo
             France: First dry cell for producing electricity
             Alfred Nobel invents dynamite (patented in Britain, 1867)
             US: Cyrus Field lays the first Trans-Atlantic Cable under Atlantic Ocean, connects Europe
             to America by telegraph wire

1867   England: Antiseptic surgery begins when carbolic acid used to disinfect operating room
             Henry Sorby discovers carotene, the chemical that gives plants and animals red and
             yellow coloring
             France: Marie Curie: French chemist (1867 to 1934)

1868   Helium discovered

1869   France: Margarine patented
             Suez Canal opens
             US: Transcontinental rail route completed
             US: Chewing gum invented
             US: Thomas Alva Edison's first invention, an electrical vote recorder

1871   Africa: Henry Stanley meets David Livingstone (who discovered Zambezi River and
             Victoria Falls): the pair search for the source of the Nile

1872   Japan: Gas streetlights come to Tokyo
             Japan: First railway opens (Tokyo to Yokohama)
             Russia: Russian chemist Dmitri Mendeleyev publishes his periodic table
             Scotland: Robert Smith describes acid rain

1873   First color photographs
             Scotland: James Clark Maxwell publishes complete theory of electromagnetism

Did You Know?

Chewing gum is derived from the latex of the chicle (or sapodilla) trees of Central and South America. Chicle grows wild, and the trees are often several miles apart. The milky latex is harvested by cutting a v-shaped incision in the bark and letting the sap ooze out. The latex is then boiled to provide the gum base. Since the late 1940s, chicle latex has been partly replaced by synthetics in gum manufacturing.

1874	US: Barbed wire invented, accelerating the development of the West
1875	French: Gallium discovered; first discovery of an element Dmitri Mendeleyev predicted
1876	Germany: First practical refrigerator invented US: Alexander Graham Bell invents the telephone US: Thomas Alva Edison sets up what he calls his "invention factory" in Menlo Park, NJ

Did You Know?

To test his telephone, Alexander Graham Bell strung a wire from his lab to the bedroom, at the far end of the hall. Bending over the mouthpiece, he said, "Mr. Watson, come here, I want you." His assistant, Thomas Watson, heard the message. The rest is history.

1877	Germany: Internal combustion engine invented US: Thomas Alva Edison patents phonograph and makes first sound recording
1878	France: Rayon invented Sweden: Turbine-operated centrifugal cream separator invented US: First commercial telephone exchange opened in New Haven, CT
1879	Swedish explorer Nils Nordenskjold navigates Northeast Passage (Arctic Ocean) US: Thomas Alva Edison patents the incandescent lightbulb
1880	England: John Milne invents modern seismograph England: Practical electric lights invented
1881	Germany: Electric trolley runs in Berlin US: Vector analysis introduced; Clara Barton (1821 to 1912) establishes the American Association of the Red Cross. As with its parent group, the International Red Cross, this organization helps citizens and soldiers in times of crisis and war France: Louis Pasteur uses weakened bacteria to inoculate against anthrax

1882   England: Sir Alexander Flemming describes cell division
Germany: Robert Koch announces discovery of tuberculosis germ

1883   South Pacific: Krakatau volcano erupts and destroys two-thirds of island; estimated that 36,000 died

1885   Canadian Pacific railway opens
France: Louis Pasteur uses weakened bacteria to inoculate against rabies, and uses it to save the life of a young boy, Joseph Meister, bitten by a rabid dog
Germany: Karl Benz builds precursor of modern automobile
US: Yellowstone Park opens, world's first national park

1886   Gottlieb Wilhelm Daimler invents internal combustion engine
US: John Styth Pemberton creates Coca-Cola as a "headache tonic"; George Westinghouse invents air brake for railroad cars; William S. Burroughs develops first commercially successful mechanical adding machine

1887   US: Herman Hollerith designs a tabulating machine for use in the US Census. His Tabulating Machine Company (established in 1911) became IBM in 1924.

1888   Germany: Hertz produces and detects radio waves; Berliner invents phonograph disk
Scotland: Dunlop patents pneumatic (air-filled) tire
US: George Eastman invents first camera using roll film

Did You Know?

Blood types include A, B, AB, and O. Type O is the most common, but blood types vary by race and geography. For example, more people in central Asia and northern India have type B blood than people in other places. Among Native Americans, type B blood is very rare.

1889   France: Gustave Eiffel builds his famous tower in Paris; tallest freestanding structure of its time
First concrete-reinforced bridge built
Herman Hollerith patents first data-processing computer

1890   First zeppelin completed

1891   Edison patents Kinetoscope, first movie projector

1892   Canada: Banff, Alberta: Canada's first national park
Germany: Ehrilch isolates diphtheria bacteria
Greenland: Robert Peary explores the region

1893   Germany: Rudolph Diesel describes the diesel engine

Did You Know?

John Styth Pemberton, a pharmacist, trademarked a medicine he called "French Wine Coca—Ideal Nerve and Tonic Stimulant," "Coca-Cola" for short. One day, a man with a terrible headache hauled himself into a drugstore and asked for a Coca-Cola. Usually druggists stirred such headache remedies into water. In this case, however, the soda jerk mixed the syrup in seltzer. The customer liked the carbonated version better than the uncarbonated one; other customers agreed. From then on, Coca-Cola was served as a carbonated drink.

1894	Coin-operated movie machines appear in New York City; London, Berlin, and Paris shortly thereafter Java ape-man discovered, now known as first specimen of *Homo erectus*

Did You Know?

Thomas Edison defined genius as "one percent inspiration and 99 percent perspiration."

1895	France: Auguste and Louis Lumiere premiere motion pictures at a cafe in Paris Germany: Roentgen discovers x-rays Italy: Marconi invents wireless telegraphy US: First hand-held Kodak camera

Did You Know?

One of the Lumieres' most effective films featured a mail train rushing at viewers, causing audiences to recoil in fear.

1896	Rudolph Diesel demonstrates the diesel engine England: Marconi receives first wireless patent France: Becquerel discovers natural radioactivity Sweden: Greenhouse effect discovered
1897	England: Thomson discovers electron Germany: Braun invents cathode-ray tube oscilloscope
1898	Denmark: Poulsen invents magnetic wire recorder, precursor to modern tape recorder France: Pierre and Marie Curie discover radium and polonium

Italy: Camillo Golgi describes the Golgi apparatus
First identification of a virus

1900   Gamma rays discovered
Graf von Zeppelin invents the first rigid airship
Germany: Max Planck proposes "quantum theory," first step in the discovery of the atom;
David Hilbert proposes his famous list of twenty-three unsolved problems
US: Eastman introduces his Brownie camera; it cost $1, could be taken anywhere, and
was so simple a child could use it; it revolutionized photography

Did You Know?

*Kodak sold 250,000 Brownie cameras in 1900 alone; with some minor changes,
the camera stayed on the market for the next 80 years.*

1901   Biologist Karl Landsteiner discovers blood antigens
England: Fingerprint system introduced
Marconi sends a radio signal across the Atlantic
Ferdinand Graf von Zeppelin builds the first successful dirigible
Satori Kato invents instant coffee

1902   Egypt: First Aswan Dam completed
France: Leon-Philippe Teisserenc de Bort discovers the stratosphere
Italy: Guiseppe Mercalli invents Mercalli Intensity Scale for measuring intensity of
earthquakes
Martinique, West Indies: Mt. Pelée erupts and wipes out city of St. Pierre; 40,000
dead
Spark plug invented
US: Willis Carrier invents air conditioning

Did You Know?

*The Mercalli Intensity Scale uses numbers to show the intensity of an earthquake:
I indicates earthquakes that aren't felt at all; XII denotes earthquakes that cause
total destruction.*

1903   France: Edouard Benedictus invents safety glass
France: Marie and Pierre Curie share Nobel Prize for Physics with Antoine Henri
Becquerel
US: Mary Anderson invents windshield wipers; Ford Motor Company established; John
Muir starts the Sierra Club; Orville Wright makes first flight at Kitty Hawk, NC
(December 17)

1904
Austria: First musical radio transmission
England: John Fleming develops the first vacuum tube, a device for changing alternating current to direct current
Ingalls building, first concrete skyscraper
Neon lights debut
Rubber improved
Rutherford and Soddy's general theory of radioactivity
US: First national wildlife refuge, Pelican Island in Florida; National Audubon society established

1905
Einstein publishes the first version of his *Special Theory of Relativity*
US: Last outbreak of yellow fever in the US

Did You Know?

Einstein showed that the nature of small particles in liquid ("Brownian motion") can be explained by assuming that the liquid is made of molecules. He also developed his special theory of relativity and the law $E = mc^2$ (energy = mass times square of speed of light).

1906
Cloud chamber created
England: Richard Olhman establishes the existence of earth's core; U.M.S. *Dreadnought*, first modern battleship, launched; Biochemist Frederick Hopkins proves link between growth and diet
Roald Amundsen, Norwegian explorer, fixes magnetic North Pole
Russia: Paper chromatography, the beginning of modern chemical analysis
US: San Francisco earthquake accompanied by fire destroys over 4 square miles; more than 500 dead or missing
Vitamins recognized as essential to health

1907
US: Lee De Forest patents Audion vacuum tube, a device for magnifying with electronic signals
France: Bicycle dealer Paul Cornu builds the first helicopter, which flies for twenty seconds at one foot off the ground and then breaks up on landing

1908
Jacques Brandenberger invents cellophane
Germany: Haber develops a cheap process for making ammonia from nitrogen in the air
Gideon Sundback invents the zipper
Hugh Moore invents the paper cup
Italy: Messina, Sicily totally destroyed by earthquake; 70,000 to 100,000 killed
US: Henry Ford develops the assembly line; first Model T Ford cost $850; Hotel Statler in Buffalo is first to have an unheard of luxury—a private bathroom in every room

1909
Chromosomes established as carriers of heredity
Croatia: Boundary between earth's crust and mantle discovered

Robert E. Peary and Matthew Henson reach the North Pole
US: Leo Baekeland patents Bakelite, the first truly successful plastic

Did You Know?

Four of every five earthquakes occur along the so-called Ring of Fire along the Pacific Ocean, which includes parts of Indonesia, Japan, Alaska, the Rocky Mountains, Central America, and the Andes.

1910　　　Africa: Large scale coffee growing in Kenya

1911　　　Denmark: Heinke Onnes discovers superconductivity (awarded Nobel Prize for his work in 1913)
England: Rutherford discovers the proton and creates nuclear theory
Europe: First use of aircraft as offensive weapon, Turkish-Italian War
South Pole: Norwegian explorer Roald Amundsen reaches the Pole

Did You Know?

The boundary between earth's crust and mantle is now known as Moho after its Croatian discoverer, Mohorovicic.

1912　　　Germany: Alfred Wegener proposes theory of continental drift

1913　　　Congo: Albert Schweitzer opens a hospital
Geiger counter used to measure radioactivity
Igor Sikorsky flies first multiengined plane
US: Construction begins on Lincoln Highway (US 30), nation's first coast-to-coast paved road
Arthur Wynne creates the first crossword puzzles

1914　　　US: First transcontinental telephone call

1915　　　Einstein completes his general theory of relativity
Italy: Avezzano earthquake leaves 29,980 dead
Tractors introduced

1916　　　Einstein publishes the complete version of his *General Theory of Relativity*
Tank developed for use in WWI

1917　　　Sigmund Freud's *Introduction to Psychoanalysis*
US: Clarence Birdseye develops freezing as a method of preserving food

Did You Know?

Admiral Peary's claim to have reached the pole has been disputed from the beginning—as was the claim made by his former colleague, Dr. Frederick Cook, who has been generally dismissed as a charlatan. The credit ultimately went to Peary, a claim officially backed by the US Congress. But recent scholarship, including evidence culled from the journals and diaries of both Cook and Peary, has cast doubt on both explorers' veracity. If it is the case that neither reached the pole, then the credit goes to Joseph Fletcher, who landed a US Air Force C-47 plane there in 1952.

1918   Worldwide influenza epidemic strikes; by 1920, nearly 20 million are dead; in US alone, 500,000 perish
US: Grand Canyon National Park and Acadia National Park established; parks open to auto traffic; AT&T introduces dial telephones; telephone operators threaten to strike

Did You Know?

The theory of continental drift proposes that a single continent (Pangaea) split into present-day continents, which have drifted away from each other.

1919   Alcock and Brown make first transatlantic nonstop flight
Germany: World's first sustained daily airline passenger service, Berlin to Weimar
Ernest Rutherford splits atom for first time

1920   China: Gansu Province earthquake, magnitude 8.6, kills 100,000
Harvey Cushing makes advances in brain surgery
US: First New York to San Francisco airmail flight; world's first radio station goes on air (KDKA, Pittsburgh); scientist A. A. Michelson becomes first to measure the diameter of a distant star, Betelgeuse; "Tommy Gun," the Thompson portable submachine gun, is demonstrated at a national gun show in Ohio; soon to become the weapon of choice for bootlegging gangsters
Trojan condoms debut

1921   Joseph Block invents whistling teakettle
France: Etienne Oehmichen makes first helicopter flight; BCG tuberculosis vaccine
Andrew Olsen invents the pop-up tissue box
Switzerland: Hermann Rorschach's inkblot test for studying human personality debuts; psychiatrist Carl Jung's *Psychological Types* introduces concepts of "introvert" and "extrovert" personality types

US: KDKA Pittsburgh transmits first regular radio programs in US; Albert Einstein wins the Nobel Prize for Physics for his discovery of the photoelectric effect and his overall theoretical work
Western Union begins wirephoto service
The word "robot," coined by Capek, enters English

1922   Denmark: Niels Bohr publishes theory that electrons orbit an atom's nucleus in concentric circles; receives Nobel Prize for Physics
First 3D movie; requires eyeglasses with one red and one green lens
George Squier invents Muzak
US: First portable radio and first car radio; first lab transmission of a television picture signal

1923   First transcontinental airplane flight, from New York to San Diego (26 hours, 50 minutes)
Austria: Sigmund Freud's *The Ego and the Id*
Frederick G. Banting and John J. R. Macleod win Nobel Prize in medicine for discovering insulin
Japan: Earthquake destroys third of Tokyo and most of Yokohama. More than 140,000 killed
Robert A. Millikan isolates and measures the electron and verifies photoelectric effect
Garrett Morgan invents the traffic light
US: Vladimir Zworykin applies for a patent for his television system, after inventing a key component for television, the iconoscope, a precursor of the cathode ray (picture) tube;
Frank Epperson invents popsicles (first called *epsicles*)
Whooping cough vaccine created
First wireless telephone call, sent via radio waves, made from New York to London

1924   First use of insecticides
France: de Broglie publishes his theory that particles, such as electrons, also have wave nature

Scotland: John Logie Baird transmits human features by television

South Africa: Raymond Arthur Dart discovers the first skull of australopithecus; one of the major finds of century

US: Edwin Hubble shows that galaxies are "island universes"—giant aggregations of stars as large as the Milky Way

1925   James Franck and Gustav Hertz win Nobel Prize for their discovery of the laws governing the impact of an electron upon an atom

Physicists W. K. Heisenberg and Niels Bohr develop quantum mechanics, key concept in modern physics

Mid-Atlantic Range discovered, giant mountain range in the middle of the Atlantic Ocean

Wolfgang Pauli discovers exclusion principle: Two electrons or protons described by the same number cannot exist in the same atom

US: First liquid fuel rocket invented by Robert Goddard; the rocket, 4 feet long, reaches a height of 184 feet; image of revolving windmill is transmitted from Maryland to Washington, DC, in first public demonstration of a television system, developed by Charles Francis Jenkins; photoelectric cell invented; converts light into electricity; R. A. Milliken discovers cosmic rays in upper atmosphere; modern sound recordings made Richard Adolf Zsigmondy wins Nobel Prize in chemistry for showing heterogeneous nature of colloid solutions

Vladimir Zworykin files for color television patent, which he receives in 1928

1926   Austria: Wave version of quantum mechanics discovered

Egypt: Makwar Dam on Nile River is completed

England: First compound fertilizers with nitrogen, phosphorous, and potassium; astronomer/physicist Arthur Stanley Eddington's *The Internal Constitution of the Stars;* John Baird demonstrates his mechanical television system in London

Johannes Fibiger wins Nobel Prize in medicine for discovering *Spiroptera carcinoma*

Ivan Pavlov: *Conditioned Reflexes*

Jean Baptiste Perrin wins Nobel Prize for his work on the discontinuous structure of matter

Mexico: Mayan city ruins discovered in Yucatan peninsula

Did You Know?

In 1983, the lowest temperature ever recorded on earth was at Vostok, the Soviet Station in Antarctica: −128.6° Fahrenheit!

Norway: Aerosol spray invented

Theodor Svedberg wins Nobel Prize in chemistry for work on disperse system

US: E. L. Thorndike's *The Measurement of Intelligence;* Thomas Hunt Morgan's *The Theory of the Gene;* electrical phonograph recording, "Electrola," vast improvement over tinny acoustic recording technology; A. A. Michelson measures speed of light; greatest tornado ever to strike ravages Missouri, killing 695 people; Francis Davis invents power steering

1927   China: Magnitude 8.3 earthquake kills 200,000
Heisenberg develops his uncertainty principle: It is impossible to accurately measure position and momentum of electron or proton at the same time
Iron Lung invented; helps polio victims breathe
Lev Theremin invents first electronic instrument
Transatlantic phone service links London and New York

Did You Know?

About half the size of our moon, Pluto is a ball of frozen gasses. Some scientists think that Pluto is a large comet, and not a planet at all.

US: Charles Lindbergh flies nonstop from New York to Paris; first successful demonstration of TV in US; Robert H. Goddard launches first liquid fuel rocket; Fox Studios introduces Movietone, which synchronizes motion and sound films; 7-mile long, $12 million Moffat Tunnel, carved through James Peak, CO, opens; NBC begins two radio networks; CBS formed

1928   Byrd expedition sails to Antarctica
Charles Jules Henri Nicolle wins Nobel Prize in medicine for work on typhus
England: Fleming discovers penicillin; few are interested; the world wakes up in 1945 and Fleming gets the Nobel Prize in medicine
Hans Geiger and Walther Muller make first feasible Geiger counter to measure radiation (Geiger invented the original device in 1912)
Max Knoll and Ernst Ruska invent electron microscope
Teletype machine invented
US: Walt Disney's first talking cartoon, *Steamboat Willie;* Amelia Earhart becomes first woman to fly across the Atlantic; first regularly scheduled television broadcasts, three days a week for two hours each, at station WGY in Schenectady, NY; quartz clock invented; anthropologist Margaret Mead publishes *Coming of Age in Samoa;* Hoover Dam authorized

1929   Admiral Byrd flies over South Pole
Germany: Electroencephalograph invented
Japan: Matuyama shows that earth's magnetic field reverses every few hundred million years
Jean Piaget: Developmental psychology
US: Kodak introduces 16 mm color movie film; Edwin Hubble observes that all galaxies are moving away from each other; Ernest O. Lawrence invents cyclotron; wins Nobel Prize in physics; first demonstration of color television, in New York; images are roses and US flag; Robert Goddard launches first instrumental liquid-fueled rocket

1930   England: Sir Frank Whittle patents jet engine
US: Clyde Tombaugh discovers Pluto

1931   Africa: First trans-African railway completed, from Angola to Mozambique
Harold C. Urey discovers heavy hydrogen

US: Karl Jansky discovers that radio waves are coming from space; leads to founding of radio astronomy; dentist Frederick S. McKay identifies a chemical that stained his patient's teeth; US Public Health Service expands McKay's research; discovers the chemical fluoride, which helps prevent tooth decay and doesn't discolor teeth

Did You Know?

By age 84 (in 1931), Thomas Edison had received 1,093 patents, including patents for a motion-picture projector, a telephone transmitter, and a way to make rubber from the goldenrod plant.

1932   Auguste Piccard's stratosphere balloon ascends 17.5 miles
Cockcroft develops first particle accelerator
China: Magnitude 7.6 earthquake kills approximately 70,000
England: Chadwick discovers the neutron, neutral particle about the same mass as proton
Germany: Electron microscope, x400 magnification
US: Amelia Earhart becomes first woman to fly solo across Atlantic; Anderson discovers the positron, the positively charged analog of electron

1933   US: Tennessee Valley Authority created to develop the Tennessee River for flood control, navigation, electric power, agriculture, and forestry

1934   US: Carothers invents nylon, first marketed in 1938

1935   Scotland: Robert Watt builds aircraft that detect radar
SS *Normandie* sets transatlantic speed record of 107 hours, 33 minutes
Pakistan: Earthquake at Quetta kills 30,000 to 60,000
US: R. Stanton Avery invents self-adhesive label; Amelia Earhart becomes first woman to fly solo from Hawaii to California

1936   Douglas Aviation introduces DC-3, first practical commercial passenger plane

1937   England: Coronation of Edward VI broadcast around the world
Electron microscope with x7000 magnification
France: Daniel Bovet creates the first antihistamine to block allergic reactions
US: First animated feature: Disney's *Snow White and the Seven Dwarfs;* Carlson invents xerography, the first method of photocopying; Atanasoff starts work in first electronic computer; Amelia Earhart vanishes on a flight around the world
First jet engine
Shopping cart invented
Hindenburg zeppelin crashes

1938   Ballpoint pen invented
Hahn and Meitner split uranium atom, opening the way for nuclear bombs and nuclear power

1939   Chile: Earthquake razes 50,000 square miles; about 30,000 killed
Sikorsky patents the first helicopter for mass production
Switzerland: Paul Muller discovers that DDT kills insects
US: First jet flight, 36 years after Wright Brother's flight at Kitty Hawk; TV first
broadcast publicly, from the Empire State Building; first digital computer; Einstein tells
Roosevelt it is possible to make an atomic bomb

1940   British scientists develop radar; used in Battle of Britain
Peter Carl Goldmark demonstrates first successful color television
Plutonium made; first artificial element

1941   England and Germany develop jet aircraft
England: Dacron invented
US: First push-button phone produced

Did You Know?

*In the early 1940s, engineer James Wright had been trying to develop a rubber
substitute to help the Allies during World War II. Instead of rubber, he created a
blob of sticky stuff that bounced when he dropped it. It had no use, but
everyone liked to play with it. A few years later, Peter Hodgson decided to try to
market this odd clay. He called it "Silly Putty" and featured it in a 1949 toy store
catalog. Silly Putty was an instant hit.*

1942   US: First HMO; Manhattan Project created to build an atomic bomb to help end World
War II
Enrico Fermi builds first nuclear reactor

1943   Penicillin produced on a large scale

1944   US: International Bank for Reconstruction and Development (later the World Bank) and
the International Monetary Fund (IMF) created at a conference at Bretton Wood; first
antihistamines commercially sold; IBM makes mechanical calculating machine; DNA
shown to carry heredity characteristics

1945   US: First computer "bug": A moth gets into Harvard's Mark II computer; birth of the
atomic age as the first bomb is tested at Los Alamos, NM (July 16); Edwin Peterson
invents answering machine

Did You Know?

*When the first atom bomb was set off, Dr. J. Robert Oppenheimer, the physicist
in charge of building the bomb in the "Manhattan Project," recited two lines
from the Hindu Bhagavad-Gita: "I am become death, the shatterer of worlds."*

1946   South Pacific: US tests atomic bomb at Bikini Atoll in Marshall Islands; continuing US and French nuclear testing on Pacific islands causes massive resentment
US: ENIAC, first all-electronic digital computer, has vacuum tubes arranged to display decimal numerals

1947   Dennis Gabor invents *holography*, a method of recording and displaying three-dimensional objects
England: First atomic power station
Radiocarbon dating perfected
US: Transistor invented (Bell labs); first drive-in banking (Chicago); first around-the-world commercial air service (PanAm); Chuck Yeager is first to break the sound barrier, flying an X-1 rocket-plane

1948   Big Bang Theory of Universe developed
Jaguar sports car, capable of reaching a speed of 120 mph, put into production
Goldmark develops the 33⅓-rpm long-playing phonograph record
"Steady-state" theory of the universe proposed
Switzerland: Velcro invented (patented 1955)
Transistor invented
US: Centigrade renamed Celsius after its inventor, Anders Celsius

Did You Know?

According to the Big Bang Theory, the universe began with something like an explosion, which caused all parts of the universe to rush away from one another—the expansion of the universe.

1949   US: First paper copier
USSR: America's atomic monopoly ends when Russia detonates its own device

1950   India: Earthquake affects 30,000 square miles in Assam; 20,000 to 30,000 believed killed
US: DDT contamination thins eagle eggshells and decimates the population; Earl John Hilton invents credit card; Clinton Riggs invents yield sign

1951   US: First color TV sold

1952   England: Smog blamed for 4,000 deaths in London
US: Hydrogen bomb detonated, driven by nuclear fusion, not fission (November 1); link between smoking and lung cancer first proposed

1953   Edmund Hillary and Tenzing Norkay reach peak of Mount Everest
US: IBM releases its first computer, the 701; James Watson and Francis Crick publish their discovery of the molecular model of DNA
USSR: Moscow announces explosion of hydrogen bomb

| 1954 | Richard Herrick becomes first person to live with a transplanted kidney; donor was his identical twin
US: *Nautilus,* first atomic submarine, launched; Dr. Jonas Salk starts inoculating children against polio |

| 1955 | Link between exposure to asbestos and lung cancer established
Transistor radio invented
Albert Sabin develops oral polio vaccine |

Did You Know?

Fortunately, today it is difficult to imagine the terror the very word "polio" could inspire. An infectious viral disease of the central nervous system, poliomyelitis causes weakness, paralysis, and even death. In 1952, there were nearly 60,000 cases of polio; after Sabin created an oral vaccine, only a few cases are reported each year.

| 1956 | England: Nuclear power first generated on a viable scale for industry
Neutrino detected
South Pacific: First aerial H-bomb, equivalent to 10 million tons of TNT, tested over Namu islet, Bikini Atoll (May 21)
US: First practical videotape recorder |

| 1957 | Bubble wrap invented
Laika, a small dog, becomes the first living creature in space
US: Boeing builds first 707 jet; replica of the *Mayflower* sails from England to Plymouth, MA, in fifty-four days; superconductivity theory; basic laser invented; patented in 1986 after a long struggle
USSR: *Sputnik I* and *II* launched; first artificial satellites; they weigh 184 lb. and measure 23 inches across |

| 1958 | Modem invented
US: NASA established to administer space program; Pan Am begins daily transatlantic jet service (October 26); James Van Allen discovers belts of radiation that surround earth in space, now known as Van Allen belts; first experimental nuclear power plant opens |

| 1959 | Antarctica: Antarctic Treaty limits exploitation of Antarctica
Hovercraft demonstrated
First robot marketed
Tanganyika: Louis Leakey finds 600,000-year-old skull
US: Texas Instruments invents the microchip; American Medical Association sanctions hypnosis as medical aid
St. Lawrence Seaway opens, allowing ocean ships to reach Midwest (April 25) |

1960
Aluminum cans first used commercially
ATM invented
Coal supplies forty-five percent of US energy needs
Enovid 10 is introduced as oral contraceptive
France: Detonates its first atomic bomb
Laser perfected
Typesetting by computer begins
World fisheries catch reaches 40 million tons
US: 2,000 electronic computers bought; Xerox 914 copier sparks revolution in paperwork reproduction; theory of seafloor spreading

1961
Acetaminophen tablets gain FDA approval
Coffee-mate nondairy creamer created
England: Louis Leakey and Mary Leakey discover *Homo habilis* in northern Tanzania
Kodachrome II color film introduced
Lippes Loop intrauterine contraceptive invented
US: Murray Gell-Mann and Israeli Yu'val Ne'eman independently develop a method of classifying heavy sub-atoms, particles that come to be known as "eight-fold way"; Alan B. Shepard, Jr. rockets 116.5 miles up in 302-mile trip (May 5); Virgil Grissom becomes second American astronaut making 118-mile-high, 303-mile-long rocket flight (July 21); TWA is first airline to show in-flight movies; first IBM Selectric typewriters sold; Federal Communications Commission approves stereo broadcasting on FM
USSR fires fifty-megaton hydrogen bomb, biggest explosion in history (October 29); Yuri Gagarin becomes first man in space (April 12)

1962
England: Neil Bartlett shows that noble gasses can form compounds
US: John H. Glenn, Jr. is first American to orbit Earth—three times in 4 hours 55 minutes (February 20); *Telstar I* launched (July 10); first successful measles vaccine; Polaroid introduces color film; *Mariner 2* first probe to reach another planet, Venus; Petrified Forest National Park established; Rachel Carson's *Silent Spring* sparks environmental movement; American Airlines inaugurates a system (SABRE) for airline reservation, thus linking thousands of agencies, reservation terminals, and ticket desks

1963
Audiocassettes introduced
US: Eastman Kodak introduces Instamatic cameras; Michael E. De Bakey implants artificial heart in human for first time at Houston hospital; plastic device functions and patient lives for four days; Valium first sold; Maarten Schmidt, first astronomer to recognize a quasar; Congress passes first Clean Air Act; Phillips introduces compact cassette tape
USSR: Valentine Tereshkova becomes first woman in space

1964
Methadone helps rehabilitate heroin addicts
Ranger VII returns with first close-up pictures of Mars
Touch-tone phones introduced
US: Surgeon General's Report links smoking to cancer and other diseases (January 11); Wilderness Act protects remaining undeveloped lands; Alaska suffers strongest earthquake ever to strike North America, followed by seismic wave 50 feet high that traveled 8,445 miles at 450 miles per hour; 117 killed; Xerox introduces fax machines

1965 Sony introduces Betamax
US: Congress requires health warning on cigarette packages; astronaut Edward White walks in space from *Gemini 4;* scientists prove radio waves pervade space, thus proving to most that Big Bang really occurred

Did You Know?

Named for the Roman goddess of love, Venus is second only to the moon in brightness. Because it is between the earth and sun, Venus is seen either as the Morning Star or Evening Star.

1966 US: First Winnebago RV; Rare and Endangered Species Act; fiber optics used to transmit data

1967 England: Jocelyn Bell-Burnell discovers the first-known pulsar
Computer language Logo is developed
South Africa: Dr. Christiaan N. Barnard and team of South African surgeons perform world's first successful human heart transplant; patient dies eighteen days later

Did You Know?

Bears on Kodiak Island somehow knew that the 1964 quake was about to strike. They woke from hibernation two weeks early and instead of looking for food, ran from the area where the quake would strike.

US: Kroger installs first retail bar code scanner (Cincinnati supermarket); Virgil Grissom, Edward White II, and Roger Chaffee killed in spacecraft fire during simulated launch (January 27)

1968 *Apollo 8,* with three astronauts, orbits the moon and returns
USSR: First supersonic airliner

1969 US: Neil Armstrong becomes first human to walk on the moon (July 20); Chemical Bank (NY) installs first ATM; first computer-to-computer message: UC-Berkeley professor tries to send the words "log in" to a Stanford computer, but it crashes after the "g"; ARPANET, first general-purpose computer network, created by the Defense Department; Hurricane Camille, described as "the greatest storm of any kind ever to affect the mainland of the US," claims 256 lives

1970 China: Earthquake magnitude 7.7 quake kills 15,621
US: Disaster averted when crippled *Apollo 13* returns to earth safely; Intel creates microprocessor; microcomputers developed; First Earth Day, April 22; Environmental Protection Agency established; Boeing 747 jets go into service

1971   US: First Auto Train; *Mariner 9* first spacecraft to orbit another planet, Mars; first microprocessor, Intel 4004

1972   US: Clean Water Act; Oregon passes first recycling laws

1973   US: Space station *Skylab 4* launched; first genetic engineering

Did You Know?

Our only natural satellite, the moon is the brightest object in the night sky.

1974   Crack cocaine hits public awareness
Lucy, 3 million-year-old skeleton, is discovered; skeleton proves that human ancestors walked erect (October 17)
US: Lap and shoulder belts required in all new American cars; Rowland and Molinas warn that chloroflurocarbons produced by spray cans and air conditioners are destroying the ozone layer

KEY DOCUMENT

As he set foot on the moon on July 20, 1969, Neil Armstrong said: "That's one small step for man, one giant leap for mankind." Minutes later, Armstrong was joined by Edwin ("Buzz") Aldrin. The two strode across the moon's surface for 2 hours and 14 minutes while a TV camera they had set up 50 feet from the *Eagle* transmitted their historic walk to a captivated audience some 250,000 miles away.

1975   Apollo and Soyuz spacecraft take off for U.S.-Soviet linkup in space
US: Bill Gates and Paul Allen establish Microsoft to sell their BASIC as operating software for the Altair computer; IBM introduces first laser printer
USSR: Space probe transmits pictures from surface of Venus

1976   China: Worst earthquake to hit China in twentieth century; devastates 20-square-mile area of city, leaving 242,000 confirmed dead
First commercial supersonic jet, the Concorde, cuts flight time between New York and Paris from 7 hours to 3 hours, 25 minutes
First major computer-assisted mathematical proof shows that a map can be colored with four colors in such a way that no two regions of the same color share a common border
US: Steve Jobs and Steve Wozniak build the first Apple computer in their garage; mysterious disease that eventually claims twenty-nine lives strikes American Legion convention in Philadelphia; *Viking* space probe transmits pictures from Mars

1977   Five rings around Uranus are discovered
Scientists identify new bacterium as cause of mysterious "Legionnaire's disease"
Scientists report using bacteria in lab to make insulin
US: Space shuttle *Enterprise* completes its first manned flight; chemist Arthur Fry invents
Post-Its; ocean vents discovered, surrounded by exotic life forms based on sulfur, not oxygen

Did You Know?

*Steven Jobs and Stephen Wozniak's Altair 8800, the first true PC, was sold in
Popular Electronics magazine as a do-it-yourself kit. It was a tremendous hit, but
no one expected the groundswell reaction to the Altair. Although it wasn't the first
microcomputer people could buy, it did start the modern microcomputer industry.*

1978   Cell phones first tested
England: Louise Brown becomes first baby conceived outside her mother's body, the
product of in vitro fertilization
Iran: Earthquake leaves 25,000 dead
Sweden: First nation to curb aerosol sprays to halt destruction of the ozone
US: Love Canal evacuated after hazardous waste dumps discovered
Ultrasound techniques developed to view fetuses in the womb

1979   Smallpox eradicated
US: Intel produces the 8088 microprocessor, brains of the first IBM personal computer;
key cards replace metal keys in the Westin Peachtree Plaza, Atlanta; nuclear power plant
accident at Three Mile Island, PA, releases radiation; Space probe *Voyager I* reveals that
Jupiter has rings

Did You Know?

*Fully assembled, the Apple I computer cost $666.66. About 600 machines
sold—a huge success.*

1980   China: Scientists clone a fish
Classification of all finite simple groups started in 1830, is completed, perhaps the longest
proof in the history of mathematics
India: First satellite goes into orbit
Mexico: First giant panda cub born into captivity
US: Mount St. Helens in Washington state erupts, 8 people killed, blast heard 200 miles
away; Alan Guth develops the theory of inflationary universe, an explanation of how the
Big Bang occurred; Martin Cline transfers functioning gene from one mouse to another
USSR: Soviet cosmonauts return to earth from *Salyut 6* space station; set a record 185
days in space

Did You Know?

The magnitude of the Mount St. Helens eruption went far beyond predictions. When the volcano erupted at 8:32 AM, the blast had the power of 500 atomic bomb explosions. Forests 17 miles away were flattened; 400 million tons of debris shot into the atmosphere. About 2 million animals died and 200 square miles of habitat were destroyed. Forty-seven people died trying to escape the gas clouds chasing them at 200 miles per hour.

1981	AIDS is first identified France: World's fastest train, TGV Switzerland: Mammals first cloned US: IBM sells personal computers to general public; the *Columbia* is first reusable space shuttle
1982	Compact disc players created England: 20 million elm trees killed by Dutch Elm disease First permanent artificial heart is transplanted *Pioneer 10* is first spacecraft to leave the solar system
1983	First computer "mouse" Scientists studying the South Pole find a decrease in the ozone layer Ice cores in Greenland and Antarctica reveal the earth's climate for past 250,000 years US: Sally Ride becomes first American woman to fly in space, aboard the *Challenger;* Barney Clark, first person to receive artificial heart, dies 112 days after surgery; genes for Duchenne muscular dystrophy and Huntington's disease identified; start of cellular phone networks
1984	India: More than 2,000 people die from toxic fumes from US-owned Union Carbide plant in Bhopal US: Danny Schectman and coworkers discover first quasicrystal, a "crystal" that violates the symmetry rules of all other crystals; Motorola introduces first commercial cell phones
1985	England: Scientists discover a "hole" in the ozone layer over Antarctica; screening of blood donations for HIV virus Mexico: Earthquake registering 8.1 on Richter scale devastates part of Mexico City and three coastal states; 25,000 killed New Zealand declared a nuclear-free zone Remains of the luxury liner *Titanic* found and photographed
1986	South Pacific: Treaty of Rarotonga sets up South Pacific Nuclear-Free Zone US: Space shuttle *Challenger* explodes on liftoff, killing crew; I-80 becomes first coast-to-coast interstate highway under one number; Rutan and Yeager make first nonstop flight around the world, takes 9 days USSR: Nuclear accident at Chernobyl causes 133,000 to be evacuated US: *Voyager 2* discovers ten more moons by Uranus

Did You Know?

Seventy-three seconds after lift-off, the space shuttle Challenger *exploded, engulfed in a huge fireball. One rocket booster separated and violently continued to fire as the* Challenger *plummeted to the ocean. All seven crew members were killed. People around the world were shocked and devastated. After much study, a special commission discovered that launch conditions, mechanical failure, and poor decision making had caused the accident.*

1987	China and USSR: Worst fire in history burns more than 3 million acres of China's timber reserves and up to 15 million acres in USSR England: Work begins on Channel Tunnel ("Chunnel") from Britain to France Five billionth inhabitant of earth born
1988	Armenia: Earthquake measuring 6.9 on the Richter scale kills nearly 55,000, injures 15,000, and leaves at least 500,000 homeless Prozac is first marketed
1989	The World Wide Web begins at the Conseil European pour la Recherche Nucleaire World Wide Web revolutionizes the Internet; millions begin logging on US: San Francisco earthquake measuring 7.1 on Richter scale kills 67 and injures over 3,000. Over 100,000 buildings damaged or destroyed and damage cost city billions of dollars; Space probe *Voyager 2* flies by Neptune, farthest planet from the sun at that time, and takes pictures; Exxon *Valdez* grounds in Prince William Sound, Alaska, leaking 35,000 tons of oil
1990	Iran: Earthquake measuring 7.7 on Richter scale destroys cities and villages in Caspian Sea area; at least 50,000 dead, over 60,000 injured, and 400,000 homeless US: Hubble telescope launched into space, plagued with problems from the start; Clegg and coworkers isolate DNA and a gene for photosynthesis from a fossilized 17-million-year-old leaf; mathematicians discover the largest known prime number, 65,087 digits
1991	Middle East: Iraq dumps over a million tons of oil from occupied Kuwait into the Persian Gulf Prototype for high-definition television created
1992	Tim Berners-Lee devises *hypertext* and the language HTTP US: Gopher, first popular way to navigate the Internet; *Magellan Venus* orbiter maps ninety-five percent of the planet's surface
1993	US: Crew of space shuttle *Endeavor* successfully repairs the main lens of the Hubble Space Telescope; midwest floods cause $15 million in damage, forcing 40,000 people from their homes and killing 50
1994	FDA approves first genetically-engineered tomato Europe: Channel Tunnel ("Chunnel") opens

1995 DVDs introduced
France: Nuclear device in Pacific exploded, causing wide protests
US: Yellowstone Park restocked with fourteen Canadian timber wolves; Southwest becomes first airline to offer system-wide ticketless travel; Craig Venter publishes complete base sequence for all the genes of a free-living organism, a bacteria; Andrew Wiles publishes a corrected version of his 1993 proof of Fermat's last theorem

1996 England: Alarm over mad cow disease
Global warming climbs to record highs
Switzerland: Scientists announce the first planet known to orbit an ordinary star other than the sun
US: Bomb mars Summer Olympic games in Atlanta; *Galileo* spacecraft probes the atmosphere of Jupiter and reports on its composition and weather; Hubble telescope used to make the first images of a star (Betelguese) other than the sun that shows the star's disc

Did You Know?

Hypertext *are the words you click to go to another site.*

1997 England: Ian Wilmut clones a sheep, whom he names "Dolly"
Hale-Bopp Comet is closest it will be to earth until 4397
Iran: Earthquake measuring 7.1 on Richter scale leaves more than 1,500 people dead and at least 4,460 injured
Mars Pathfinder lands on Mars and sends back astonishing photographs
Montserrat: Soufriere Hills volcano kills twenty and leaves two-thirds of Montserrat uninhabitable
US: Spacecraft begins exploration of Mars; Russian *Mir* space station and US space shuttle *Atlantis* linked; US company launches first commercial spy satellite; first artificial chromosome created

1998 Afghanistan: Magnitude 7.1 earthquake kills 5,000; later that year, another quake in same area kills 2,300
Astronomers conclude universe is still expanding
India: Three atomic tests conducted despite worldwide disapproval
Pakistan: Five nuclear tests in response to India's
US: *Voyager I* becomes the most distant artificial object, 6.5 billion miles from earth; John Glenn returns to space in a shuttle becoming oldest human in space; FDA approves Viagra, male impotence drug; scientists find evidence that life on earth existed 3.85 billion years ago

1999 China: First spacecraft launched
Colombia: 1,124 dead and 4,000 injured in magnitude 6 earthquake
First nonstop balloon flight around world completed in twenty days

Malaysia: Petronas Twin Towers in Kuala Lumpur become world's tallest building, rising 1,483 feet, 33 feet higher than the Sears Tower in Chicago

"Melissa" computer virus spreads through the Internet

Taiwan: 2,295 killed and 8,729 injured in earthquake

Did You Know?

How tall is tall? The Eiffel Tower is 984 feet; the Great Pyramid at Giza, 480 feet; the Statue of Liberty, 305 feet, and the Leaning Tower of Pisa, 179 feet.

Turkey: Magnitude 7.4 earthquake kills 17,000, injures 43,000

Last full crew leaves 13-year-old Russian space station *Mir*

US: NASA accidentally loses $125 million spacecraft as it orbits Mars; number of electronic airplane tickets exceeds paper tickets; first directional atom laser; periodical table extended to include elements 116 and 118; cattle and mice cloned

Ji Qiang finds fossil of earliest known ancestor to mammals, almost a "missing link" between mammals and reptiles from 120 million years ago

2000   Scientists crack genetic code of human life; "Today we are learning the language in which God created life," US President Bill Clinton says